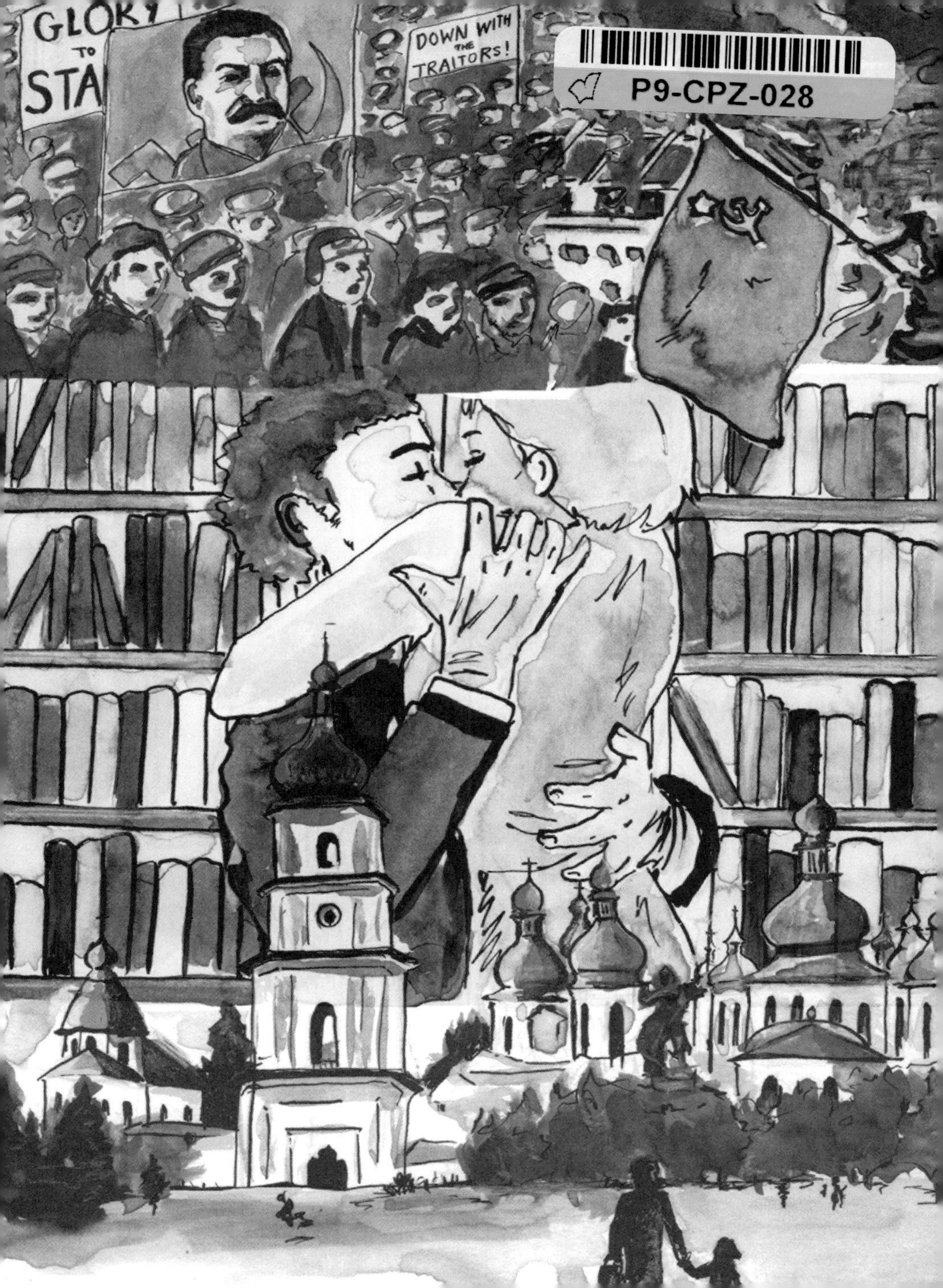
GLORY TO STA
DOWN WITH THE TRAITORS!

Soviet Daughter
A Graphic Revolution

Julia Alekseyeva

Edited by Elly Blue
Designed by Joe Biel

First published January 10, 2017

Microcosm Publishing
2752 N Williams Ave.
Portland, OR 97227
www.microcosmpublishing.com

ISBN 978-1-62106-969-0

First Published
First printing of 3,000 copies

Distributed by Legato / Perseus Books Group and Turnaround, U.K.

Printed on post-consumer paper with sustainable inks in the U.S.

Library of Congress Cataloging-in-Publication Data

Names: Alekseyeva, Julia, author.
Title: Soviet daughter : a graphic revolution / Julia Alekseyeva.
Description: First edition. | Portland, OR : Microcosm Publishing, [2016] |
    Graphic novel.
Identifiers: LCCN 2016014093 (print) | LCCN 2016016705 (ebook) | ISBN
    9781621069690 (pbk.) | ISBN 9781621067658 (epdf) | ISBN 9781621060765
    (epub) | ISBN 9781621068969 (mobi)
Classification: LCC PS3601.L35335 S68 2017 (print) | LCC PS3601.L35335
    (ebook) | DDC 741.5/973--dc23
LC record available at https://lccn.loc.gov/2016014093

SOVIET DAUGHTER

DAUGHTER

A Graphic Revolution

JULIA ALEKSEYEVA

MICROCOSM PUBLISHING
PORTLAND, OR

Table of Contents

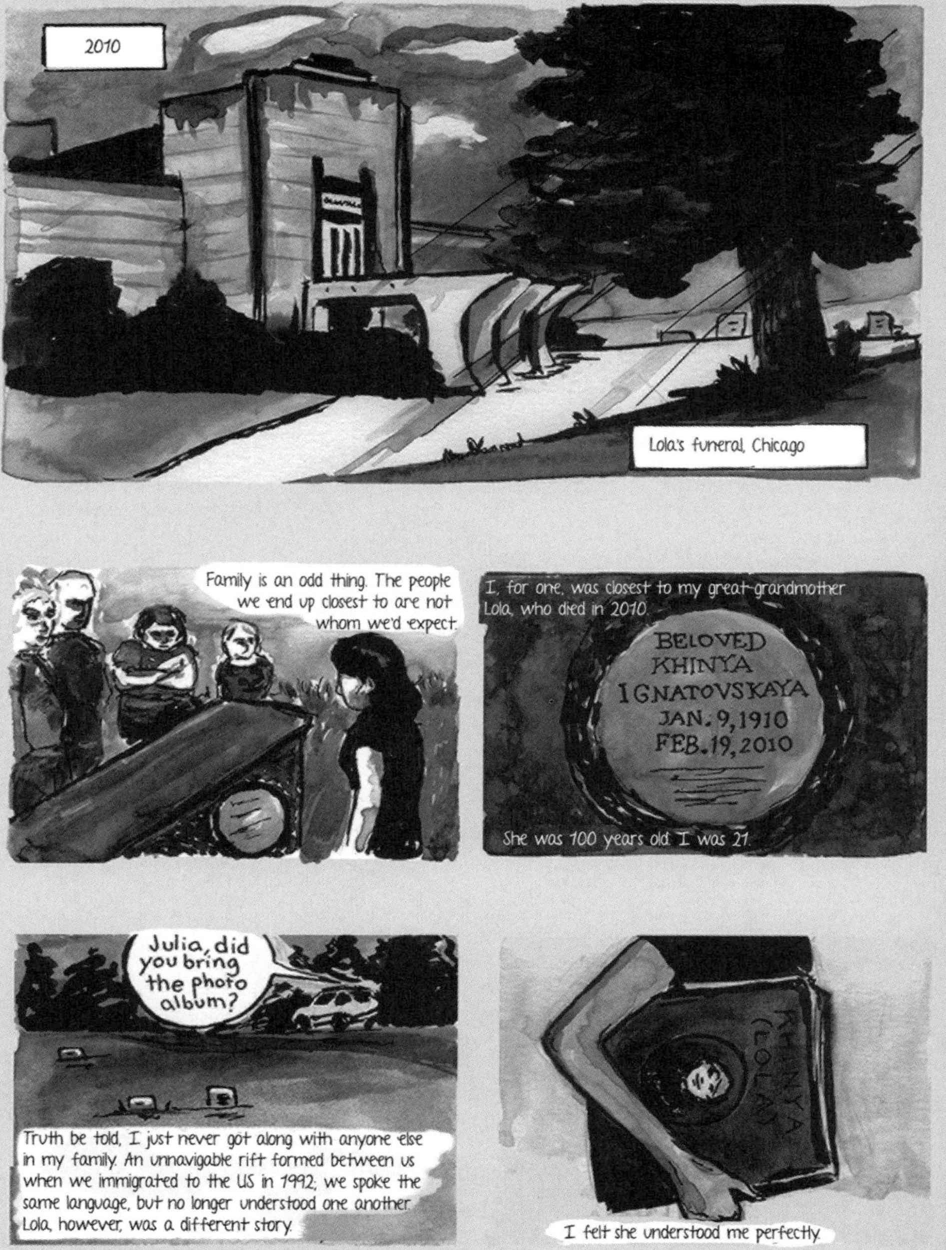
2010
Lola's funeral, Chicago
Family is an odd thing. The people we end up closest to are not whom we'd expect.
I, for one, was closest to my great-grandmother Lola, who died in 2010.
BELOVED KHINYA IGNATOVSKAYA JAN. 9, 1910 FEB. 19, 2010
She was 100 years old. I was 21.
Julia, did you bring the photo album?
Truth be told, I just never got along with anyone else in my family. An unnavigable rift formed between us when we immigrated to the US in 1992; we spoke the same language, but no longer understood one another. Lola, however, was a different story.
KHINYA (LOLA)
I felt she understood me perfectly.

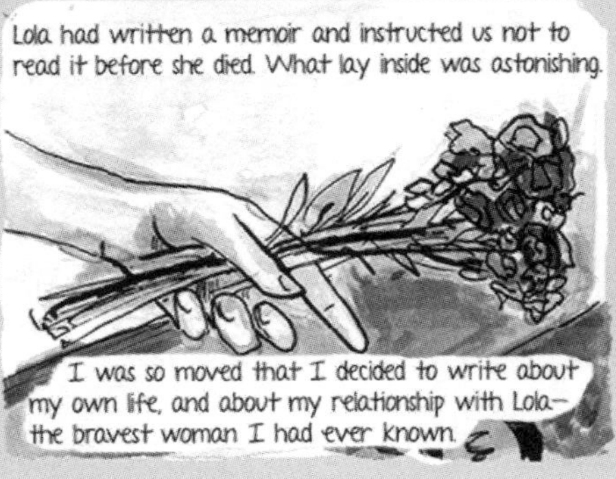
Lola had written a memoir and instructed us not to read it before she died. What lay inside was astonishing.
I was so moved that I decided to write about my own life, and about my relationship with Lola—the bravest woman I had ever known.

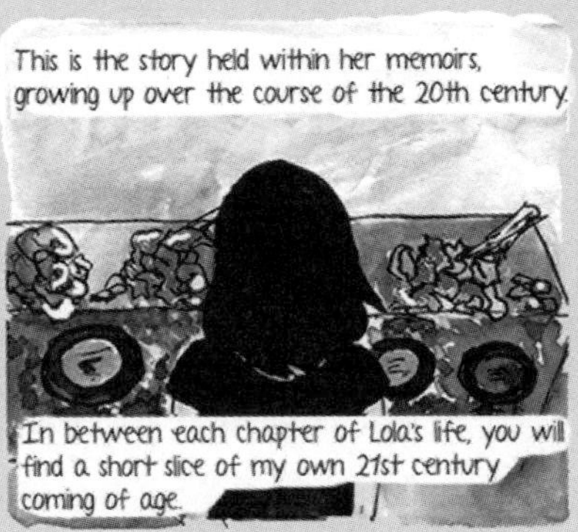
This is the story held within her memoirs, growing up over the course of the 20th century.
In between each chapter of Lola's life, you will find a short slice of my own 21st century coming of age.

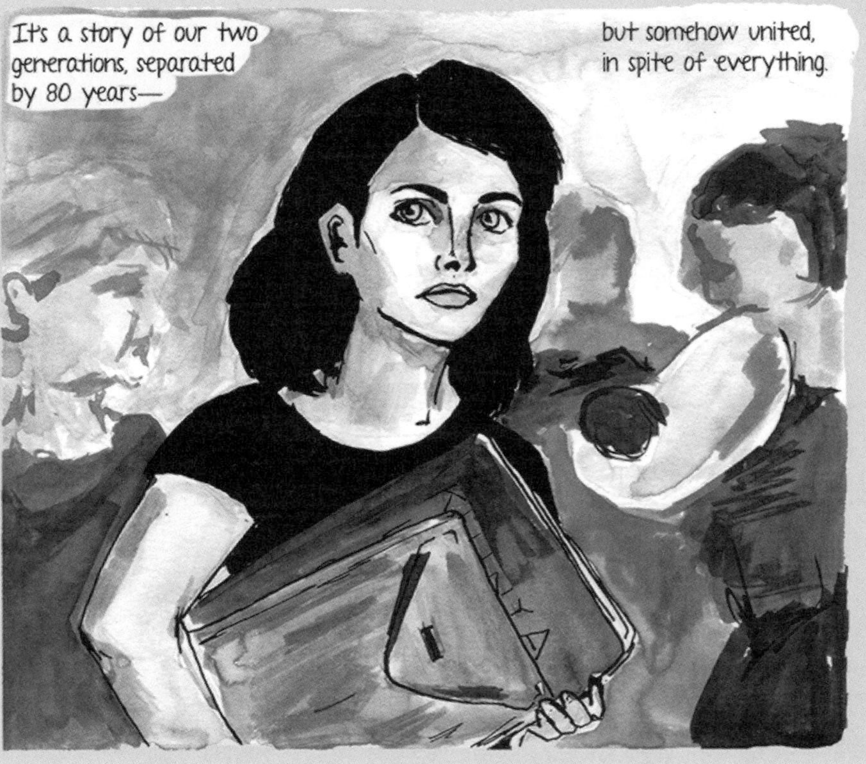
It's a story of our two generations, separated by 80 years—
but somehow united, in spite of everything.

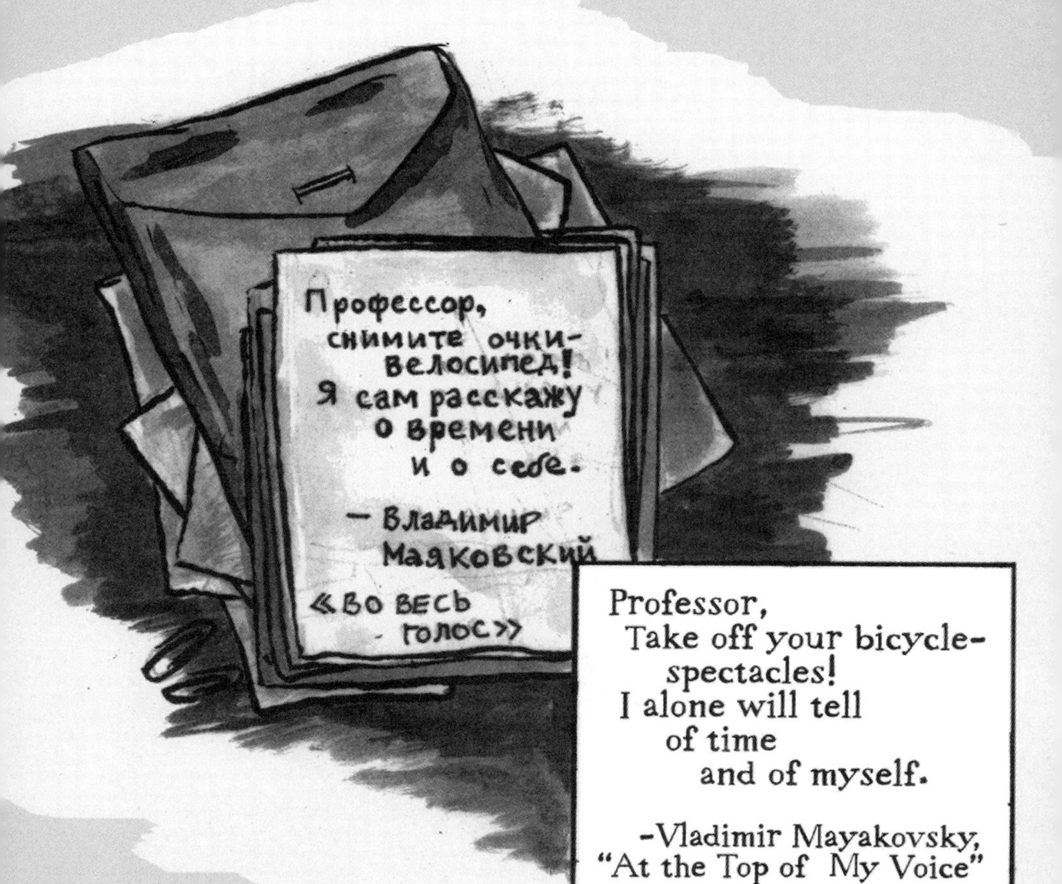
Профессор,
снимите очки-
велосипед!
Я сам расскажу
о времени
и о себе.
— Владимир
Маяковский
«Во весь
голос»
Professor,
Take off your bicycle-
spectacles!
I alone will tell
of time
and of myself.
-Vladimir Mayakovsky,
"At the Top of My Voice"

Chapter 1: 1910-1917

My father Avram was born in 1886, in a village called Ignatovka. This became my family's surname: Ignatovsky for boys, Ignatovskaya for girls.

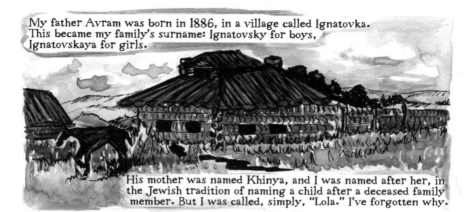

His mother was named Khinya, and I was named after her, in the Jewish tradition of naming a child after a deceased family member. But I was called, simply, "Lola." I've forgotten why.

In 1905, my father left for Kiev to become a jeweler,

and in 1906, he married my mother Khasa. She came from a slightly wealthier family.

Jews were technically not allowed to live in Kiev (the rules for Jewish settlement changed constantly), so after my older brother Vladimir was born, my mother was sent away to the town of Dnepropetrovsk with the baby,

Shhh...

while my father stayed on, living in the outskirts of the city—the only place Jews were allowed to live on a permit.

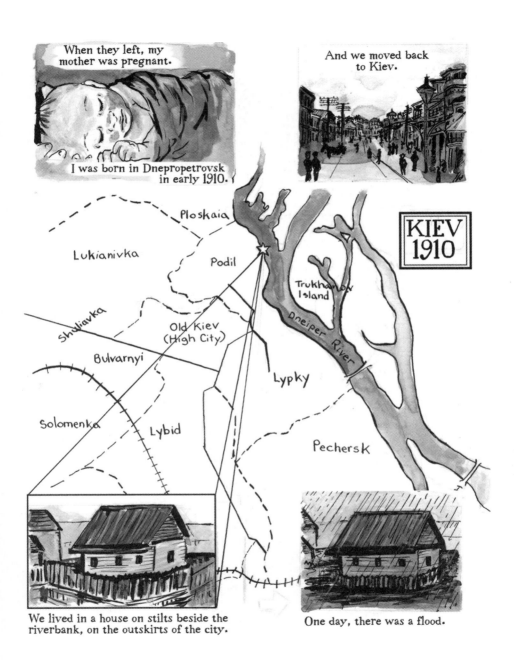

When they left, my mother was pregnant.

I was born in Dnepropetrovsk in early 1910.

And we moved back to Kiev.

KIEV 1910

Ploskaia

Lukianivka

Podil

Shuliavka

Trukhanov Island

Old Kiev (High City)

Dneiper River

Bulvarnyi

Lypky

Solomenka

Lybid

Pechersk

We lived in a house on stilts beside the riverbank, on the outskirts of the city.

One day, there was a flood.

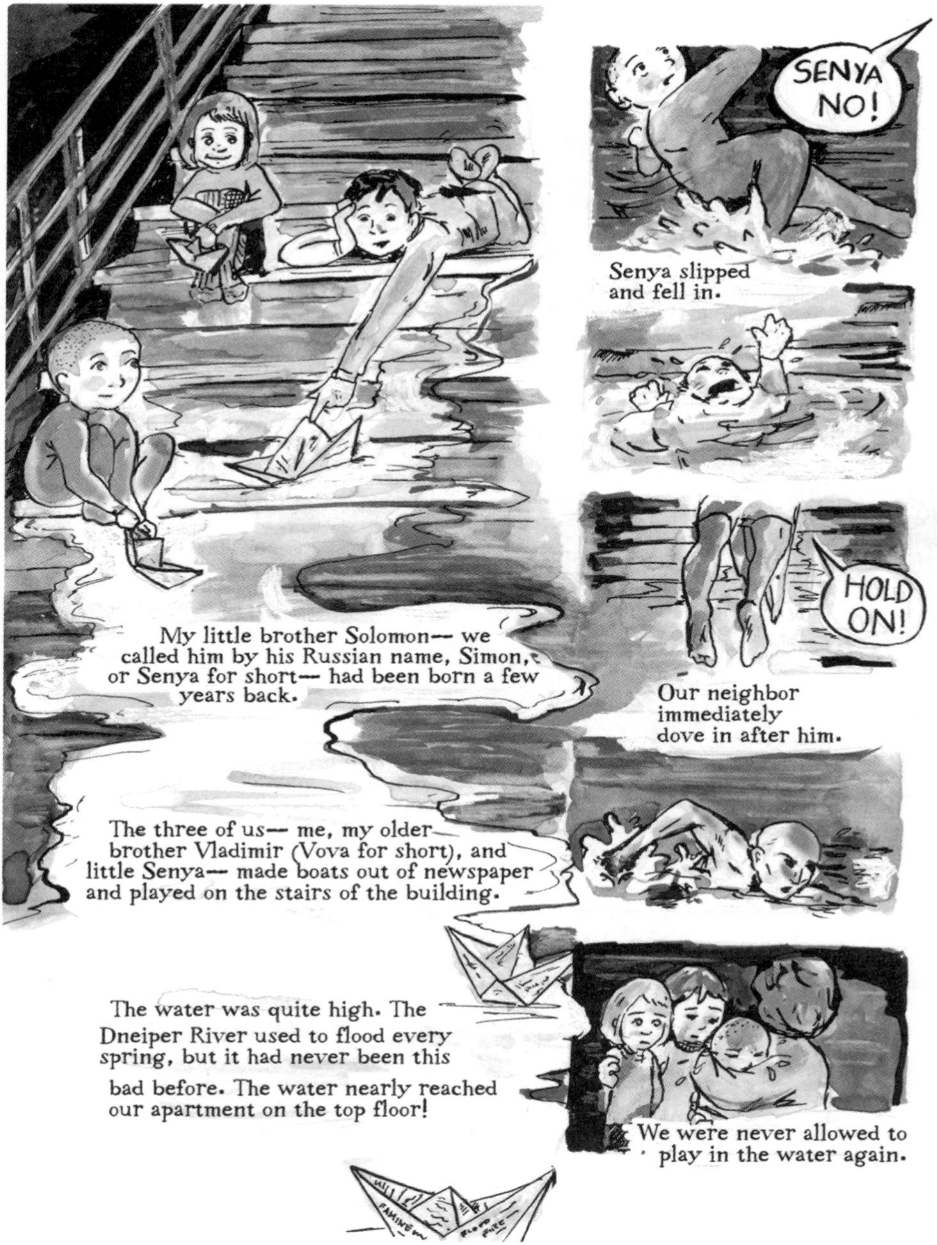
My little brother Solomon— we called him by his Russian name, Simon, or Senya for short— had been born a few years back.
The three of us— me, my older brother Vladimir (Vova for short), and little Senya— made boats out of newspaper and played on the stairs of the building.
The water was quite high. The Dneiper River used to flood every spring, but it had never been this bad before. The water nearly reached our apartment on the top floor!
SENYA NO!
Senya slipped and fell in.
HOLD ON!
Our neighbor immediately dove in after him.
We were never allowed to play in the water again.

We had to scrape to get by, but were happy in our own way.

My father, like most Jews, was not particularly devout, but he often read us the stories of Sholem Aleichem, a folk writer considered the Yiddish Mark Twain.

"Amazing!" she said. "You have a quotation for everything! Maybe you can find one about how people separated themselves into Jews and Gentiles, into landowners and beggars?"

"Now, now! I think you've gone too far, my daughter!" And I gave her to understand that the world had been there that way since the Creation.

"Why should the world be like that?" she asked me.
"Because that's the way God created it."
"Why did He create it like that?"

"Eh! If we begin asking questions, why this and why that, it's a story without an end!" I said.

"That's why God gave us reason, so we could ask questions."

"We have a custom that when a hen begins to crow like a rooster, you should take it immediately to the slaughterer. As we say in the prayers: 'He giveth the rooster knowledge to discern the dawn from the night.'"

"Haven't you two prattled enough?" my Golde called from the house. "The borscht is on the table for an hour, and he's chanting prayers!"

"Another voice is heard from!" I said. "Not for nothing did our sages say, 'The fool has seven traits'— a woman has nine yards of talk. We are talking about serious matters, and along she comes with her dairy borscht!"

In the few years after I was born, Papa would read us any news about the Beilis Affair that he could find.

Mendel Beilis was a Jewish man framed for the murder of a Ukrainian boy under the charge of "Blood Libel."* He spent several years in prison but was eventually acquitted.

*A claim that Jews kidnapped and murdered Christian children to use their blood for holiday rituals

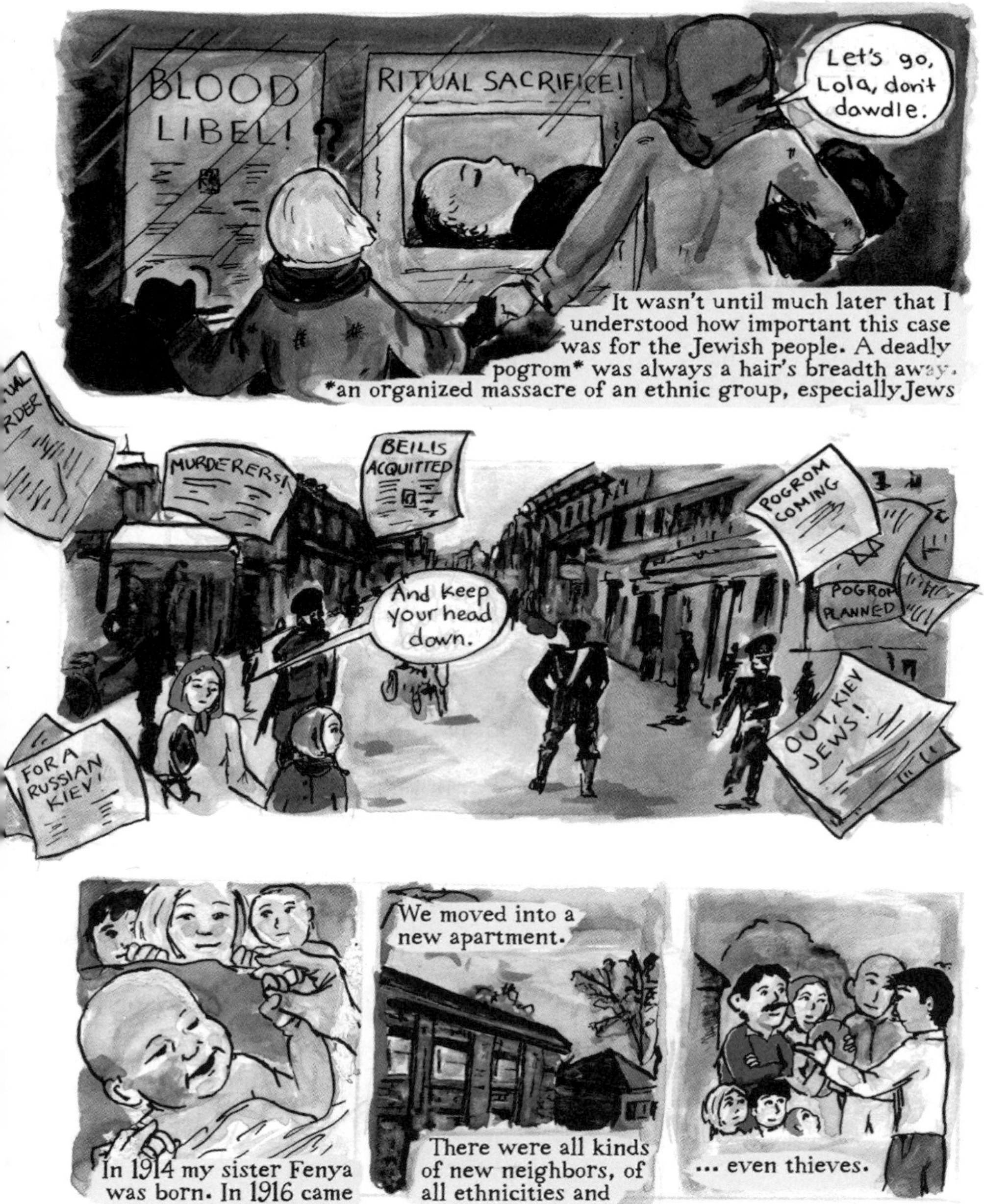
BLOOD LIBEL!
RITUAL SACRIFICE!
Let's go, Lola, don't dawdle.
It wasn't until much later that I understood how important this case was for the Jewish people. A deadly pogrom* was always a hair's breadth away.
*an organized massacre of an ethnic group, especially Jews
MURDERERS!
BEILIS ACQUITTED
POGROM COMING
POGROM PLANNED
And keep your head down.
FOR A RUSSIAN KIEV!
OUT, KIEV JEWS!
In 1914 my sister Fenya was born. In 1916 came my sister Lyuba.
We moved into a new apartment.
There were all kinds of new neighbors, of all ethnicities and vocations...
... even thieves.

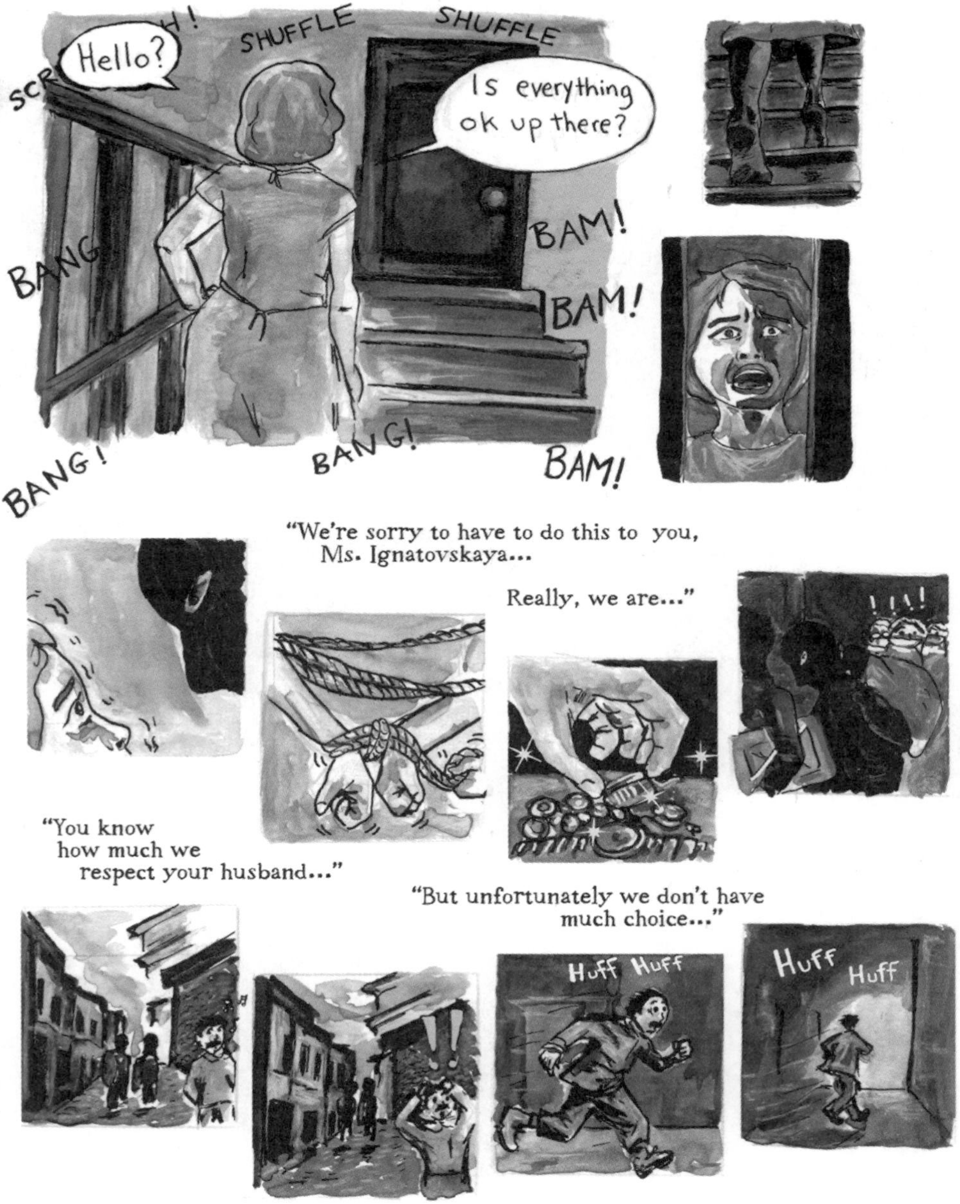
Hello?
SHUFFLE
SHUFFLE
Is everything ok up there?
BANG
BAM!
BAM!
BANG!
BANG!
BAM!
"We're sorry to have to do this to you, Ms. Ignatovskaya...
Really, we are..."
!!!!
"You know how much we respect your husband..."
"But unfortunately we don't have much choice..."
Huff Huff
Huff Huff

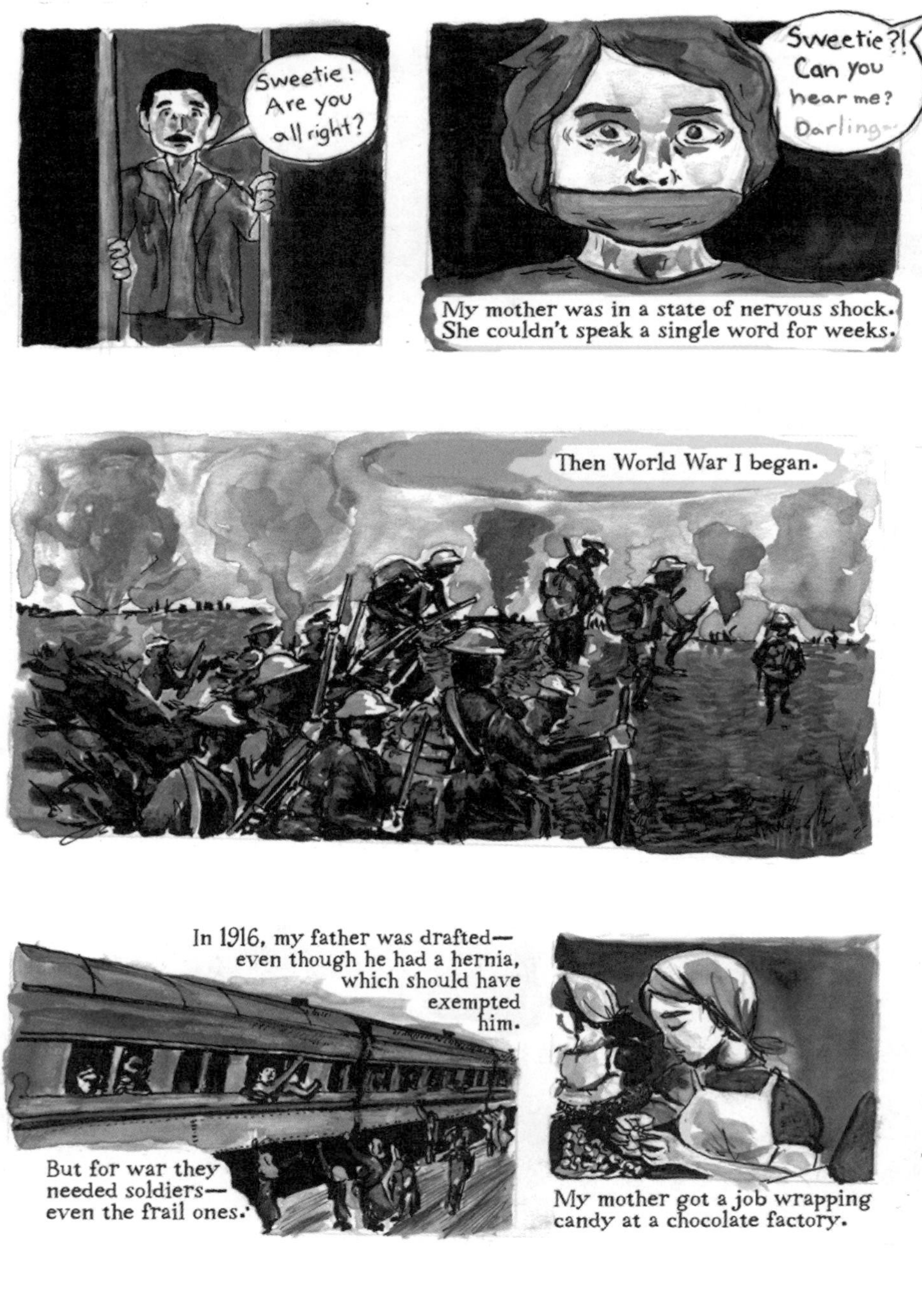
Sweetie! Are you all right?
Sweetie?! Can you hear me? Darling...
My mother was in a state of nervous shock. She couldn't speak a single word for weeks.
Then World War I began.
In 1916, my father was drafted—even though he had a hernia, which should have exempted him.
But for war they needed soldiers—even the frail ones.
My mother got a job wrapping candy at a chocolate factory.

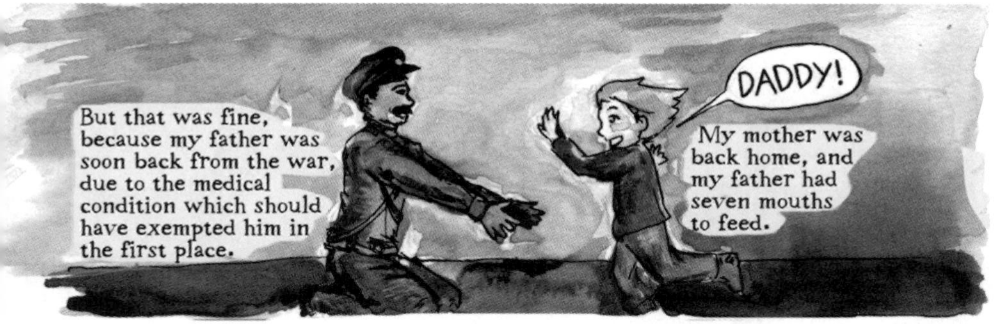
But that was fine, because my father was soon back from the war, due to the medical condition which should have exempted him in the first place.
DADDY!
My mother was back home, and my father had seven mouths to feed.

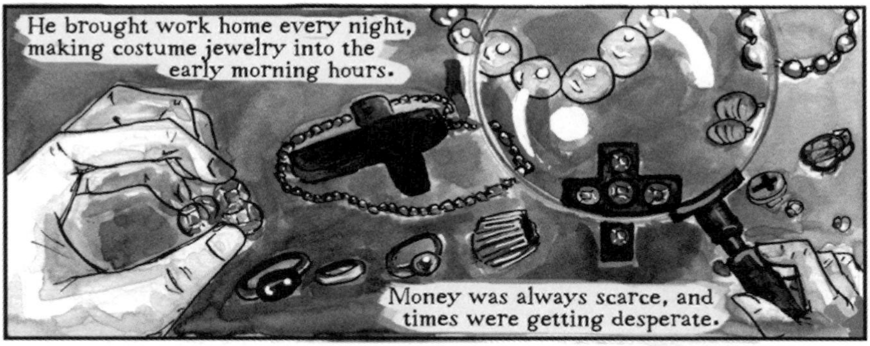
He brought work home every night, making costume jewelry into the early morning hours.
Money was always scarce, and times were getting desperate.

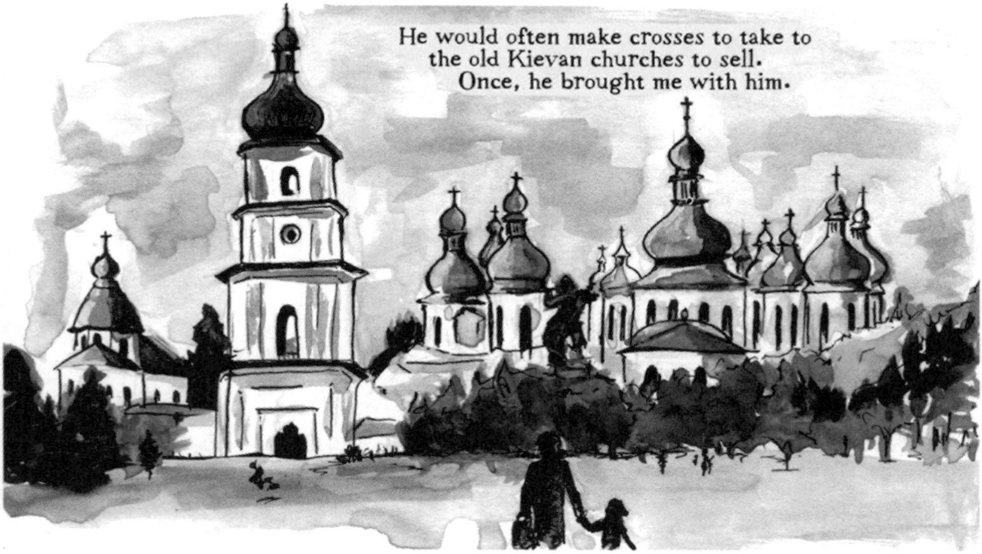
He would often make crosses to take to the old Kievan churches to sell. Once, he brought me with him.

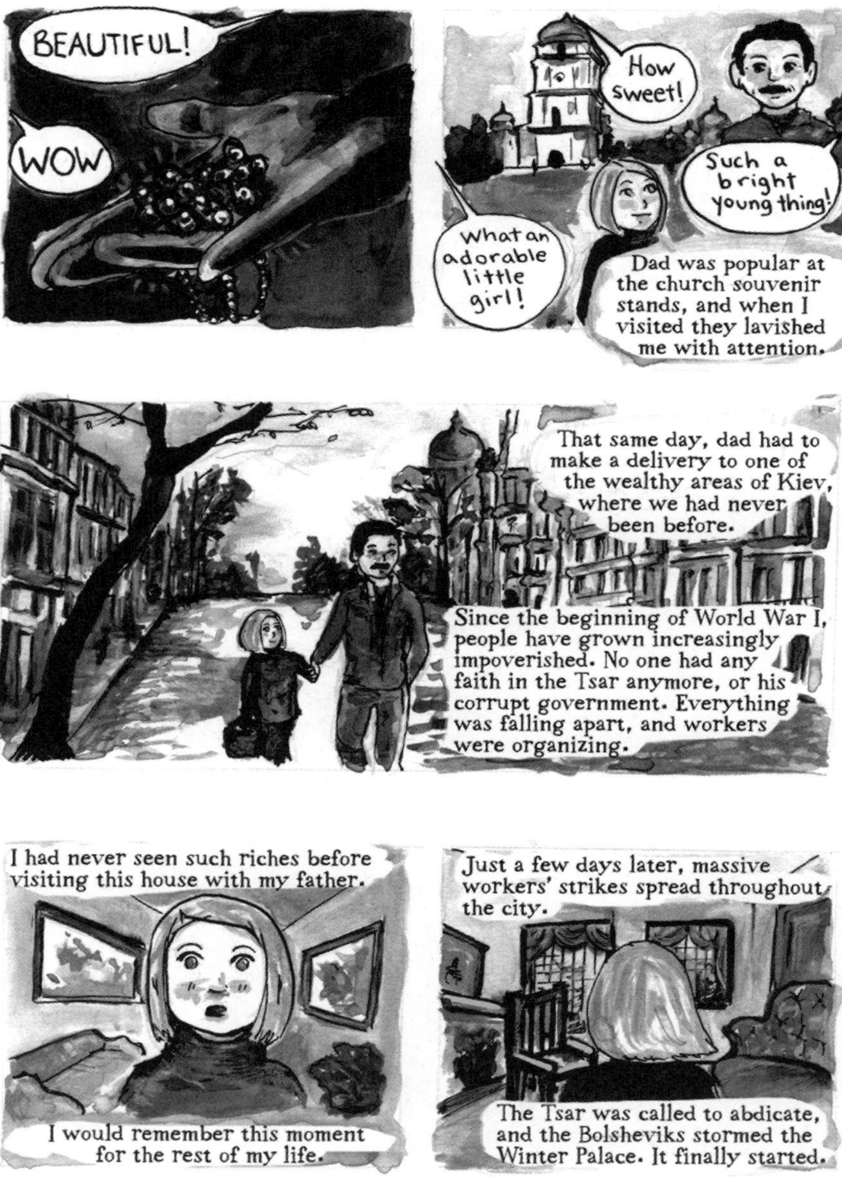
BEAUTIFUL!
WOW
How sweet!
Such a bright young thing!
What an adorable little girl!
Dad was popular at the church souvenir stands, and when I visited they lavished me with attention.
That same day, dad had to make a delivery to one of the wealthy areas of Kiev, where we had never been before.
Since the beginning of World War I, people have grown increasingly impoverished. No one had any faith in the Tsar anymore, or his corrupt government. Everything was falling apart, and workers were organizing.
I had never seen such riches before visiting this house with my father.
I would remember this moment for the rest of my life.
Just a few days later, massive workers' strikes spread throughout the city.
The Tsar was called to abdicate, and the Bolsheviks stormed the Winter Palace. It finally started.

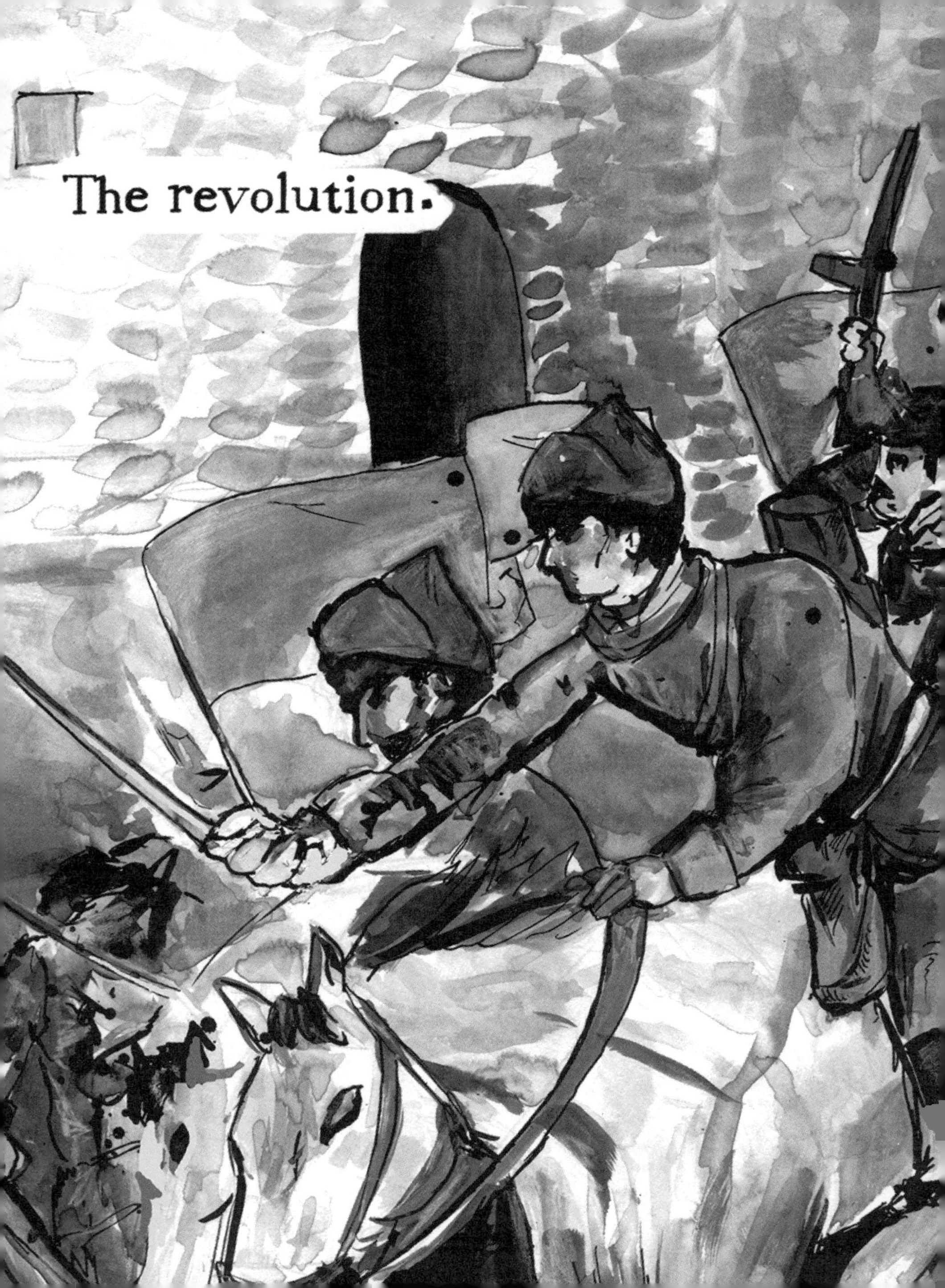
The revolution.

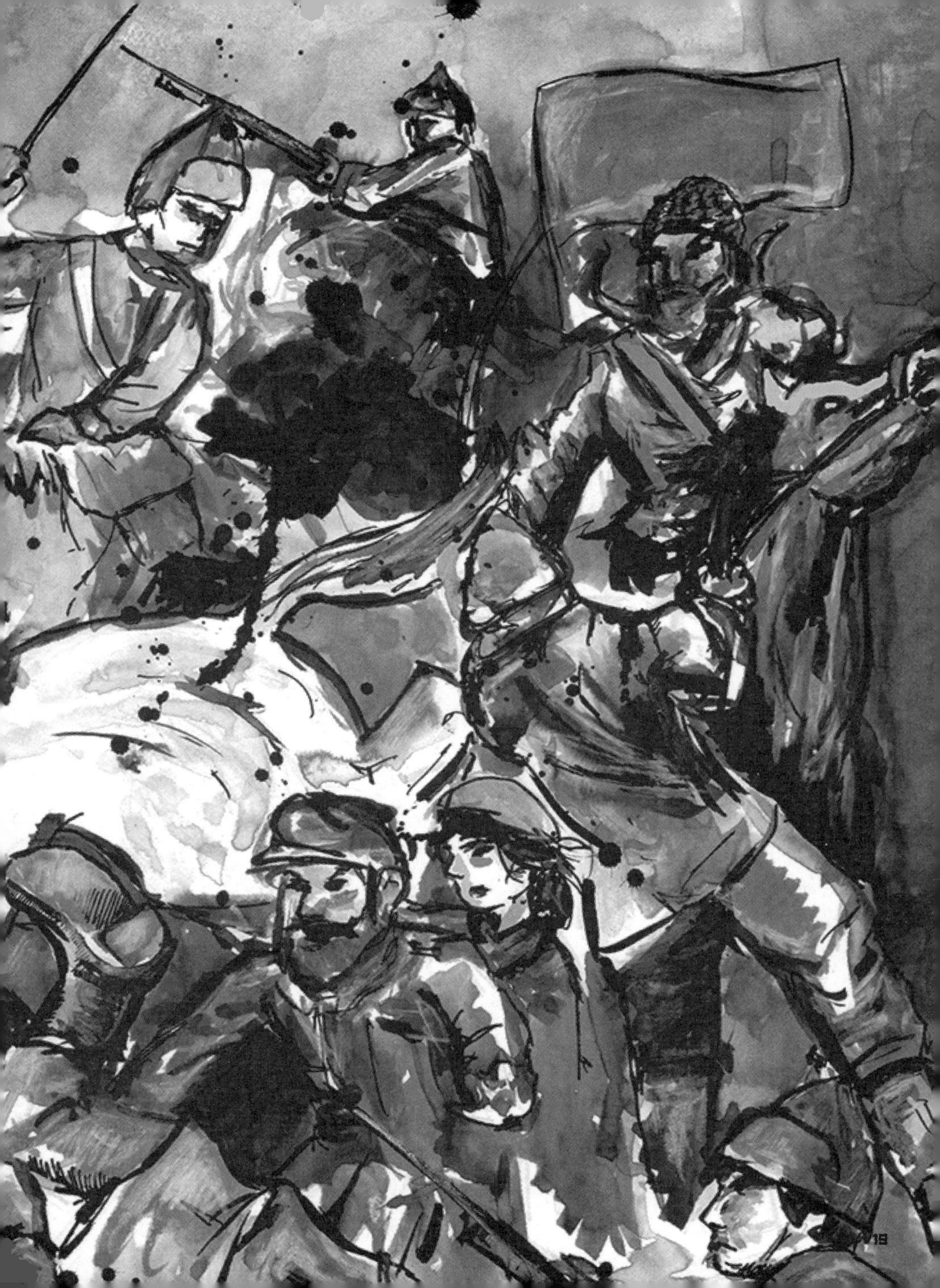

Interlude

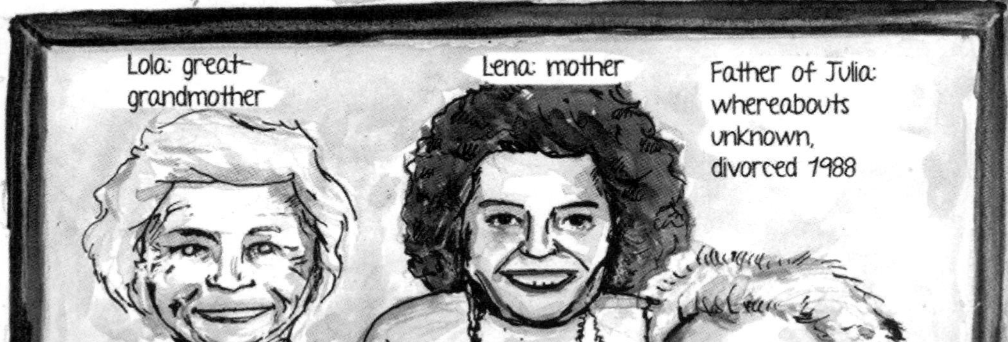
Lola: great-grandmother
Lena: mother
Father of Julia: whereabouts unknown, divorced 1988
Julia (Self)
Tanya: grandmother
Vladimir: grandfather

1992

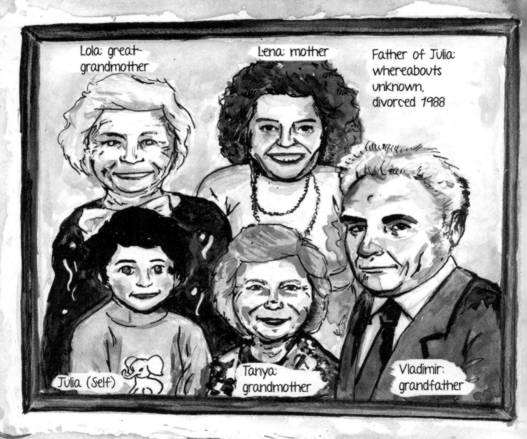

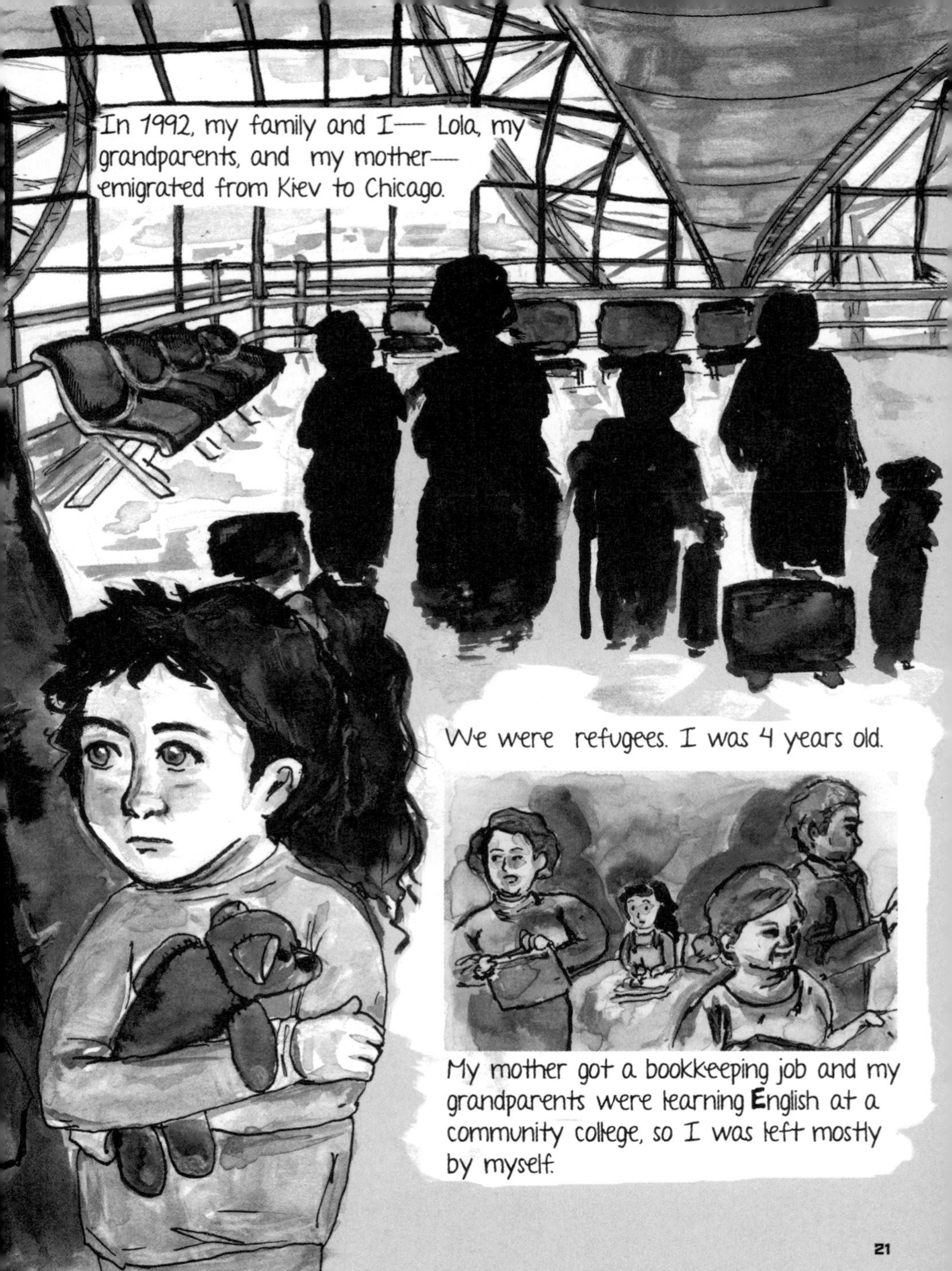
In 1992, my family and I— Lola, my grandparents, and my mother— emigrated from Kiev to Chicago.
We were refugees. I was 4 years old.
My mother got a bookkeeping job and my grandparents were learning English at a community college, so I was left mostly by myself.

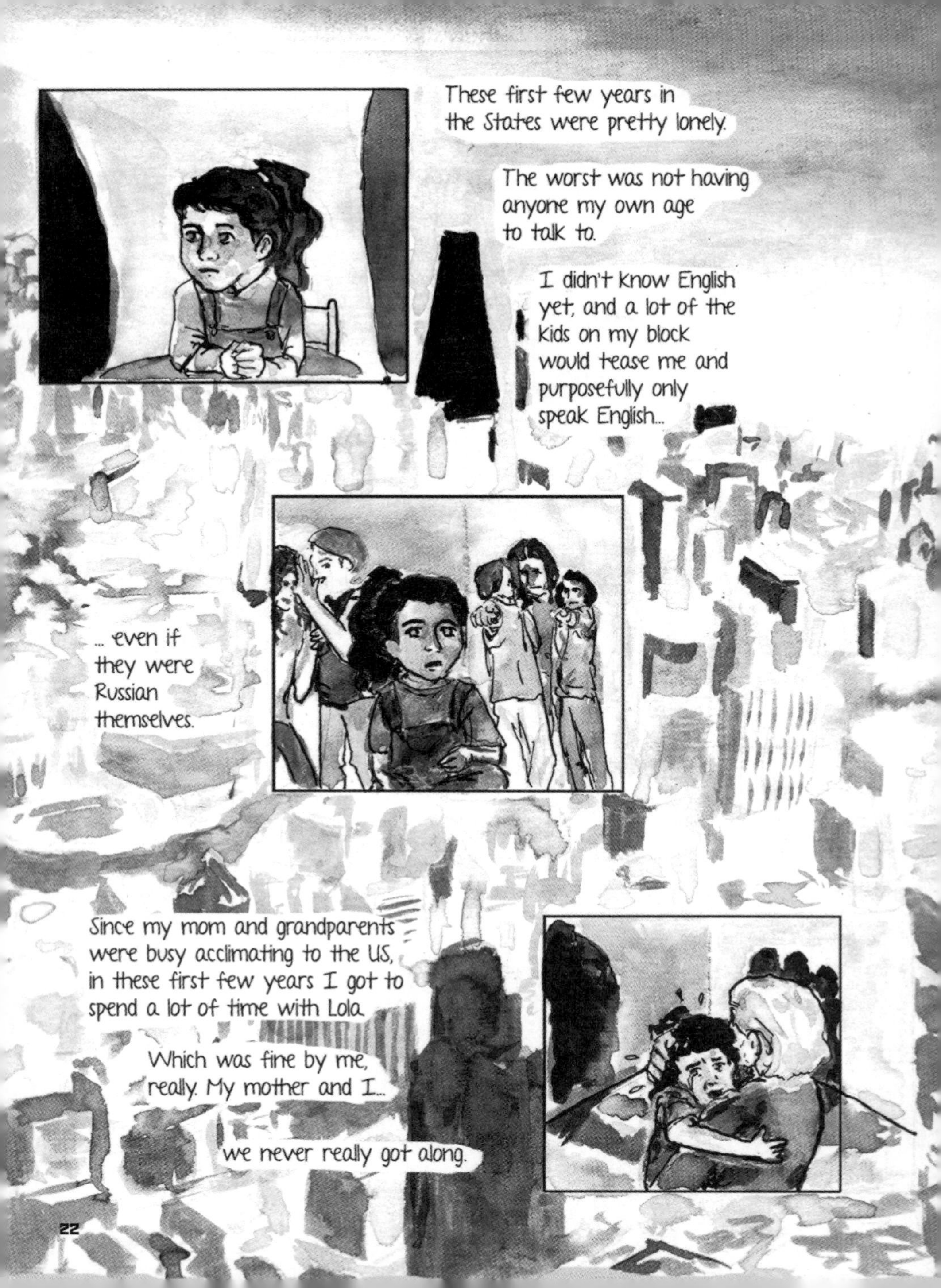
These first few years in the States were pretty lonely.
The worst was not having anyone my own age to talk to.
I didn't know English yet, and a lot of the kids on my block would tease me and purposefully only speak English...
... even if they were Russian themselves.
Since my mom and grandparents were busy acclimating to the US, in these first few years I got to spend a lot of time with Lola.
Which was fine by me, really. My mother and I...
we never really got along.

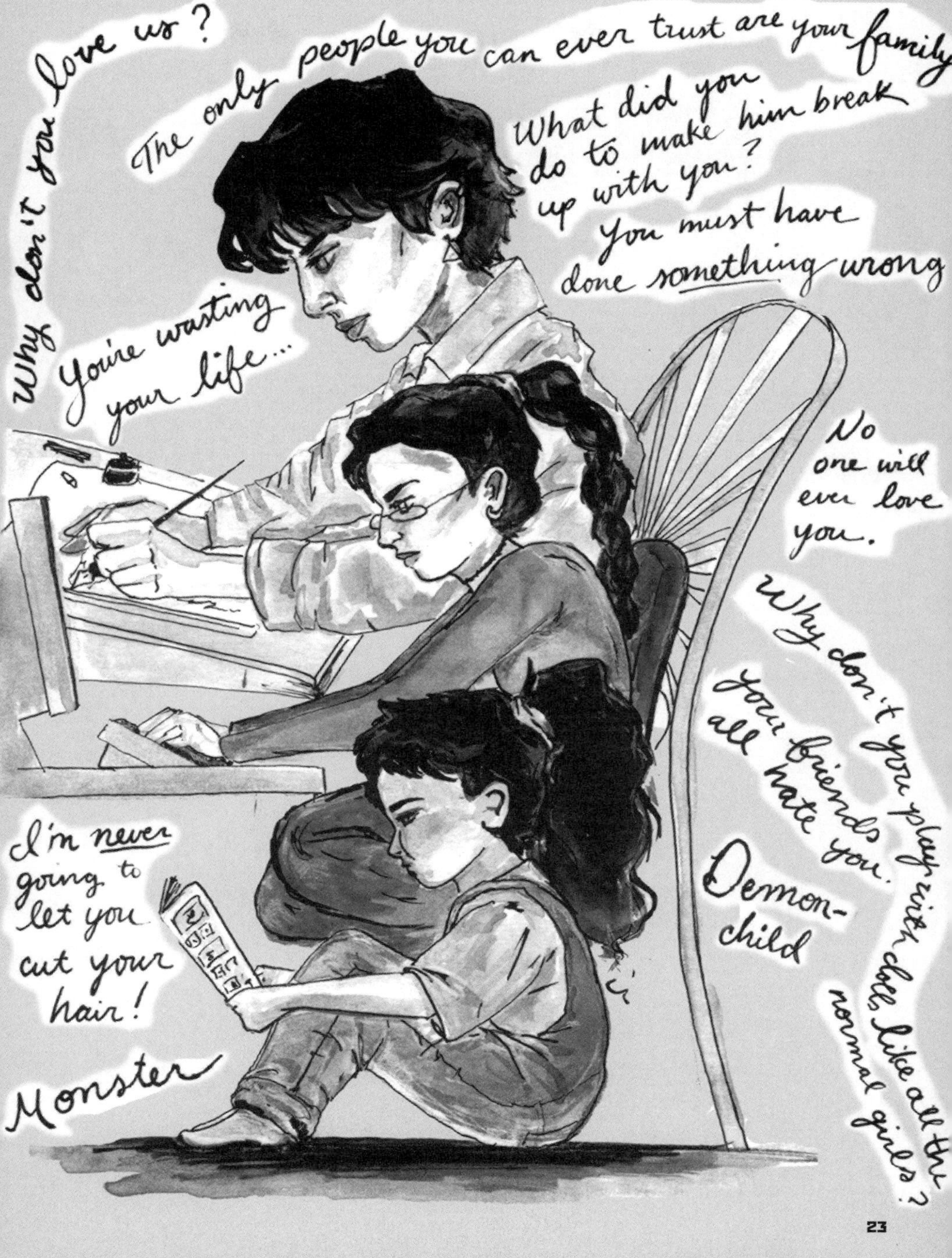
Why don't you love us?
The only people you can ever trust are your family
What did you do to make him break up with you?
You must have done something wrong
You're wasting your life...
No one will ever love you.
Why don't you play with dolls like all the normal girls?
Your friends all hate you.
Demon-child
I'm never going to let you cut your hair!
Monster

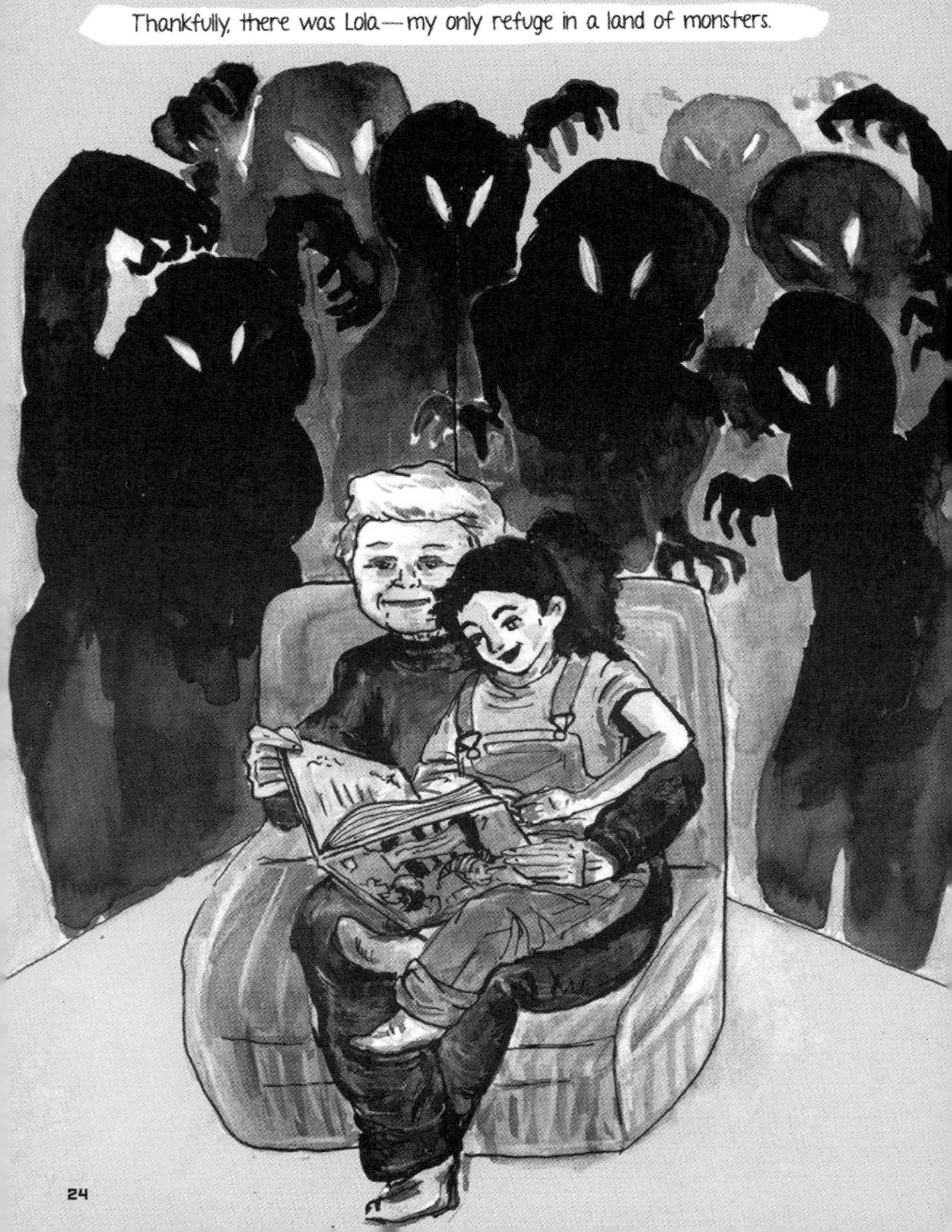
Thankfully, there was Lola—my only refuge in a land of monsters.

Chapter 2: 1917-1920

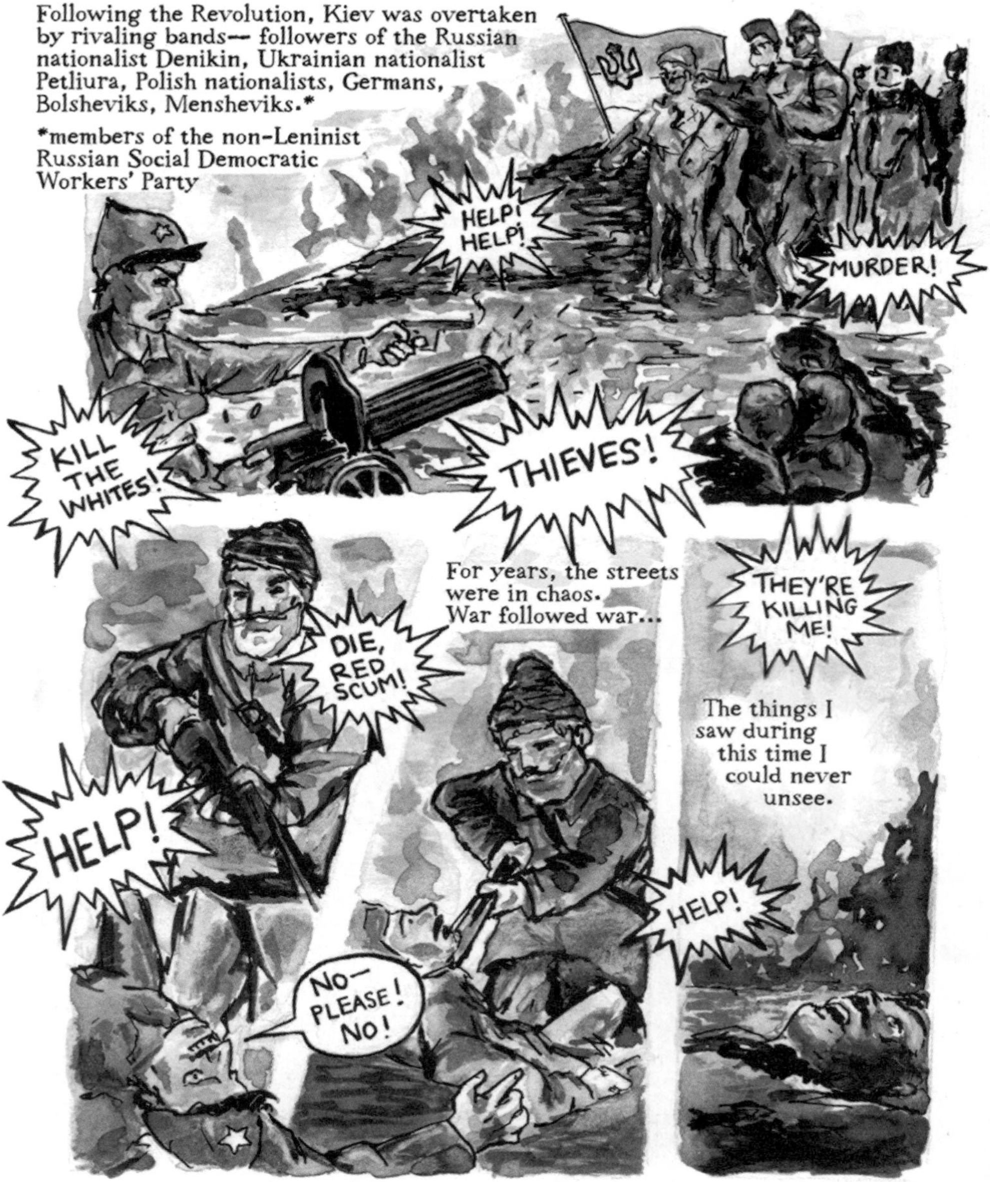
Following the Revolution, Kiev was overtaken by rivaling bands— followers of the Russian nationalist Denikin, Ukrainian nationalist Petliura, Polish nationalists, Germans, Bolsheviks, Mensheviks.*
*members of the non-Leninist Russian Social Democratic Workers' Party
HELP! HELP!
MURDER!
KILL THE WHITES!
THIEVES!
For years, the streets were in chaos. War followed war...
DIE, RED SCUM!
HELP!
NO— PLEASE! NO!
THEY'RE KILLING ME!
The things I saw during this time I could never unsee.
HELP!

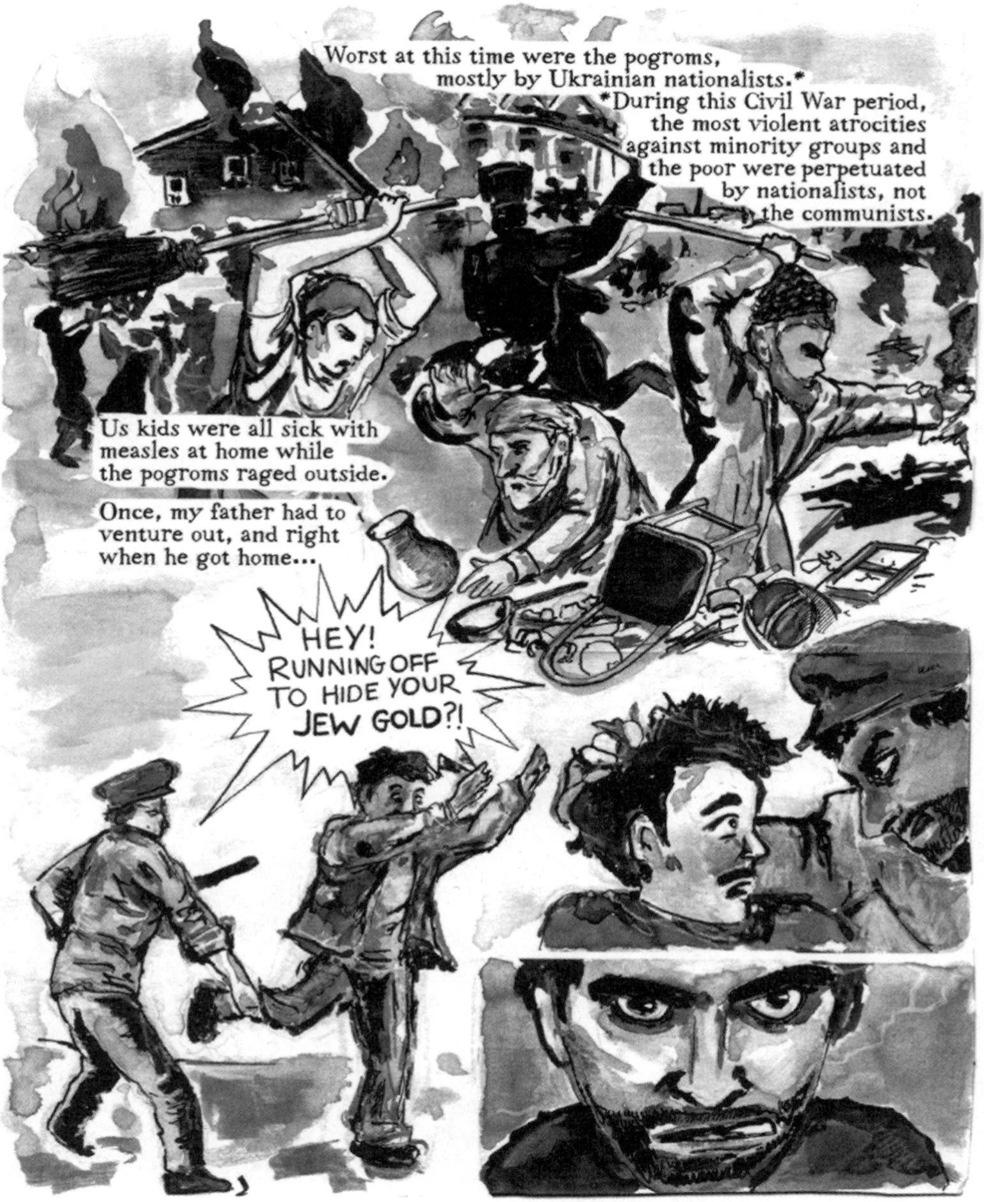

Worst at this time were the pogroms, mostly by Ukrainian nationalists.*
*During this Civil War period, the most violent atrocities against minority groups and the poor were perpetuated by nationalists, not the communists.
Us kids were all sick with measles at home while the pogroms raged outside.
Once, my father had to venture out, and right when he got home...
HEY! RUNNING OFF TO HIDE YOUR JEW GOLD?!

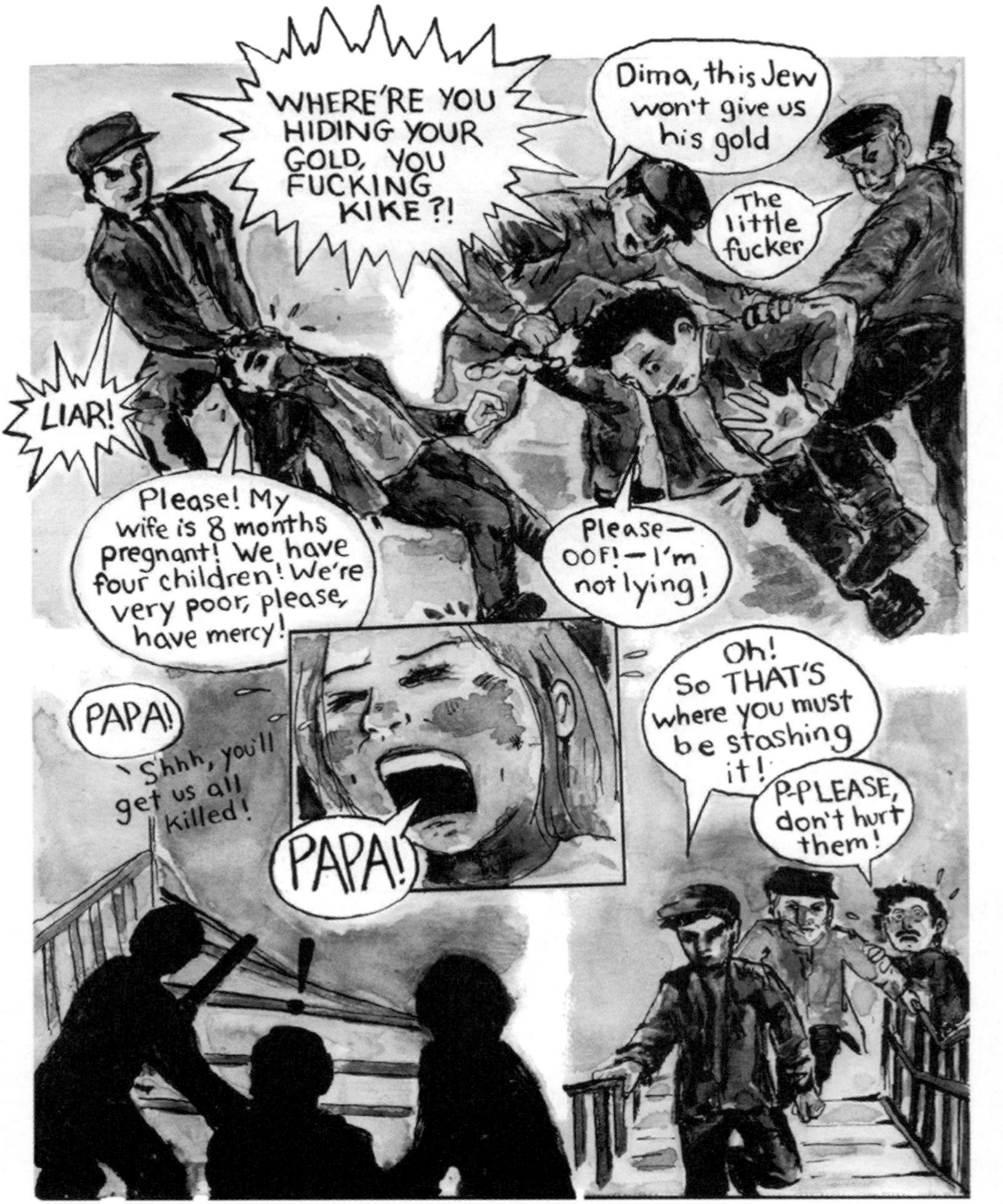
WHERE'RE YOU HIDING YOUR GOLD, YOU FUCKING KIKE?!
Dima, this Jew won't give us his gold
The little fucker
LIAR!
Please! My wife is 8 months pregnant! We have four children! We're very poor, please, have mercy!
Please— OOF!—I'm not lying!
PAPA!
Shhh, you'll get us all killed!
PAPA!
Oh! So THAT'S where you must be stashing it!
P-PLEASE, don't hurt them!

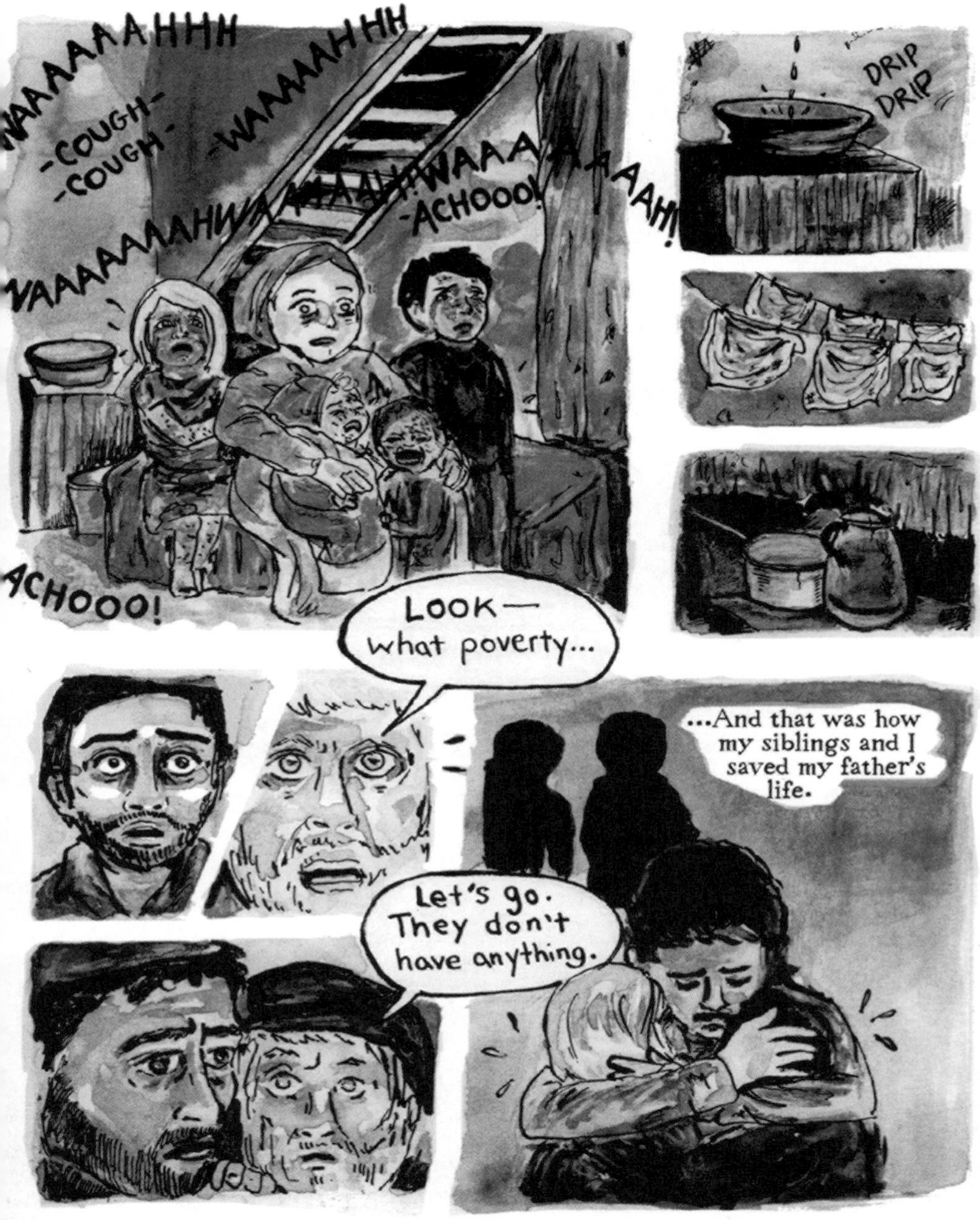
WAAAAAAAHHHH
-COUGH-
-COUGH-
-WAAAAAAHHH
WAAAA-A-AAAH!
-ACHOOO!
AAAAAAAAHWAAAAAAAH
WAAAA
ACHOOO!
DRIP
DRIP
LOOK— what poverty...
...And that was how my siblings and I saved my father's life.
Let's go. They don't have anything.

The Civil War continued, a wholesale destruction of people. The ruling parties changed often.

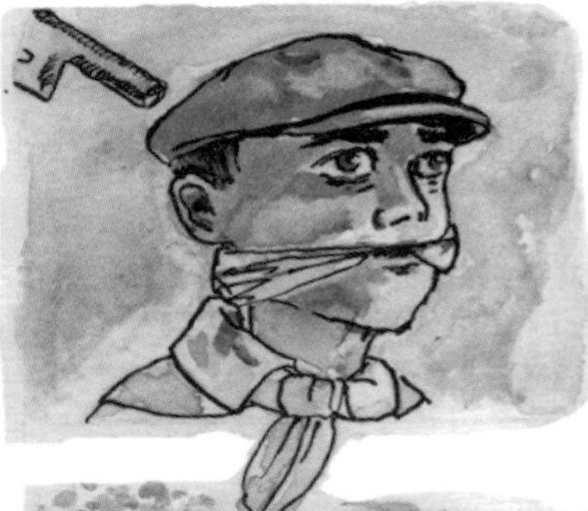

It was said that the new komsomols* were kidnapped by the White Army, their bodies tied together, and thrown into the Dneiper River to drown.

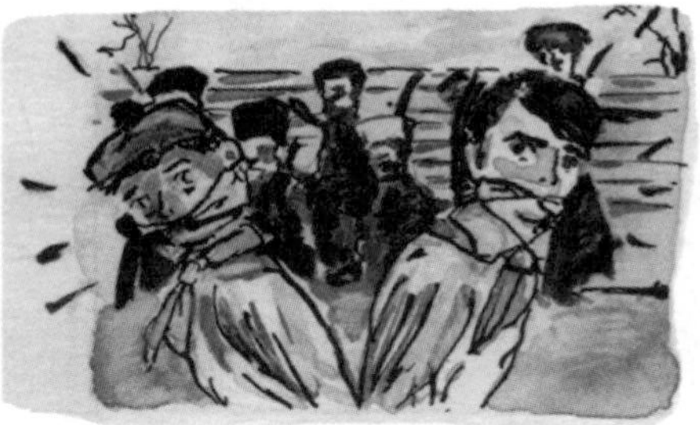

*Youth division of the communist party

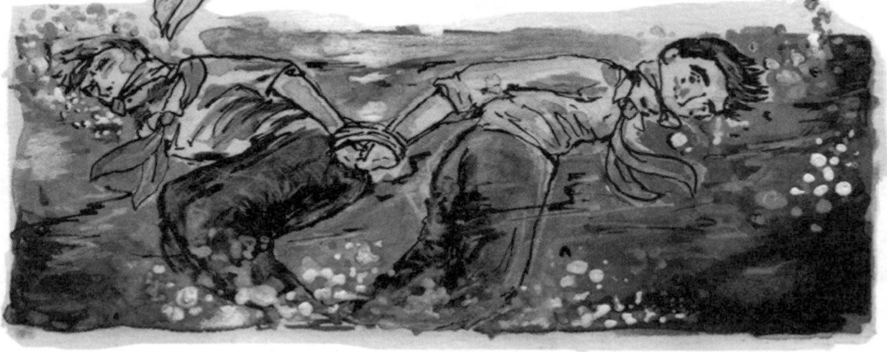

They were so young. Others, no older than they, were "baptized by fire."

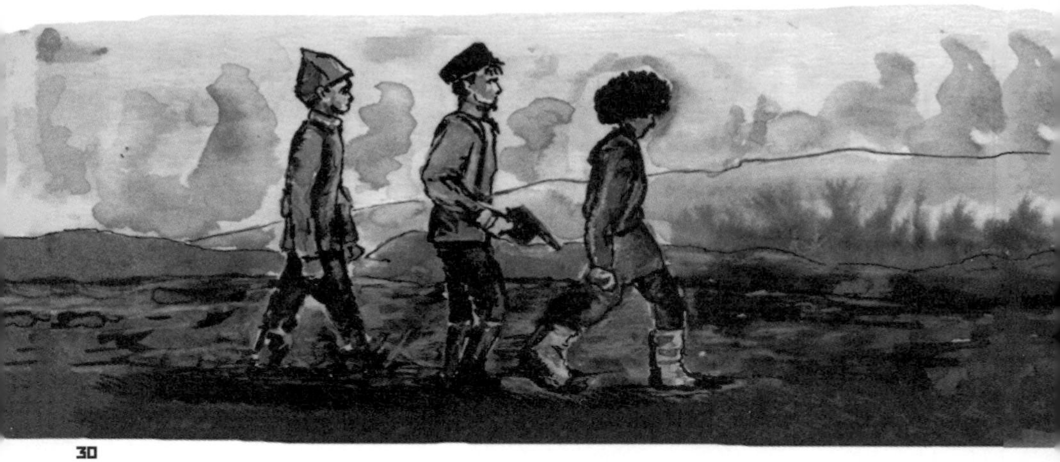

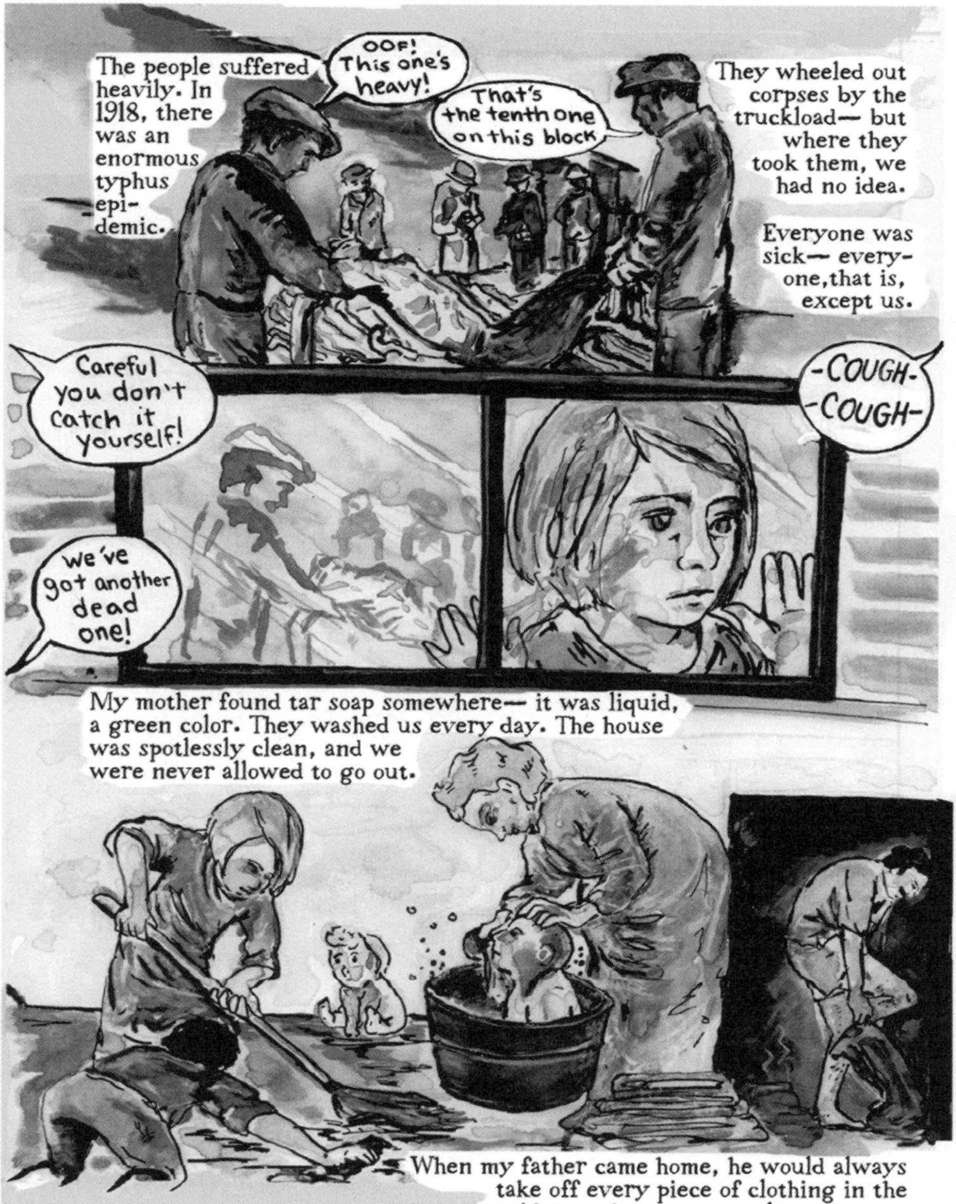
The people suffered heavily. In 1918, there was an enormous typhus epi-demic.
OOF! This one's heavy!
That's the tenth one on this block
They wheeled out corpses by the truckload— but where they took them, we had no idea.
Everyone was sick— every-one, that is, except us.
Careful you don't catch it yourself!
-COUGH- -COUGH-
we've got another dead one!
My mother found tar soap somewhere— it was liquid, a green color. They washed us every day. The house was spotlessly clean, and we were never allowed to go out.
When my father came home, he would always take off every piece of clothing in the corridor, and put on a spotless new set.

Finally, the typhus epidemic ended, and Kiev was cleared of all rivaling bands. And the hunger began.

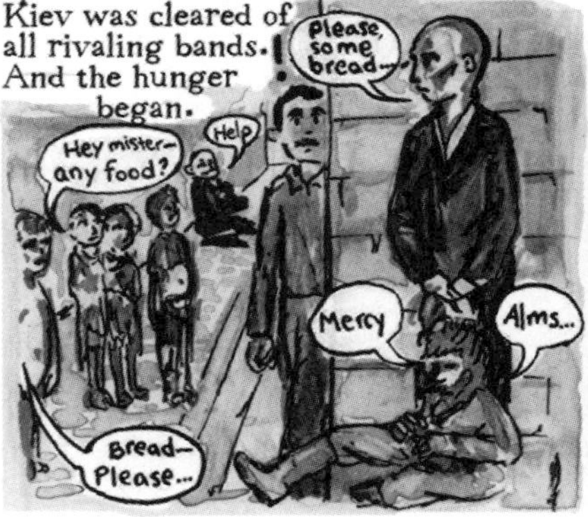
Please, some bread...
Hey mister– any food?
Help
Mercy
Alms...
Bread– Please...

For my father's landlord, it was too much to bear, and he took his own life.

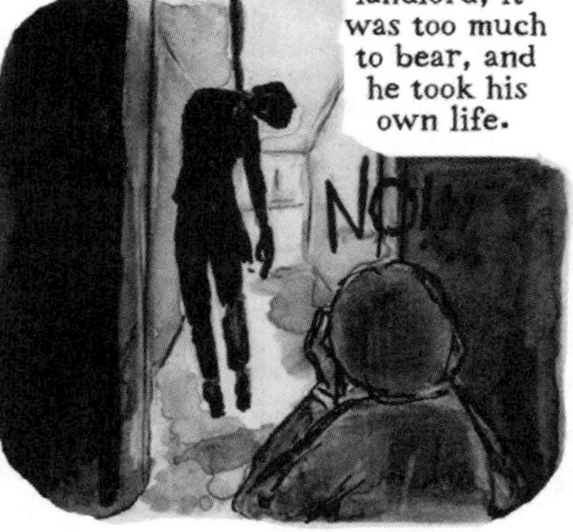
NO!

There was some humor amidst the terror. One night, my father woke up when a burglar crawled through our window...

In his confusion, he thought our apartment was flooding and my brother Vova was trying to escape.

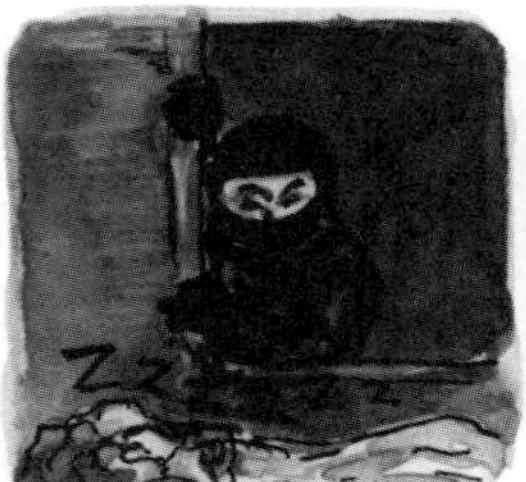

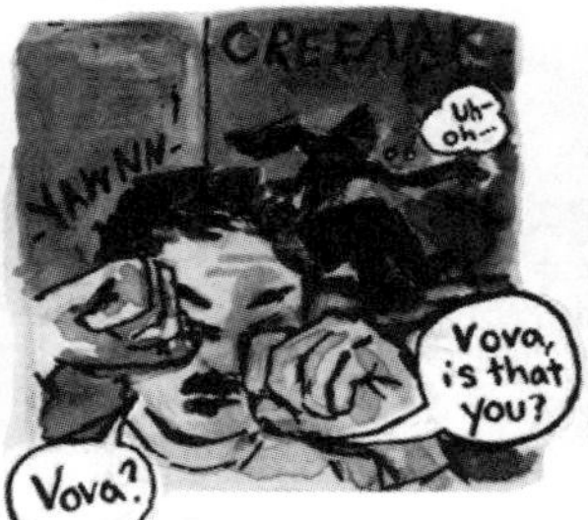
CREEAAK
Uh-oh...
YAWNN
Vova, is that you?
Vova?

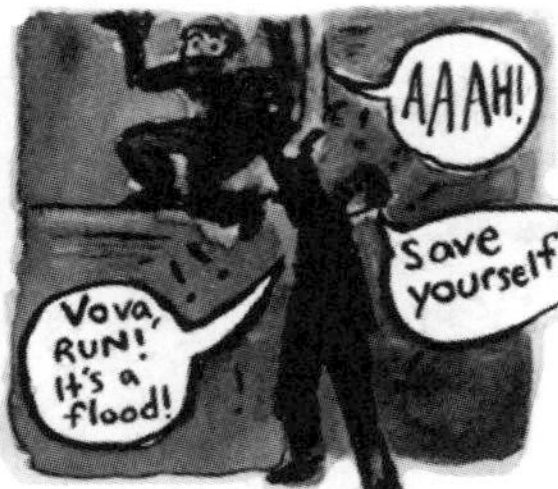
AAAH!
Save yourself!
Vova, RUN! It's a flood!

We laughed and laughed.

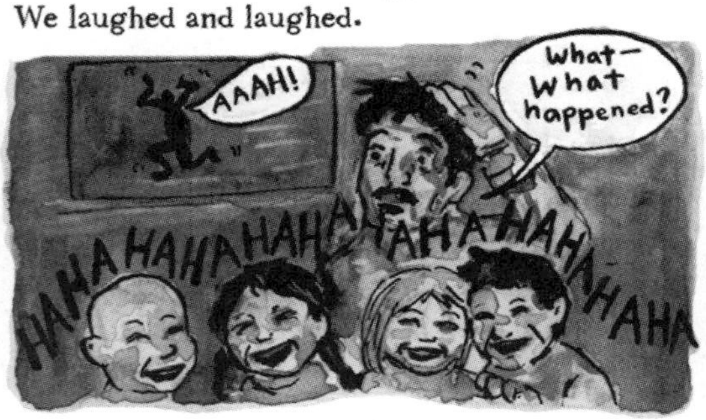
AAAH!
What– What happened?
HAHAHAHAHAHAHAHAHAHAHAHAHA

So my father built us shutters.

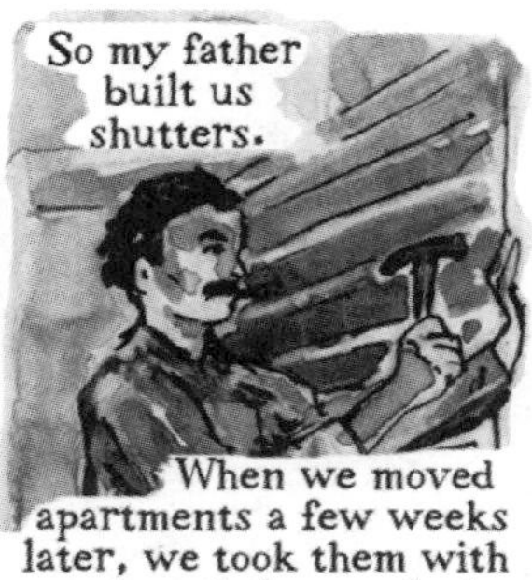

When we moved apartments a few weeks later, we took them with us and used them as beds.

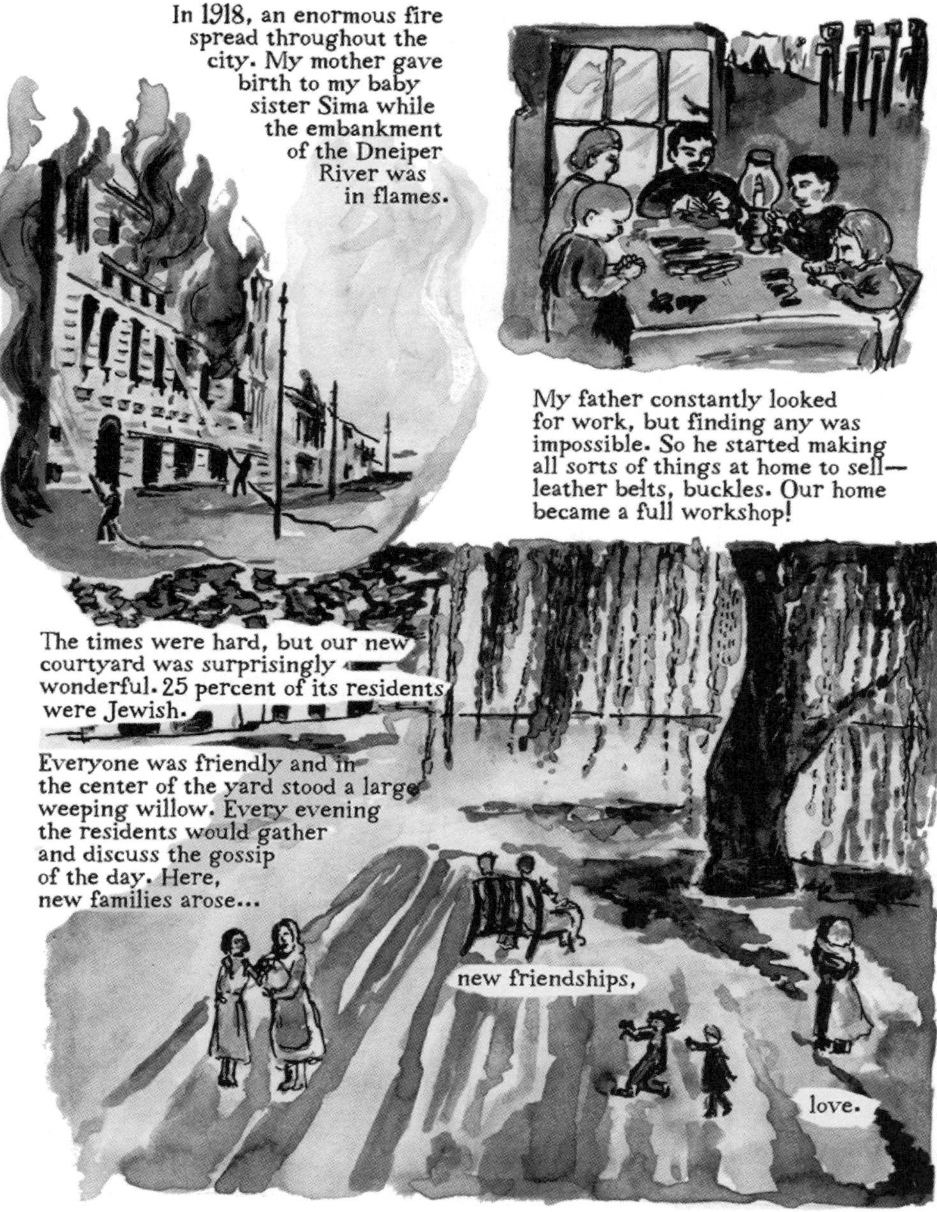
In 1918, an enormous fire spread throughout the city. My mother gave birth to my baby sister Sima while the embankment of the Dneiper River was in flames.
My father constantly looked for work, but finding any was impossible. So he started making all sorts of things at home to sell—leather belts, buckles. Our home became a full workshop!
The times were hard, but our new courtyard was surprisingly wonderful. 25 percent of its residents were Jewish.
Everyone was friendly and in the center of the yard stood a large weeping willow. Every evening the residents would gather and discuss the gossip of the day. Here, new families arose...
new friendships,
love.

Interlude

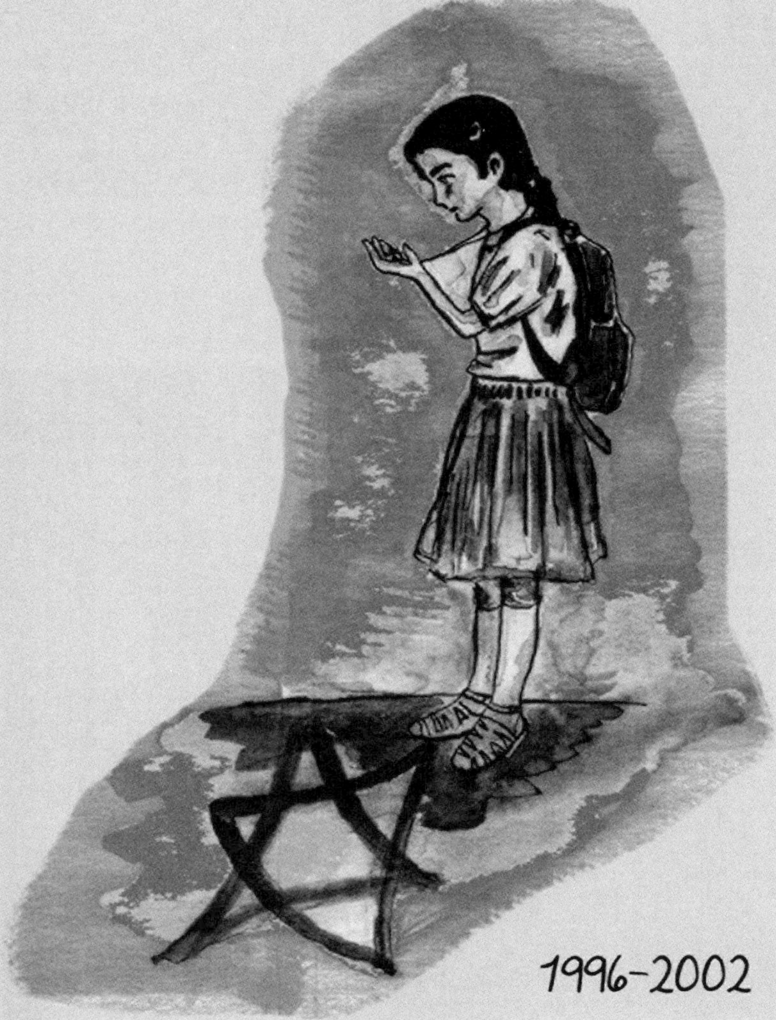

1996–2002

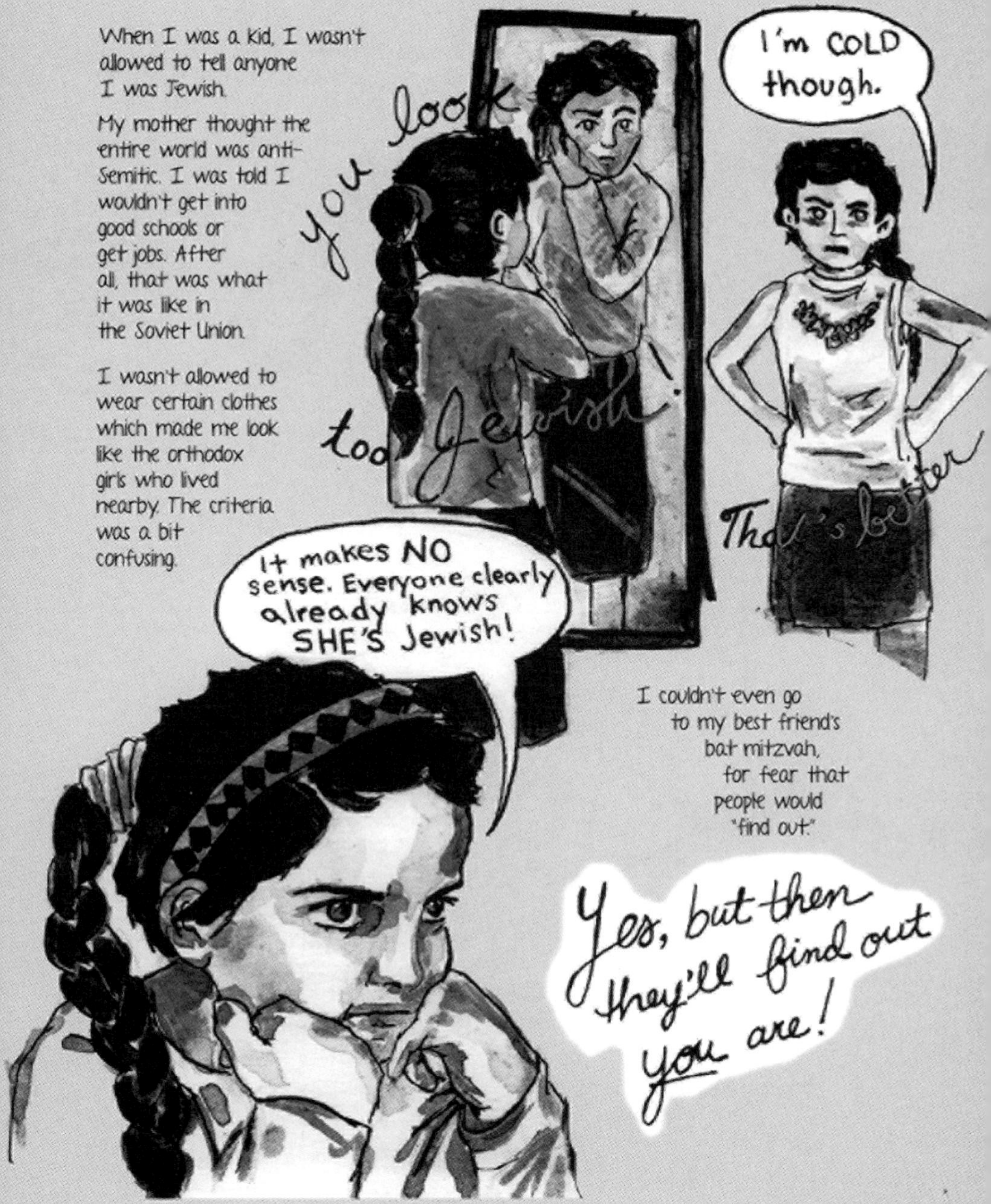
When I was a Kid, I wasn't allowed to tell anyone I was Jewish.
My mother thought the entire world was anti-Semitic. I was told I wouldn't get into good schools or get jobs. After all, that was what it was like in the Soviet Union.
I wasn't allowed to wear certain clothes which made me look like the orthodox girls who lived nearby. The criteria was a bit confusing.
you look too Jewish!
I'm COLD though.
That's better
It makes NO sense. Everyone clearly already knows SHE'S Jewish!
I couldn't even go to my best friend's bat mitzvah, for fear that people would "find out."
Yes, but then they'll find out you are!

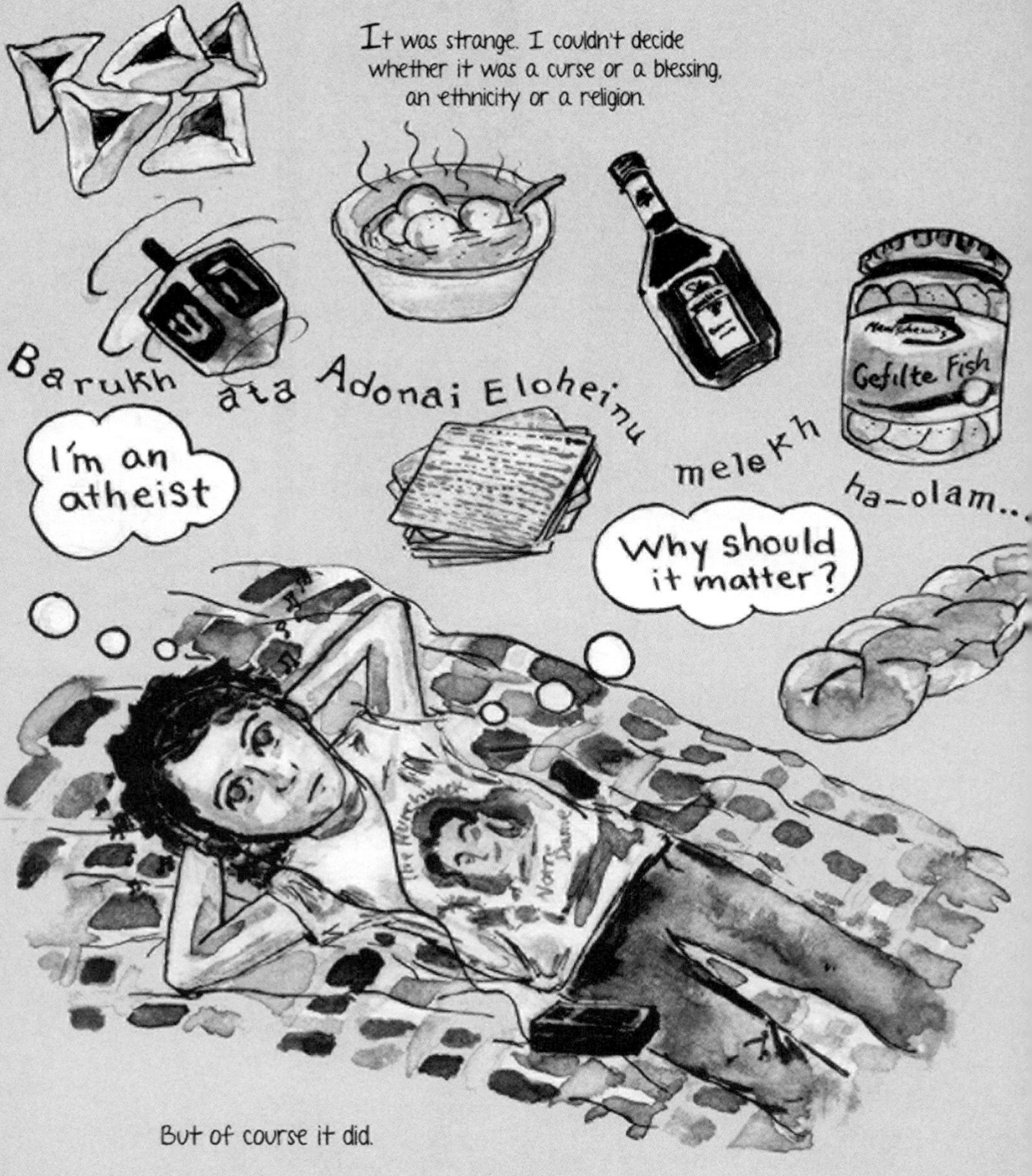
It was strange. I couldn't decide whether it was a curse or a blessing, an ethnicity or a religion.
Gefilte Fish
Barukh ata Adonai Eloheinu melekh ha-olam...
I'm an atheist
Why should it matter?
But of course it did.

Some people think there isn't any anti-semitism left in the US.

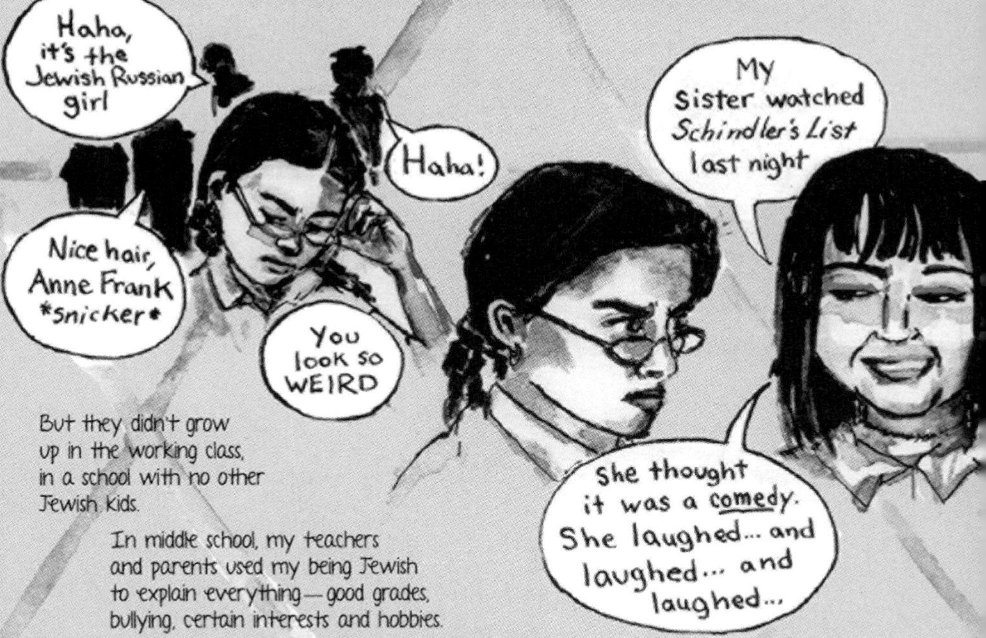

Haha, it's the Jewish Russian girl
Haha!
Nice hair, Anne Frank *snicker*
You look so WEIRD
My Sister watched *Schindler's List* last night
She thought it was a comedy. She laughed... and laughed... and laughed...

But they didn't grow up in the working class, in a school with no other Jewish kids.

In middle school, my teachers and parents used my being Jewish to explain everything—good grades, bullying, certain interests and hobbies.

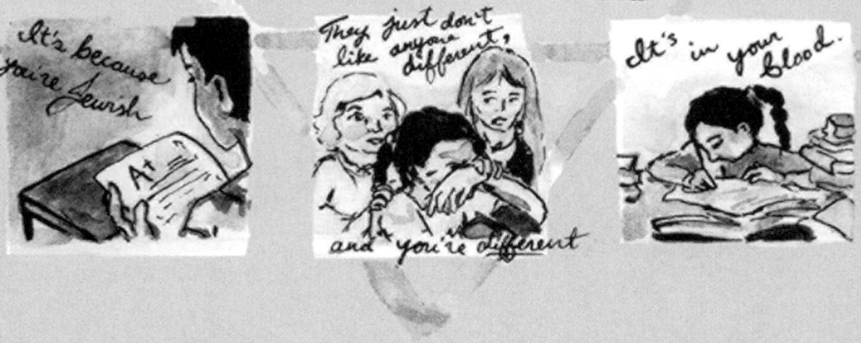

It's because you're Jewish
A+
They just don't like anyone different, and you're different
It's in your blood.

What did it mean to be Jewish? I didn't know. It felt, more than anything, like a ball and chain.

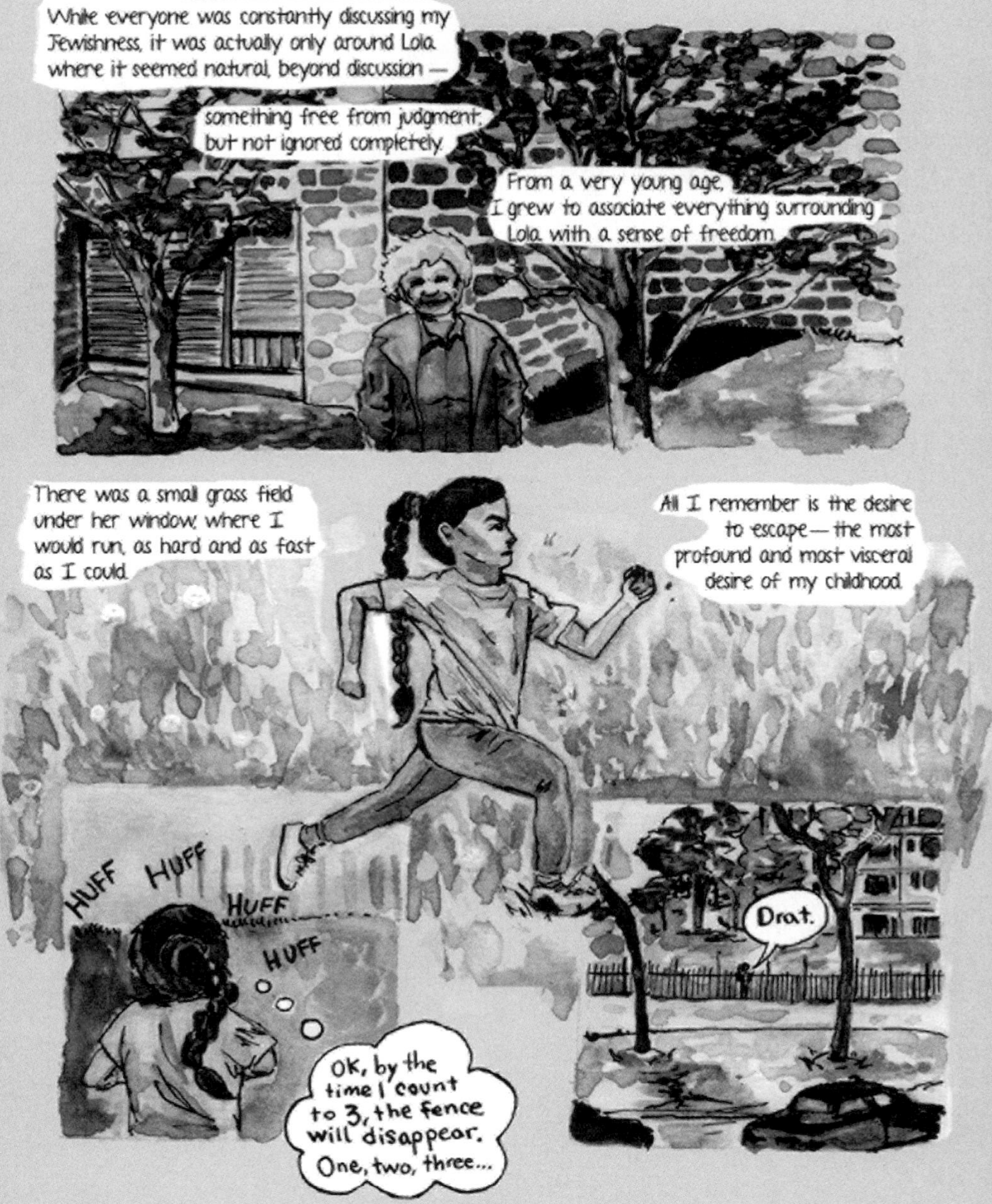
While everyone was constantly discussing my Jewishness, it was actually only around Lola where it seemed natural, beyond discussion —
something free from judgment, but not ignored completely.
From a very young age, I grew to associate everything surrounding Lola with a sense of freedom.
There was a small grass field under her window, where I would run, as hard and as fast as I could.
All I remember is the desire to escape — the most profound and most visceral desire of my childhood.
HUFF HUFF
HUFF
HUFF
OK, by the time I count to 3, the fence will disappear. One, two, three...
Drat.

Chapter 3: 1920-1925

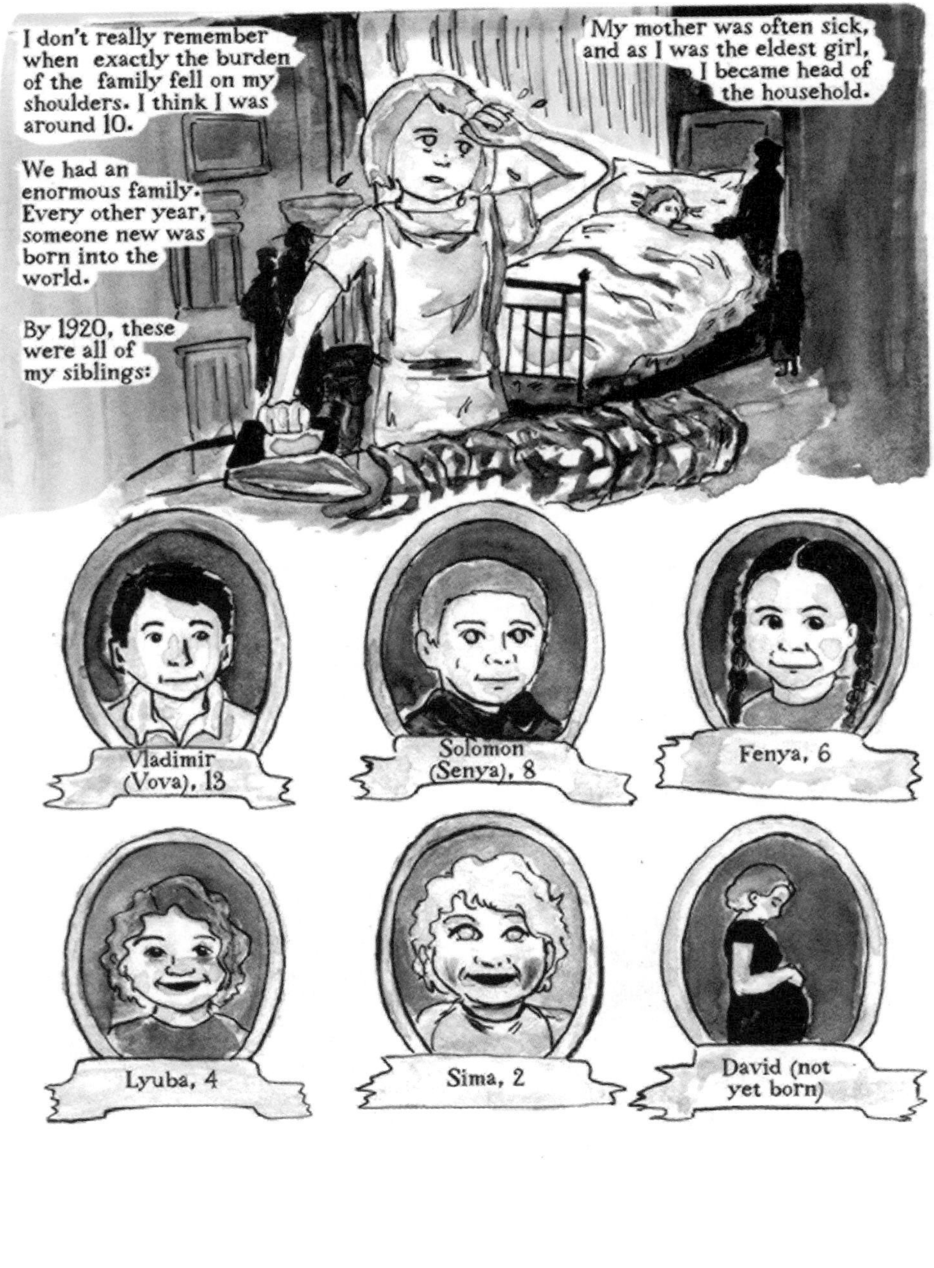
I don't really remember when exactly the burden of the family fell on my shoulders. I think I was around 10.
We had an enormous family. Every other year, someone new was born into the world.
By 1920, these were all of my siblings:
My mother was often sick, and as I was the eldest girl, I became head of the household.
Vladimir (Vova), 13
Solomon (Senya), 8
Fenya, 6
Lyuba, 4
Sima, 2
David (not yet born)

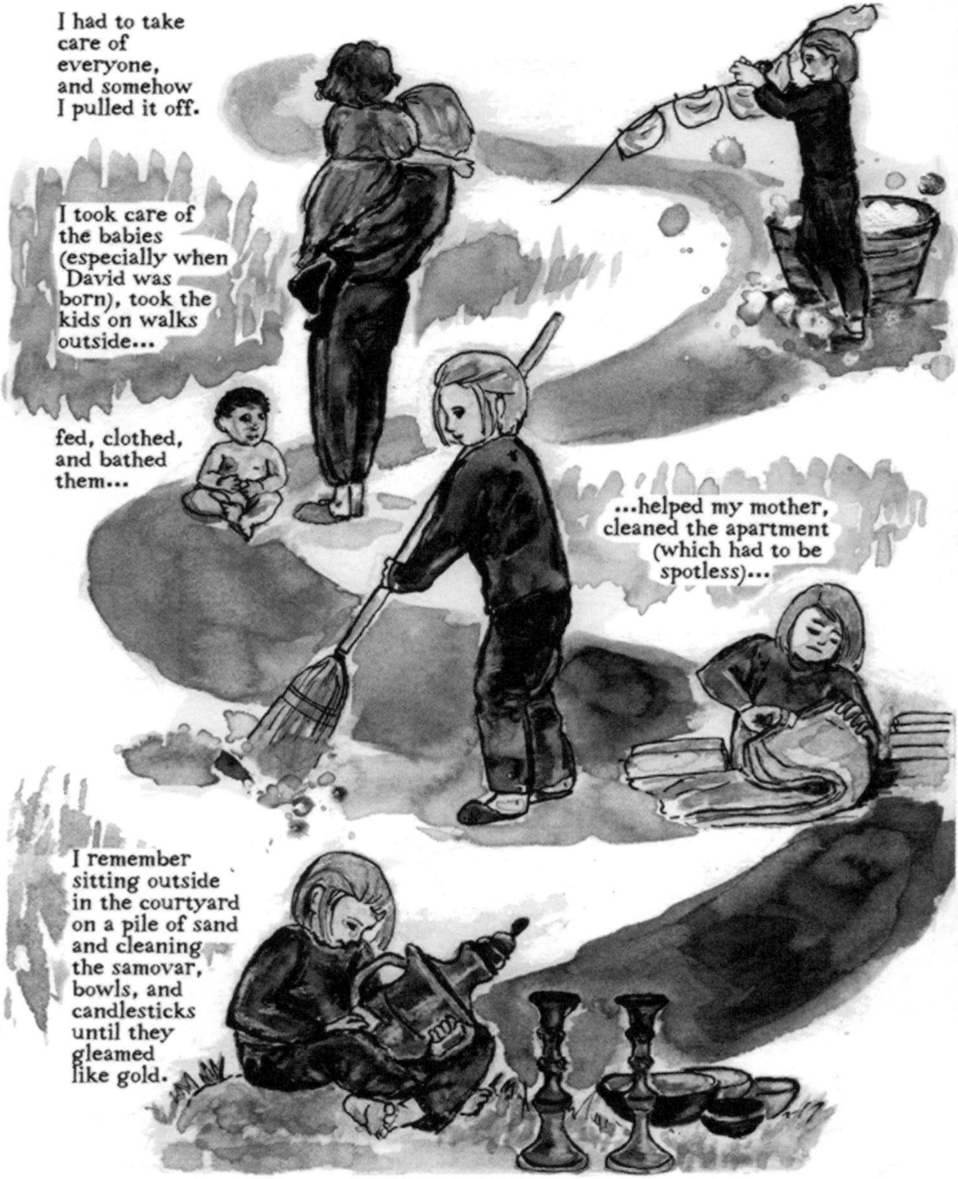
I had to take care of everyone, and somehow I pulled it off.
I took care of the babies (especially when David was born), took the kids on walks outside...
fed, clothed, and bathed them...
...helped my mother, cleaned the apartment (which had to be spotless)...
I remember sitting outside in the courtyard on a pile of sand and cleaning the samovar, bowls, and candlesticks until they gleamed like gold.

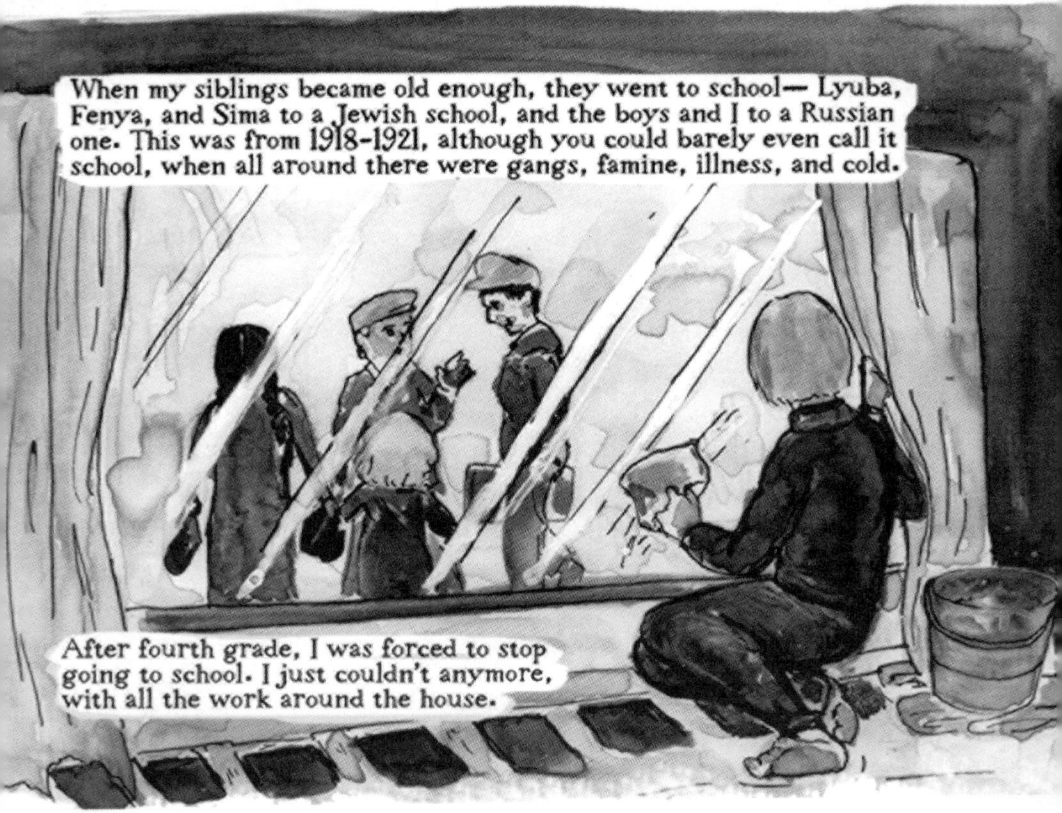
When my siblings became old enough, they went to school— Lyuba, Fenya, and Sima to a Jewish school, and the boys and I to a Russian one. This was from 1918-1921, although you could barely even call it school, when all around there were gangs, famine, illness, and cold.
After fourth grade, I was forced to stop going to school. I just couldn't anymore, with all the work around the house.

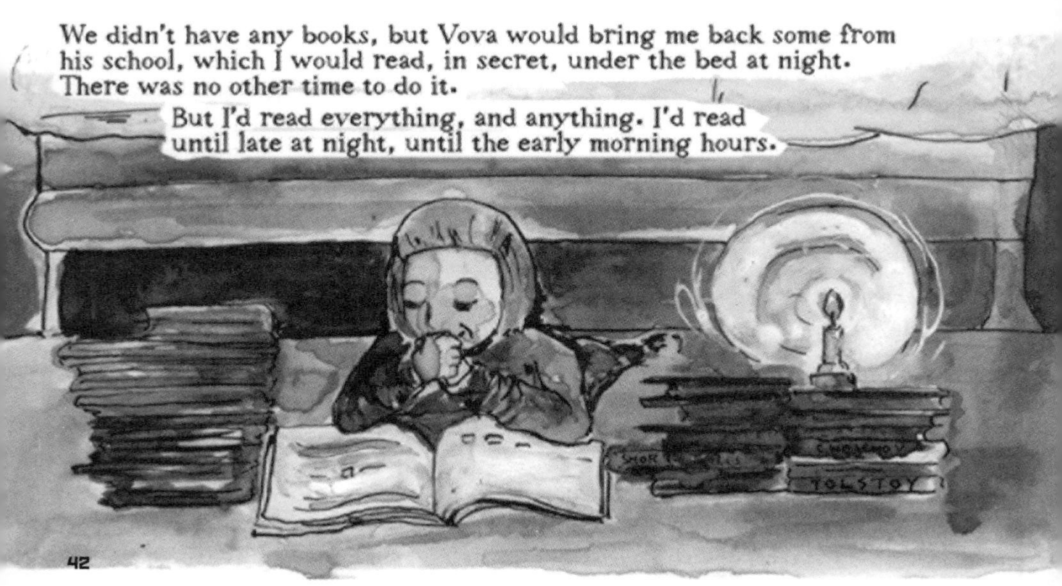
We didn't have any books, but Vova would bring me back some from his school, which I would read, in secret, under the bed at night. There was no other time to do it.
But I'd read everything, and anything. I'd read until late at night, until the early morning hours.
TOLSTOY

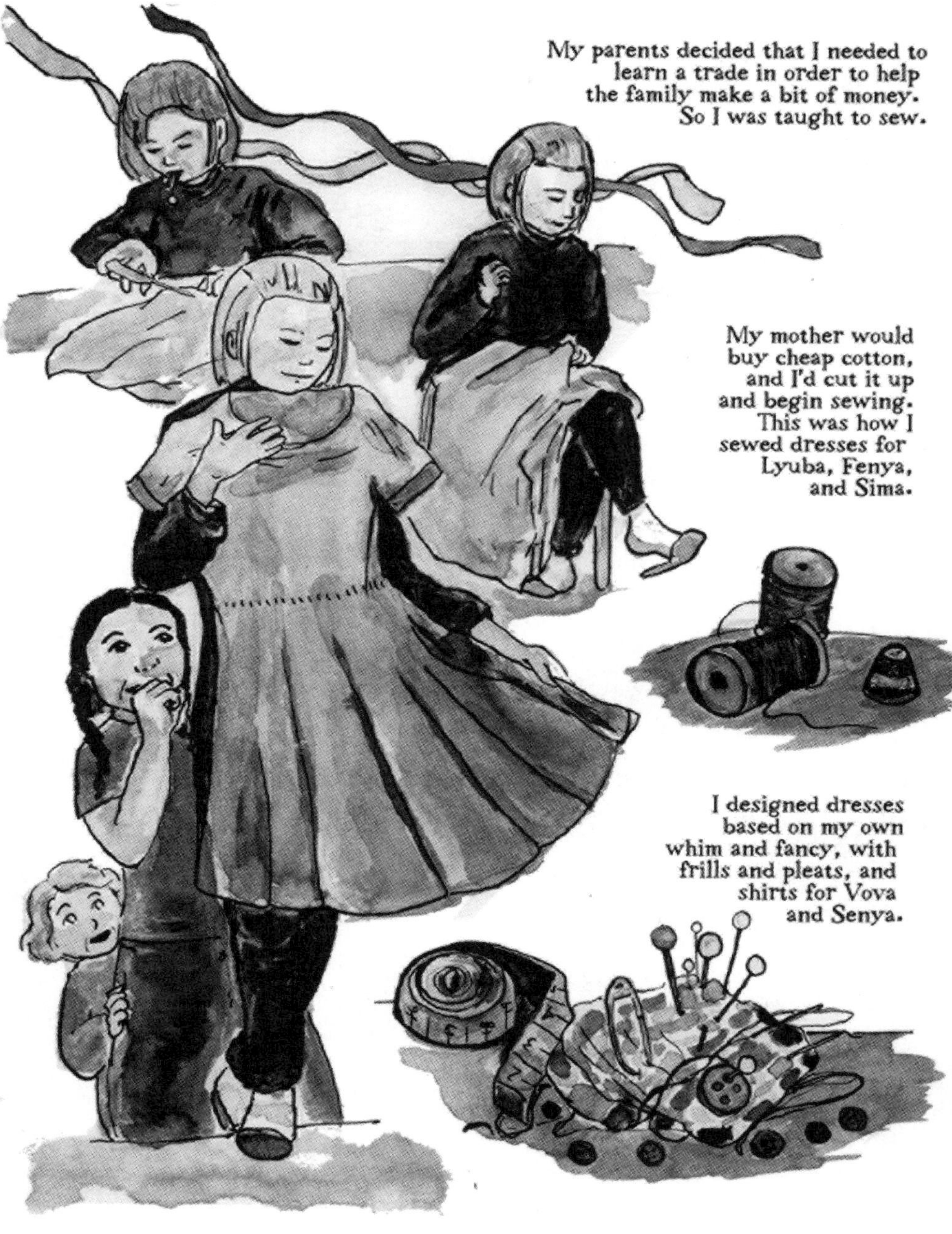
My parents decided that I needed to learn a trade in order to help the family make a bit of money. So I was taught to sew.
My mother would buy cheap cotton, and I'd cut it up and begin sewing. This was how I sewed dresses for Lyuba, Fenya, and Sima.
I designed dresses based on my own whim and fancy, with frills and pleats, and shirts for Vova and Senya.

I wasn't a very good seamstress, but
I was efficient. In one day I could:

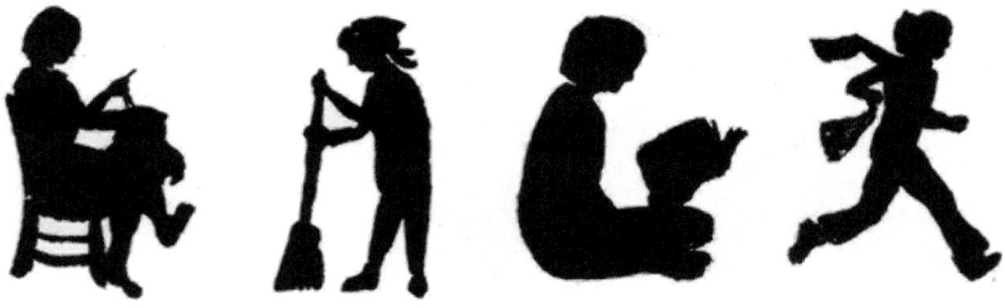

sew two dresses, clean the house, and read or go out with friends in the evenings.

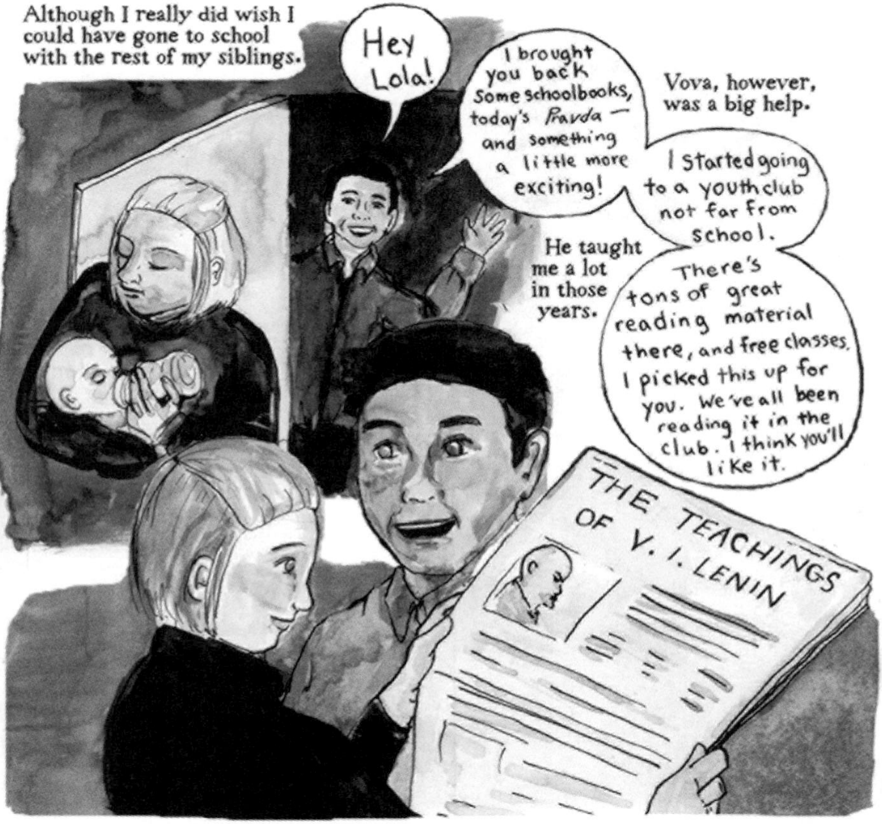

Although I really did wish I could have gone to school with the rest of my siblings.
Hey Lola!
I brought you back Some schoolbooks, today's Pravda — and something a little more exciting!
Vova, however, was a big help.
I started going to a youth club not far from school.
He taught me a lot in those years.
There's tons of great reading material there, and free classes. I picked this up for you. We've all been reading it in the club. I think you'll like it.
THE TEACHINGS OF V. I. LENIN

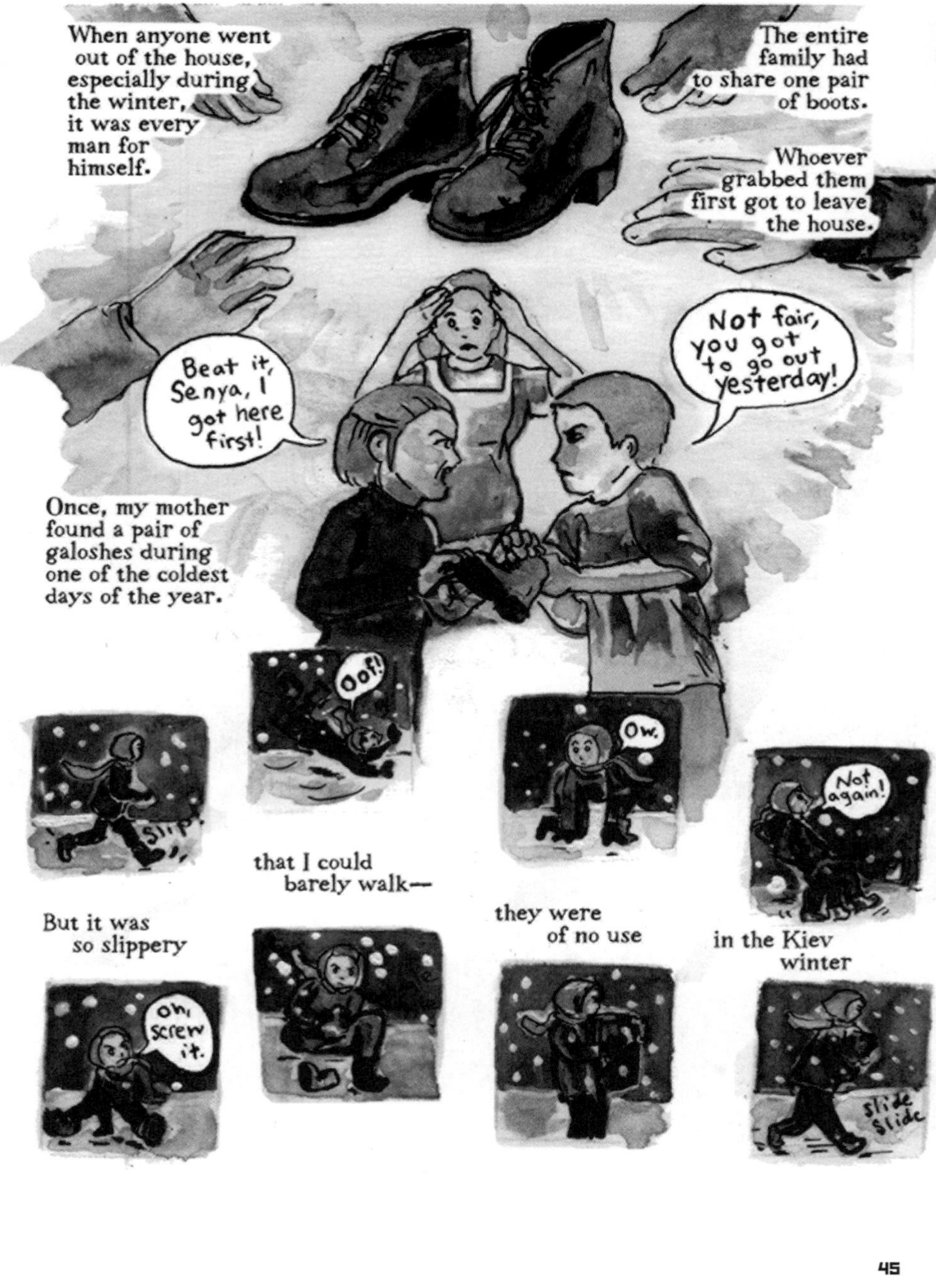
When anyone went out of the house, especially during the winter, it was every man for himself.
The entire family had to share one pair of boots.
Whoever grabbed them first got to leave the house.
Beat it, Senya, I got here first!
Not fair, you got to go out yesterday!
Once, my mother found a pair of galoshes during one of the coldest days of the year.
slip
Oof!
Ow.
Not again!
But it was so slippery
Oh, screw it.
that I could barely walk—
they were of no use
in the Kiev winter
slide slide

Interlude

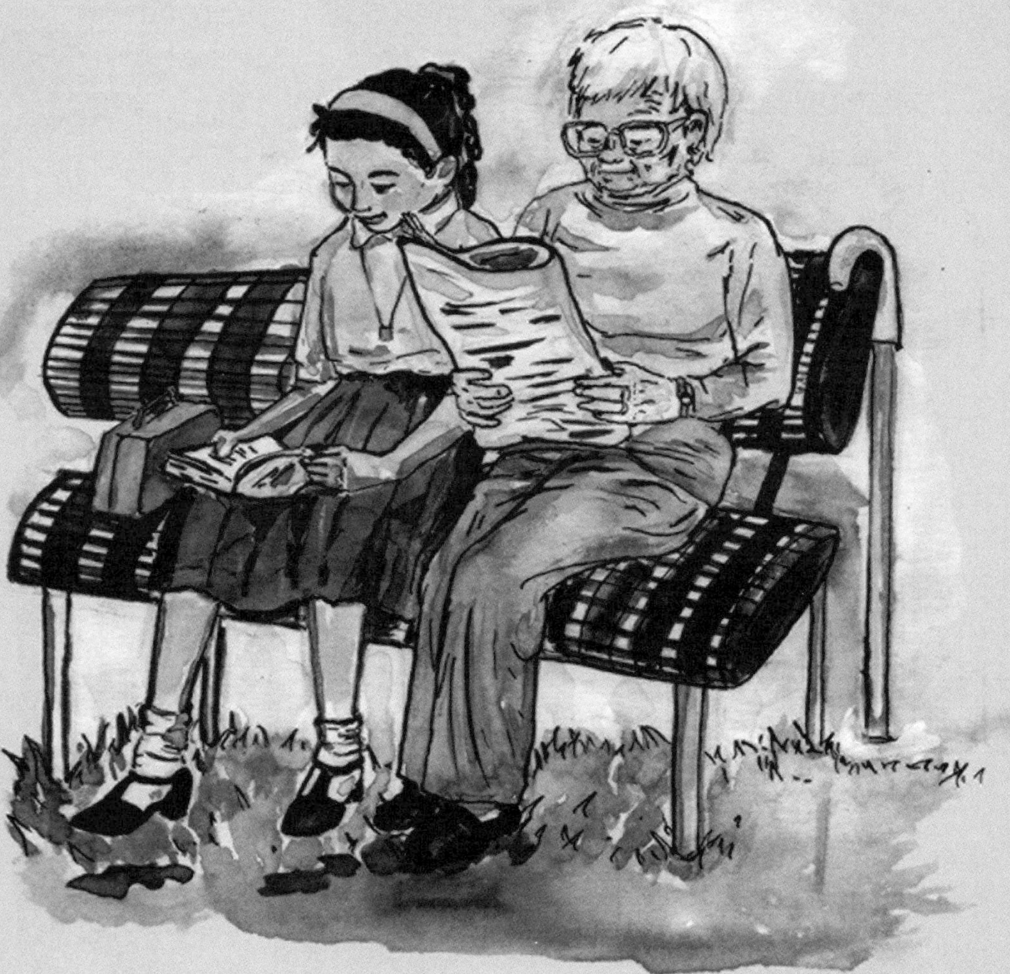

1993–2000

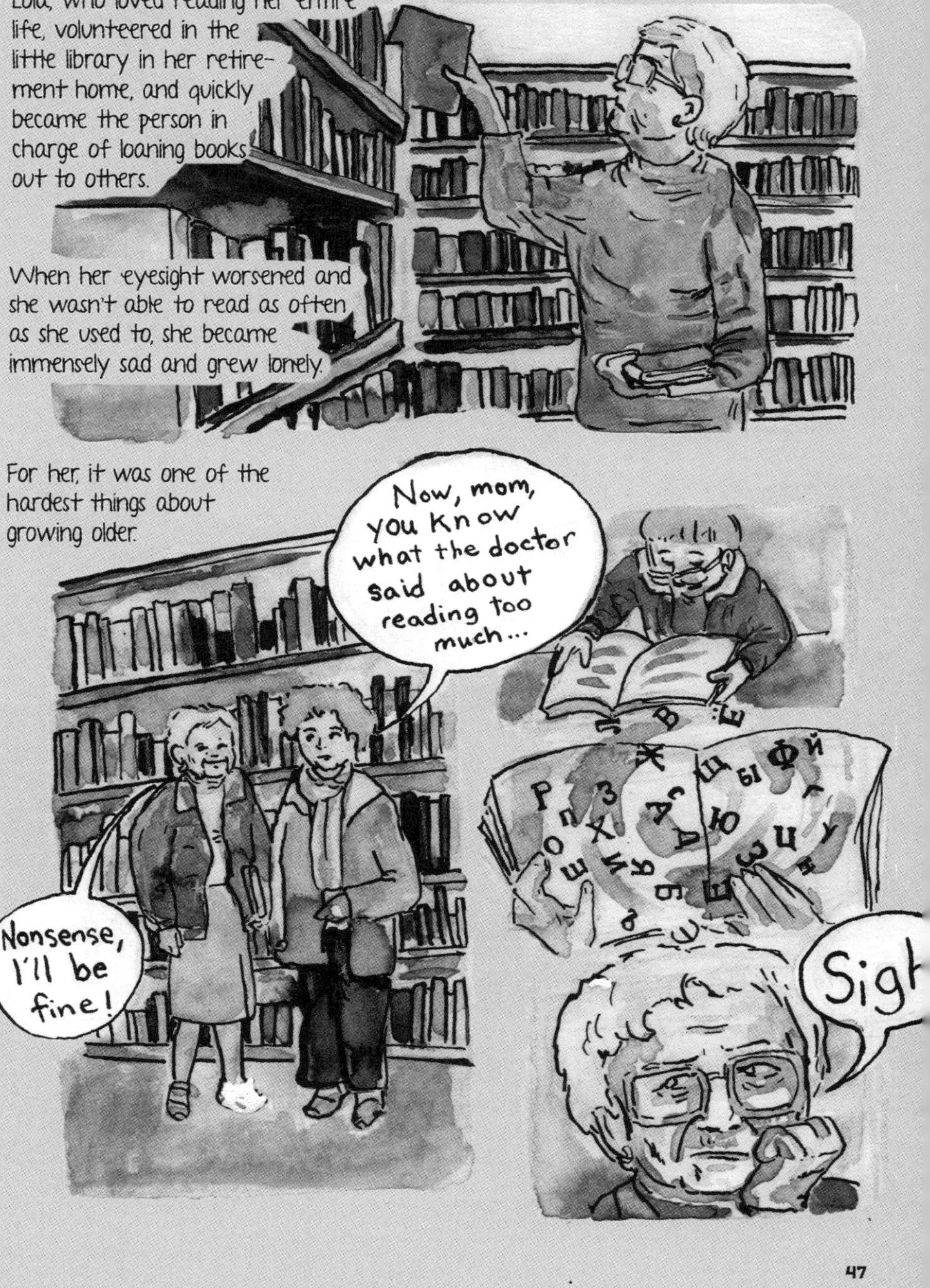
Lola, who loved reading her entire life, volunteered in the little library in her retirement home, and quickly became the person in charge of loaning books out to others.
When her eyesight worsened and she wasn't able to read as often as she used to, she became immensely sad and grew lonely.
For her, it was one of the hardest things about growing older.
Now, mom, you know what the doctor said about reading too much...
Nonsense, I'll be fine!
Sigh

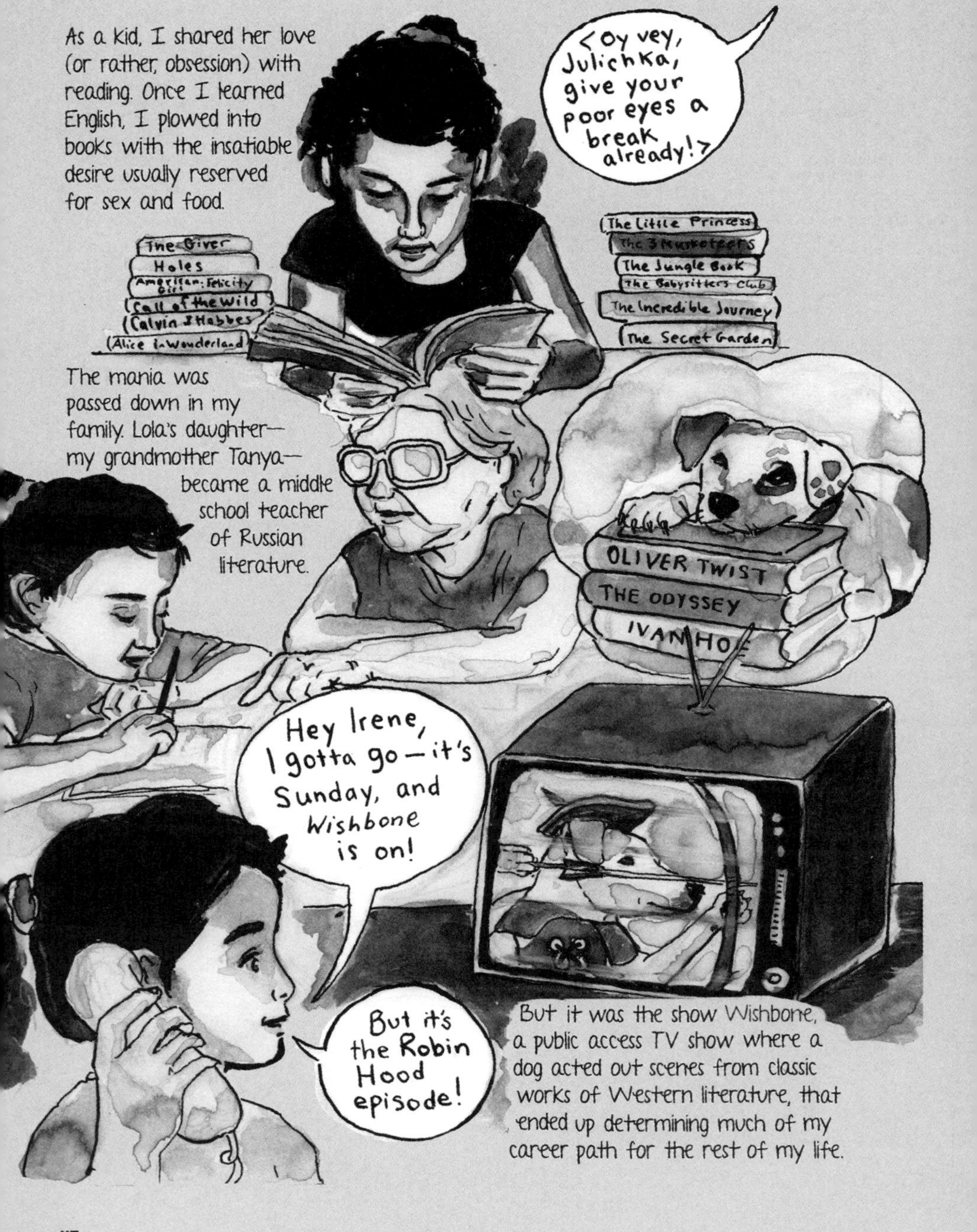
As a kid, I shared her love (or rather, obsession) with reading. Once I learned English, I plowed into books with the insatiable desire usually reserved for sex and food.
<Oy vey, Julichka, give your poor eyes a break already!>
The Giver
Holes
American Girl: Felicity
Call of the Wild
Calvin & Hobbes
Alice in Wonderland
The Little Princess
The 3 Musketeers
The Jungle Book
The Babysitters Club
The Incredible Journey
The Secret Garden
The mania was passed down in my family. Lola's daughter—my grandmother Tanya—became a middle school teacher of Russian literature.
OLIVER TWIST
THE ODYSSEY
IVANHOE
Hey Irene, I gotta go—it's Sunday, and Wishbone is on!
But it's the Robin Hood episode!
But it was the show Wishbone, a public access TV show where a dog acted out scenes from classic works of Western literature, that ended up determining much of my career path for the rest of my life.

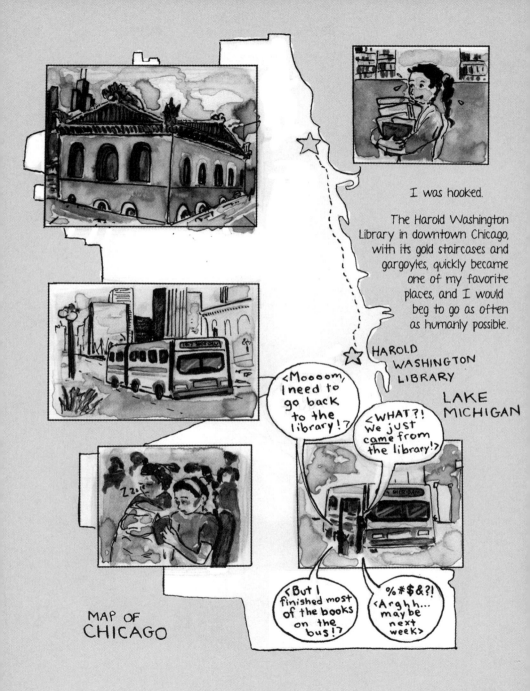

I was hooked.

The Harold Washington Library in downtown Chicago, with its gold staircases and gargoyles, quickly became one of my favorite places, and I would beg to go as often as humanly possible.

HAROLD WASHINGTON LIBRARY

LAKE MICHIGAN

‹Mooooom, I need to go back to the library!›

‹WHAT?! We just came from the library!›

‹But I finished most of the books on the bus!›

%#$&?! ‹Arghh... maybe next week›

MAP OF CHICAGO

Chapter 4: 1925–1930

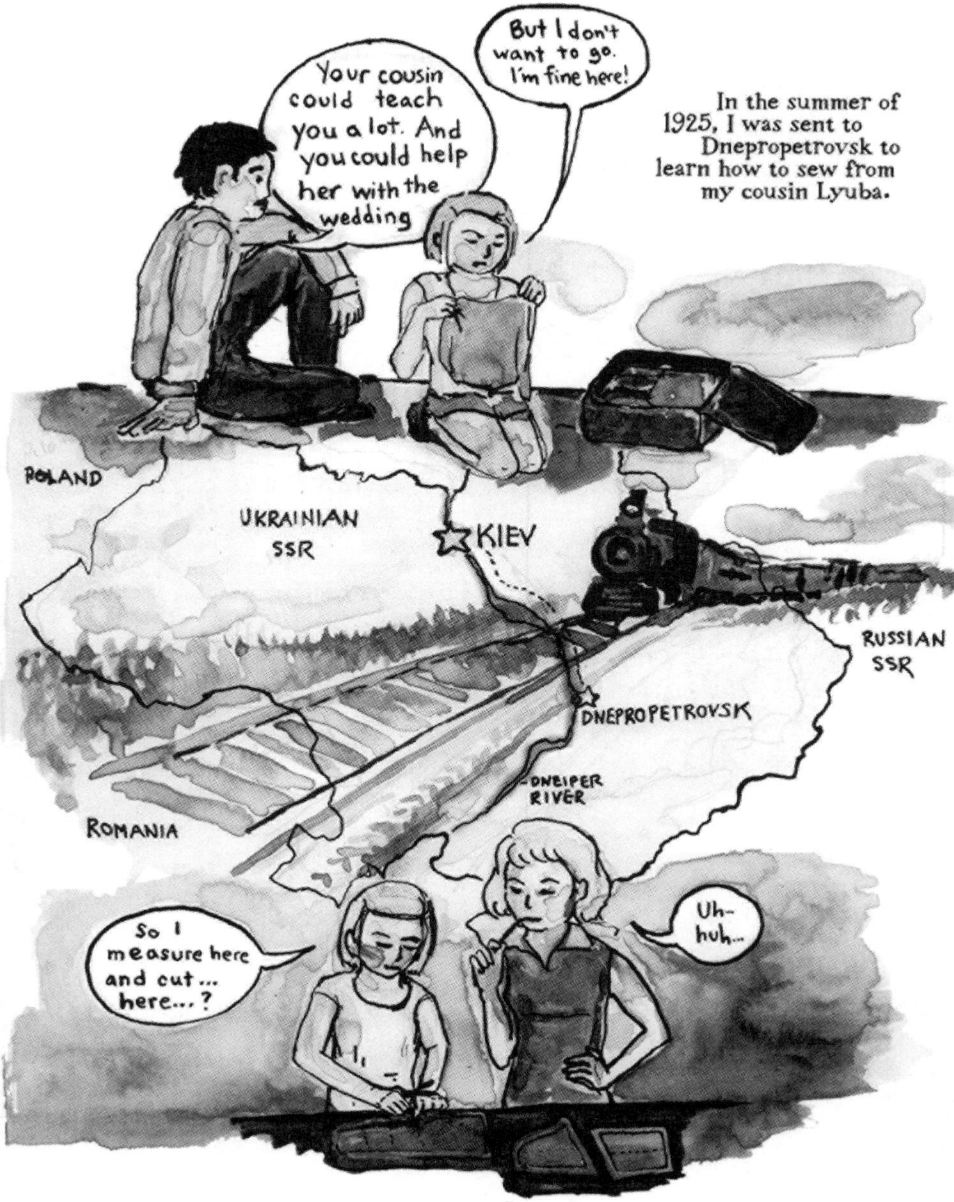
In the summer of 1925, I was sent to Dnepropetrovsk to learn how to sew from my cousin Lyuba.
Your cousin could teach you a lot. And you could help her with the wedding
But I don't want to go. I'm fine here!
POLAND
UKRAINIAN SSR
KIEV
RUSSIAN SSR
DNEPROPETROVSK
DNEIPER RIVER
ROMANIA
So I measure here and cut... here...?
Uh-huh...

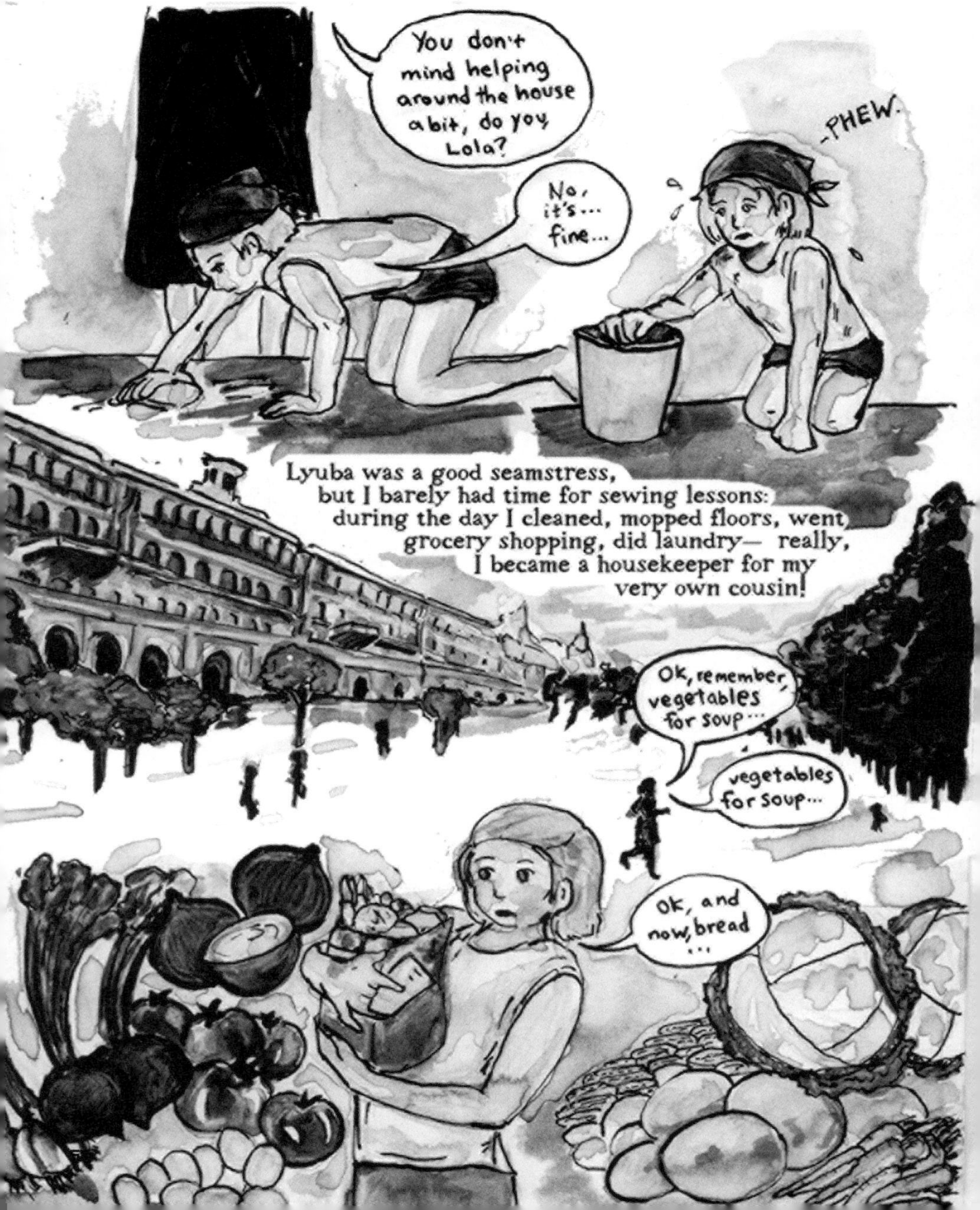
You don't mind helping around the house a bit, do you, Lola?
No, it's... fine...
-PHEW-
Lyuba was a good seamstress, but I barely had time for sewing lessons: during the day I cleaned, mopped floors, went grocery shopping, did laundry— really, I became a housekeeper for my very own cousin!
Ok, remember, vegetables for soup...
vegetables for soup...
Ok, and now, bread ...

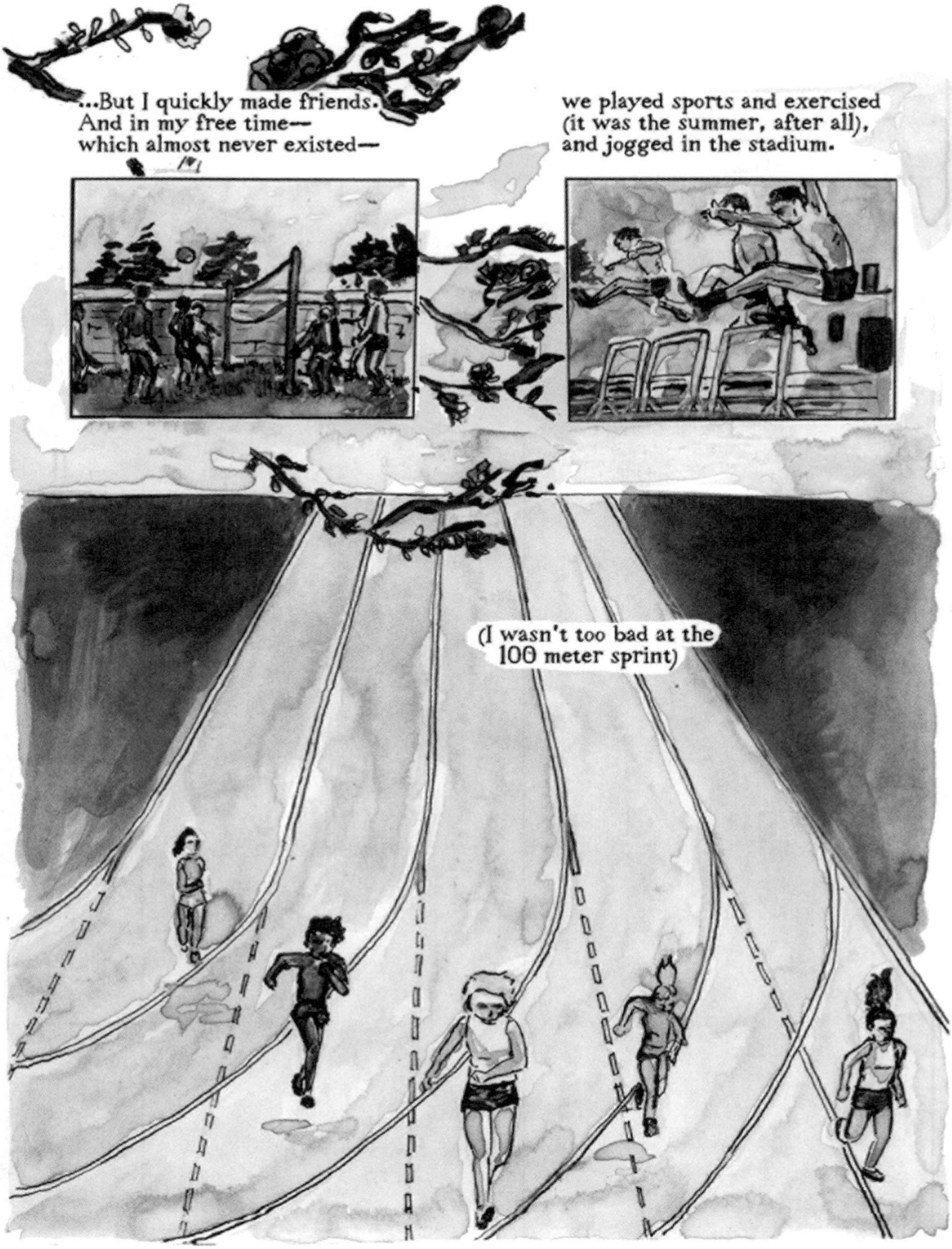
...But I quickly made friends. And in my free time— which almost never existed—
we played sports and exercised (it was the summer, after all), and jogged in the stadium.
(I wasn't too bad at the 100 meter sprint)

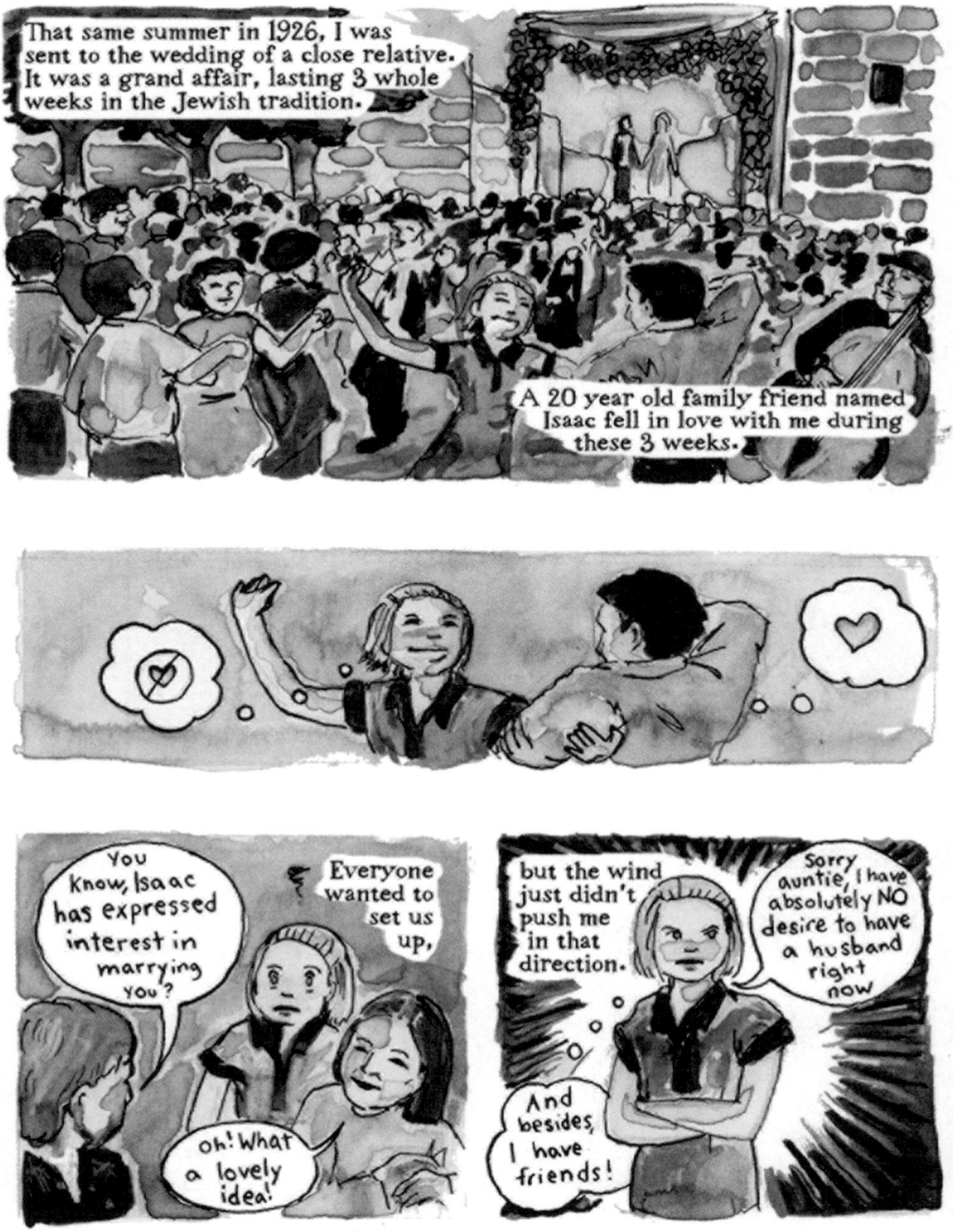
That same summer in 1926, I was sent to the wedding of a close relative. It was a grand affair, lasting 3 whole weeks in the Jewish tradition.
A 20 year old family friend named Isaac fell in love with me during these 3 weeks.
You know, Isaac has expressed interest in marrying you?
Everyone wanted to set us up,
oh! What a lovely idea!
but the wind just didn't push me in that direction.
Sorry auntie, I have absolutely NO desire to have a husband right now
And besides, I have friends!

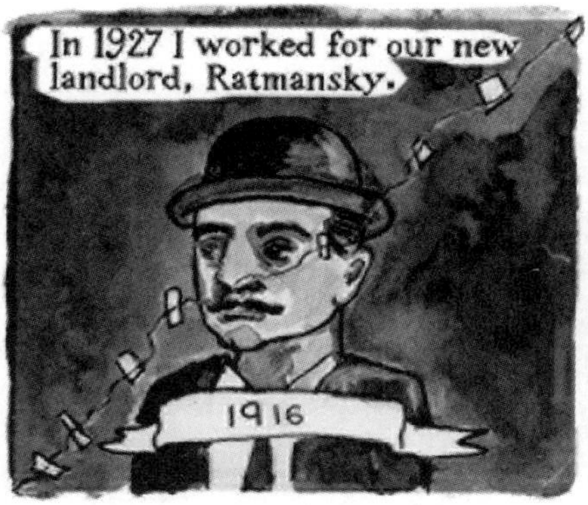
In 1927 I worked for our new landlord, Ratmansky.
1916

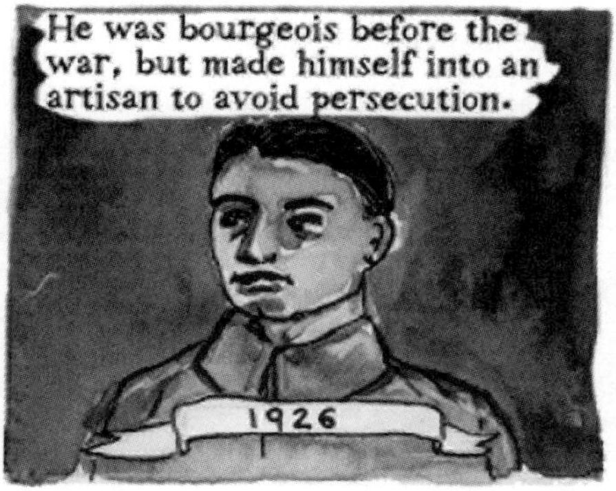
He was bourgeois before the war, but made himself into an artisan to avoid persecution.
1926

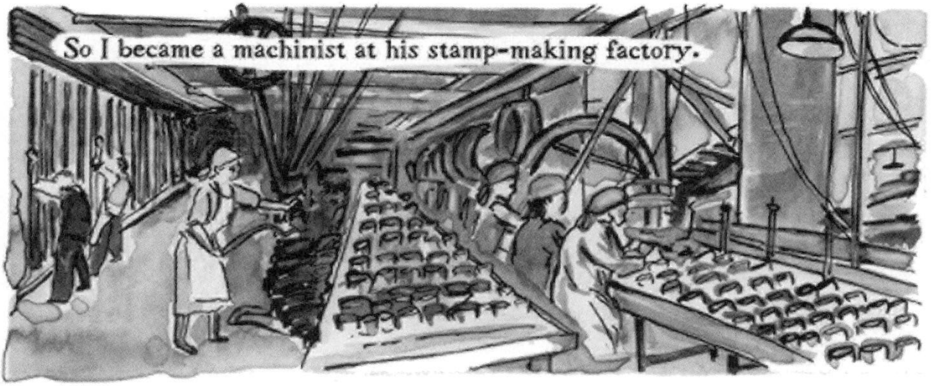
So I became a machinist at his stamp-making factory.

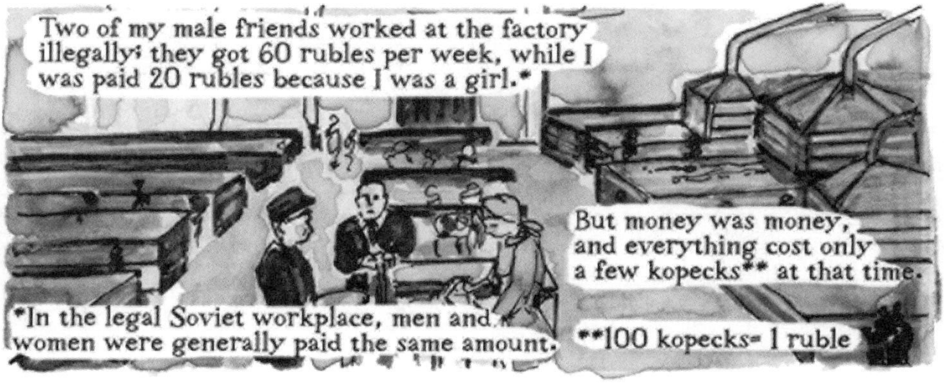
Two of my male friends worked at the factory illegally; they got 60 rubles per week, while I was paid 20 rubles because I was a girl.*
But money was money, and everything cost only a few kopecks** at that time.
*In the legal Soviet workplace, men and women were generally paid the same amount.
**100 kopecks= 1 ruble

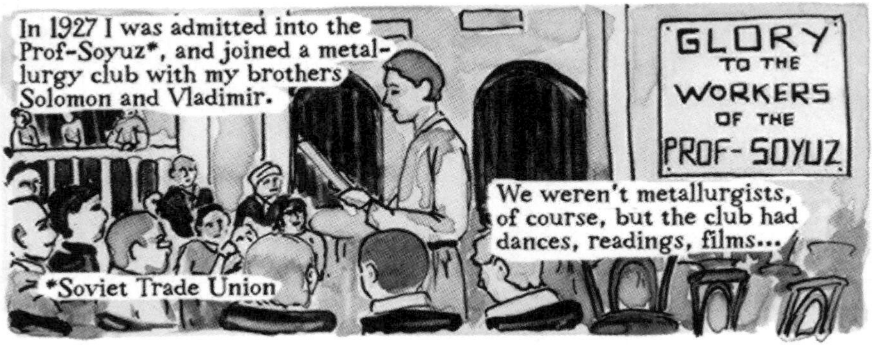
In 1927 I was admitted into the Prof-Soyuz*, and joined a metallurgy club with my brothers Solomon and Vladimir.
GLORY TO THE WORKERS OF THE PROF-SOYUZ
We weren't metallurgists, of course, but the club had dances, readings, films...
*Soviet Trade Union

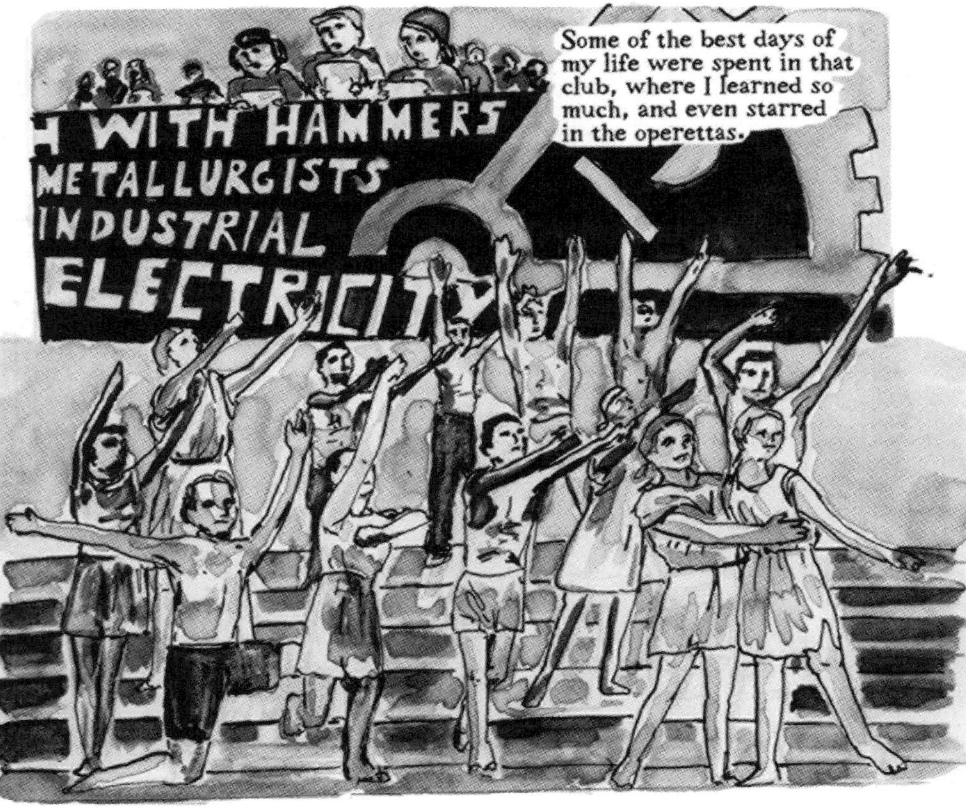
Some of the best days of my life were spent in that club, where I learned so much, and even starred in the operettas.
H WITH HAMMERS
METALLURGISTS
INDUSTRIAL
ELECTRICITY

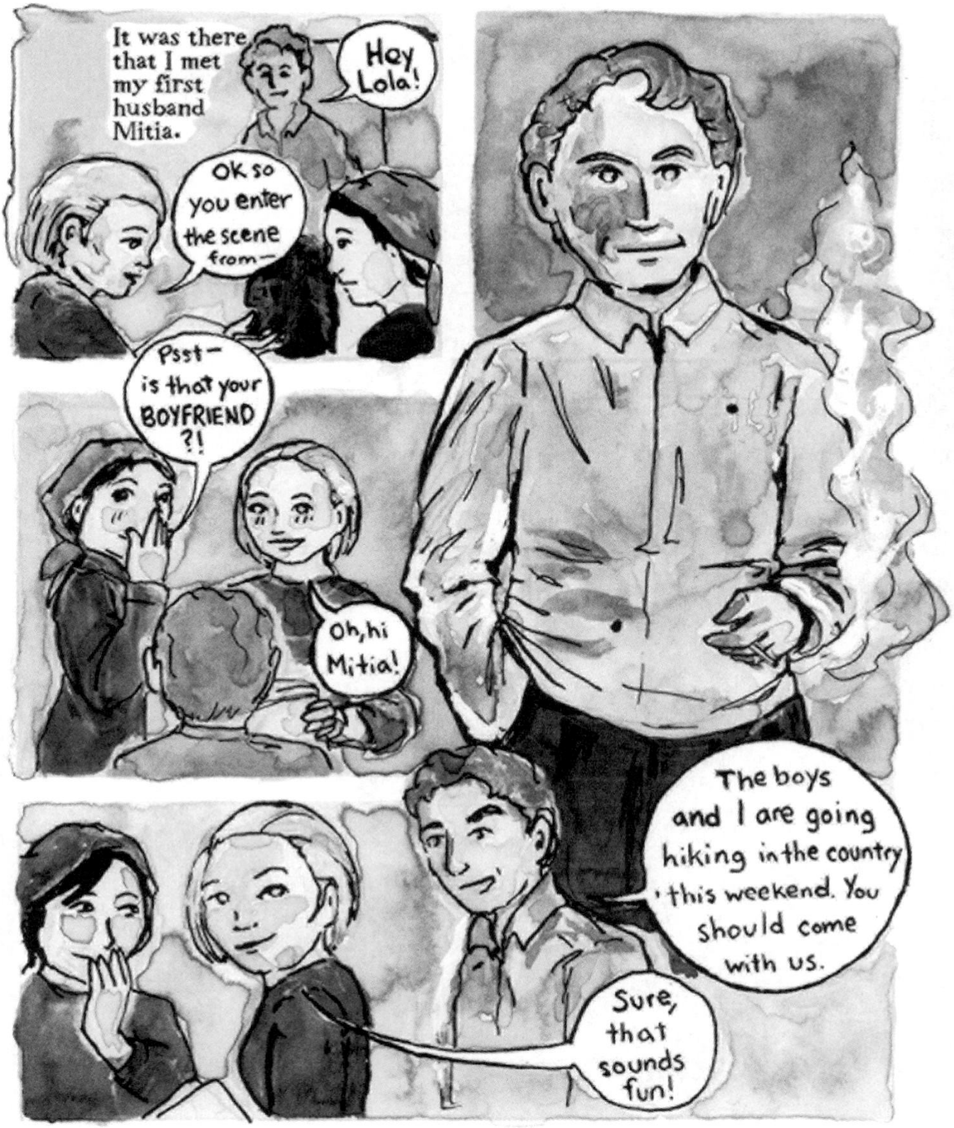
It was there that I met my first husband Mitia.
Hey Lola!
OK so you enter the scene from—
Psst— is that your BOYFRIEND?!
Oh, hi Mitia!
The boys and I are going hiking in the country this weekend. You should come with us.
Sure, that sounds fun!

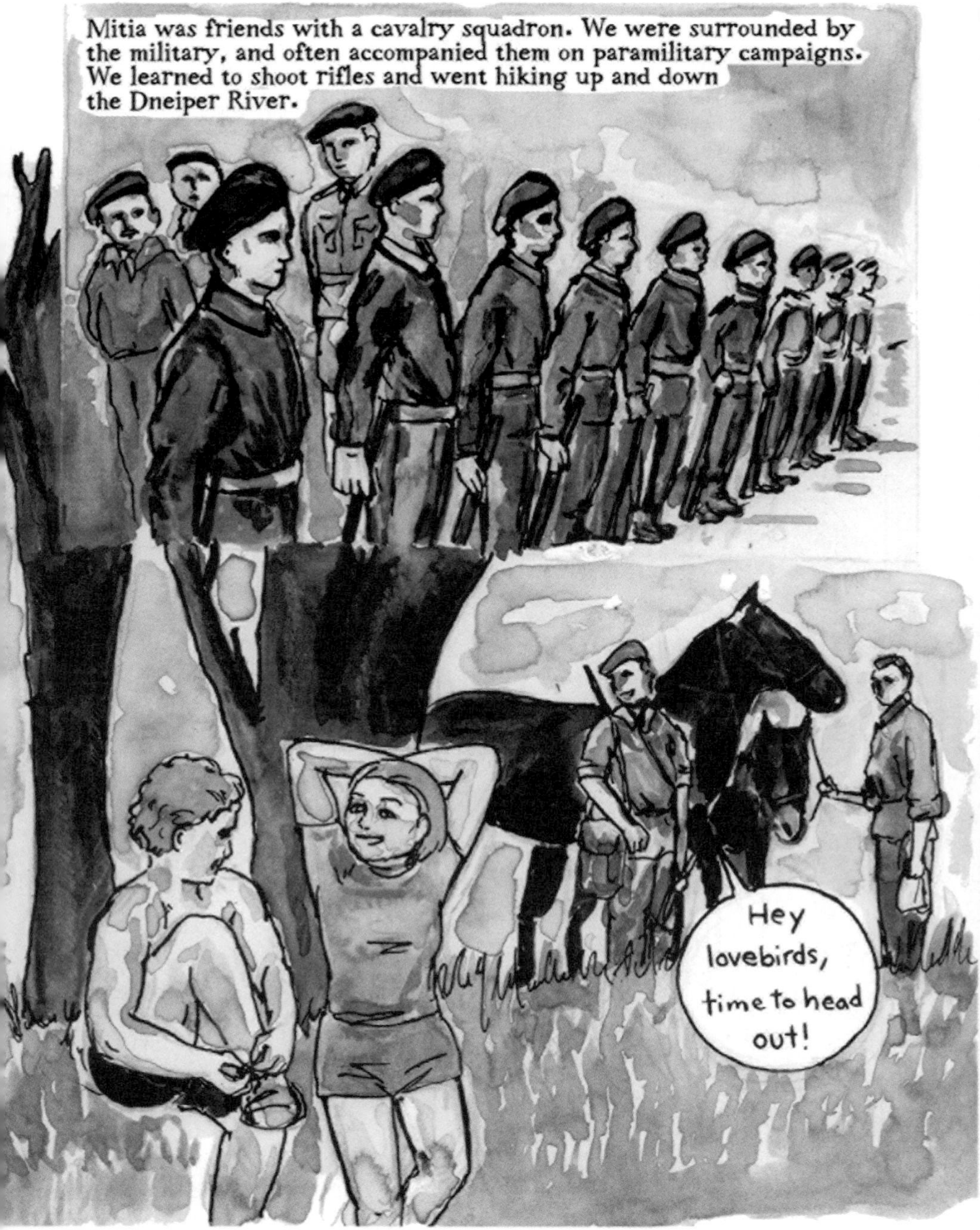
Mitia was friends with a cavalry squadron. We were surrounded by the military, and often accompanied them on paramilitary campaigns. We learned to shoot rifles and went hiking up and down the Dneiper River.
Hey lovebirds, time to head out!

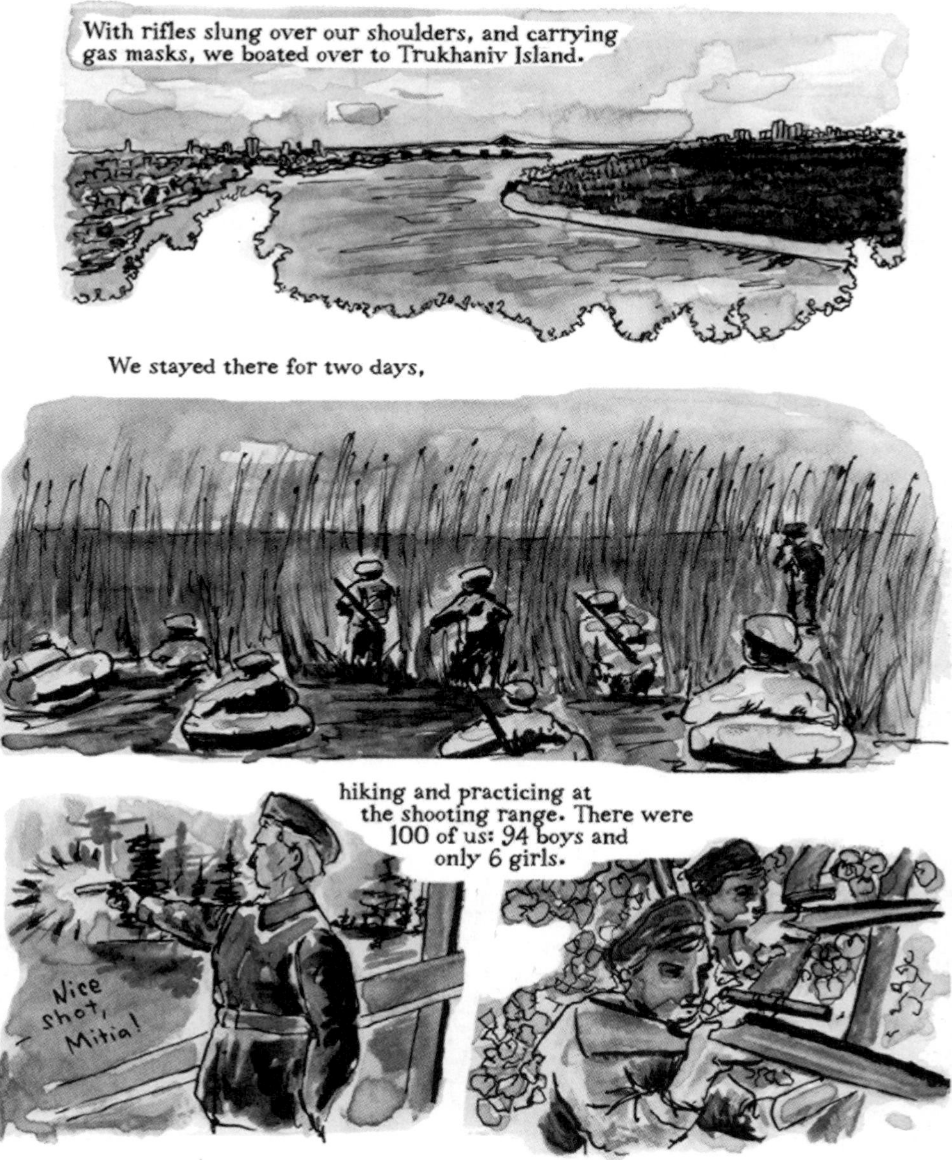
With rifles slung over our shoulders, and carrying gas masks, we boated over to Trukhaniv Island.
We stayed there for two days,
hiking and practicing at the shooting range. There were 100 of us: 94 boys and only 6 girls.
Nice shot, Mitia!

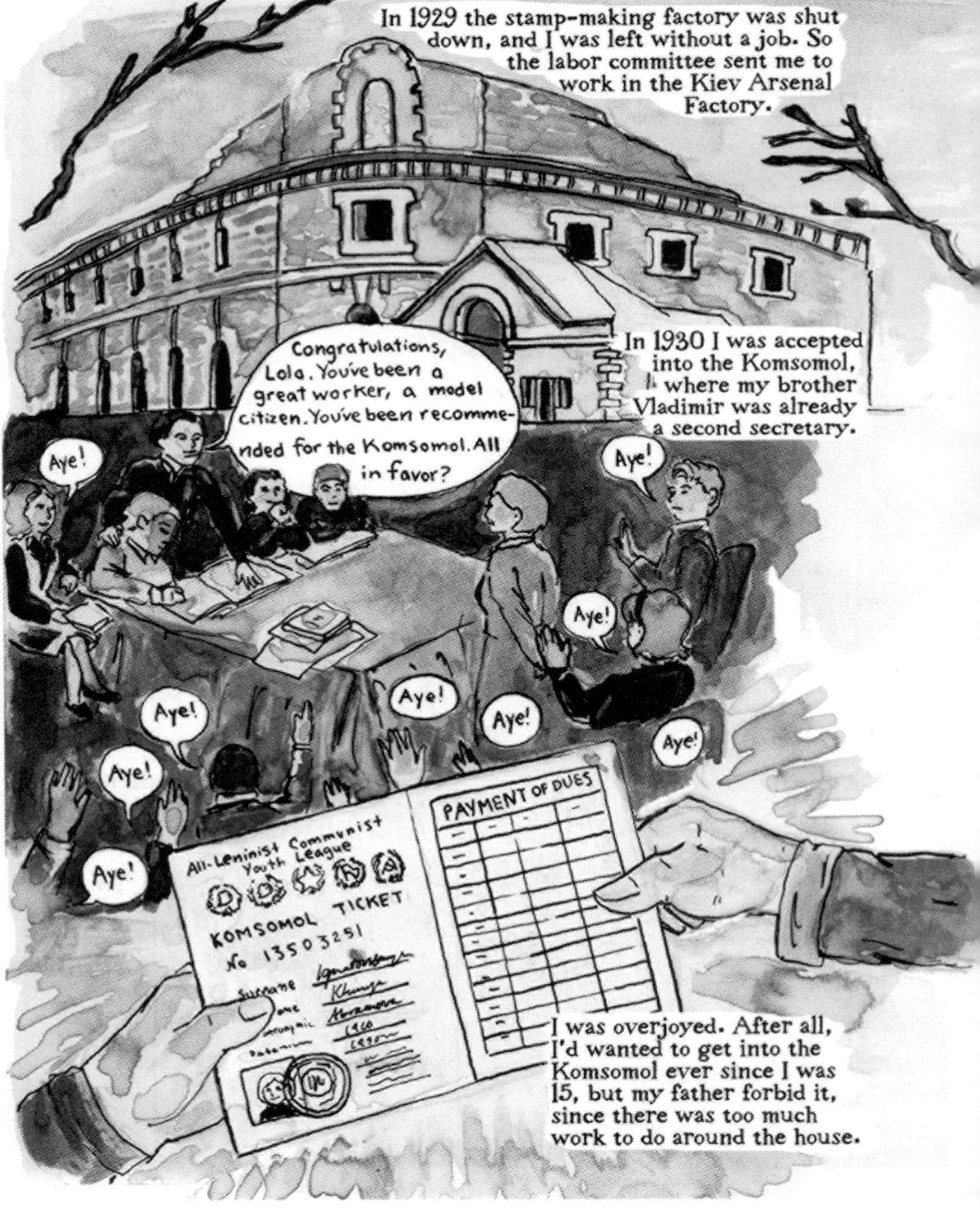
In 1929 the stamp-making factory was shut down, and I was left without a job. So the labor committee sent me to work in the Kiev Arsenal Factory.
In 1930 I was accepted into the Komsomol, where my brother Vladimir was already a second secretary.
Congratulations, Lola. You've been a great worker, a model citizen. You've been recommended for the Komsomol. All in favor?
Aye!
Aye!
Aye!
Aye!
Aye!
Aye!
Aye!
Aye!
Aye!
All-Leninist Communist Youth League
KOMSOMOL TICKET
No 13503251
PAYMENT OF DUES
I was overjoyed. After all, I'd wanted to get into the Komsomol ever since I was 15, but my father forbid it, since there was too much work to do around the house.

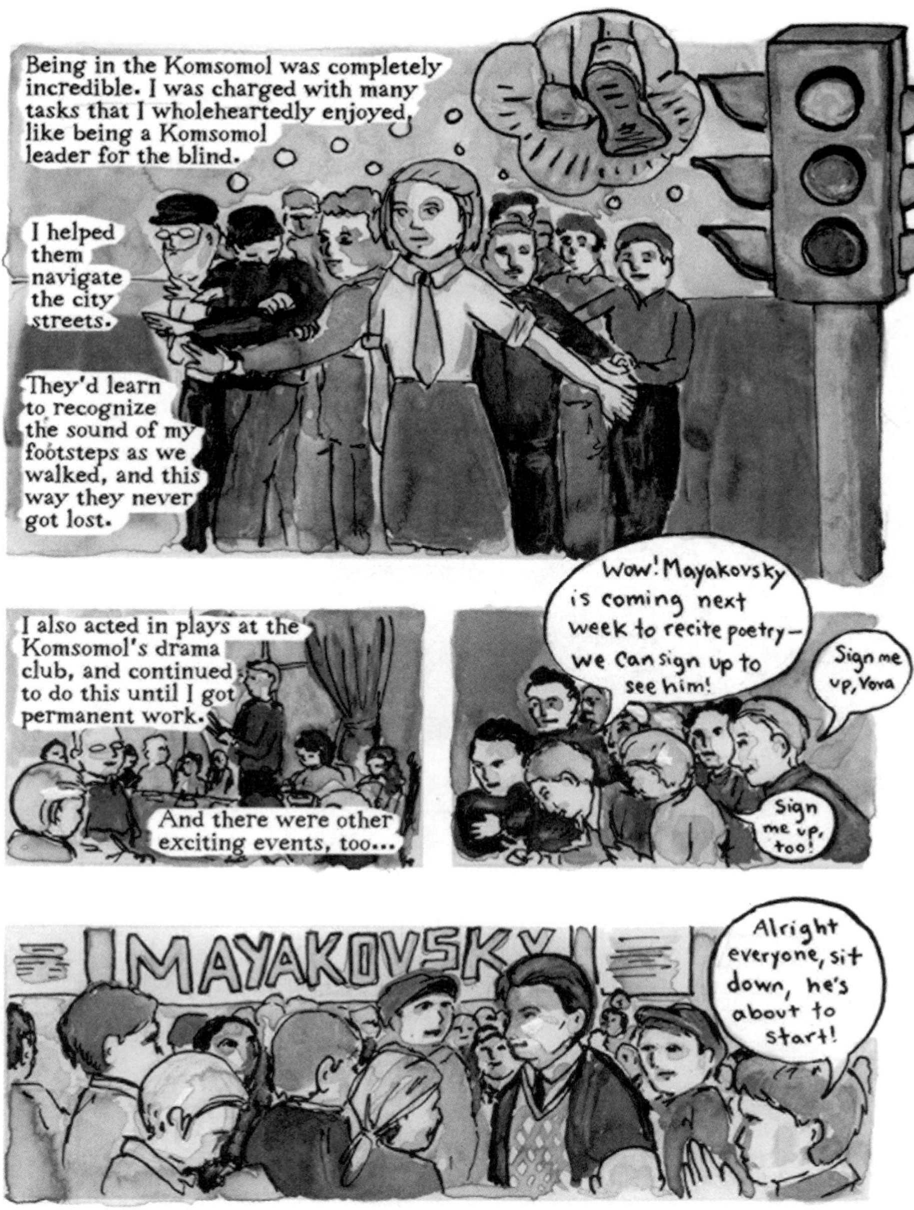
Being in the Komsomol was completely incredible. I was charged with many tasks that I wholeheartedly enjoyed, like being a Komsomol leader for the blind.
I helped them navigate the city streets.
They'd learn to recognize the sound of my footsteps as we walked, and this way they never got lost.
I also acted in plays at the Komsomol's drama club, and continued to do this until I got permanent work.
And there were other exciting events, too...
Wow! Mayakovsky is coming next week to recite poetry— we can sign up to see him!
Sign me up, Vova
Sign me up, too!
MAYAKOVSKY
Alright everyone, sit down, he's about to start!

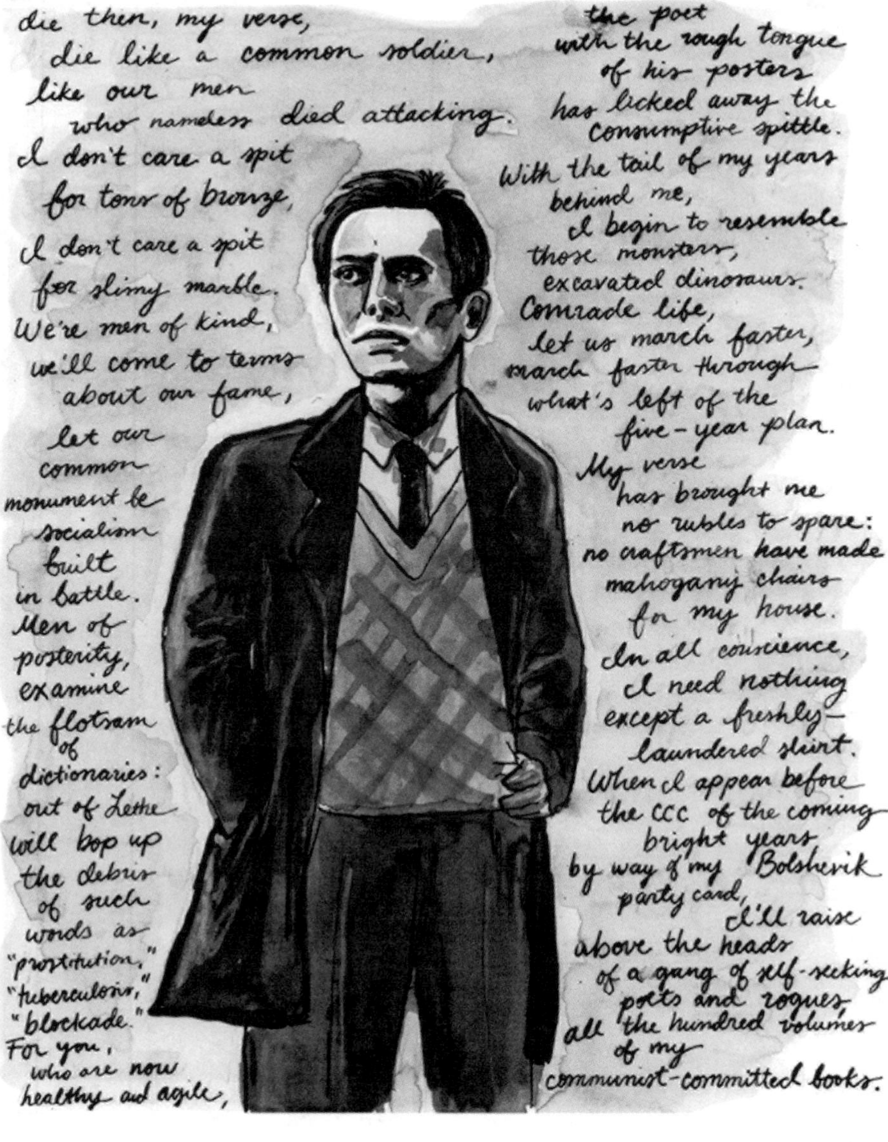
die then, my verse,
die like a common soldier,
like our men
who nameless died attacking.
I don't care a spit
for tons of bronze,
I don't care a spit
for slimy marble.
We're men of kind,
we'll come to terms
about our fame,
let our
common
monument be
socialism
built
in battle.
Men of
posterity,
examine
the flotsam
of
dictionaries:
out of Lethe
will bop up
the debris
of such
words as
"prostitution,"
"tuberculosis,"
"blockade."
For you,
who are now
healthy and agile,
the poet
with the rough tongue
of his posters
has licked away the
consumptive spittle.
With the tail of my years
behind me,
I begin to resemble
those monsters,
excavated dinosaurs.
Comrade life,
let us march faster,
march faster through
what's left of the
five-year plan.
My verse
has brought me
no rubles to spare:
no craftsmen have made
mahogany chairs
for my house.
In all conscience,
I need nothing
except a freshly-
laundered shirt.
When I appear before
the CCC of the coming
bright years
by way of my Bolshevik
party card,
I'll raise
above the heads
of a gang of self-seeking
poets and rogues,
all the hundred volumes
of my
communist-committed books.

Interlude

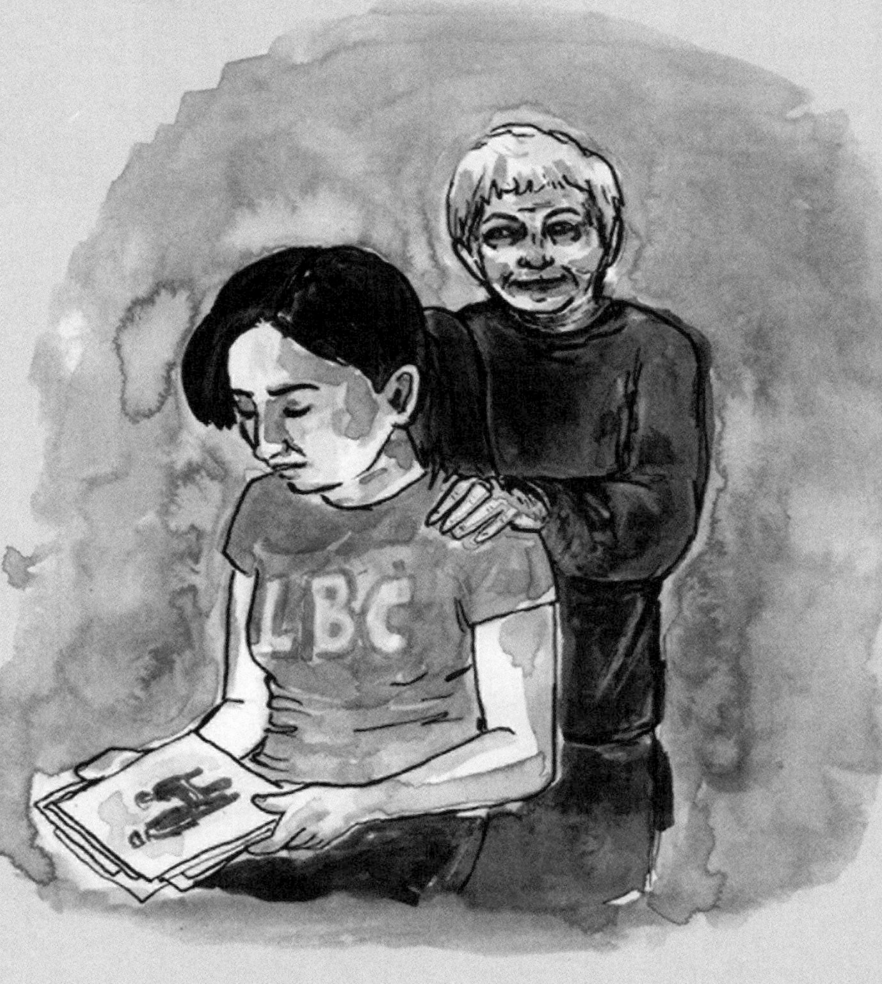
LBC

Summer 2008

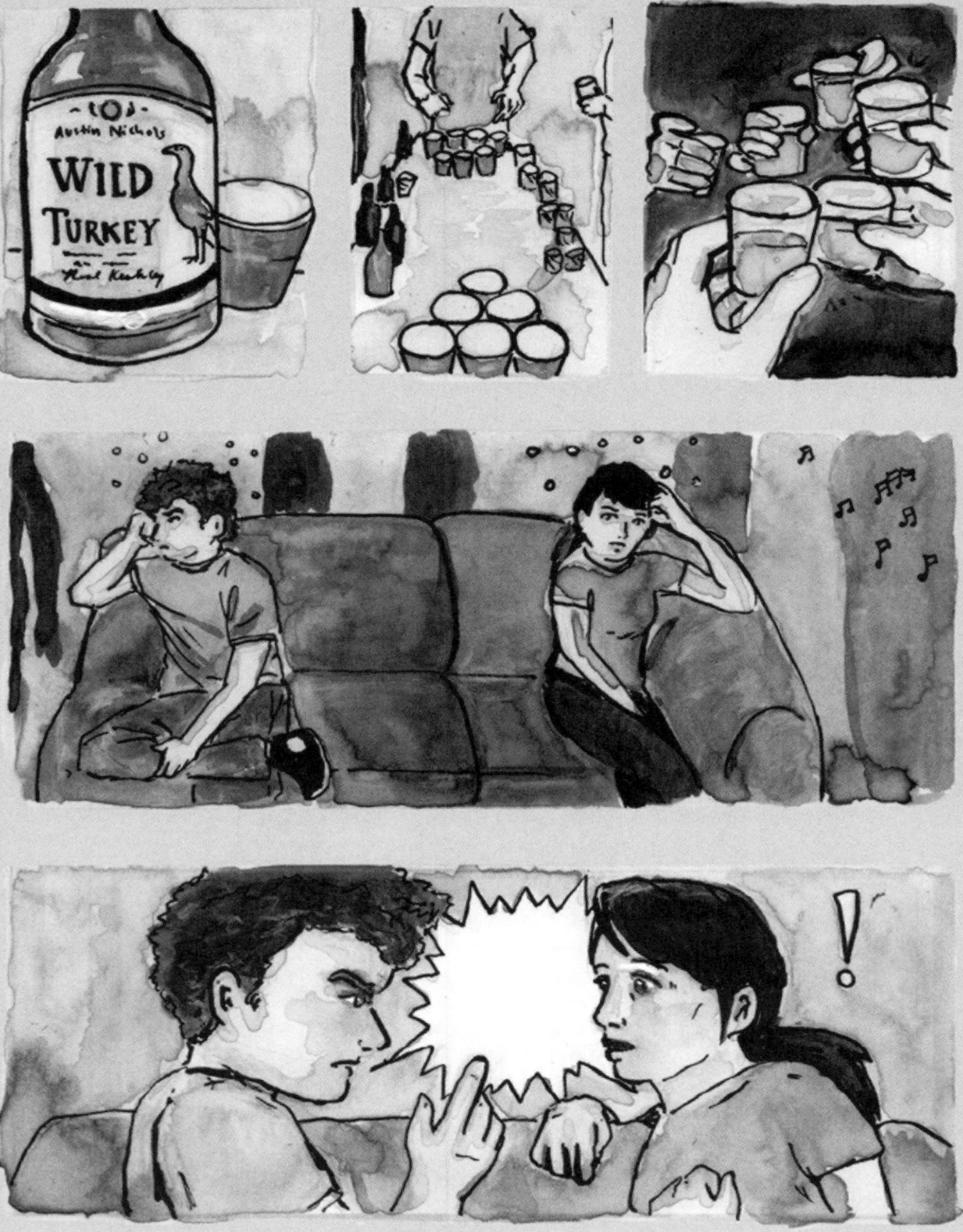
Austin Nichols
WILD TURKEY
!

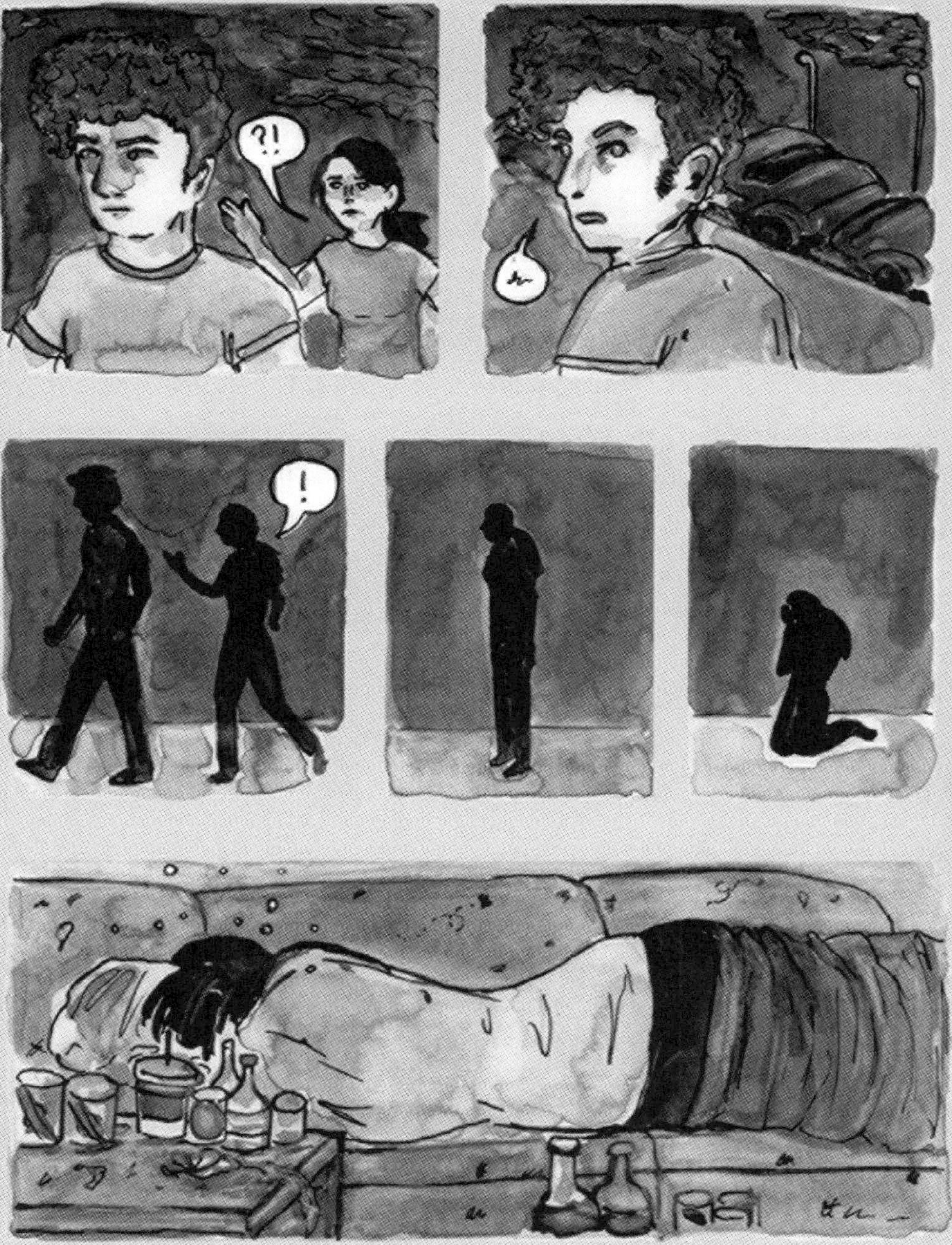
?!
!

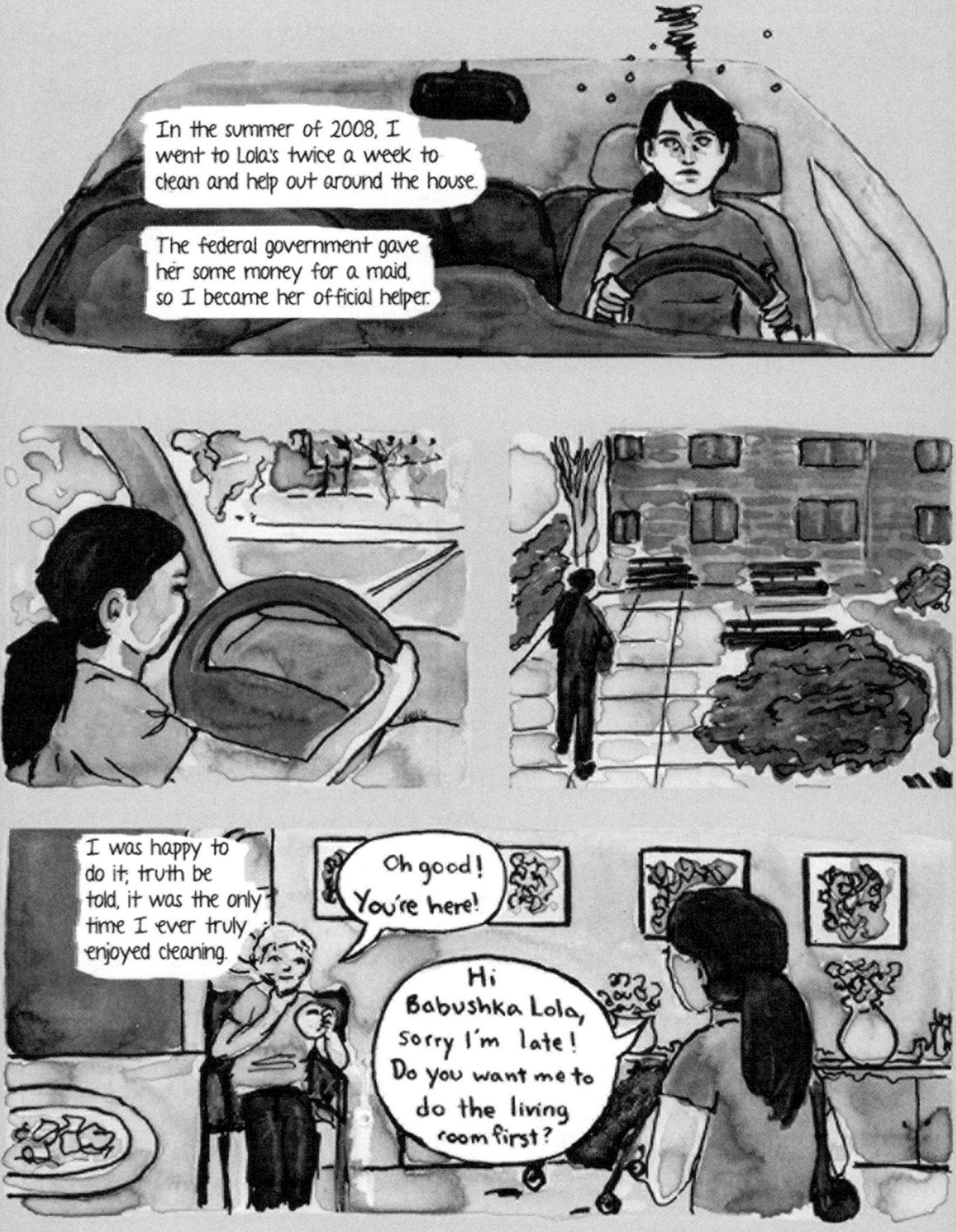
In the summer of 2008, I went to Lola's twice a week to clean and help out around the house.
The federal government gave her some money for a maid, so I became her official helper.
I was happy to do it; truth be told, it was the only time I ever truly enjoyed cleaning.
Oh good! You're here!
Hi Babushka Lola, sorry I'm late! Do you want me to do the living room first?

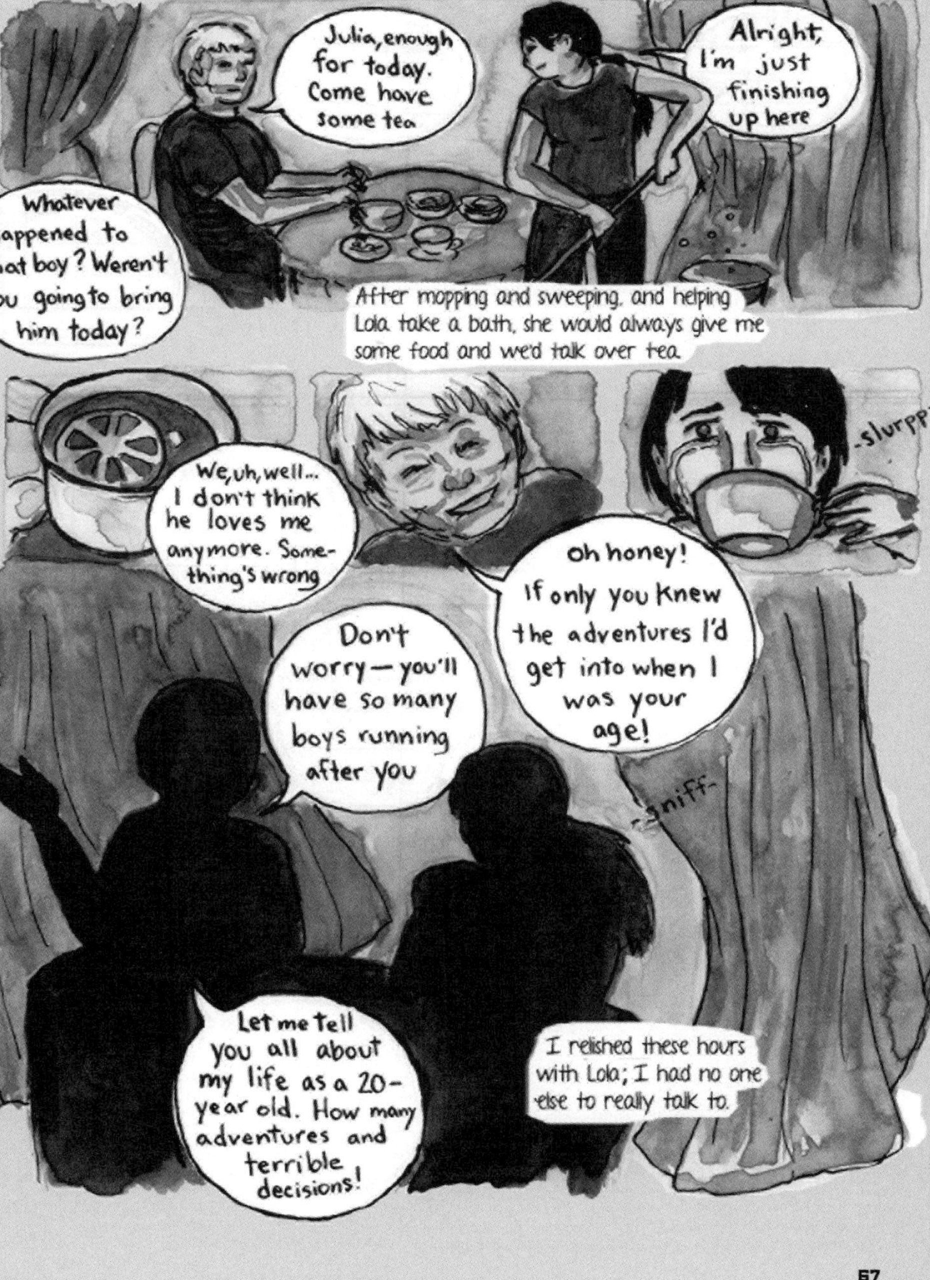
Julia, enough for today. Come have some tea
Alright, I'm just finishing up here
Whatever happened to that boy? Weren't you going to bring him today?
After mopping and sweeping, and helping Lola take a bath, she would always give me some food and we'd talk over tea.
We, uh, well... I don't think he loves me anymore. Some-thing's wrong
-slurpp-
Oh honey! If only you knew the adventures I'd get into when I was your age!
Don't worry—you'll have so many boys running after you
-sniff-
Let me tell you all about my life as a 20-year old. How many adventures and terrible decisions!
I relished these hours with Lola; I had no one else to really talk to.

Chapter 5: 1930-1933

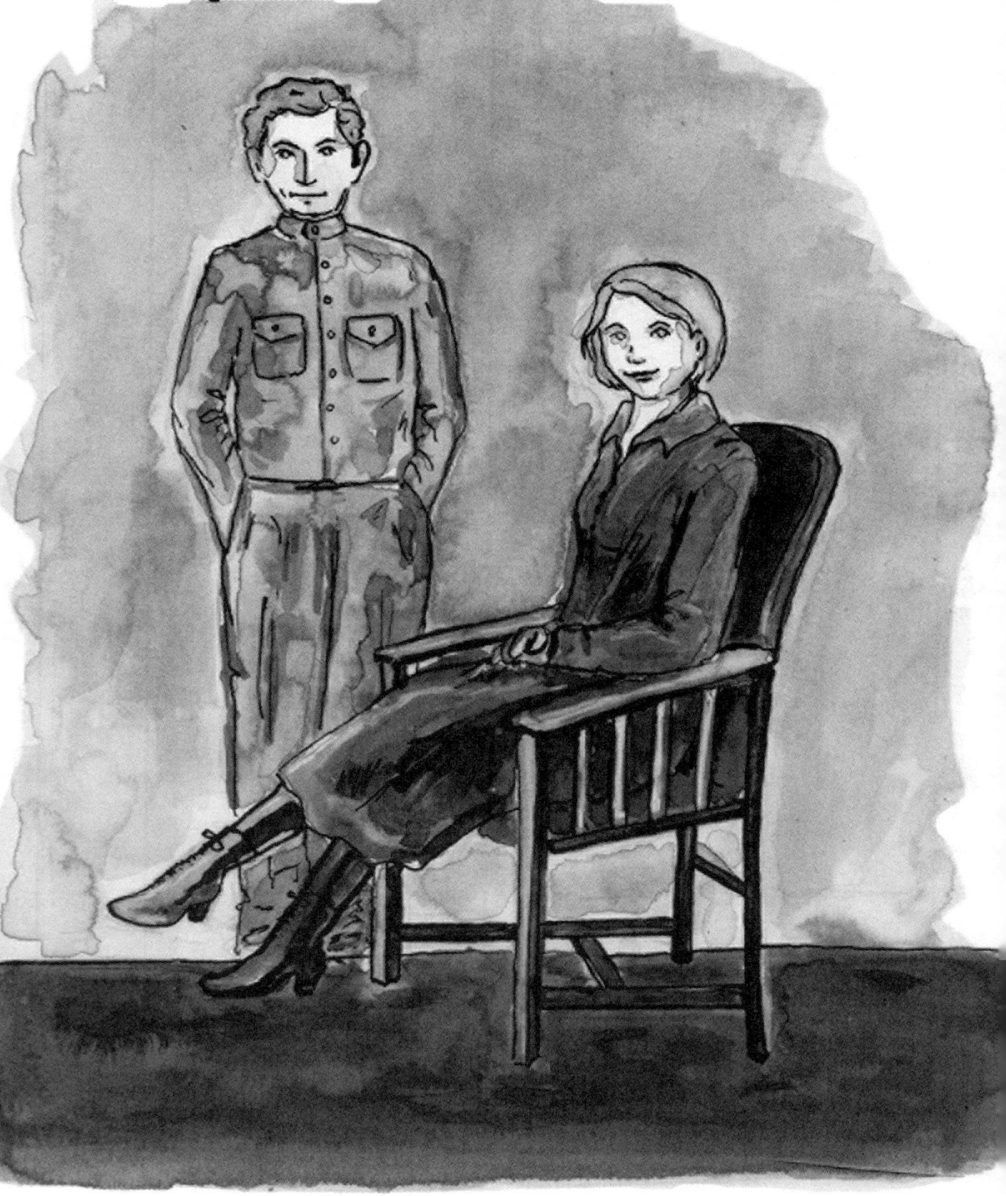

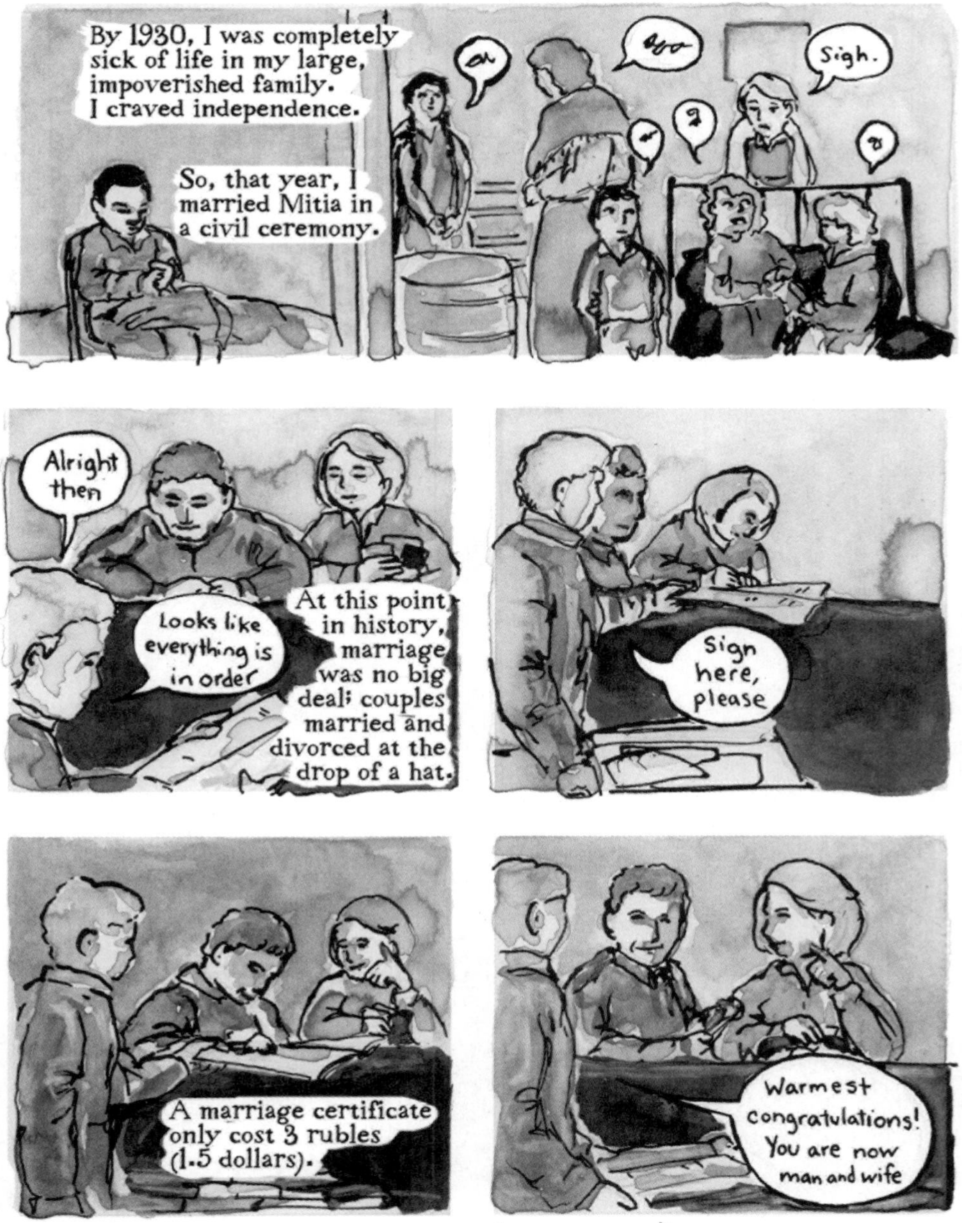
By 1930, I was completely sick of life in my large, impoverished family. I craved independence.
So, that year, I married Mitia in a civil ceremony.
Sigh.
Alright then
Looks like everything is in order
At this point in history, marriage was no big deal; couples married and divorced at the drop of a hat.
Sign here, please
A marriage certificate only cost 3 rubles (1.5 dollars).
Warmest congratulations! You are now man and wife

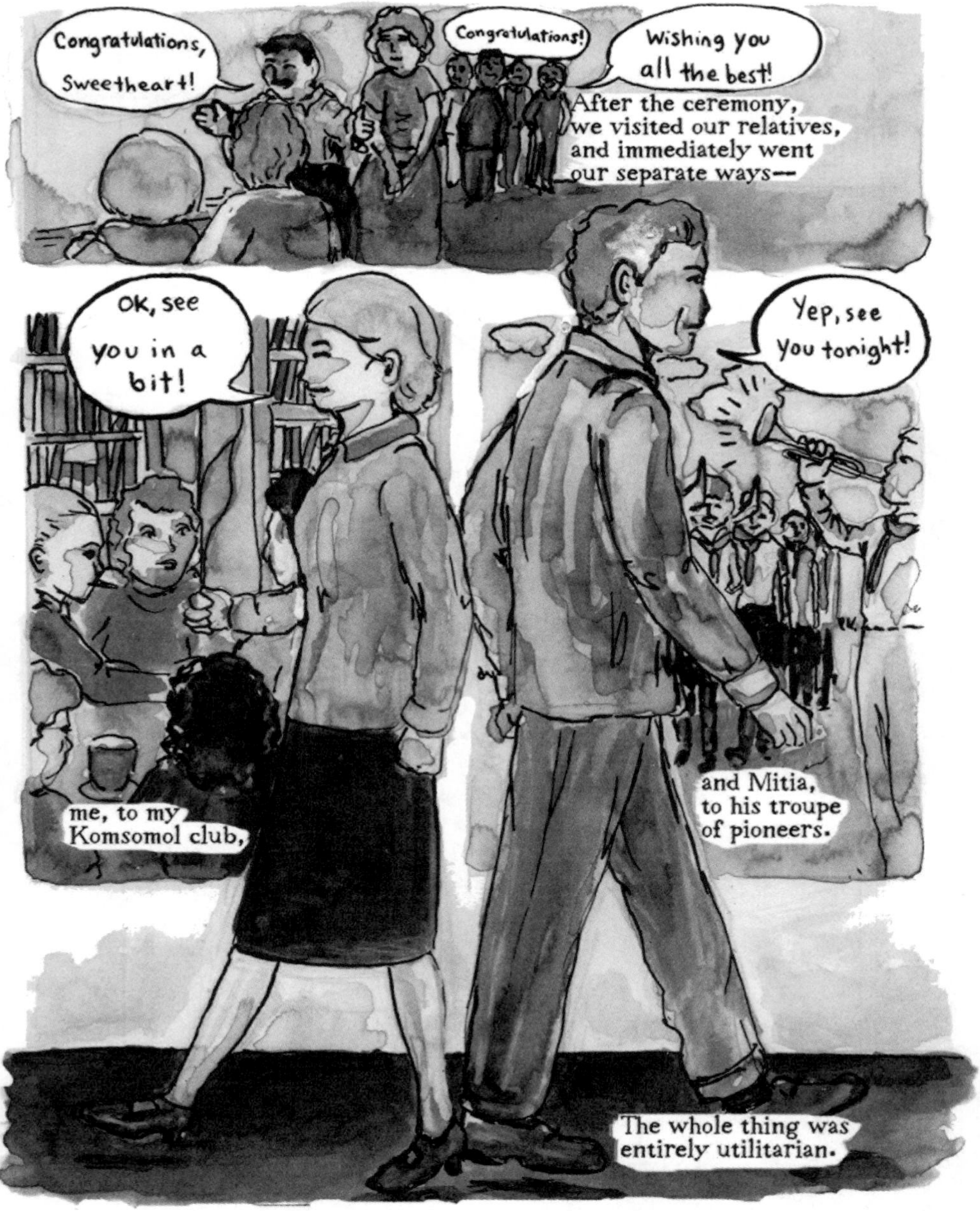
Congratulations, Sweetheart!
Congratulations!
Wishing you all the best!
After the ceremony, we visited our relatives, and immediately went our separate ways—
Ok, see you in a bit!
Yep, see you tonight!
me, to my Komsomol club,
and Mitia, to his troupe of pioneers.
The whole thing was entirely utilitarian.

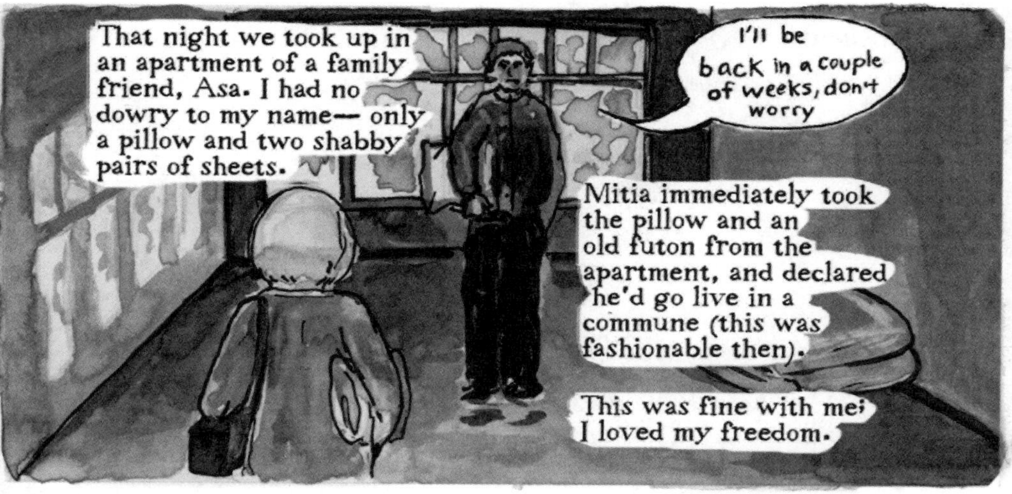
That night we took up in an apartment of a family friend, Asa. I had no dowry to my name— only a pillow and two shabby pairs of sheets.
I'll be back in a couple of weeks, don't worry
Mitia immediately took the pillow and an old futon from the apartment, and declared he'd go live in a commune (this was fashionable then).
This was fine with me; I loved my freedom.

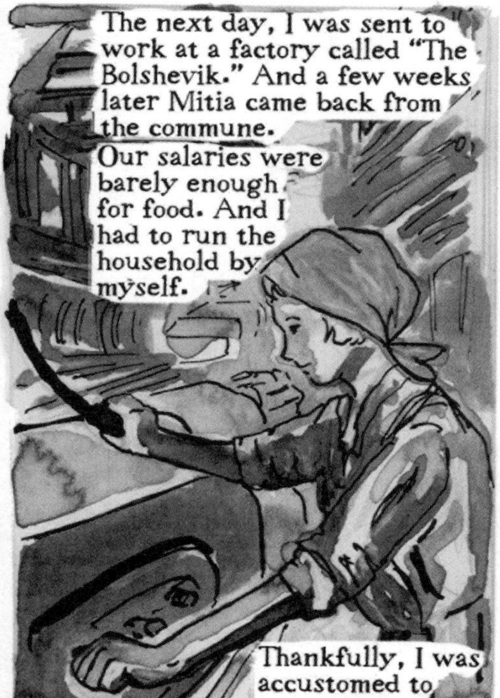
The next day, I was sent to work at a factory called "The Bolshevik." And a few weeks later Mitia came back from the commune.
Our salaries were barely enough for food. And I had to run the household by myself.
Thankfully, I was accustomed to everything.

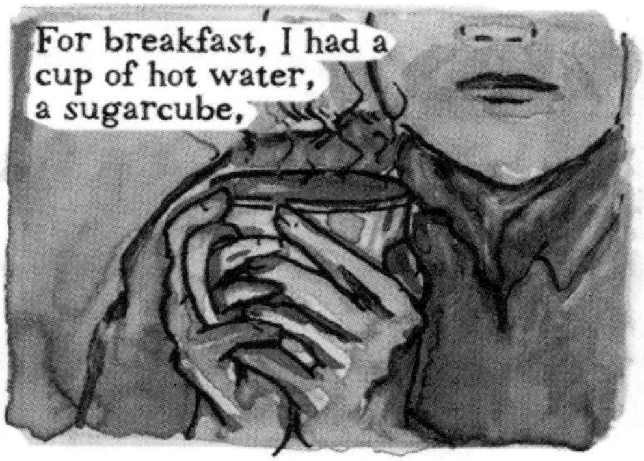
For breakfast, I had a cup of hot water, a sugarcube,

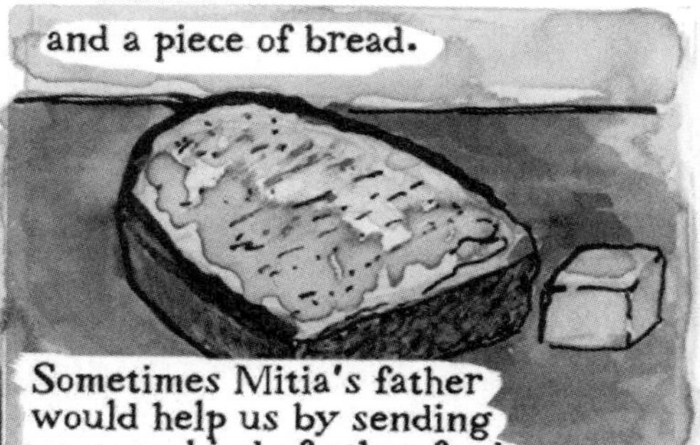
and a piece of bread.
Sometimes Mitia's father would help us by sending us some kind of other food.

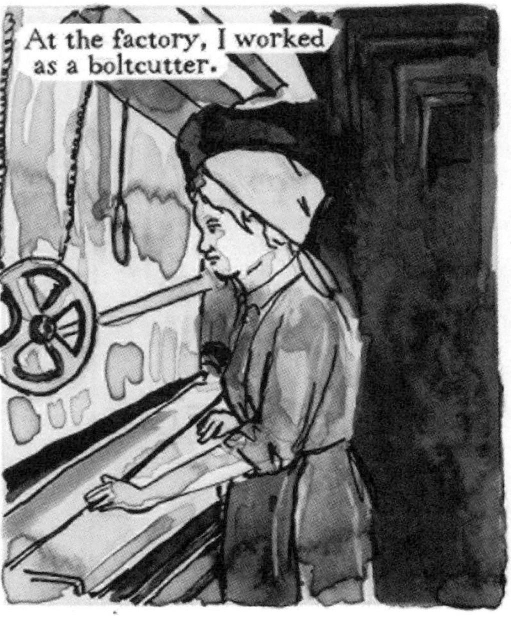
At the factory, I worked as a boltcutter.

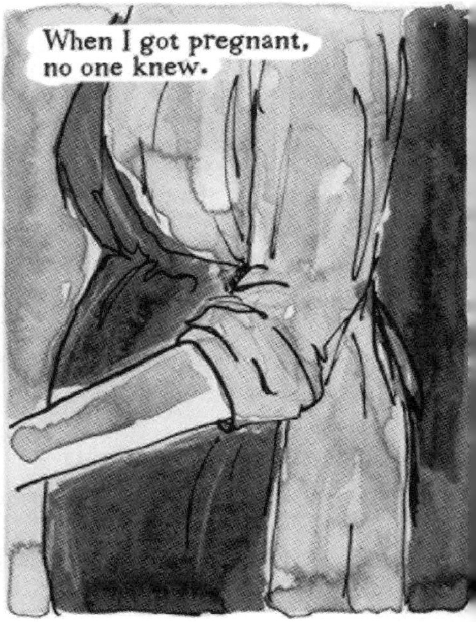
When I got pregnant, no one knew.

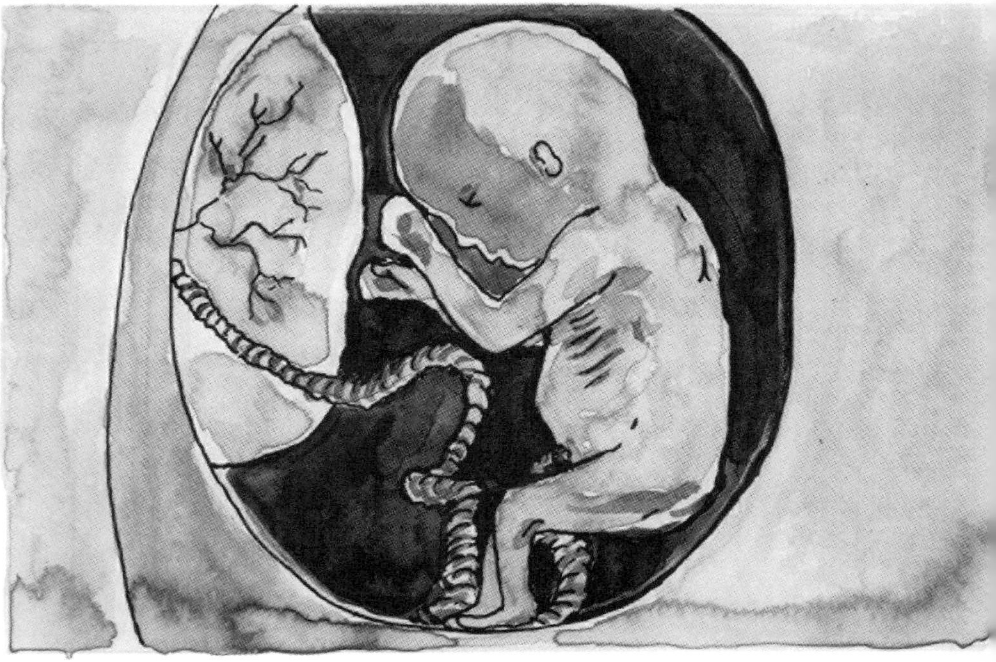

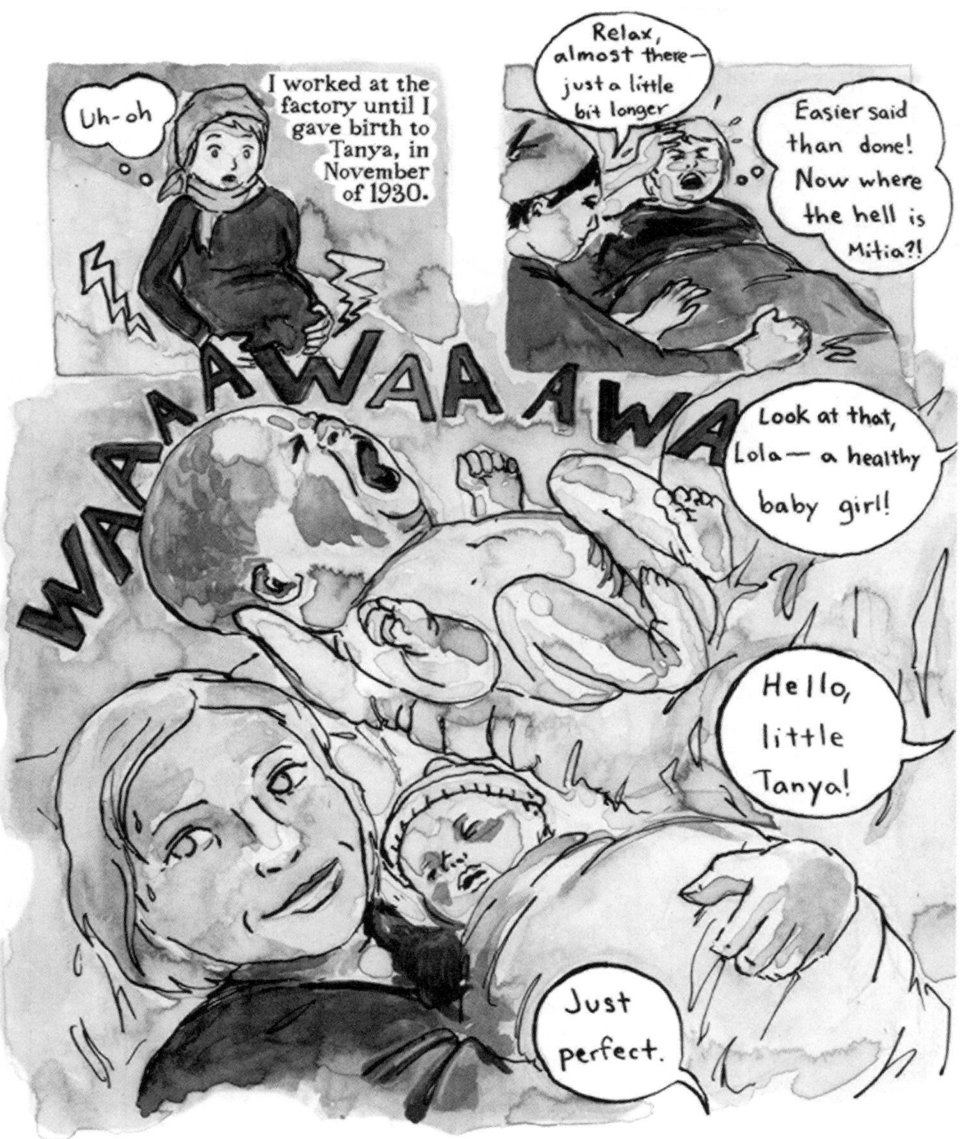

I worked at the factory until I gave birth to Tanya, in November of 1930.
Uh-oh
Relax, almost there— just a little bit longer
Easier said than done! Now where the hell is Mitia?!
WAAAWAAAWA
Look at that, Lola— a healthy baby girl!
Hello, little Tanya!
Just perfect.

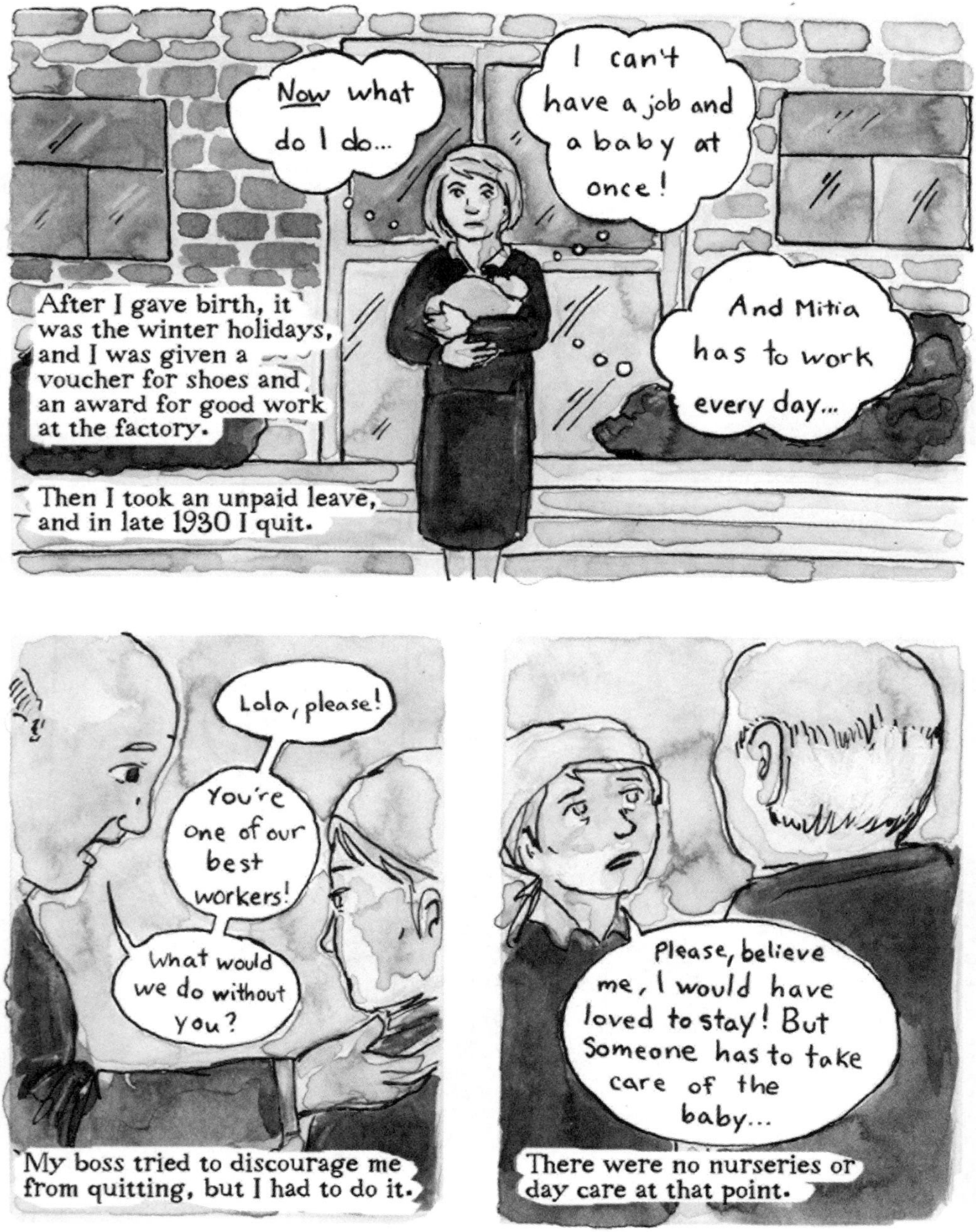
Now what do I do...
I can't have a job and a baby at once!
And Mitia has to work every day...
After I gave birth, it was the winter holidays, and I was given a voucher for shoes and an award for good work at the factory.
Then I took an unpaid leave, and in late 1930 I quit.
Lola, please!
You're one of our best workers!
What would we do without you?
My boss tried to discourage me from quitting, but I had to do it.
Please, believe me, I would have loved to stay! But Someone has to take care of the baby...
There were no nurseries or day care at that point.

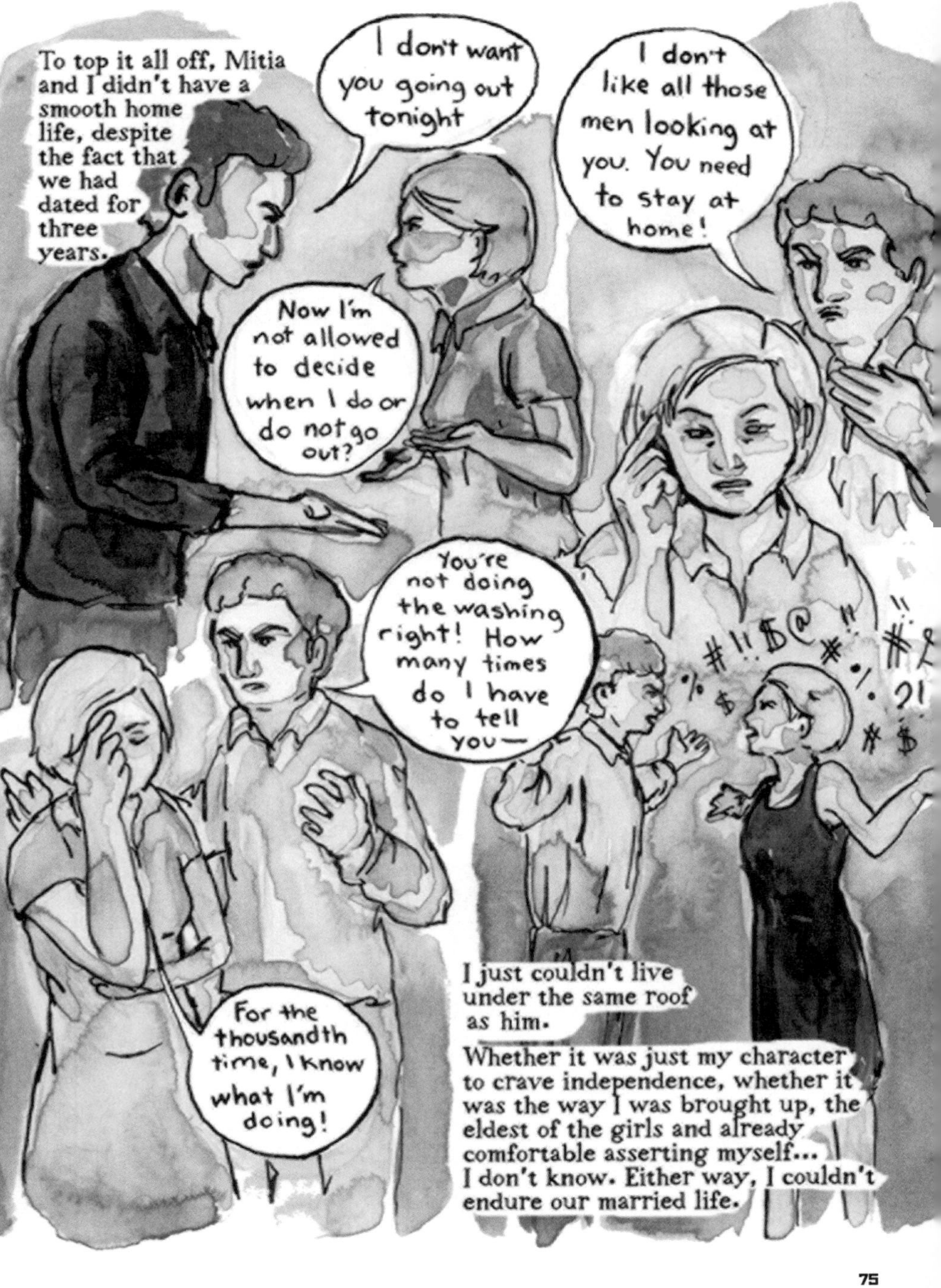
To top it all off, Mitia and I didn't have a smooth home life, despite the fact that we had dated for three years.
I don't want you going out tonight
Now I'm not allowed to decide when I do or do not go out?
I don't like all those men looking at you. You need to stay at home!
You're not doing the washing right! How many times do I have to tell you—
For the thousandth time, I know what I'm doing!
I just couldn't live under the same roof as him.
Whether it was just my character to crave independence, whether it was the way I was brought up, the eldest of the girls and already comfortable asserting myself... I don't know. Either way, I couldn't endure our married life.

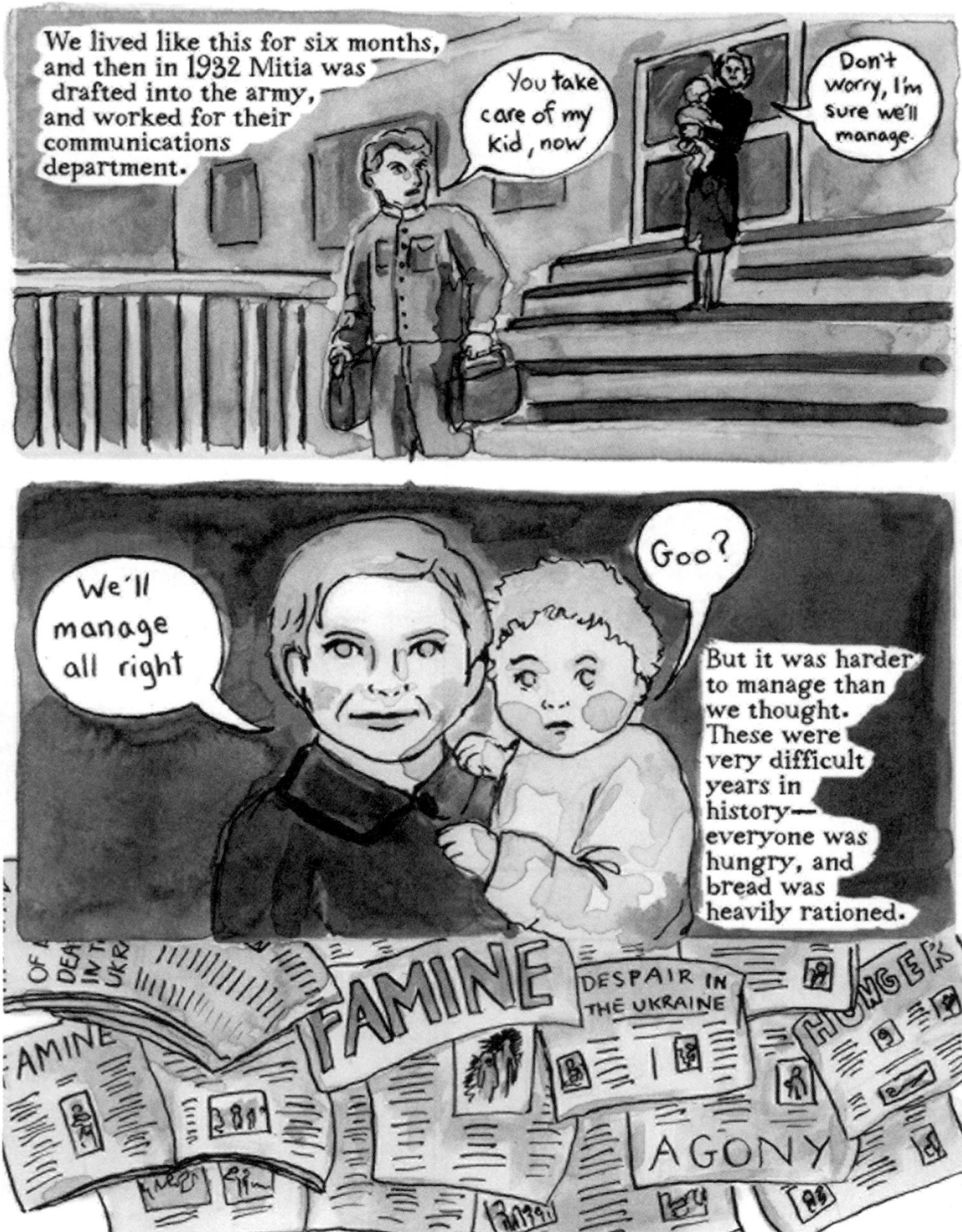
We lived like this for six months, and then in 1932 Mitia was drafted into the army, and worked for their communications department.
You take care of my kid, now
Don't worry, I'm sure we'll manage.
We'll manage all right
Goo?
But it was harder to manage than we thought. These were very difficult years in history—everyone was hungry, and bread was heavily rationed.
FAMINE
DESPAIR IN THE UKRAINE
HUNGER
AMINE
AGONY

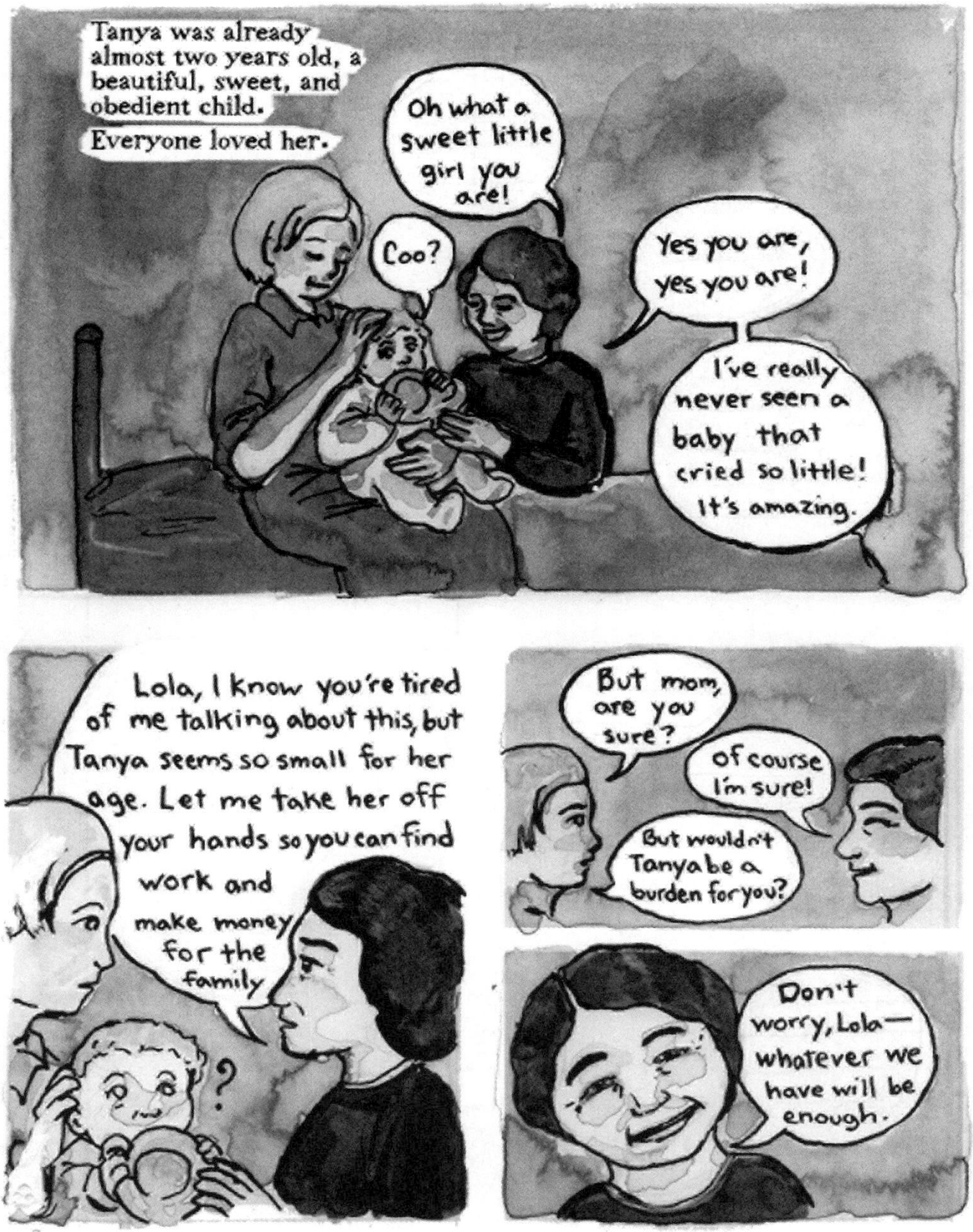
Tanya was already almost two years old, a beautiful, sweet, and obedient child.
Everyone loved her.
Oh what a sweet little girl you are!
Coo?
Yes you are, yes you are!
I've really never seen a baby that cried so little! It's amazing.
Lola, I know you're tired of me talking about this, but Tanya seems so small for her age. Let me take her off your hands so you can find work and make money for the family
?
But mom, are you sure?
Of course I'm sure!
But wouldn't Tanya be a burden for you?
Don't worry, Lola— whatever we have will be enough.

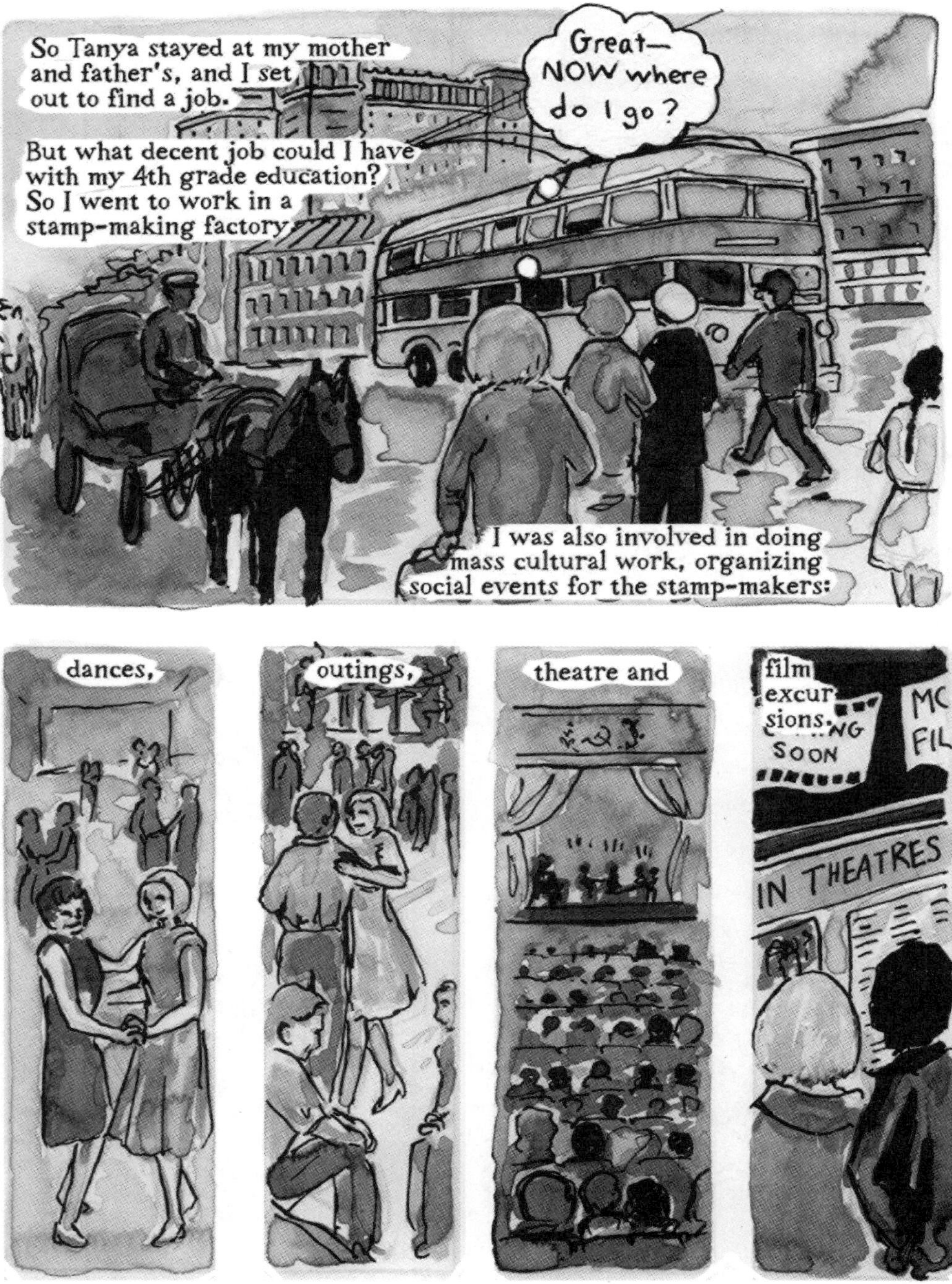
So Tanya stayed at my mother and father's, and I set out to find a job.
Great— NOW where do I go?
But what decent job could I have with my 4th grade education? So I went to work in a stamp-making factory.
I was also involved in doing mass cultural work, organizing social events for the stamp-makers:
dances,
outings,
theatre and
film excursions.
SOON
IN THEATRES

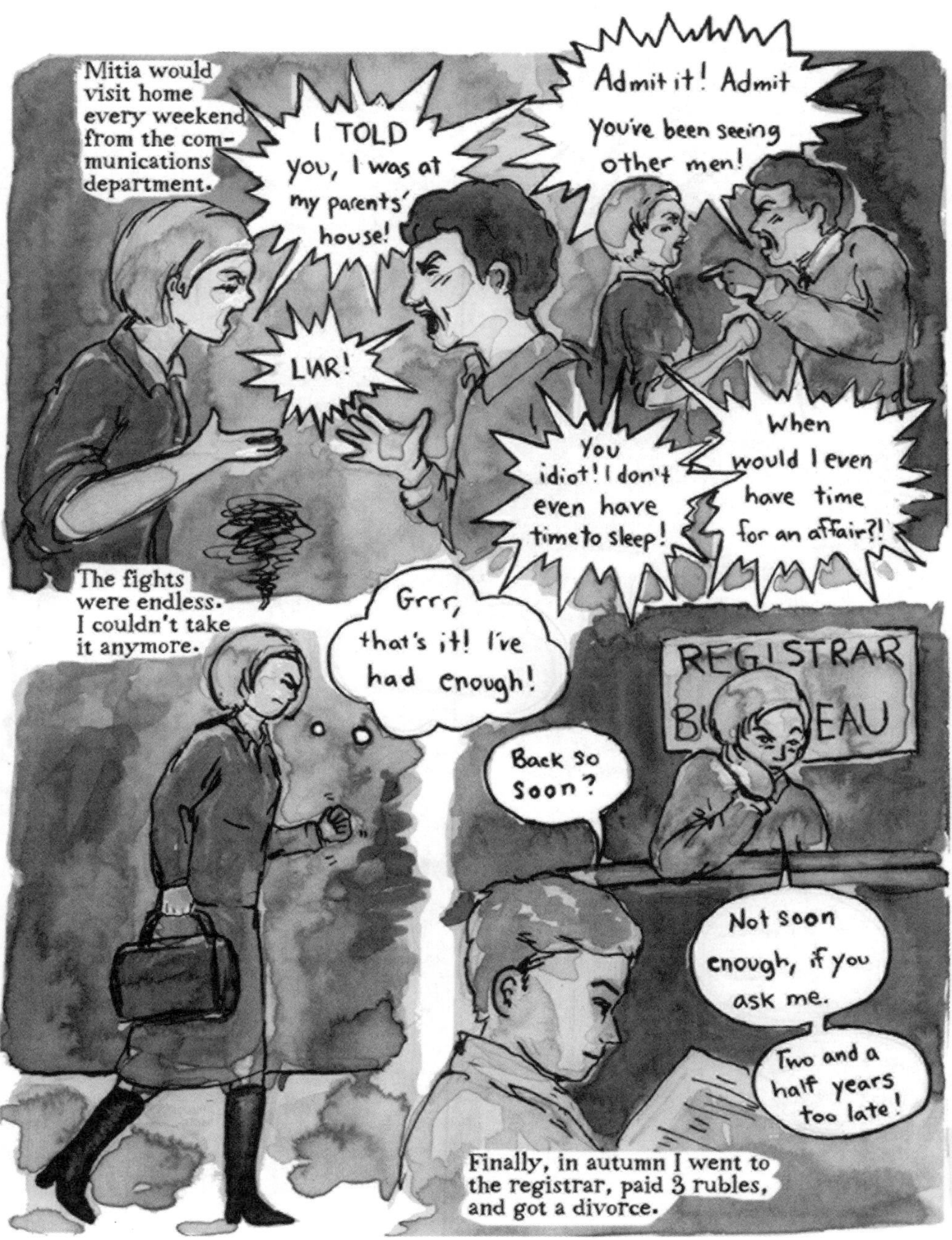

Mitia would visit home every weekend from the communications department.
I TOLD you, I was at my parents' house!
Admit it! Admit you've been seeing other men!
LIAR!
You idiot! I don't even have time to sleep!
When would I even have time for an affair?!
The fights were endless. I couldn't take it anymore.
Grrr, that's it! I've had enough!
REGISTRAR BUREAU
Back so soon?
Not soon enough, if you ask me.
Two and a half years too late!
Finally, in autumn I went to the registrar, paid 3 rubles, and got a divorce.

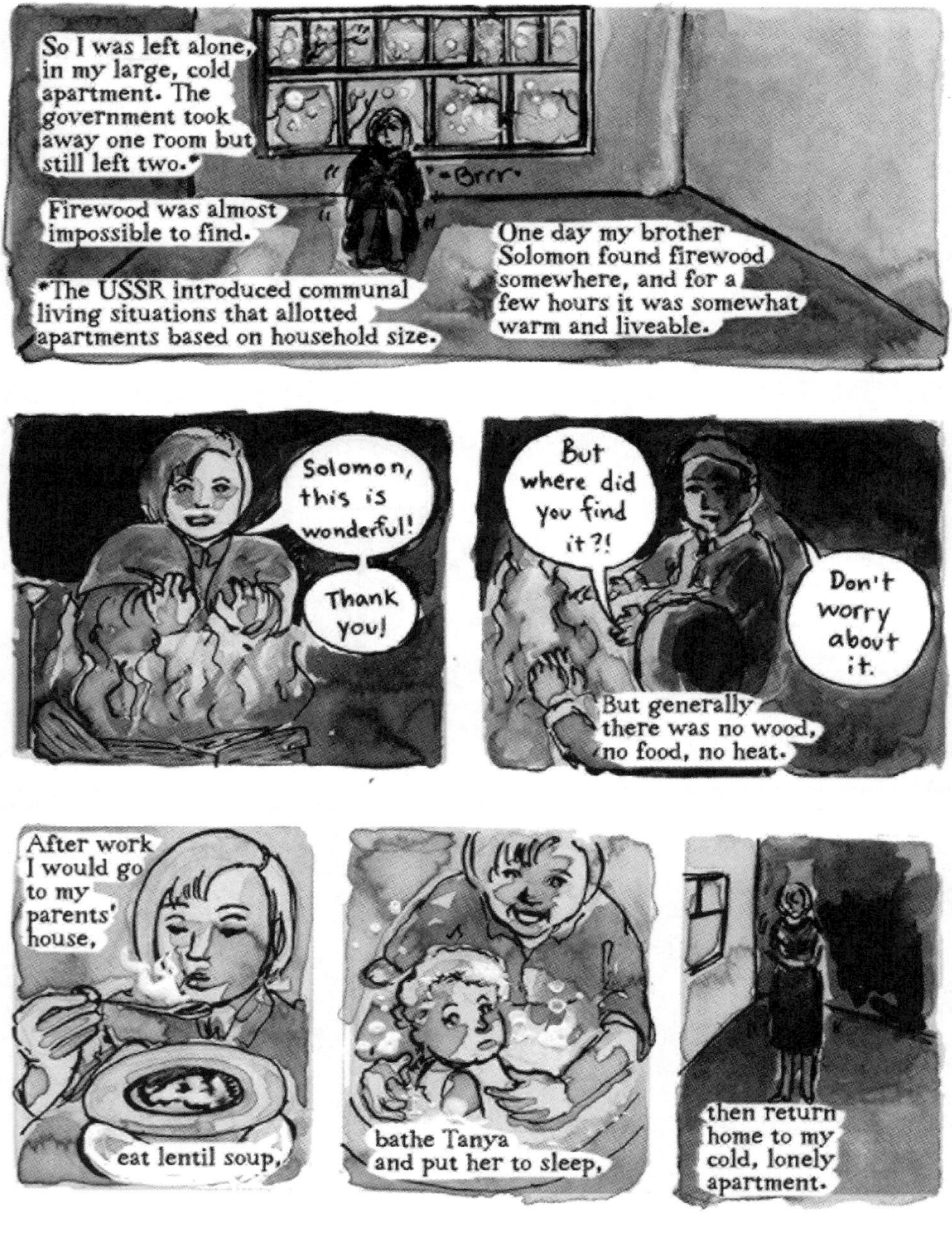
So I was left alone, in my large, cold apartment. The government took away one room but still left two.*
Brrr
Firewood was almost impossible to find.
*The USSR introduced communal living situations that allotted apartments based on household size.
One day my brother Solomon found firewood somewhere, and for a few hours it was somewhat warm and liveable.
Solomon, this is wonderful!
Thank you!
But where did you find it?!
Don't worry about it.
But generally there was no wood, no food, no heat.
After work I would go to my parents' house,
eat lentil soup,
bathe Tanya and put her to sleep,
then return home to my cold, lonely apartment.

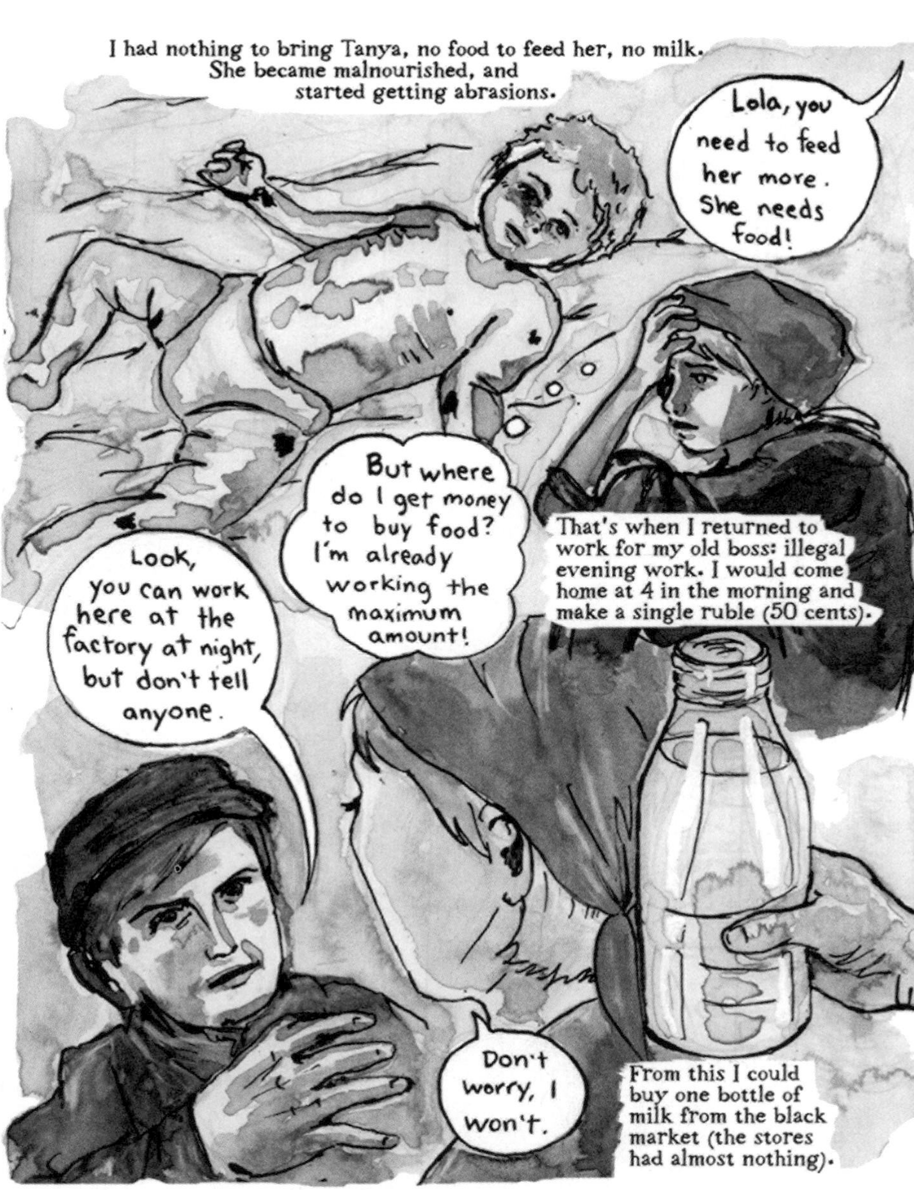

I had nothing to bring Tanya, no food to feed her, no milk. She became malnourished, and started getting abrasions.
Lola, you need to feed her more. She needs food!
But where do I get money to buy food? I'm already working the maximum amount!
That's when I returned to work for my old boss: illegal evening work. I would come home at 4 in the morning and make a single ruble (50 cents).
Look, you can work here at the factory at night, but don't tell anyone.
Don't worry, I won't.
From this I could buy one bottle of milk from the black market (the stores had almost nothing).

But that wasn't enough. Tanya stopped walking and talking.

She just listened, taking in everything, absorbing all of the information around her without saying a word.

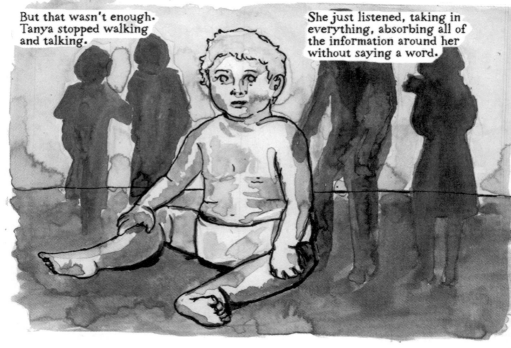

Thankfully in two years she began to talk and walk again.

Mama! Mama!

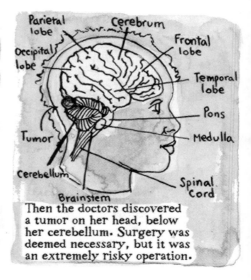

Parietal lobe

Cerebrum

Frontal lobe

Occipital lobe

Temporal lobe

Pons

Medulla

Tumor

Cerebellum

Spinal Cord

Brainstem

Then the doctors discovered a tumor on her head, below her cerebellum. Surgery was deemed necessary, but it was an extremely risky operation.

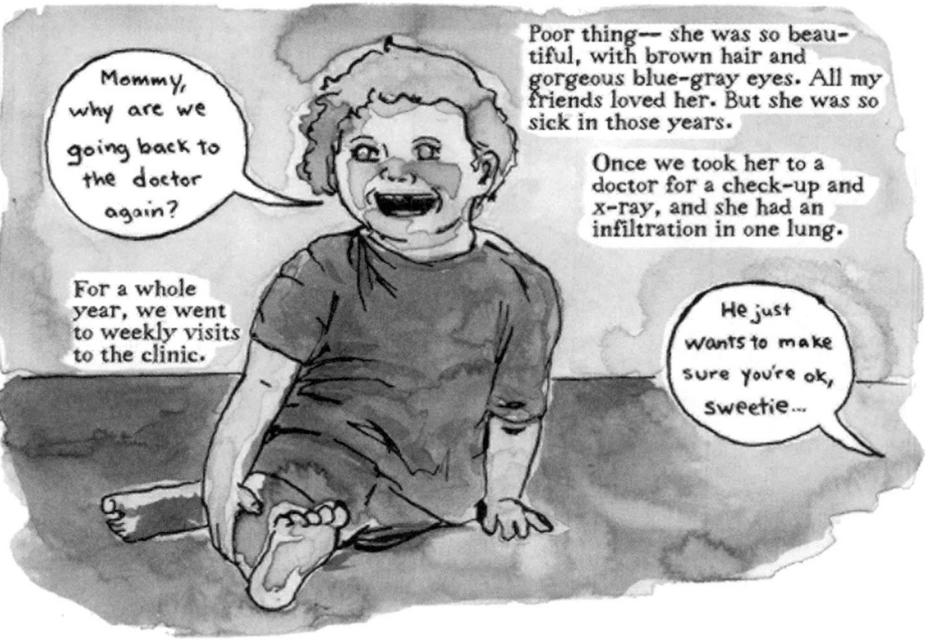
Mommy, why are we going back to the doctor again?
Poor thing— she was so beautiful, with brown hair and gorgeous blue-gray eyes. All my friends loved her. But she was so sick in those years.
Once we took her to a doctor for a check-up and x-ray, and she had an infiltration in one lung.
For a whole year, we went to weekly visits to the clinic.
He just wants to make sure you're ok, sweetie...

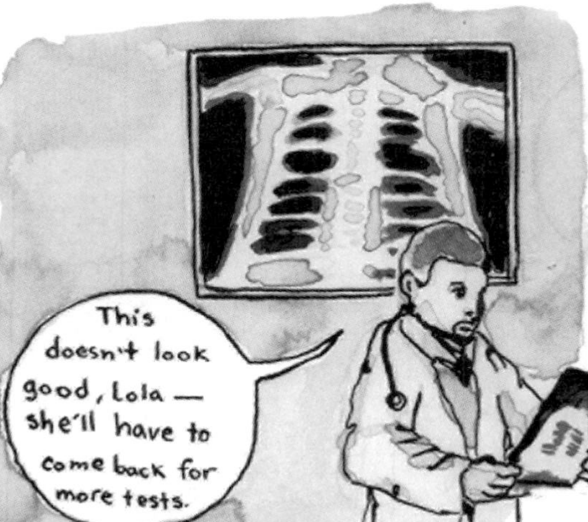
This doesn't look good, Lola — she'll have to come back for more tests.

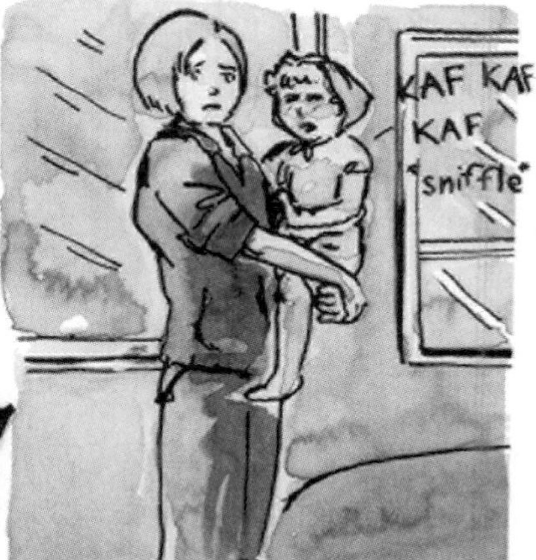
KAF KAF
KAF
sniffle

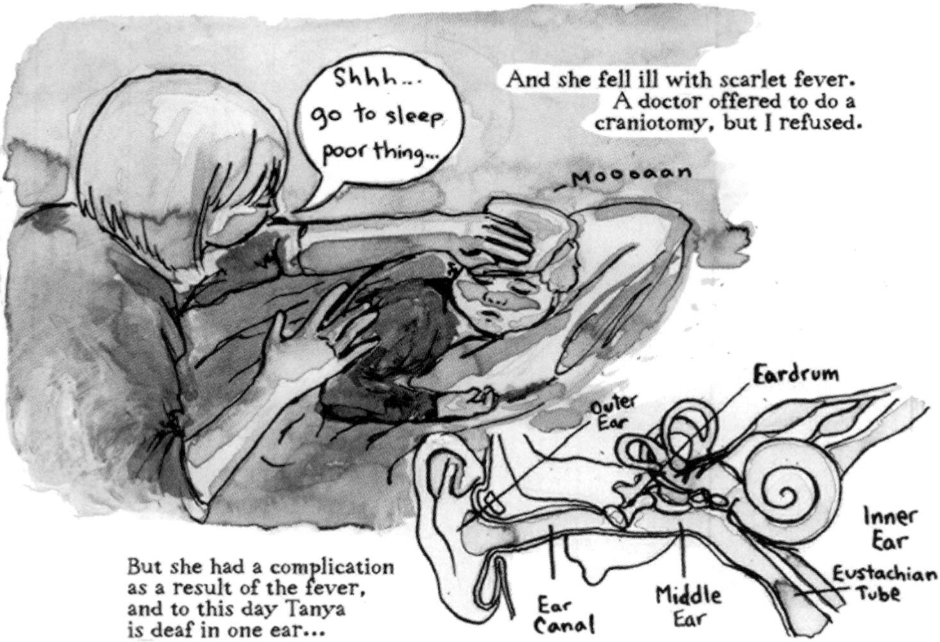
Shhh...
go to sleep
poor thing...
And she fell ill with scarlet fever. A doctor offered to do a craniotomy, but I refused.
Moooaan
Eardrum
Outer Ear
Inner Ear
Eustachian Tube
Ear Canal
Middle Ear
But she had a complication as a result of the fever, and to this day Tanya is deaf in one ear...

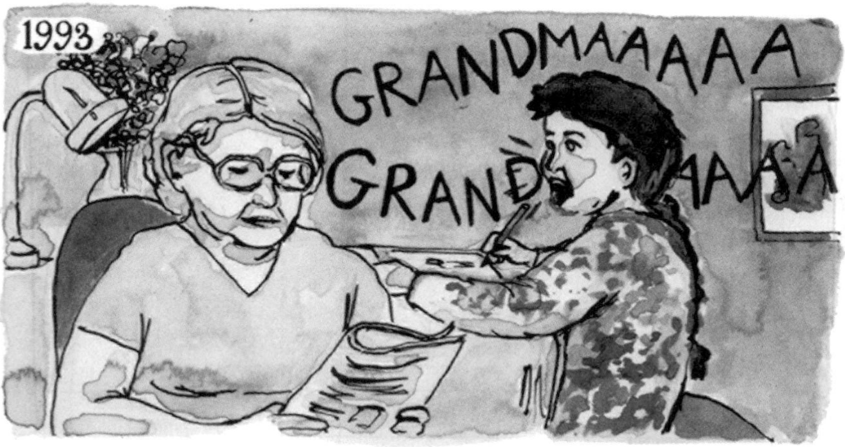
1993
GRANDMAAAAAA
GRANDMAAAA

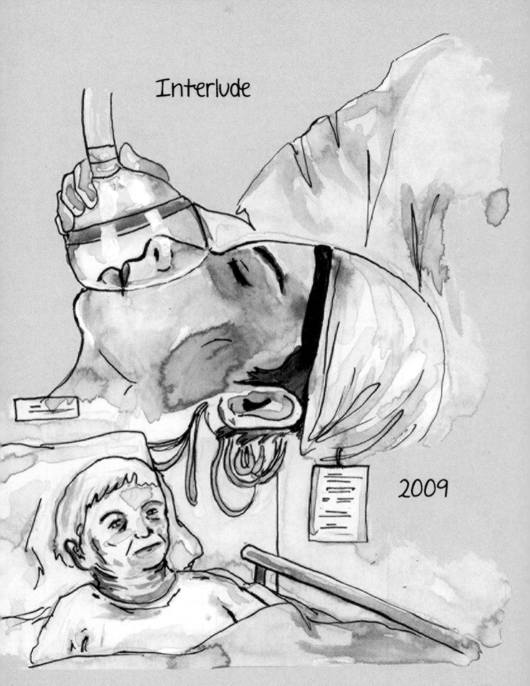

Interlude

2009

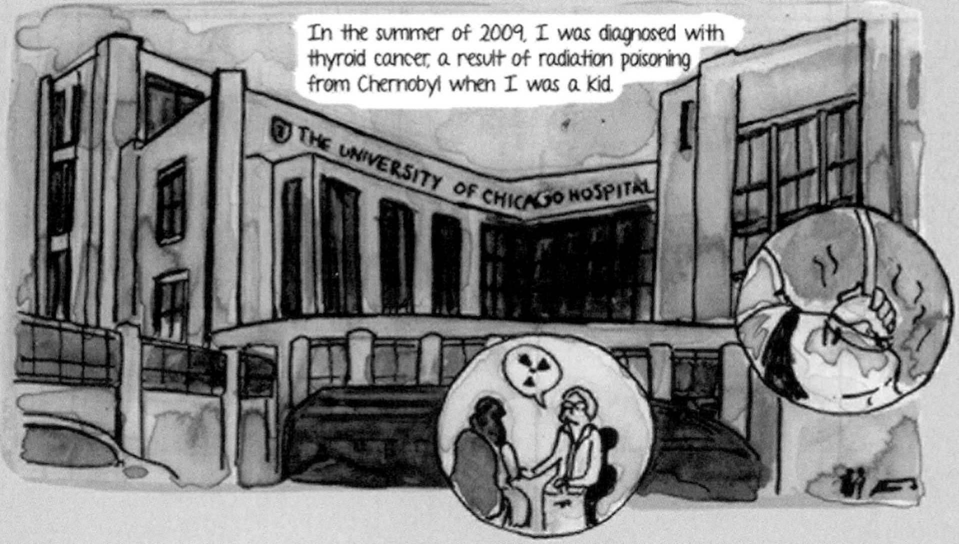
In the summer of 2009, I was diagnosed with thyroid cancer, a result of radiation poisoning from Chernobyl when I was a kid.
THE UNIVERSITY OF CHICAGO HOSPITAL

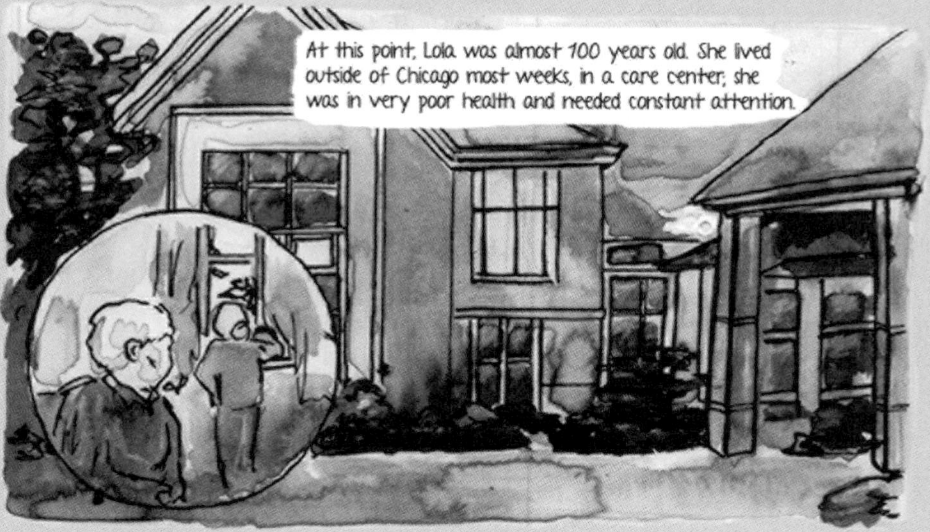
At this point, Lola was almost 100 years old. She lived outside of Chicago most weeks, in a care center; she was in very poor health and needed constant attention.

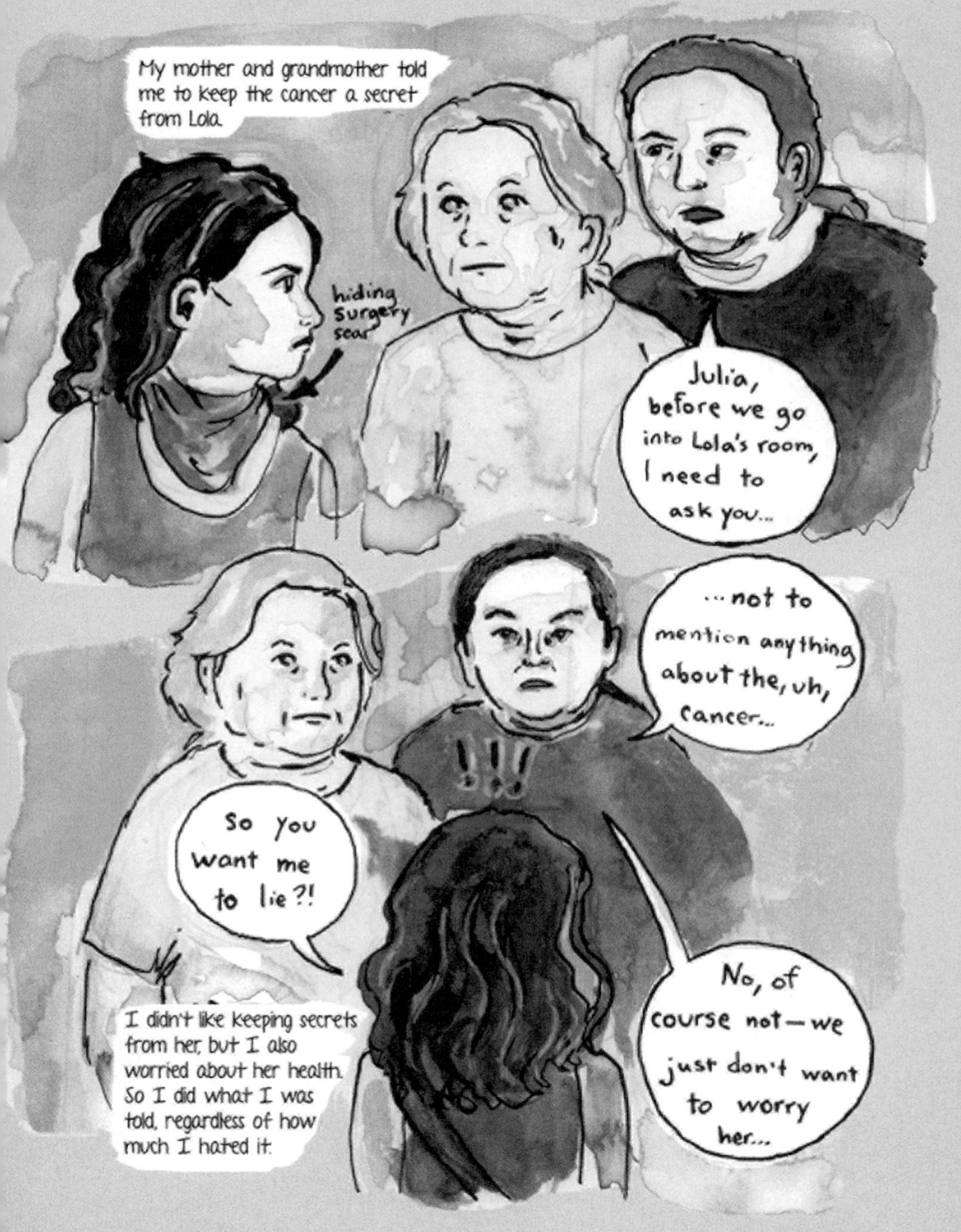

My mother and grandmother told me to keep the cancer a secret from Lola.
hiding surgery scar
Julia, before we go into Lola's room, I need to ask you...
...not to mention anything about the, uh, cancer...
!!!
So you want me to lie?!
No, of course not—we just don't want to worry her...
I didn't like keeping secrets from her, but I also worried about her health. So I did what I was told, regardless of how much I hated it.

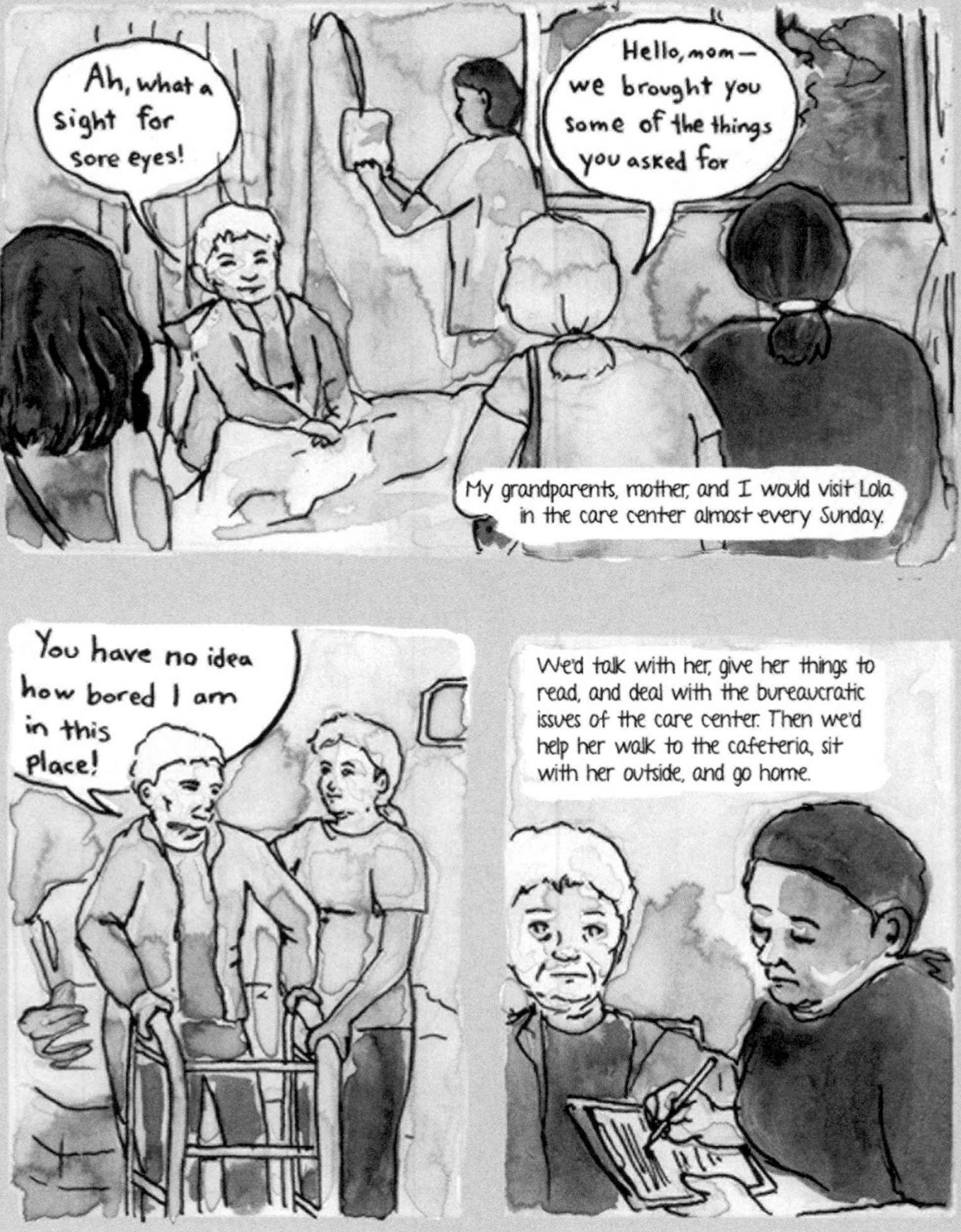
Ah, what a sight for sore eyes!
Hello, mom— we brought you some of the things you asked for
My grandparents, mother, and I would visit Lola in the care center almost every Sunday.
You have no idea how bored I am in this place!
We'd talk with her, give her things to read, and deal with the bureaucratic issues of the care center. Then we'd help her walk to the cafeteria, sit with her outside, and go home.

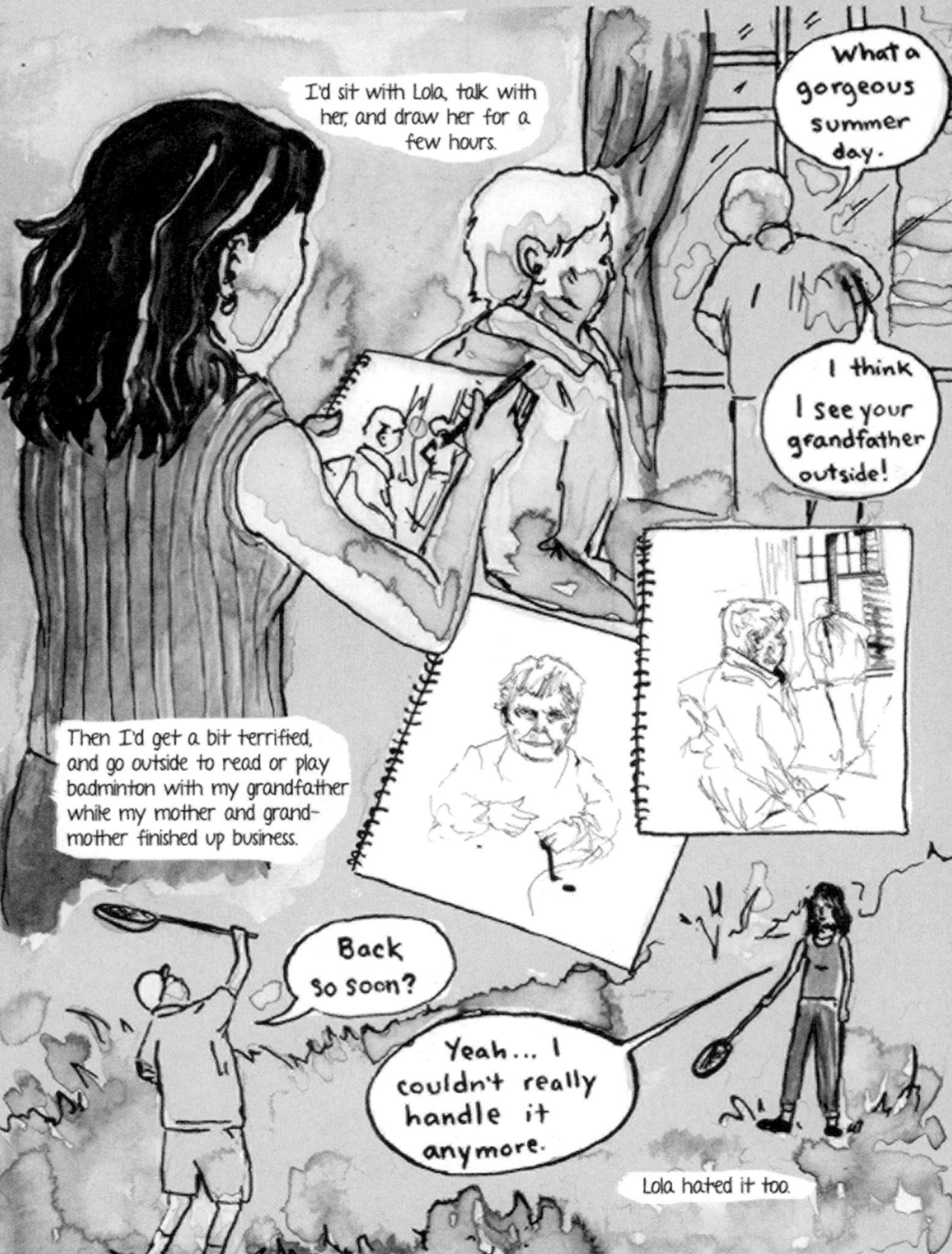
I'd sit with Lola, talk with her, and draw her for a few hours.
What a gorgeous summer day.
I think I see your grandfather outside!
Then I'd get a bit terrified, and go outside to read or play badminton with my grandfather while my mother and grand-mother finished up business.
Back so soon?
Yeah... I couldn't really handle it anymore.
Lola hated it too.

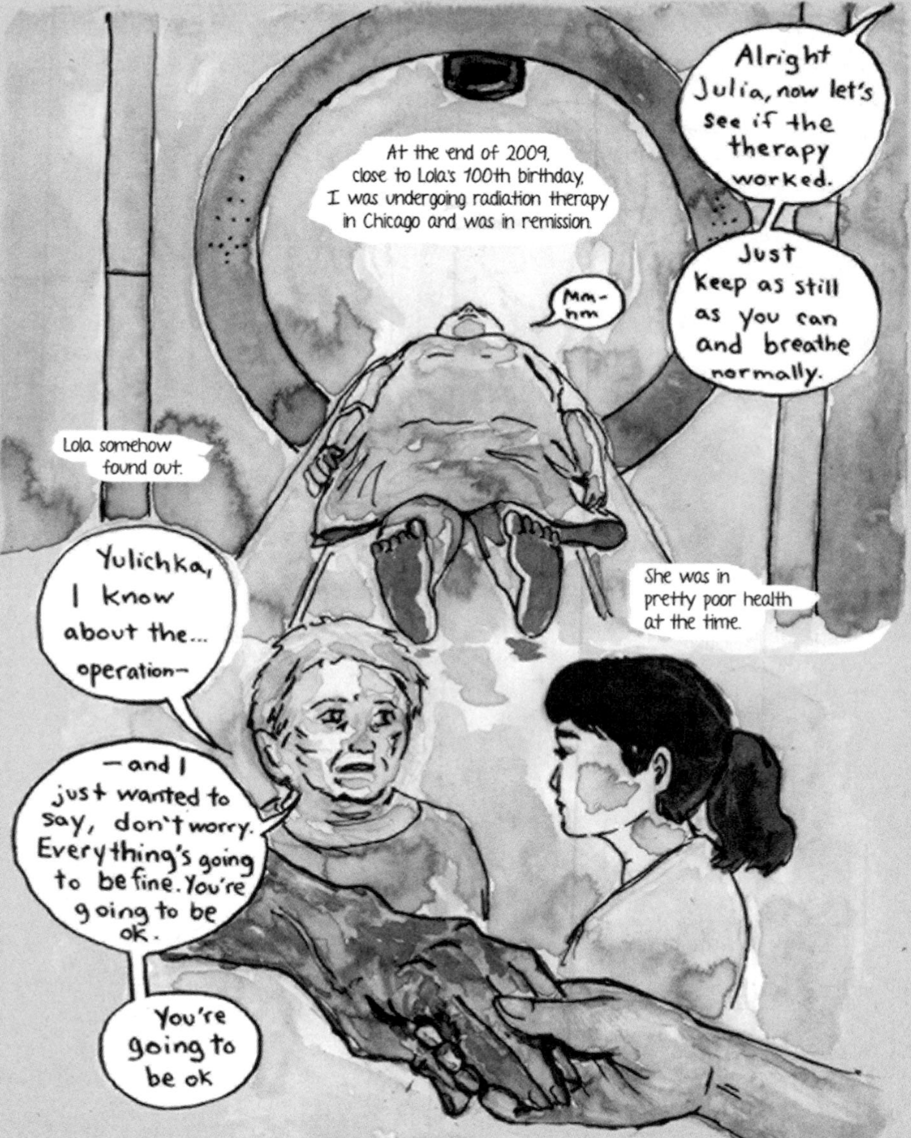
At the end of 2009, close to Lola's 100th birthday, I was undergoing radiation therapy in Chicago and was in remission.
Alright Julia, now let's see if the therapy worked.
Just keep as still as you can and breathe normally.
Mm-hm
Lola somehow found out.
She was in pretty poor health at the time.
Yulichka, I know about the... operation-
-and I just wanted to say, don't worry. Everything's going to be fine. You're going to be ok.
You're going to be ok

Chapter 6:

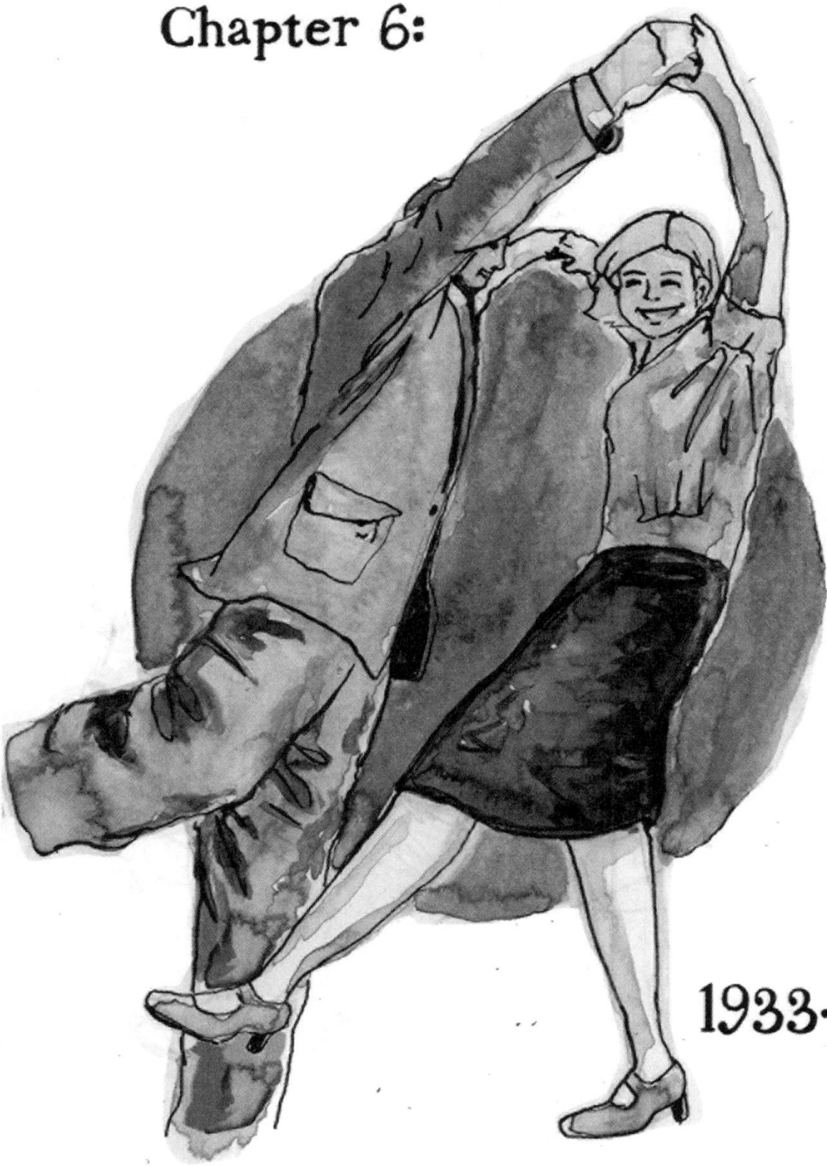

1933-1937

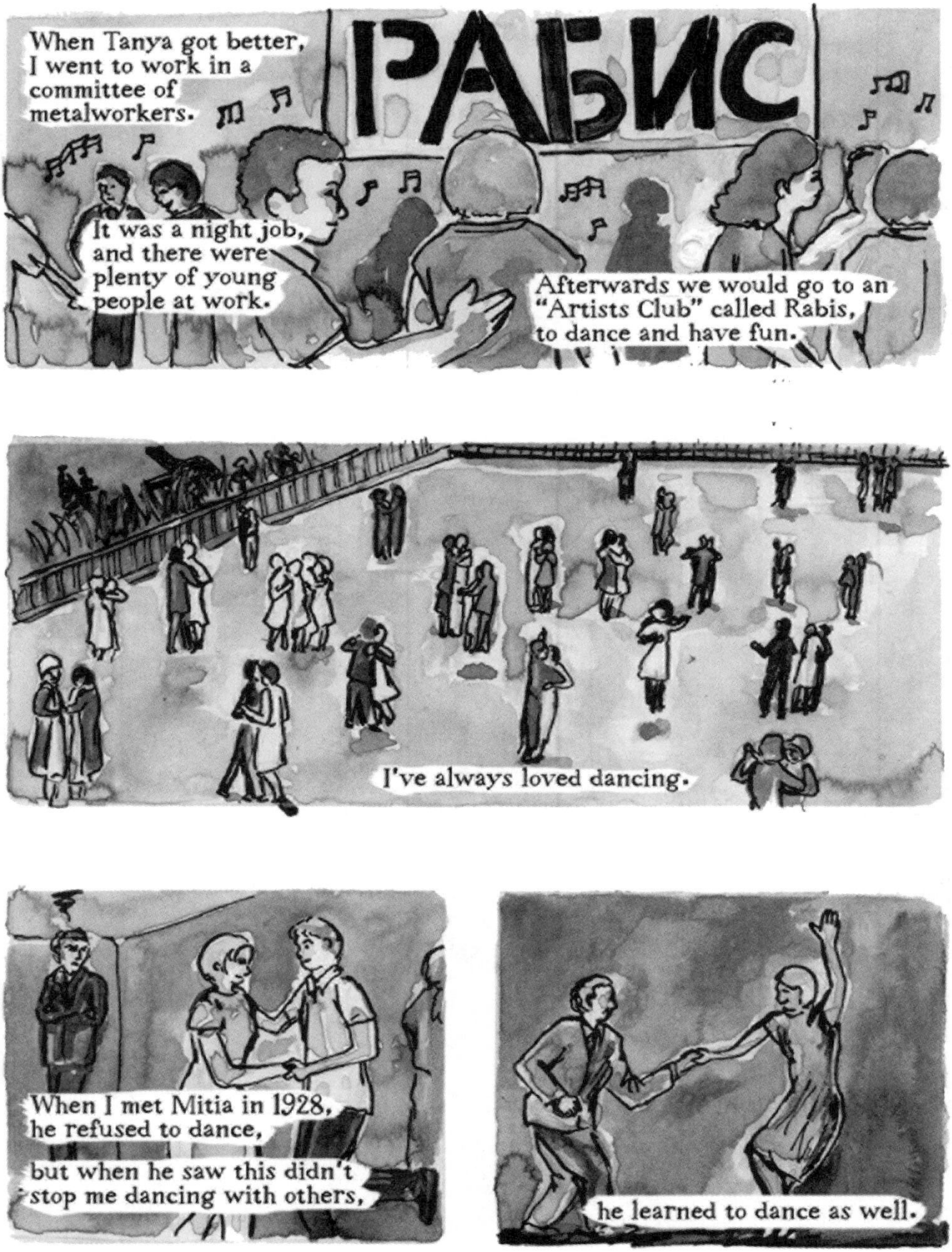

When Tanya got better, I went to work in a committee of metalworkers.
РАБИС
It was a night job, and there were plenty of young people at work.
Afterwards we would go to an "Artists Club" called Rabis, to dance and have fun.
I've always loved dancing.
When I met Mitia in 1928, he refused to dance,
but when he saw this didn't stop me dancing with others,
he learned to dance as well.

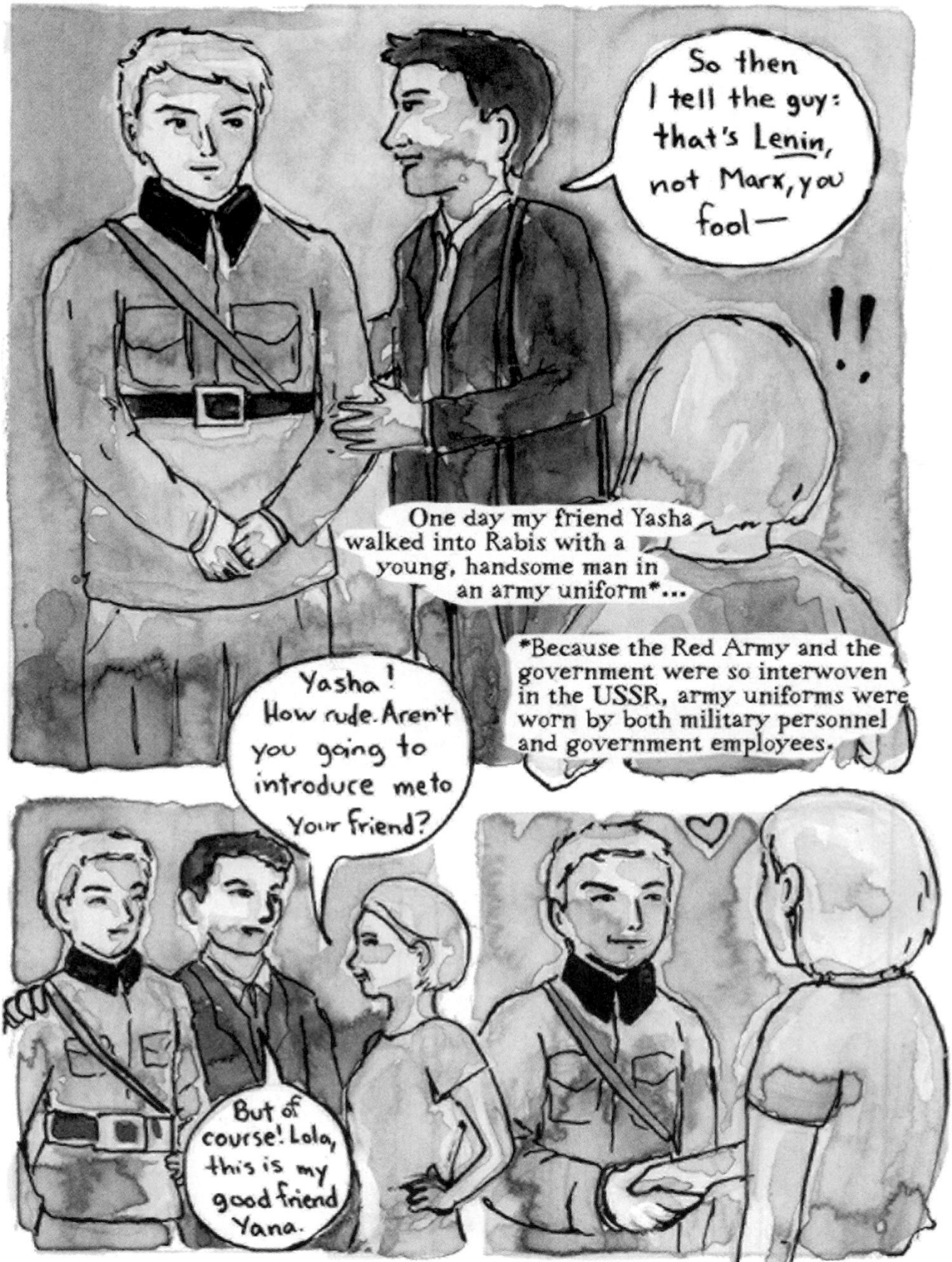
So then I tell the guy: that's Lenin, not Marx, you fool—
!!
One day my friend Yasha walked into Rabis with a young, handsome man in an army uniform*...
*Because the Red Army and the government were so interwoven in the USSR, army uniforms were worn by both military personnel and government employees.
Yasha! How rude. Aren't you going to introduce me to your friend?
But of course! Lola, this is my good friend Yana.

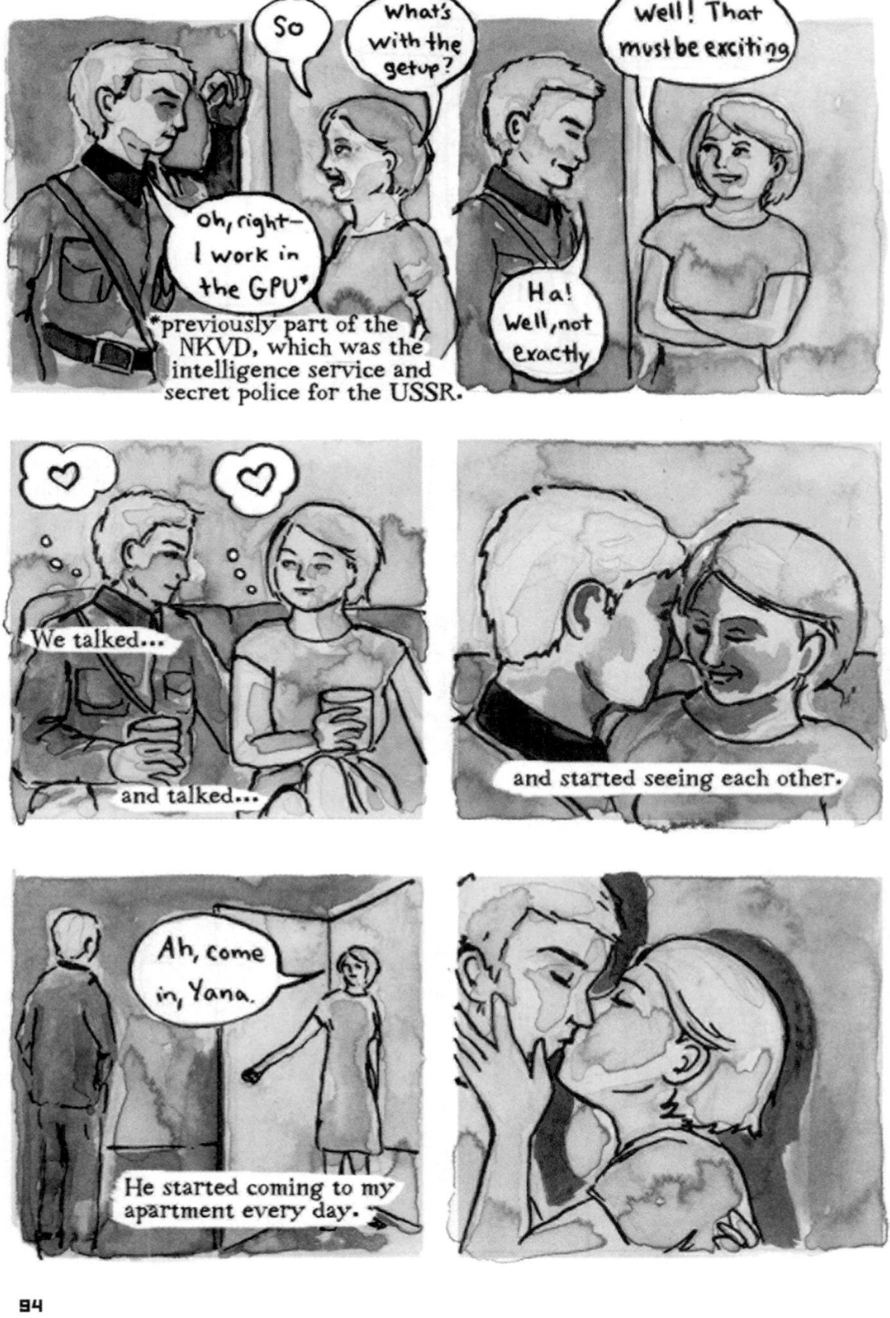
So
What's with the getup?
Oh, right— I work in the GPU*
*previously part of the NKVD, which was the intelligence service and secret police for the USSR.
Well! That must be exciting
Ha! Well, not exactly
We talked...
and talked...
and started seeing each other.
Ah, come in, Yana.
He started coming to my apartment every day.

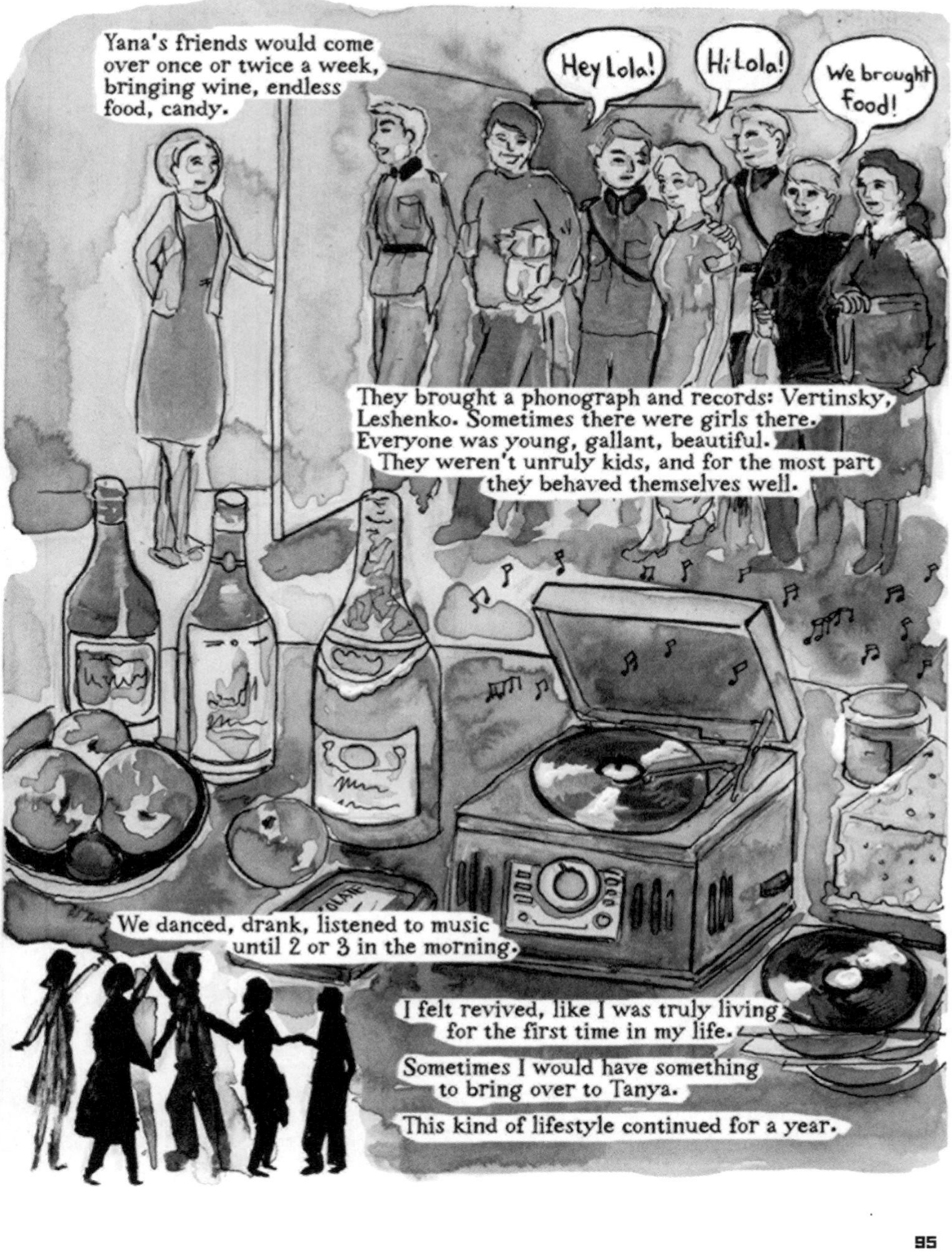

Yana's friends would come over once or twice a week, bringing wine, endless food, candy.
Hey Lola!
Hi Lola!
We brought food!
They brought a phonograph and records: Vertinsky, Leshenko. Sometimes there were girls there.
Everyone was young, gallant, beautiful.
They weren't unruly kids, and for the most part they behaved themselves well.
We danced, drank, listened to music until 2 or 3 in the morning.
I felt revived, like I was truly living for the first time in my life.
Sometimes I would have something to bring over to Tanya.
This kind of lifestyle continued for a year.

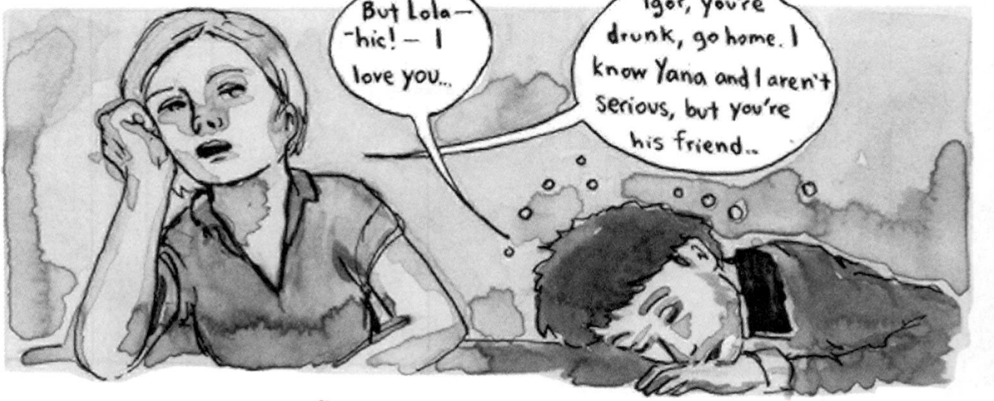
But Lola— -hic! — I love you...
Igor, you're drunk, go home. I know Yana and I aren't serious, but you're his friend...

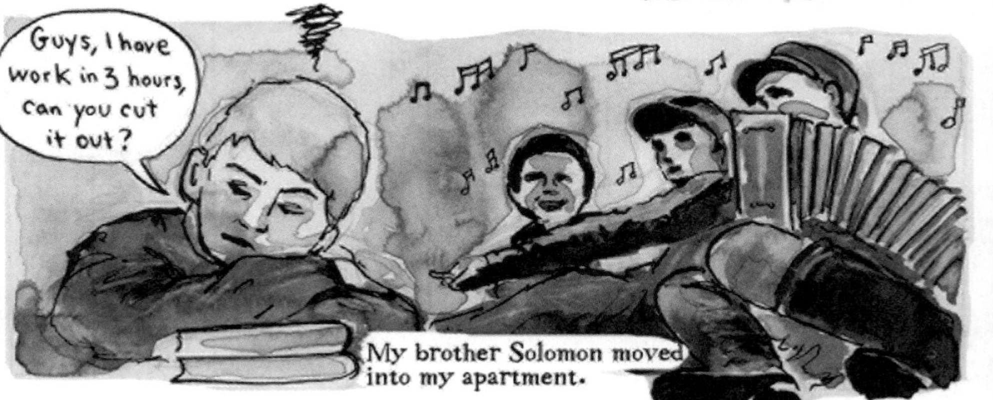
Guys, I have work in 3 hours, can you cut it out?
My brother Solomon moved into my apartment.

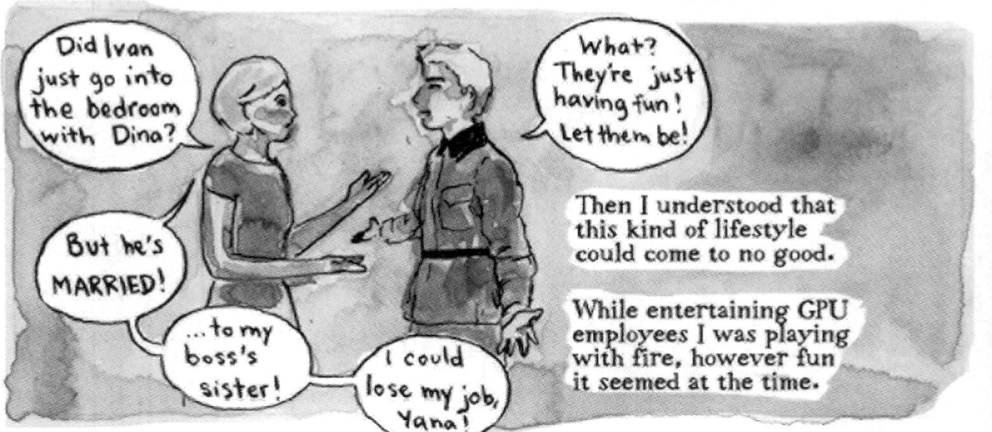
Did Ivan just go into the bedroom with Dina?
What? They're just having fun! Let them be!
But he's MARRIED!
...to my boss's sister!
I could lose my job, Yana!
Then I understood that this kind of lifestyle could come to no good.
While entertaining GPU employees I was playing with fire, however fun it seemed at the time.

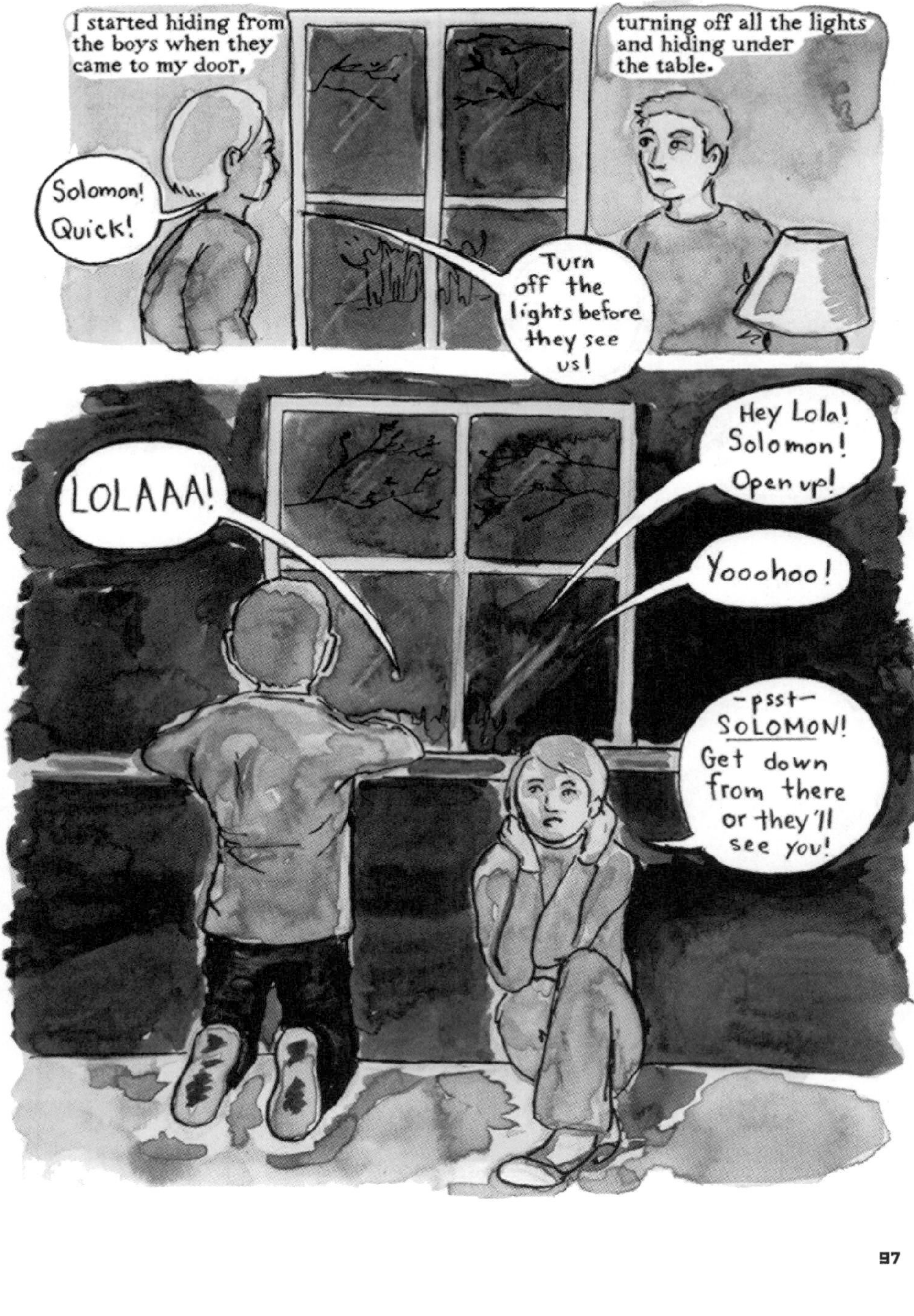
I started hiding from the boys when they came to my door,
Solomon! Quick!
Turn off the lights before they see us!
turning off all the lights and hiding under the table.
LOLAAA!
Hey Lola! Solomon! Open up!
Yooohoo!
-psst- SOLOMON! Get down from there or they'll see you!

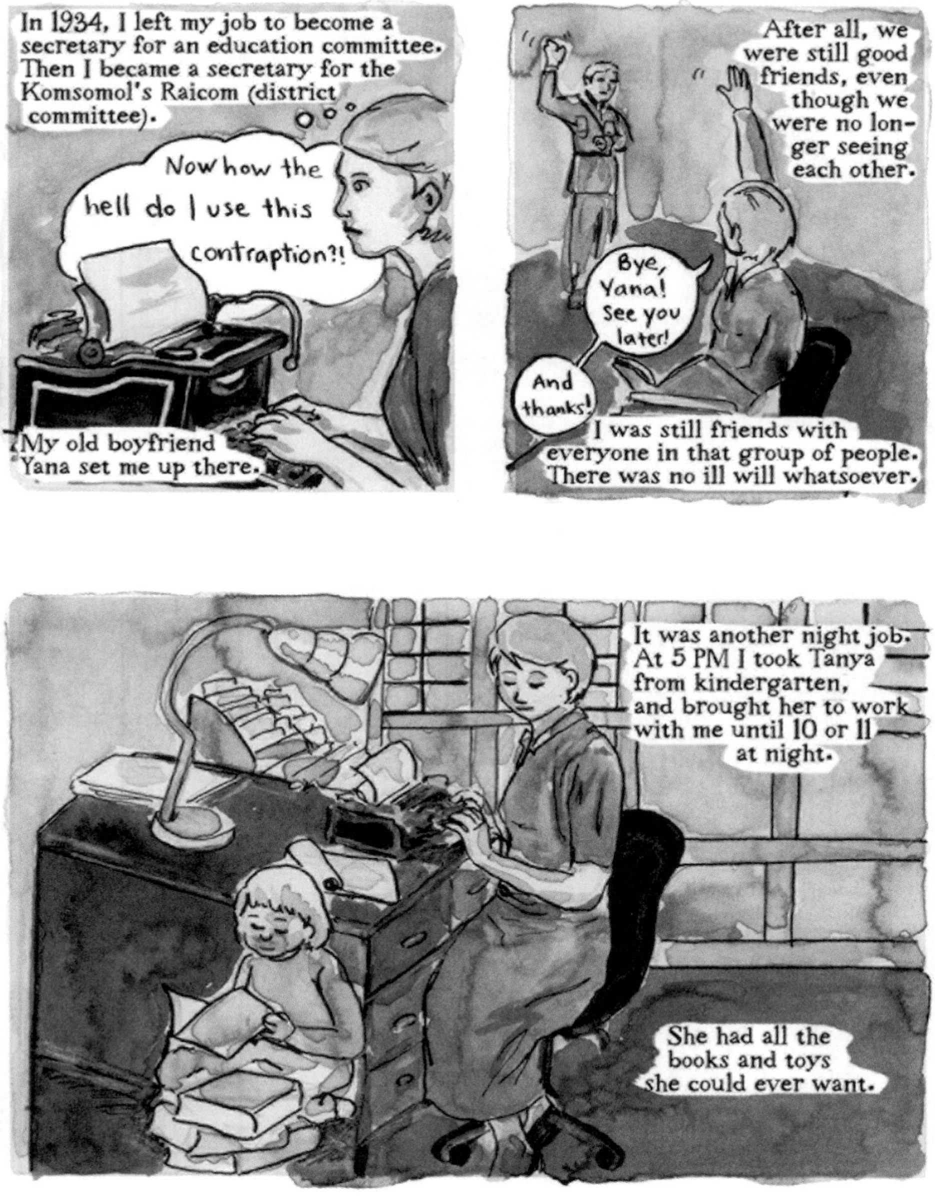
In 1934, I left my job to become a secretary for an education committee. Then I became a secretary for the Komsomol's Raicom (district committee).
Now how the hell do I use this contraption?!
My old boyfriend Yana set me up there.
After all, we were still good friends, even though we were no longer seeing each other.
Bye, Yana! See you later!
And thanks!
I was still friends with everyone in that group of people. There was no ill will whatsoever.
It was another night job. At 5 PM I took Tanya from kindergarten, and brought her to work with me until 10 or 11 at night.
She had all the books and toys she could ever want.

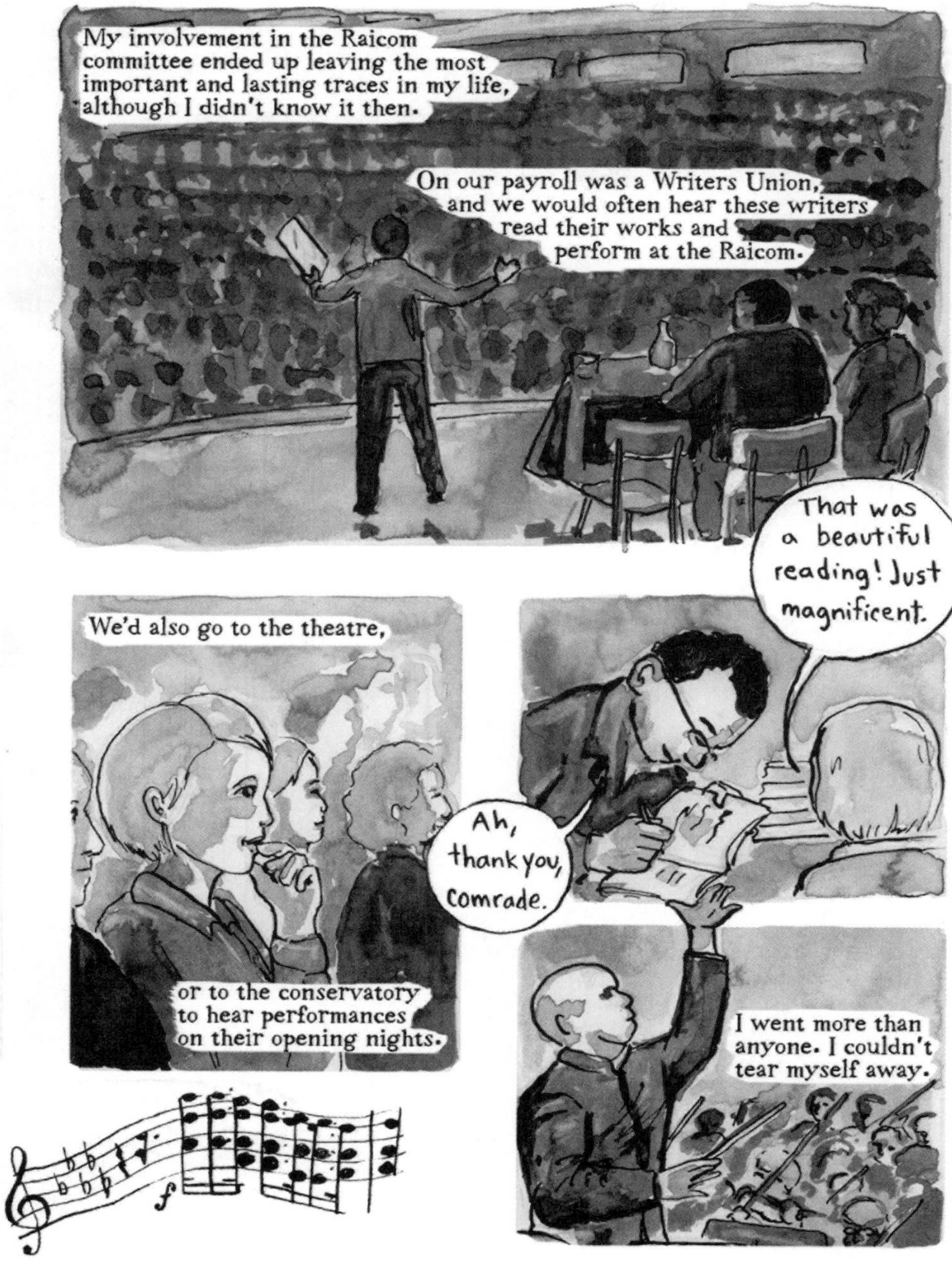
My involvement in the Raicom committee ended up leaving the most important and lasting traces in my life, although I didn't know it then.
On our payroll was a Writers Union, and we would often hear these writers read their works and perform at the Raicom.
That was a beautiful reading! Just magnificent.
Ah, thank you, comrade.
We'd also go to the theatre,
or to the conservatory to hear performances on their opening nights.
I went more than anyone. I couldn't tear myself away.

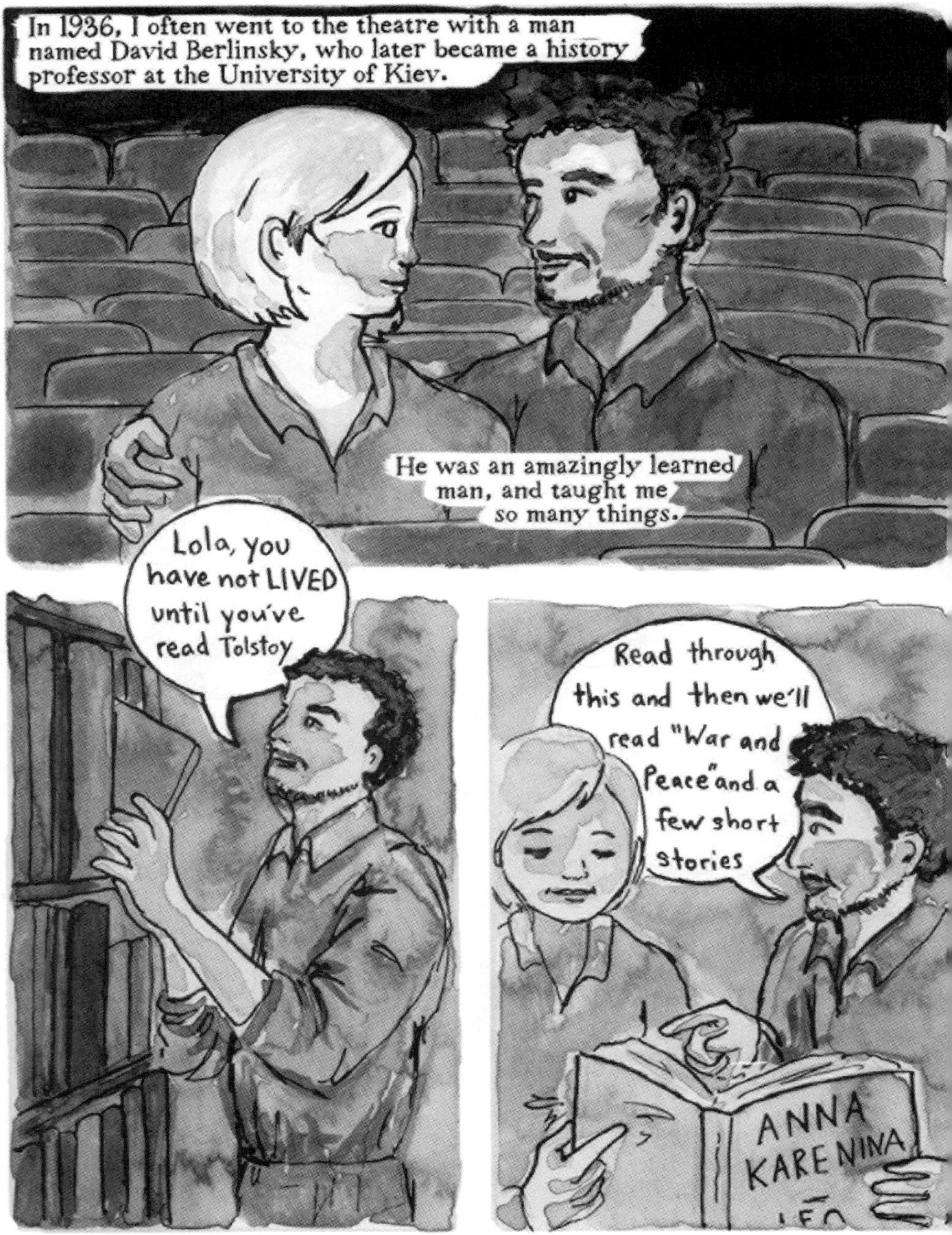

In 1936, I often went to the theatre with a man named David Berlinsky, who later became a history professor at the University of Kiev.
He was an amazingly learned man, and taught me so many things.
Lola, you have not LIVED until you've read Tolstoy
Read through this and then we'll read "War and Peace" and a few short stories
ANNA KARENINA

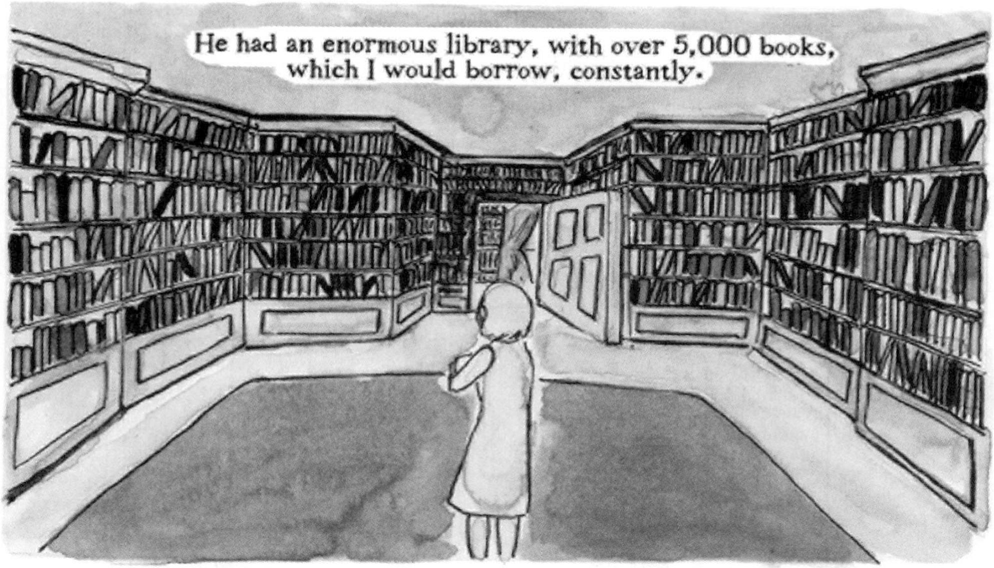
He had an enormous library, with over 5,000 books, which I would borrow, constantly.

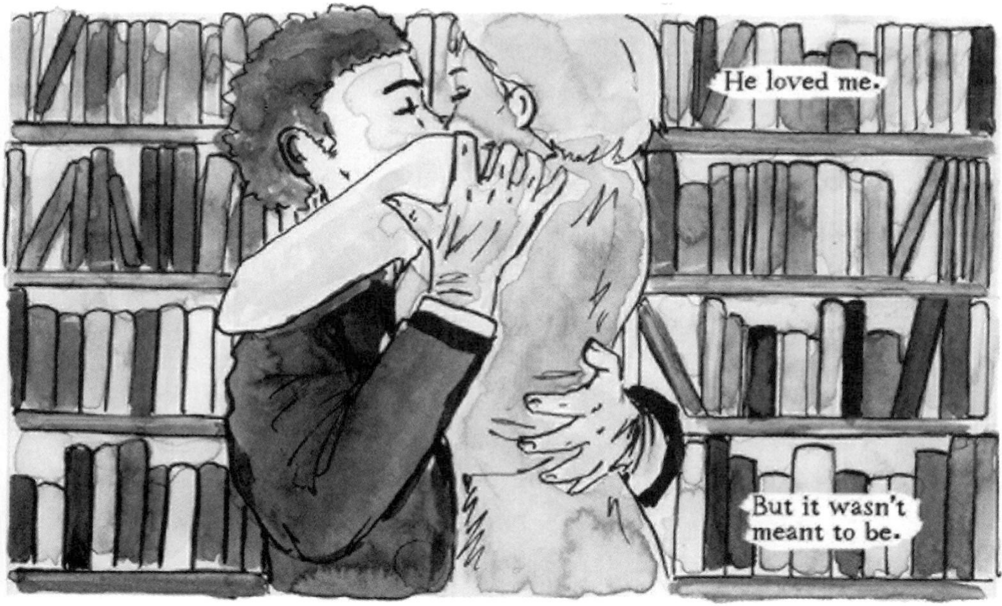
He loved me.
But it wasn't meant to be.

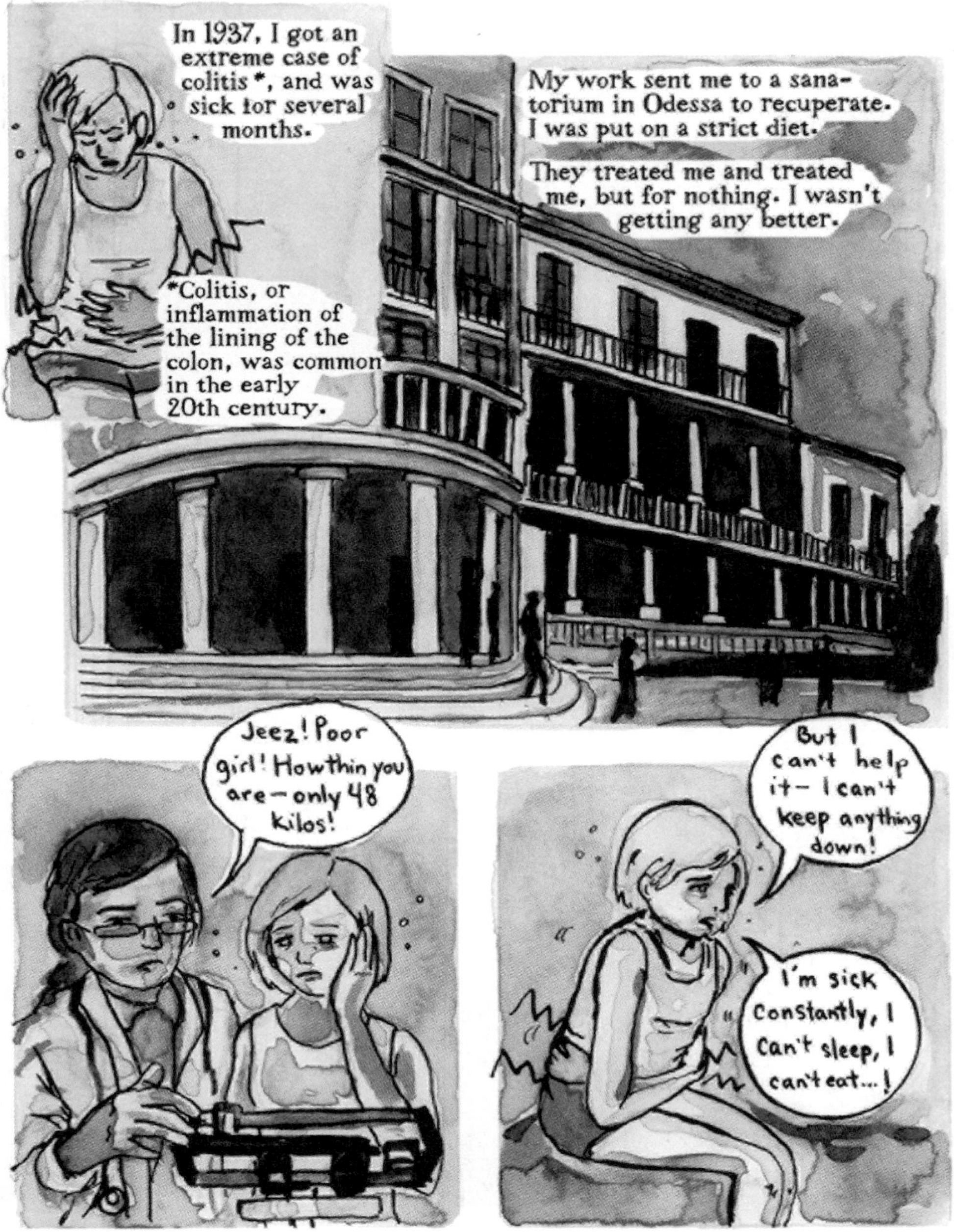
In 1937, I got an extreme case of colitis*, and was sick for several months.
My work sent me to a sanatorium in Odessa to recuperate. I was put on a strict diet.
They treated me and treated me, but for nothing. I wasn't getting any better.
*Colitis, or inflammation of the lining of the colon, was common in the early 20th century.
Jeez! Poor girl! How thin you are—only 48 kilos!
But I can't help it—I can't keep anything down!
I'm sick constantly, I can't sleep, I can't eat...!

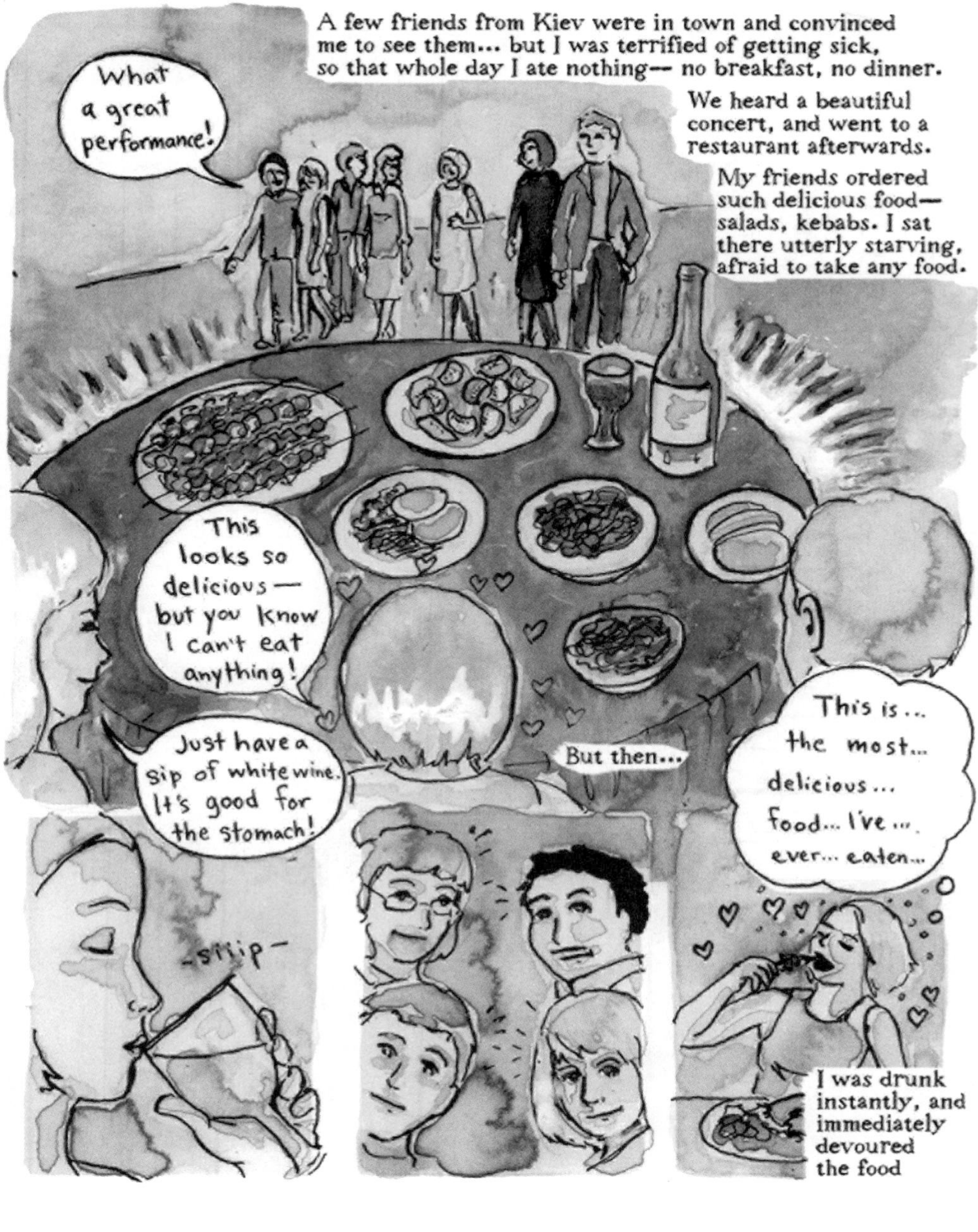

A few friends from Kiev were in town and convinced me to see them... but I was terrified of getting sick, so that whole day I ate nothing— no breakfast, no dinner.
What a great performance!
We heard a beautiful concert, and went to a restaurant afterwards.
My friends ordered such delicious food— salads, kebabs. I sat there utterly starving, afraid to take any food.
This looks so delicious— but you know I can't eat anything!
Just have a sip of white wine. It's good for the stomach!
But then...
This is... the most... delicious... food... I've... ever... eaten...
-siiip-
I was drunk instantly, and immediately devoured the food

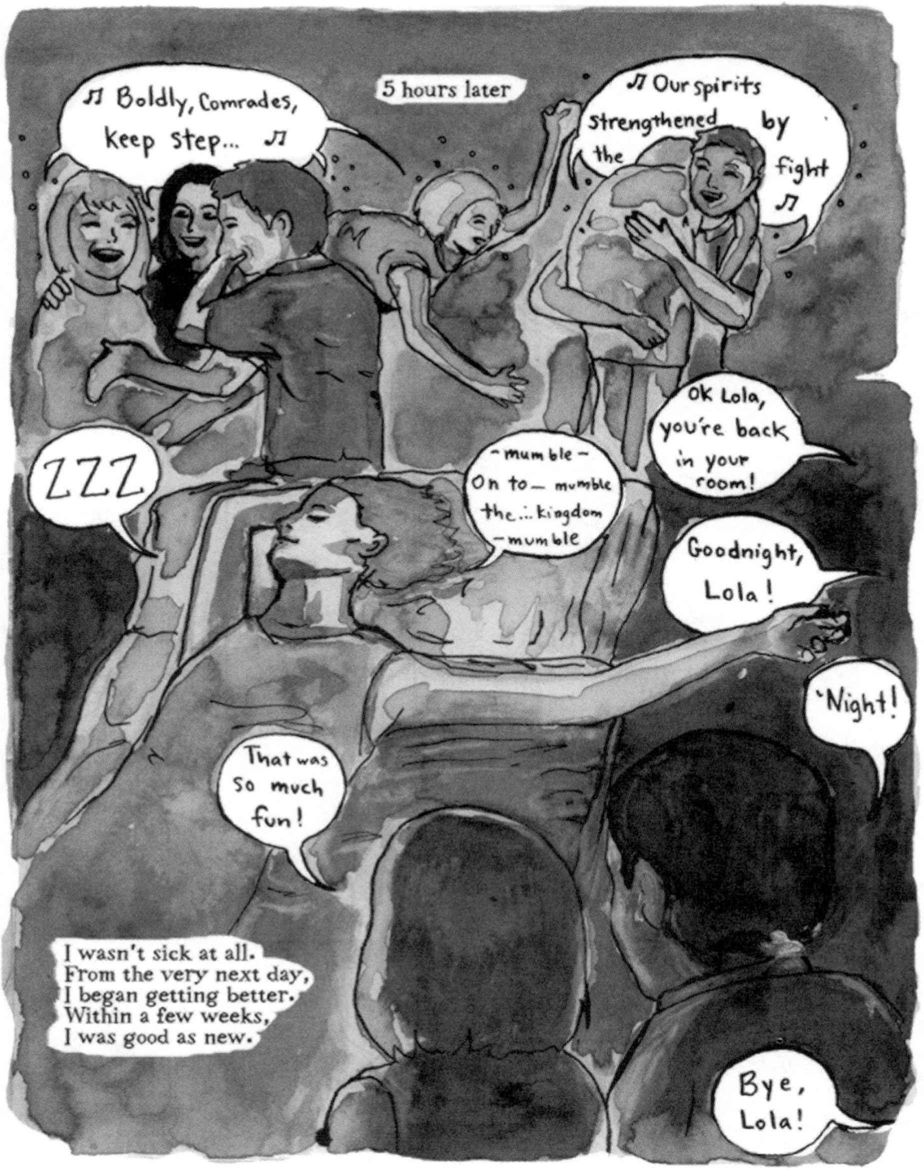
5 hours later
♫ Boldly, Comrades, keep step... ♫
♫ Our spirits strengthened by the fight ♫
ZZZ
-mumble- On to— mumble the... kingdom -mumble
Ok Lola, you're back in your room!
Goodnight, Lola!
'Night!
That was so much fun!
I wasn't sick at all.
From the very next day,
I began getting better.
Within a few weeks,
I was good as new.
Bye, Lola!

Interlude

Gay Pride Parade
Chicago, Summer '08

2008-2014

I always felt a strong generational distance from my mother, who was prudent, introverted, and conservative.

I felt an almost equal generational divide from my grandmother Tanya, who was lively but generally very cautious. My mother and grandmother followed rules; they did as they were told. They only had one or two serious relationships.

My mother thought I was absolutely crazy. I grew up feeling like a completely different breed of human.

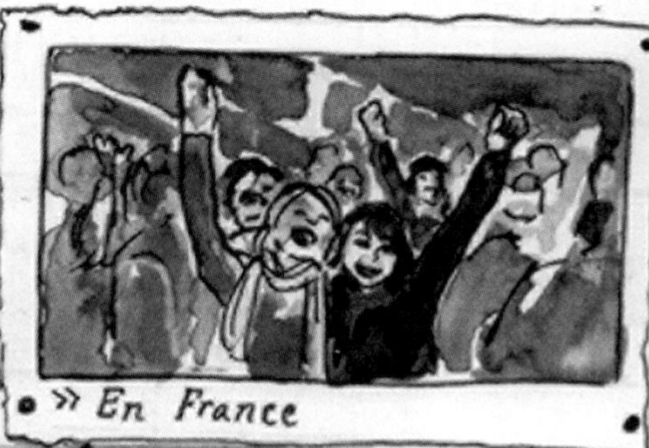

Obama election Paris, France Fall '08

» En France

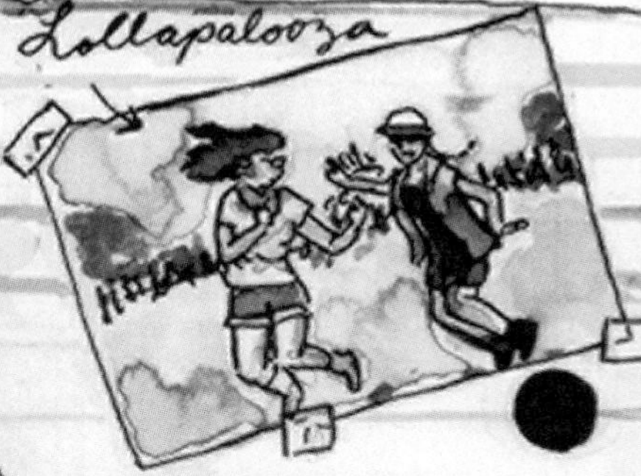

Lollapalooza

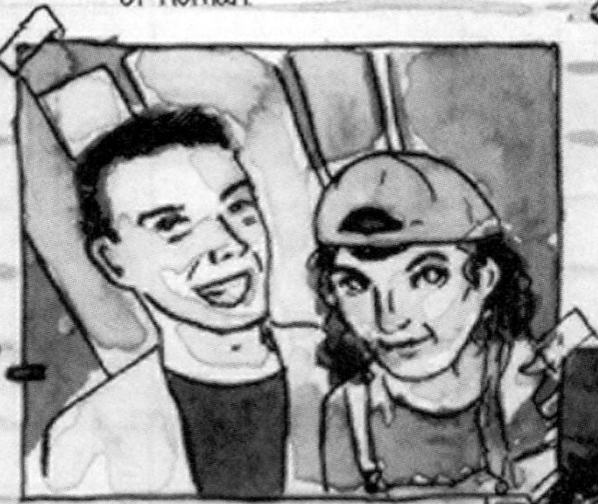

'90s party Chicago Summer '10

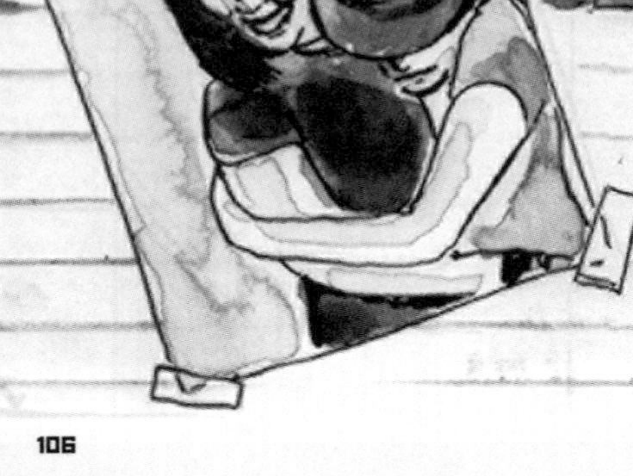

New Year's Chicago '09

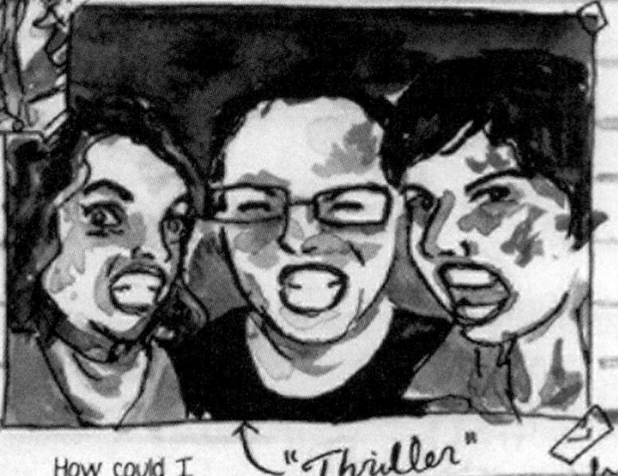

"Thriller" Zombie March Chicago Summer '09

How could I explain my desire for something other than what there was? Music, art, film, politics, books— these things restored a sense of wonder in the world that I thought my parents lacked.

Happiness wasn't quiet and calm, a few close friends, a comfortable job. It was the unknown and exciting: enormous parties, passionate and ill-fated love-affairs, spontaneous trips to far corners of the world.

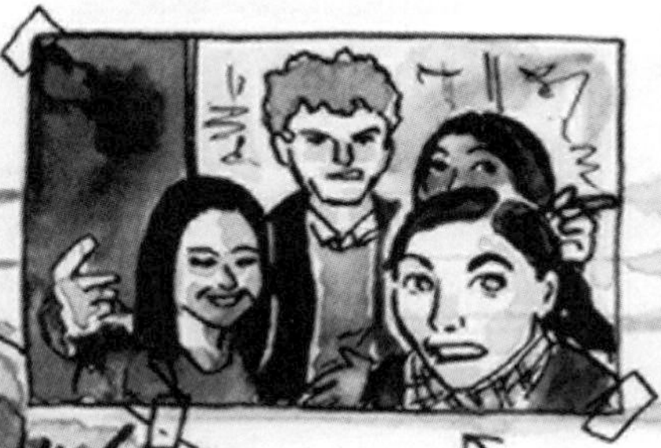

Paris, France Fall '08

It is said that Lola's generation—called the "G.I. Generation"—is closest to Generation Y ("millenials") in sentiment and personality.

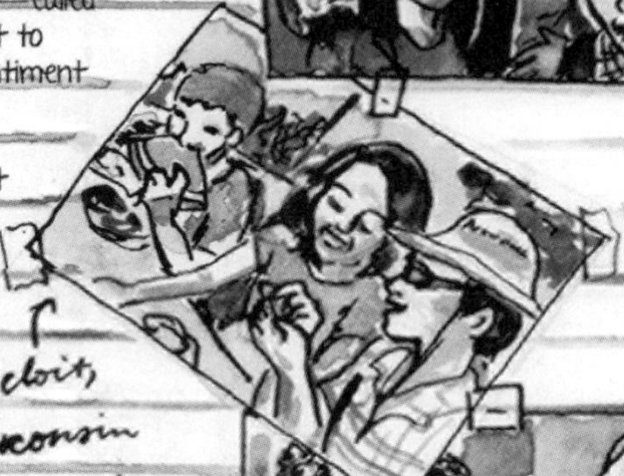

Beloit, Wisconsin Summer '09

Nowhere was this more evident than in my four-generation family.

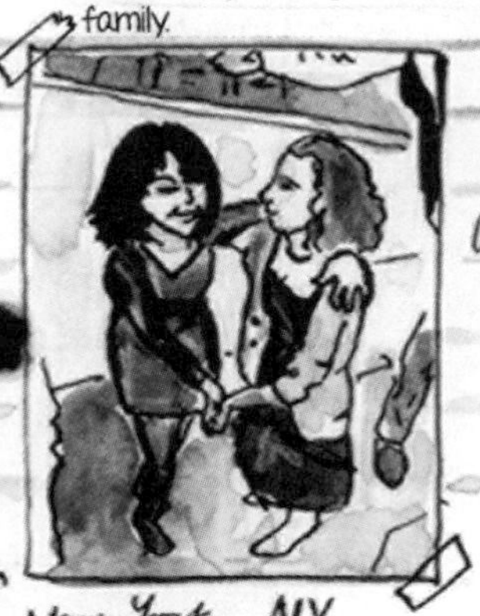

New York, NY Spring 2010

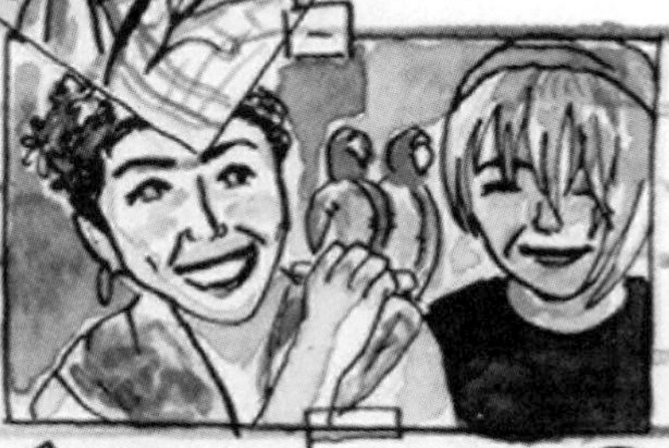

Halloween Cambridge, MA Fall '11

Of course, I didn't know this at the time Lola was alive. It was just a feeling of closeness, something that bonded the two of us more than other members of the family.

Rain Room New York, NY Summer '13

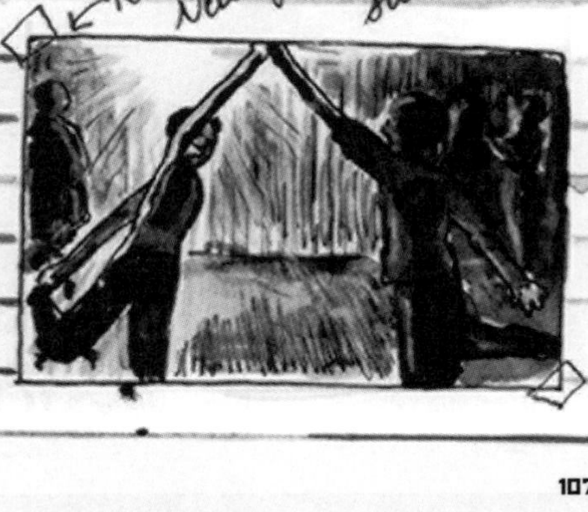

An idealism, maybe.
A desire for something—
anything—
out of the ordinary.

Chapter 7:

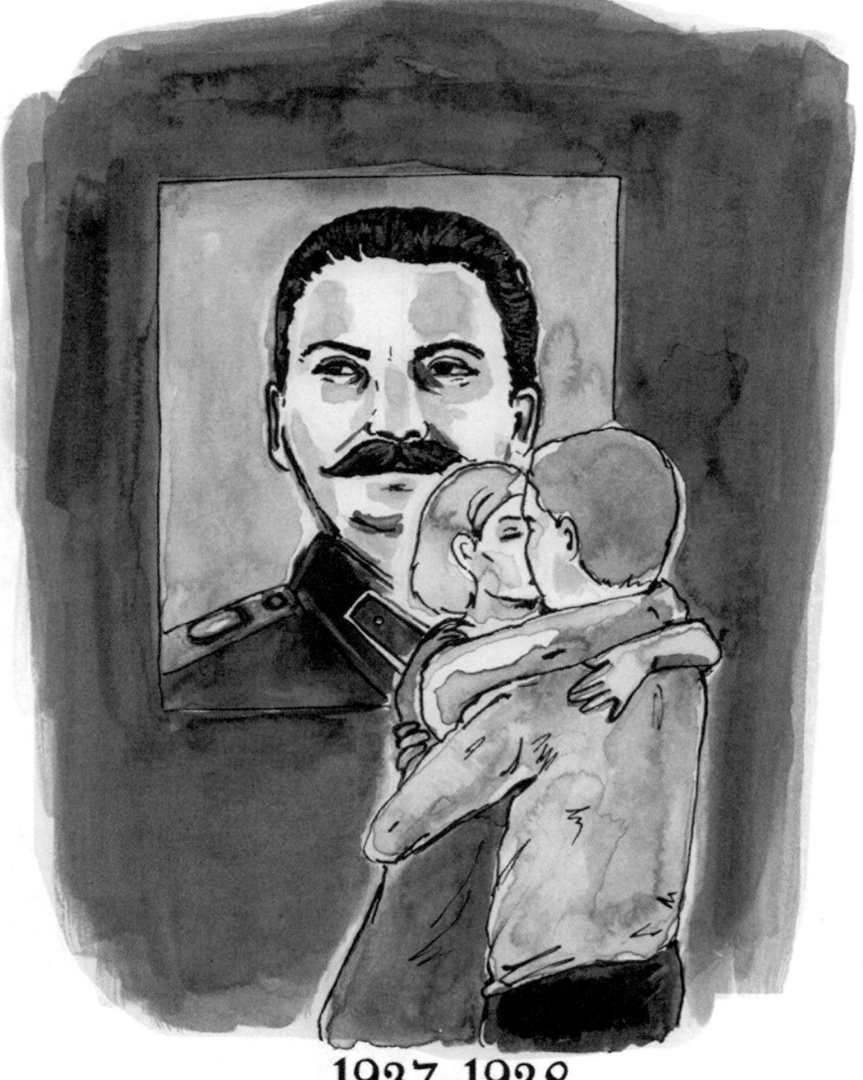

1937-1938

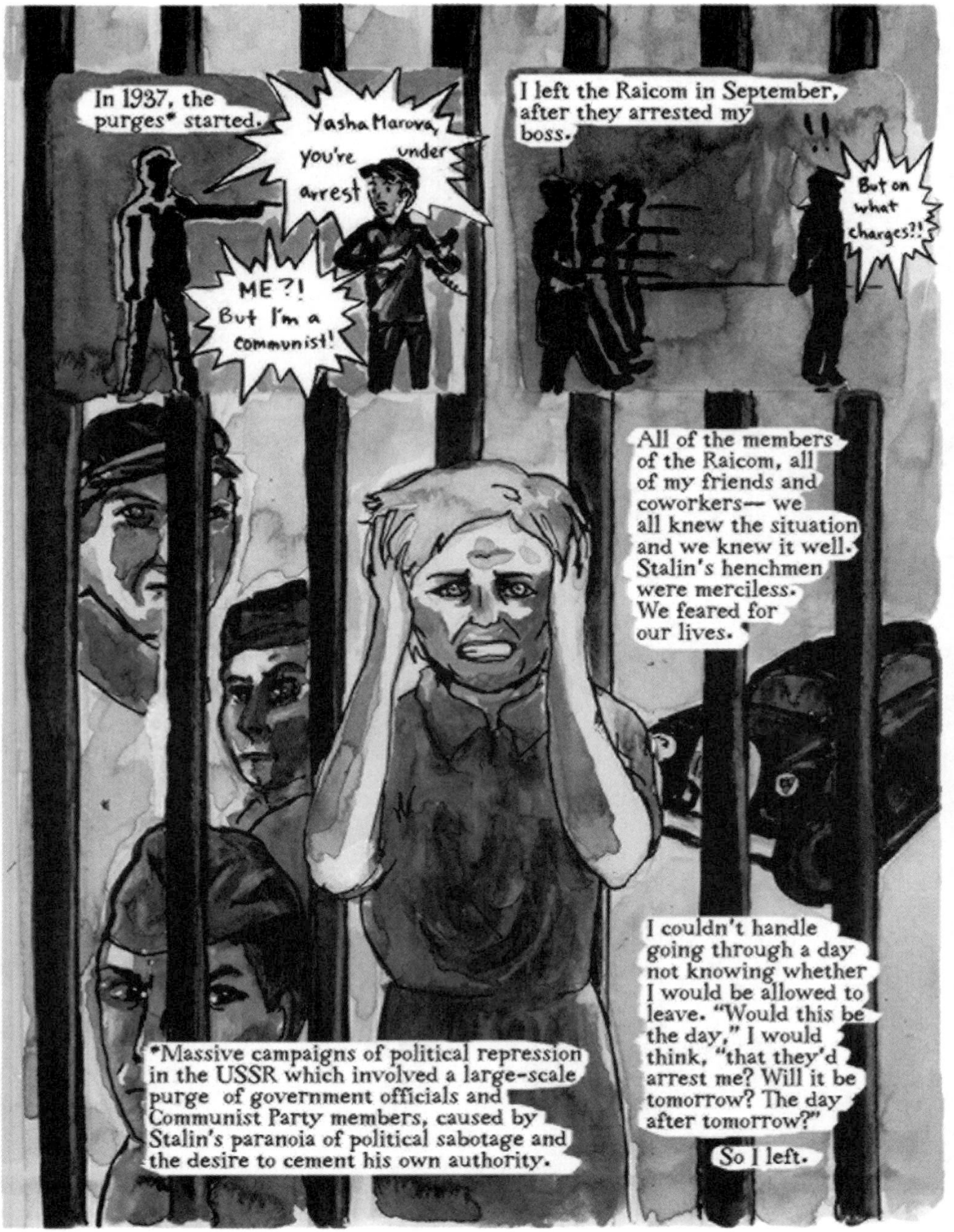
In 1937, the purges* started.
Yasha Marova, you're under arrest
ME?! But I'm a communist!
I left the Raicom in September, after they arrested my boss.
!!
But on what charges?!
All of the members of the Raicom, all of my friends and coworkers— we all knew the situation and we knew it well. Stalin's henchmen were merciless. We feared for our lives.
I couldn't handle going through a day not knowing whether I would be allowed to leave. "Would this be the day," I would think, "that they'd arrest me? Will it be tomorrow? The day after tomorrow?"
So I left.
*Massive campaigns of political repression in the USSR which involved a large-scale purge of government officials and Communist Party members, caused by Stalin's paranoia of political sabotage and the desire to cement his own authority.

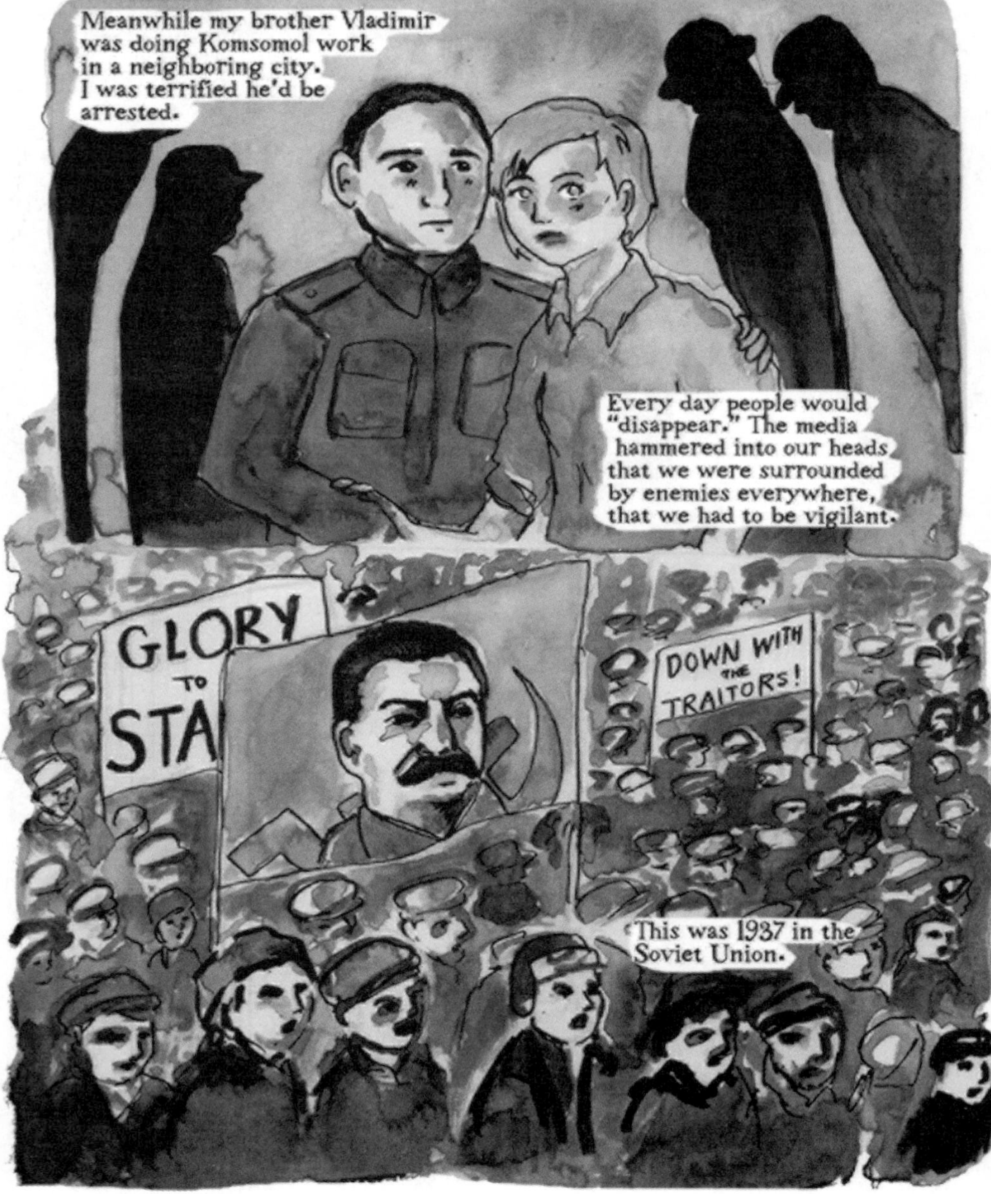
Meanwhile my brother Vladimir was doing Komsomol work in a neighboring city. I was terrified he'd be arrested.
Every day people would "disappear." The media hammered into our heads that we were surrounded by enemies everywhere, that we had to be vigilant.
GLORY TO STA
DOWN WITH THE TRAITORS!
This was 1937 in the Soviet Union.

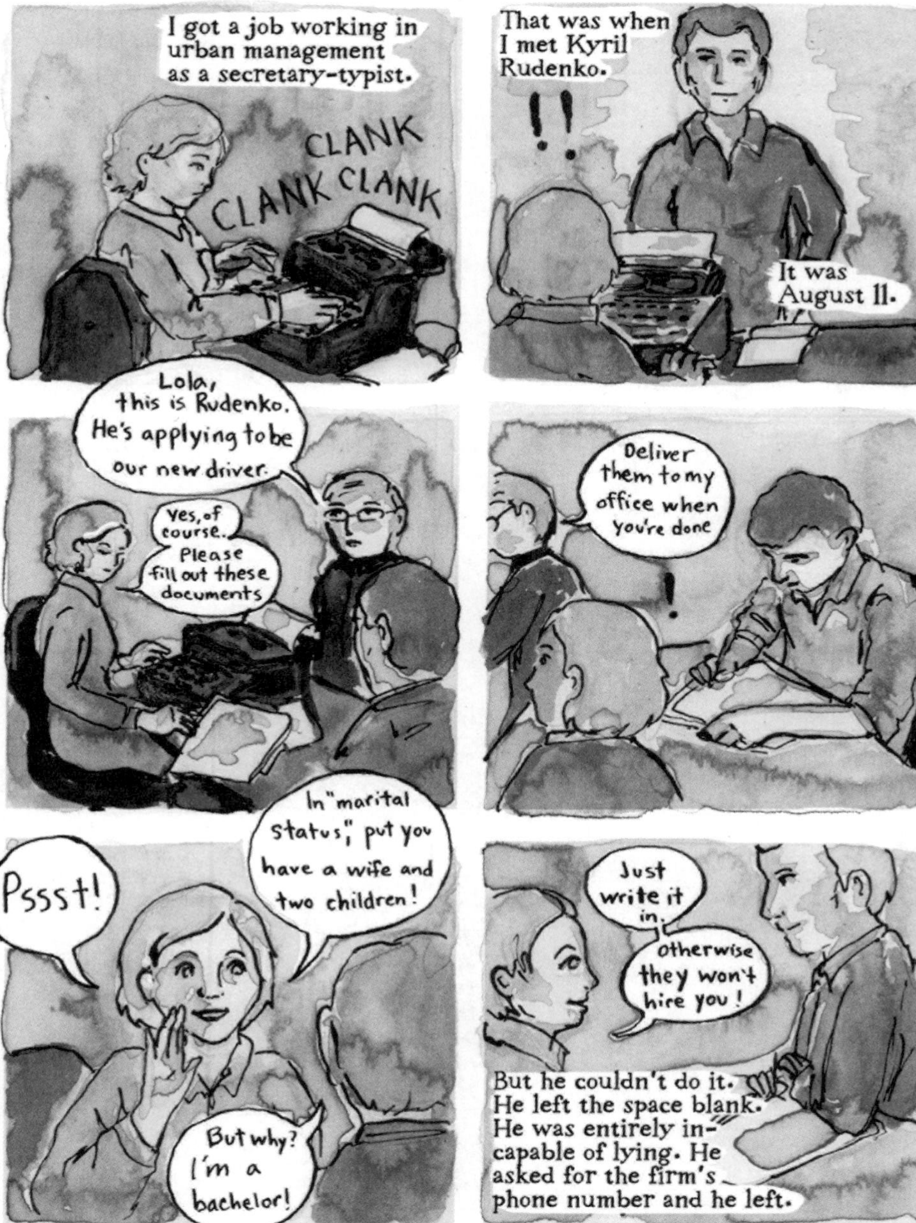
I got a job working in urban management as a secretary-typist.
CLANK CLANK CLANK
That was when I met Kyril Rudenko.
!!
It was August 11.
Lola, this is Rudenko. He's applying to be our new driver.
Yes, of course. Please fill out these documents
Deliver them to my office when you're done
!
Pssst!
In "marital status," put you have a wife and two children!
But why? I'm a bachelor!
Just write it in.
otherwise they won't hire you!
But he couldn't do it. He left the space blank. He was entirely incapable of lying. He asked for the firm's phone number and he left.

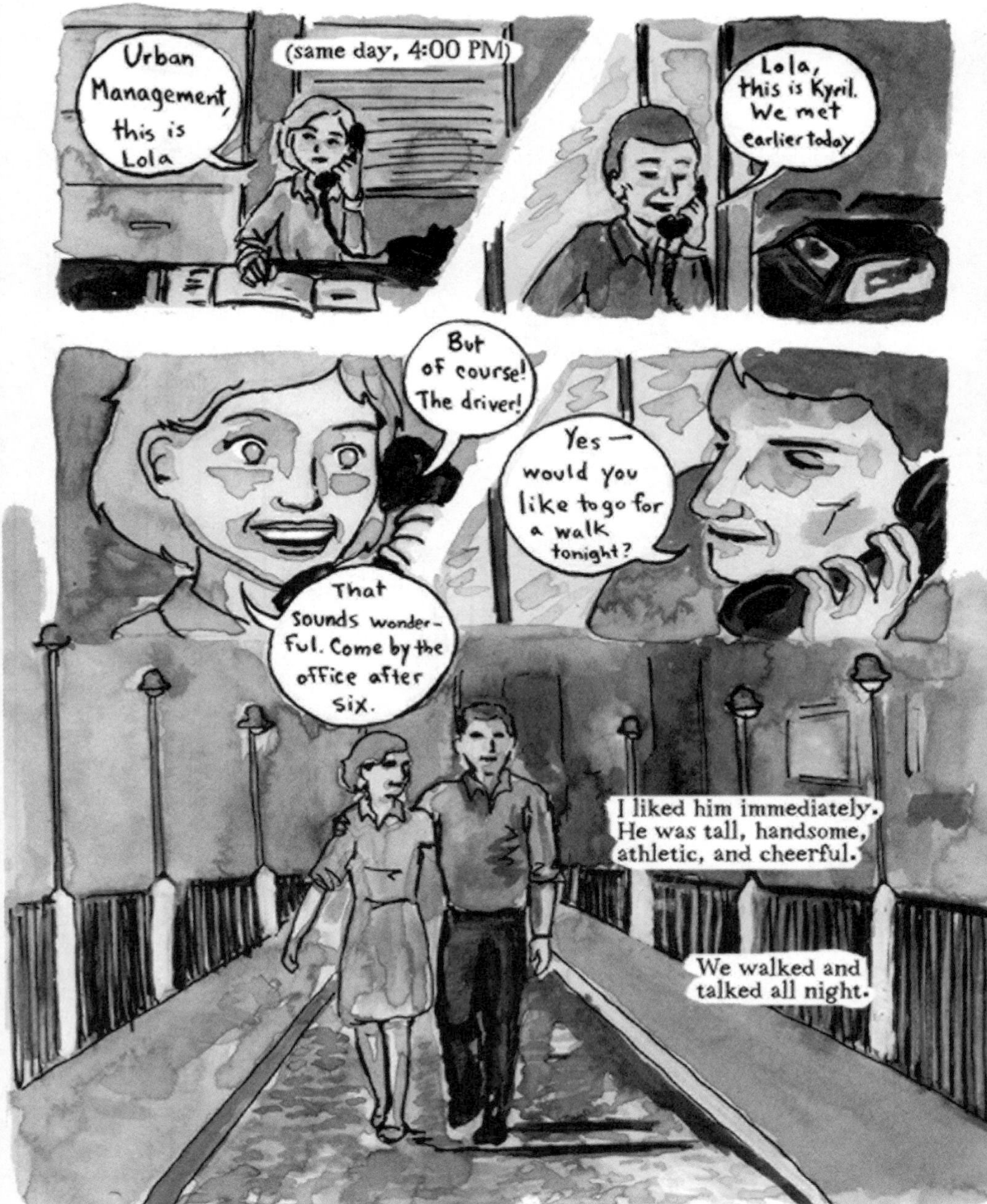
(same day, 4:00 PM)
Urban Management, this is Lola
Lola, this is Kyril. We met earlier today
But of course! The driver!
Yes— would you like to go for a walk tonight?
That sounds wonder-ful. Come by the office after six.
I liked him immediately. He was tall, handsome, athletic, and cheerful.
We walked and talked all night.

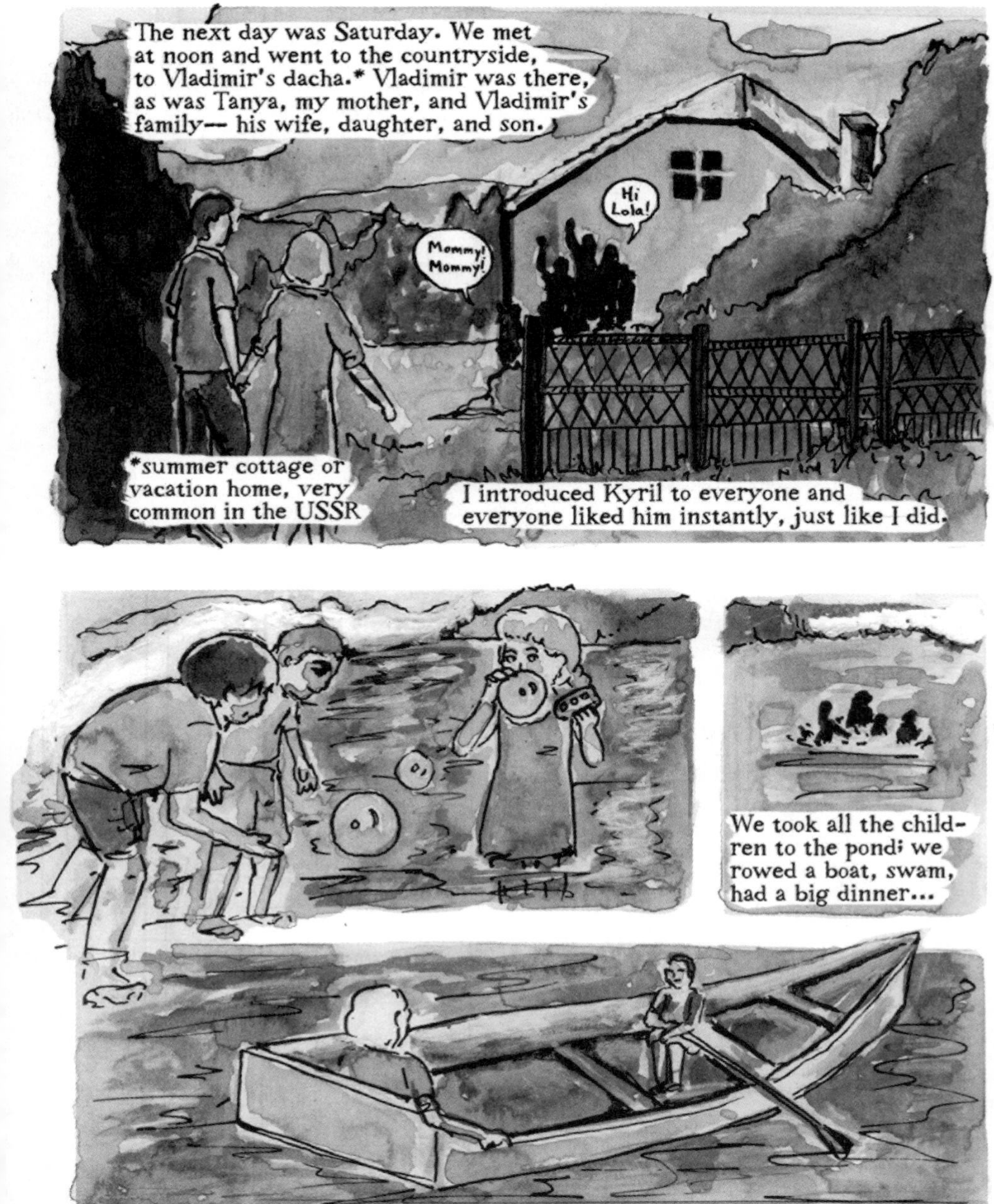
The next day was Saturday. We met at noon and went to the countryside, to Vladimir's dacha.* Vladimir was there, as was Tanya, my mother, and Vladimir's family— his wife, daughter, and son.
Hi Lola!
Mommy! Mommy!
*summer cottage or vacation home, very common in the USSR
I introduced Kyril to everyone and everyone liked him instantly, just like I did.
We took all the children to the pond; we rowed a boat, swam, had a big dinner...

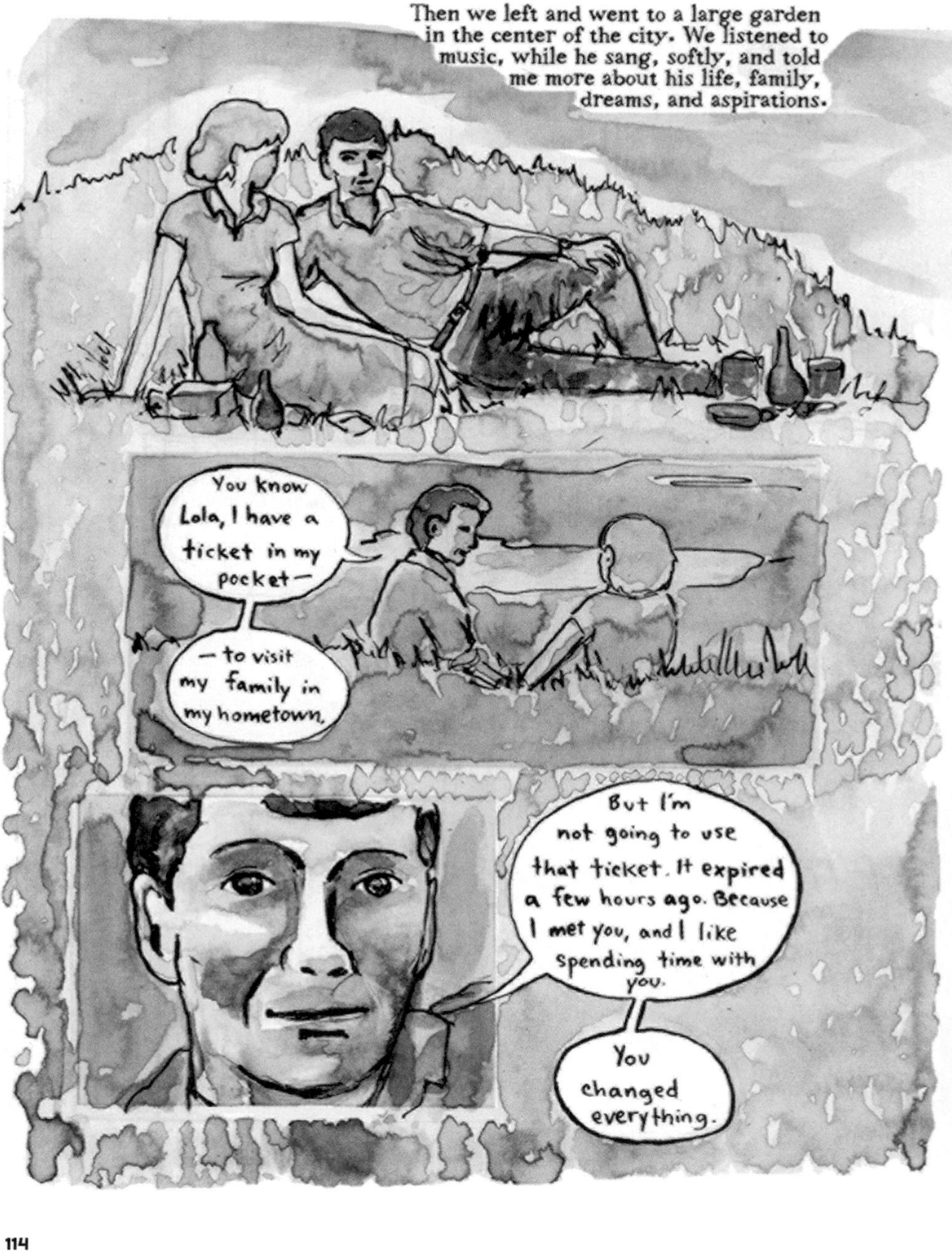
Then we left and went to a large garden in the center of the city. We listened to music, while he sang, softly, and told me more about his life, family, dreams, and aspirations.
You know Lola, I have a ticket in my pocket—
—to visit my family in my hometown.
But I'm not going to use that ticket. It expired a few hours ago. Because I met you, and I like spending time with you.
You changed everything.

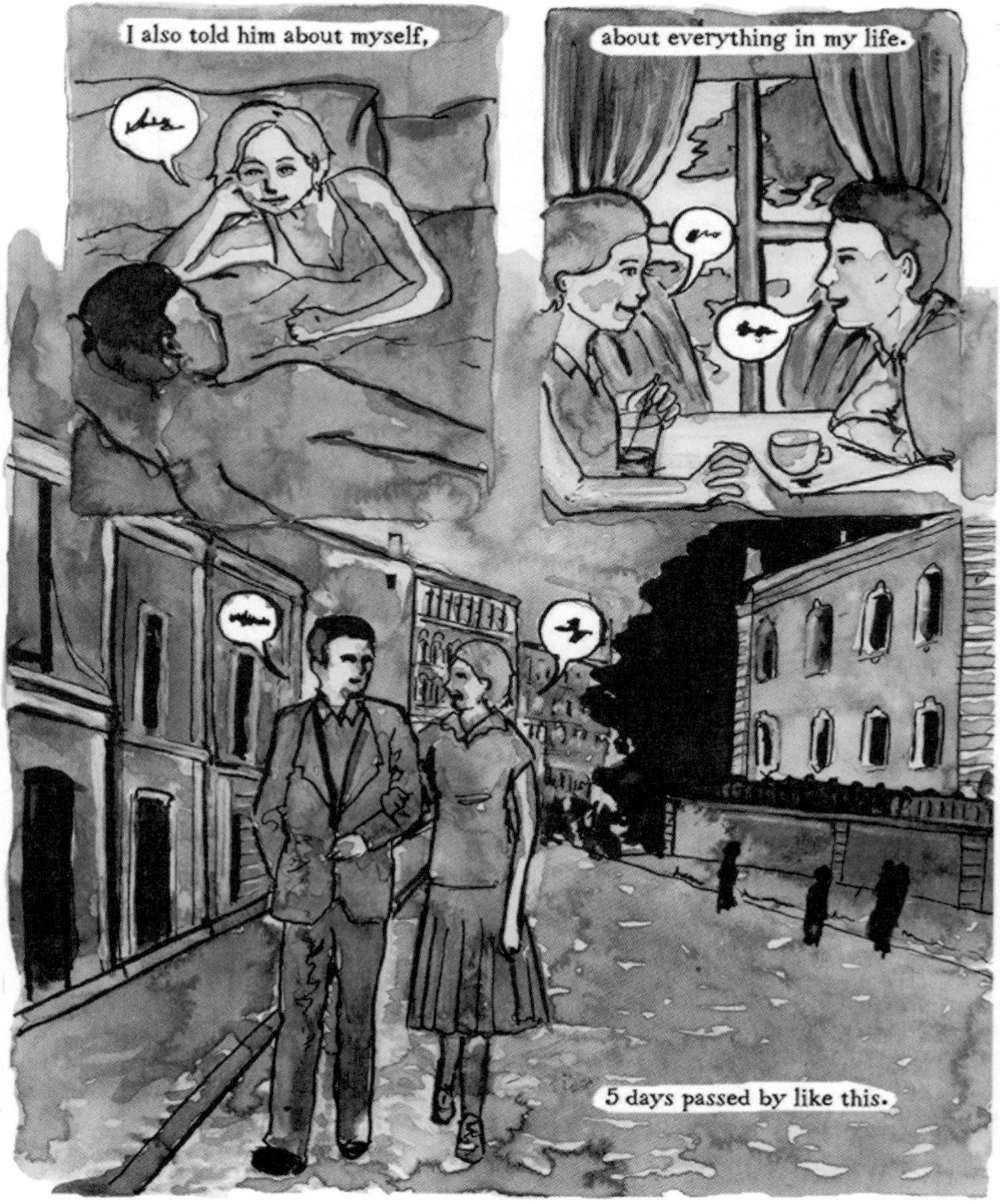

I also told him about myself,
about everything in my life.
5 days passed by like this.

On August 15, he proposed.

I liked that he was simple,
but by no means dull or boring.
He was bright. And happy.
And I said yes.

By August 17, he moved in.

On September 1st, Tanya started
going to a school directly in front
of our apartment.

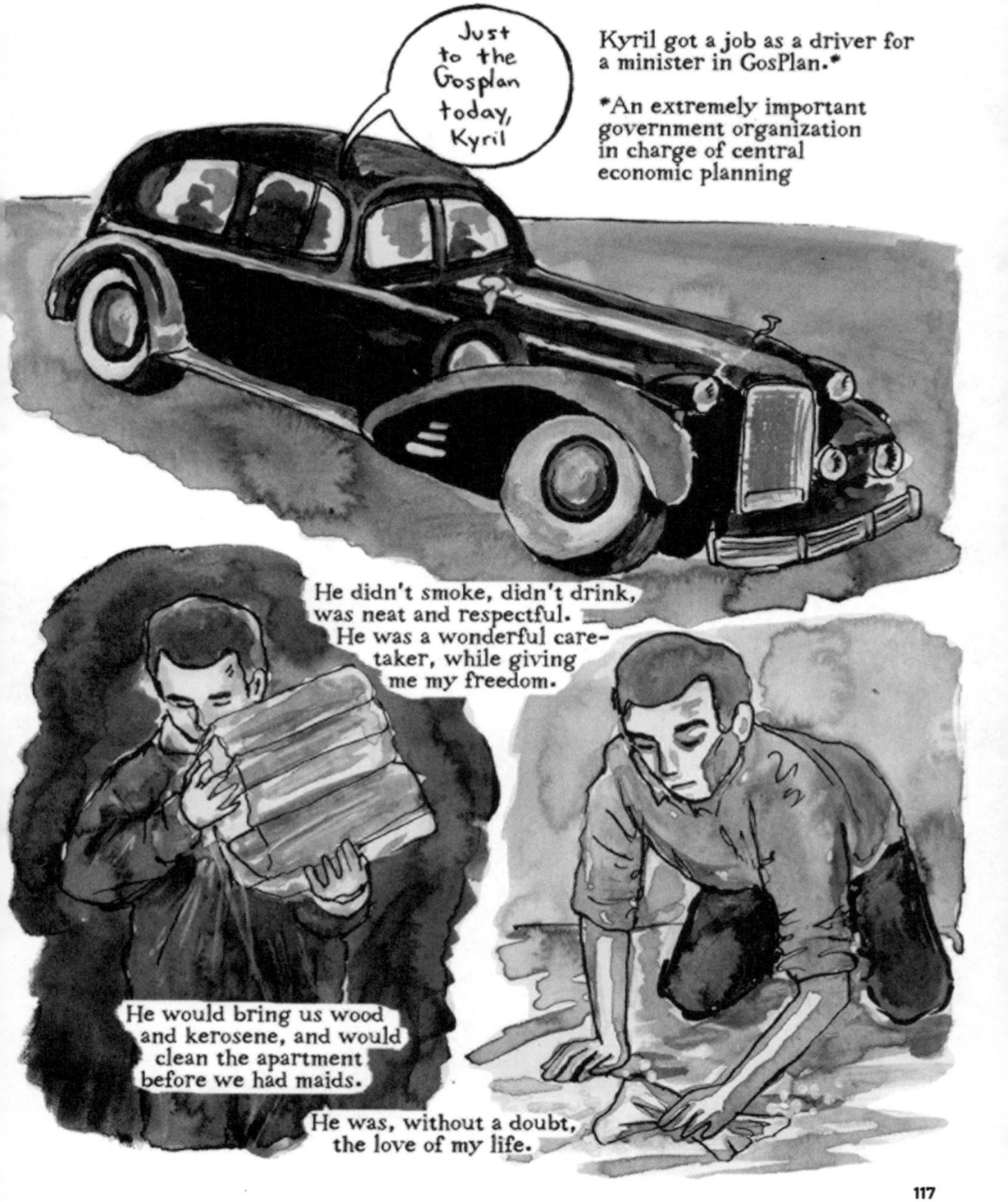
Just to the Gosplan today, Kyril
Kyril got a job as a driver for a minister in GosPlan.*
*An extremely important government organization in charge of central economic planning
He didn't smoke, didn't drink, was neat and respectful. He was a wonderful caretaker, while giving me my freedom.
He would bring us wood and kerosene, and would clean the apartment before we had maids.
He was, without a doubt, the love of my life.

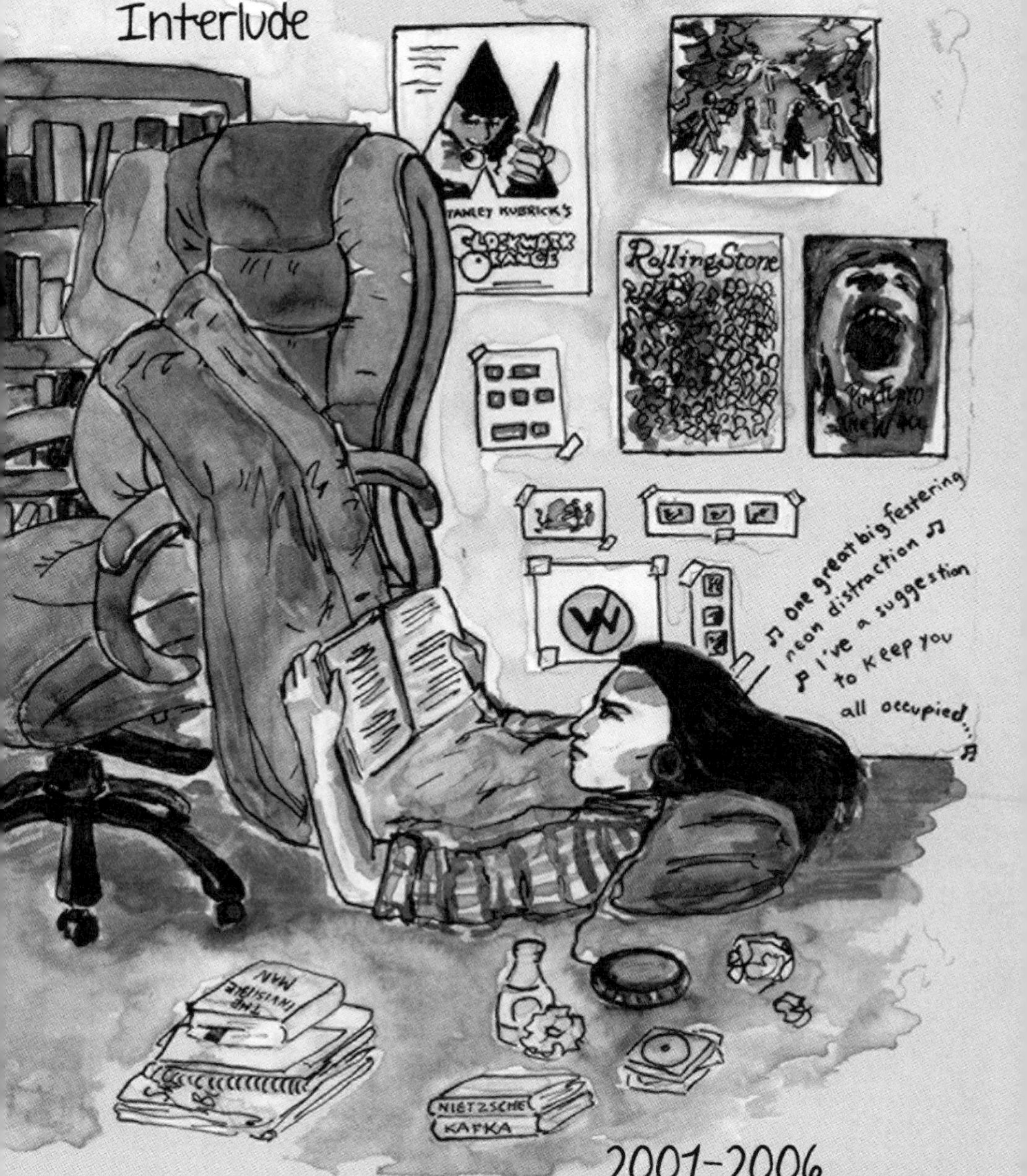
Interlude
TANLEY KUBRICK'S
CLOCKWORK ORANGE
Rolling Stone
♫ One great big festering neon distraction ♫
♫ I've a suggestion to keep you all occupied... ♫
THE INVISIBLE MAN
NIETZSCHE
KAFKA
2001–2006

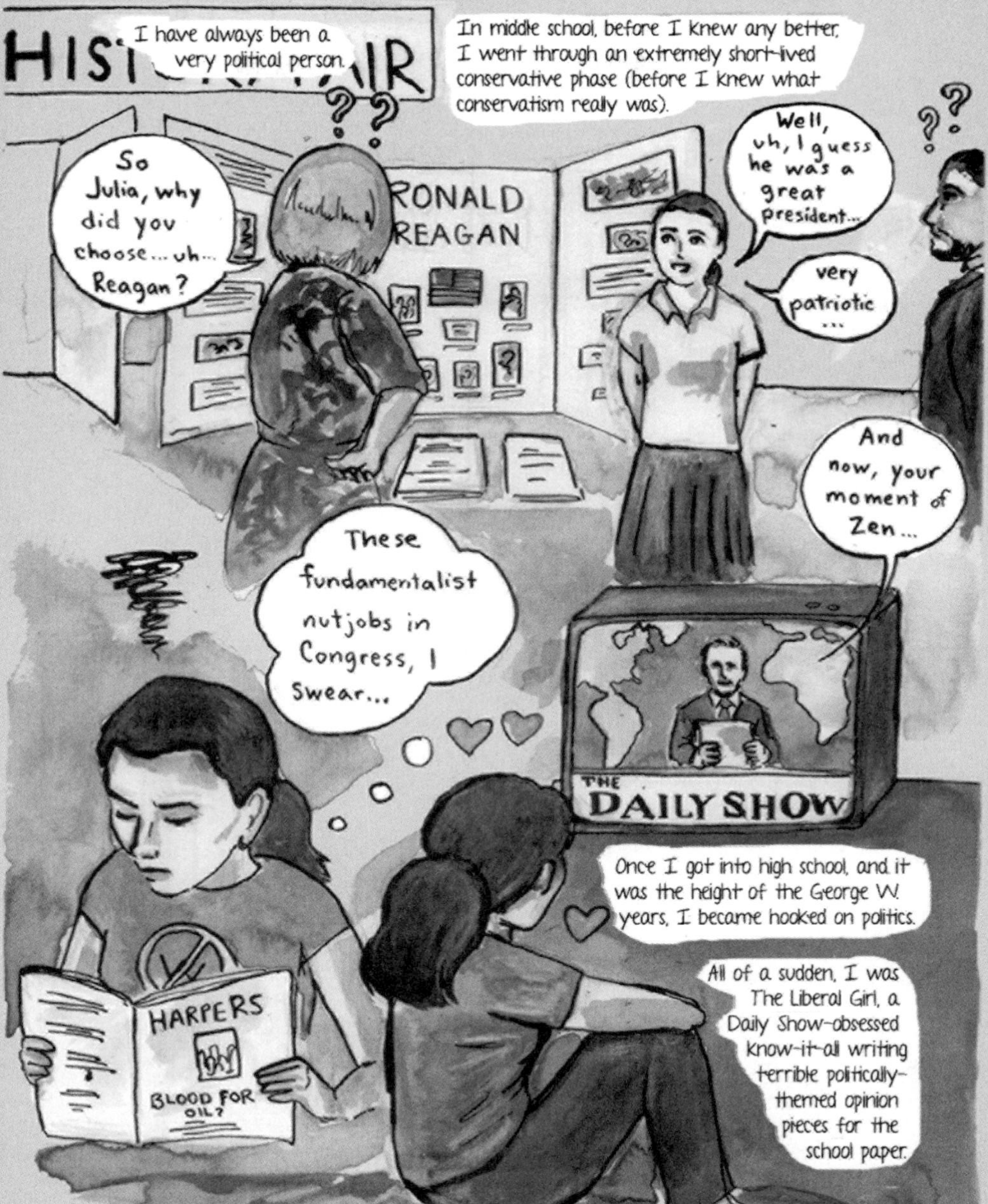
HIST... ...AIR
I have always been a very political person.
In middle school, before I knew any better, I went through an extremely short-lived conservative phase (before I knew what conservatism really was).
So Julia, why did you choose... uh... Reagan?
RONALD REAGAN
Well, uh, I guess he was a great president...
very patriotic ...
And now, your moment of Zen...
These fundamentalist nutjobs in Congress, I swear...
THE DAILY SHOW
Once I got into high school, and it was the height of the George W. years, I became hooked on politics.
HARPERS
BLOOD FOR OIL?
All of a sudden, I was The Liberal Girl, a Daily Show-obsessed know-it-all writing terrible politically-themed opinion pieces for the school paper.

Civics were especially interesting to me. I'd follow the proceedings of the US government with something between fascination and utter disdain.
ELECTION DAY!
VOTE HERE!
I had a sense of civic duty that bordered complete mania.
HERE
POLLING PLACE
My mother and grandparents were the least political people on the planet. My mother only voted for what other people told her to vote. I had no idea that Lola was as political as I was.
Do you mind if I help my mom with the machine?
She doesn't know English very well...
Um— ok, sure...
OK mom, see these blue lines? Those are Democrats.
Vote ONLY for them.
Only them?
Wait, but—
ONLY THEM.

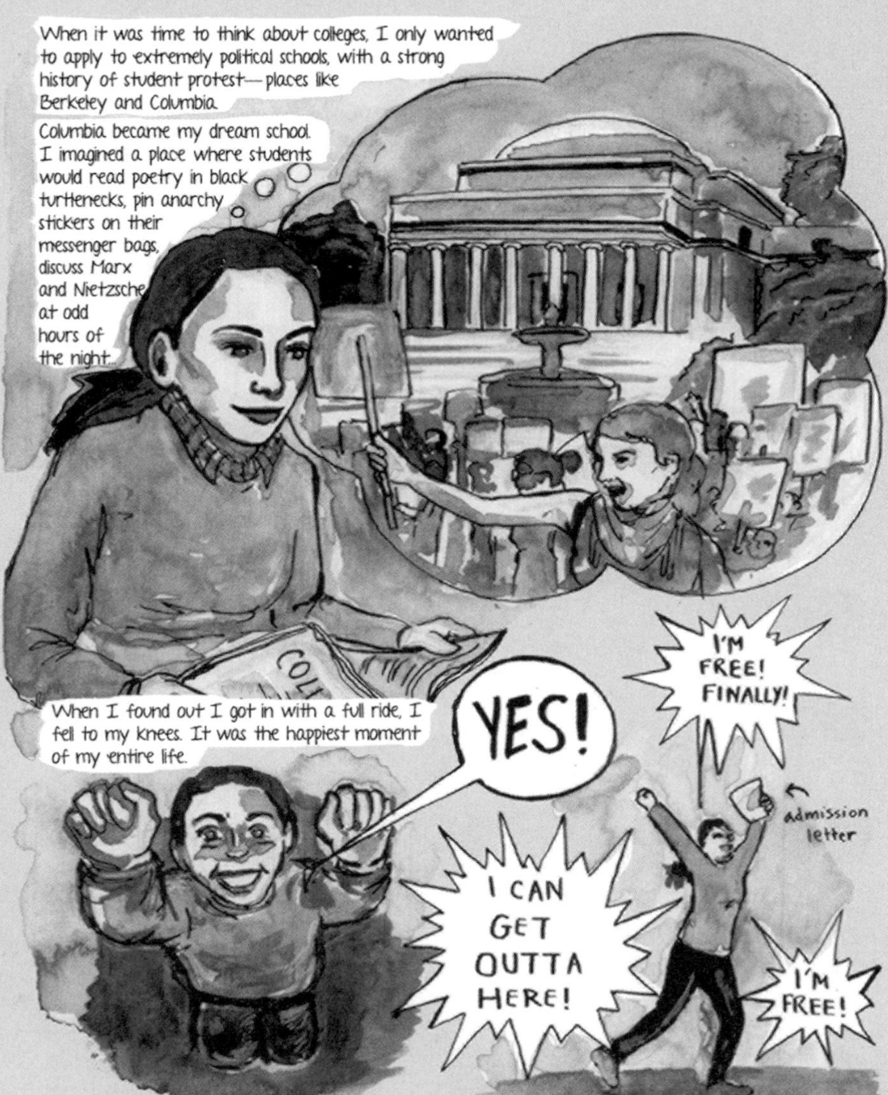
When it was time to think about colleges, I only wanted to apply to extremely political schools, with a strong history of student protest— places like Berkeley and Columbia.
Columbia became my dream school. I imagined a place where students would read poetry in black turtlenecks, pin anarchy stickers on their messenger bags, discuss Marx and Nietzsche at odd hours of the night...
When I found out I got in with a full ride, I fell to my knees. It was the happiest moment of my entire life.
YES!
I'M FREE! FINALLY!
admission letter
I CAN GET OUTTA HERE!
I'M FREE!

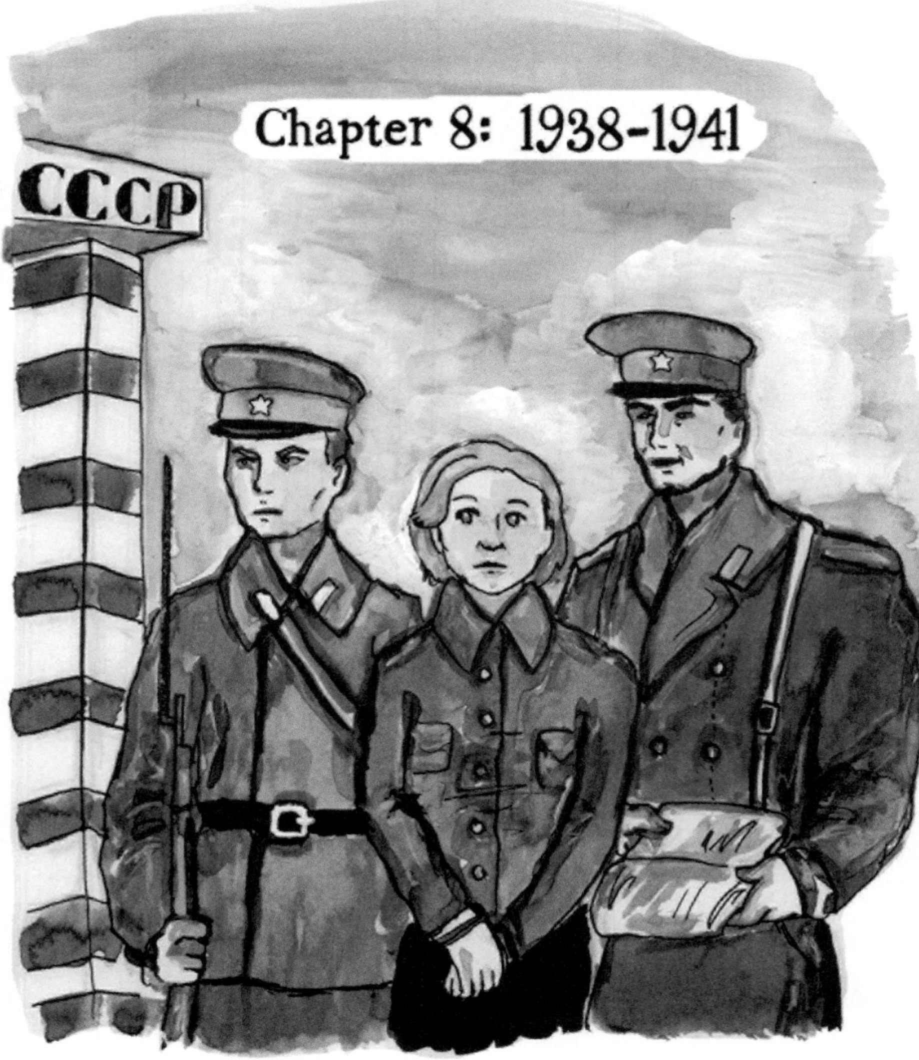
Chapter 8: 1938-1941
СССР

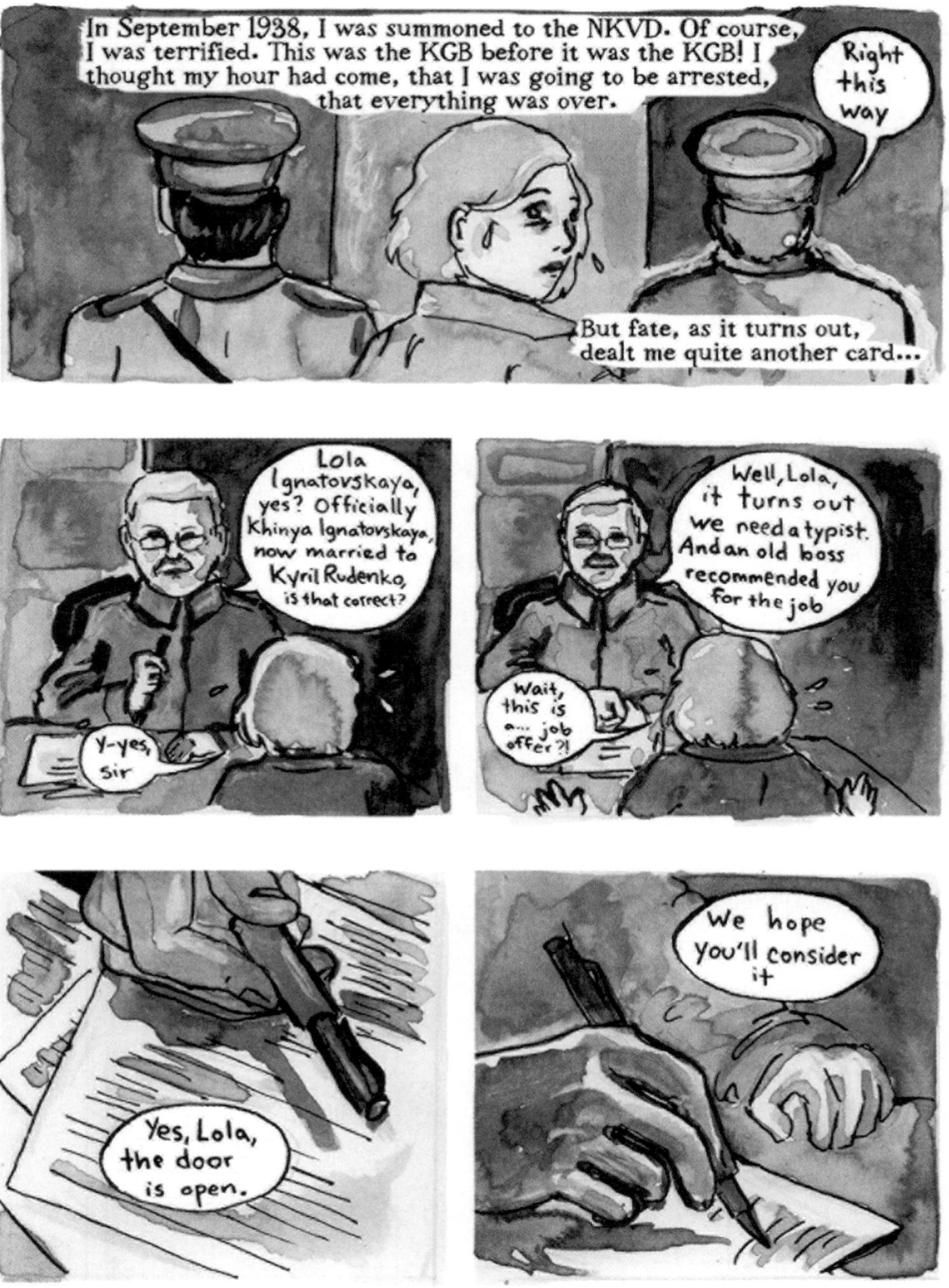

In September 1938, I was summoned to the NKVD. Of course, I was terrified. This was the KGB before it was the KGB! I thought my hour had come, that I was going to be arrested, that everything was over.
Right this way
But fate, as it turns out, dealt me quite another card...
Lola Ignatovskaya, yes? Officially Khinya Ignatovskaya, now married to Kyril Rudenko, is that correct?
Y-yes, sir
Well, Lola, it turns out we need a typist. And an old boss recommended you for the job
Wait, this is a... job offer?!
Yes, Lola, the door is open.
We hope you'll consider it

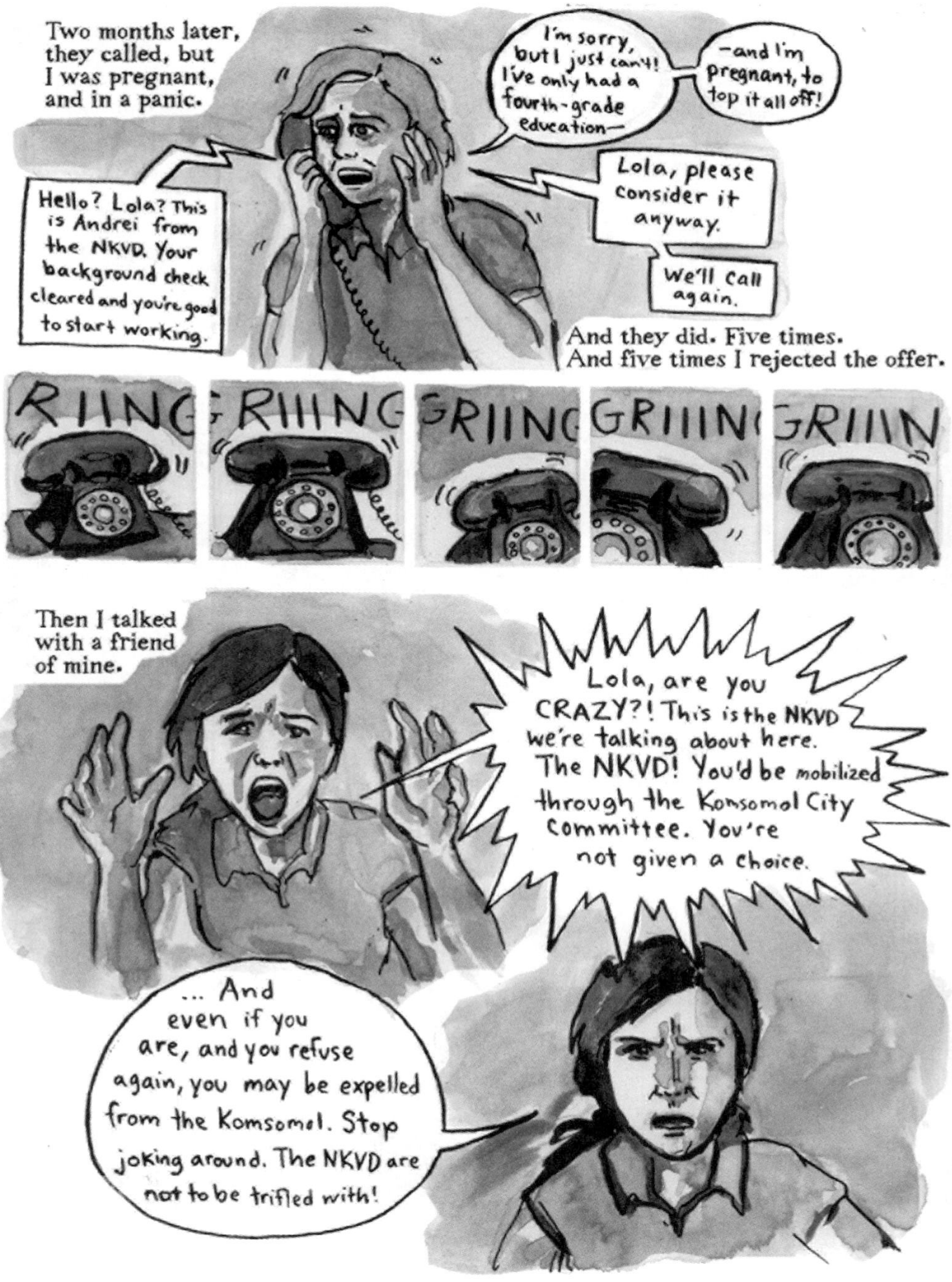
Two months later, they called, but I was pregnant, and in a panic.
Hello? Lola? This is Andrei from the NKVD. Your background check cleared and you're good to start working.
I'm sorry, but I just can't! I've only had a fourth-grade education—
—and I'm pregnant, to top it all off!
Lola, please consider it anyway.
We'll call again.
And they did. Five times. And five times I rejected the offer.
RIING
GRIIING
GRIING
GRIIIN
GRIIIN
Then I talked with a friend of mine.
Lola, are you CRAZY?! This is the NKVD we're talking about here. The NKVD! You'd be mobilized through the Konsomol City Committee. You're not given a choice.
... And even if you are, and you refuse again, you may be expelled from the Komsomol. Stop joking around. The NKVD are not to be trifled with!

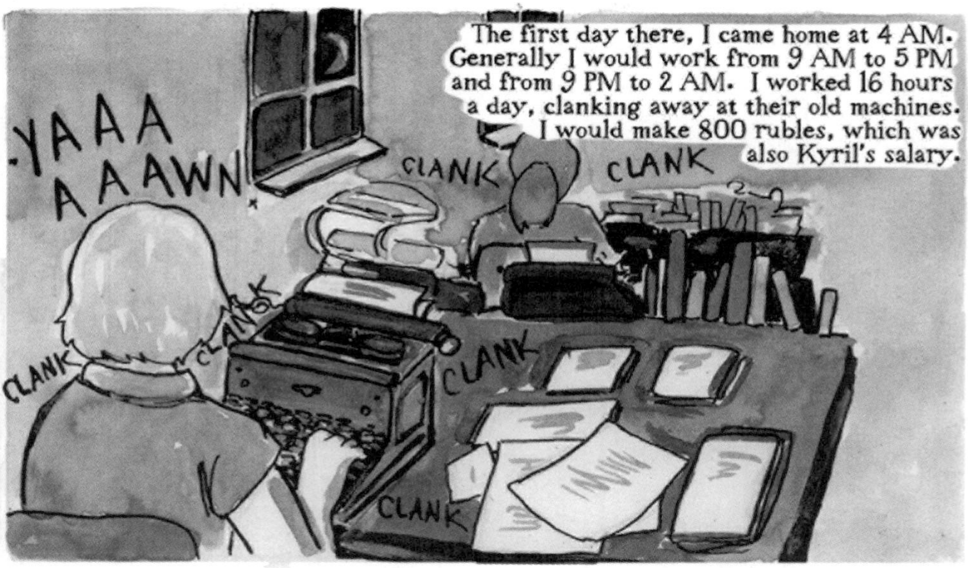
The first day there, I came home at 4 AM. Generally I would work from 9 AM to 5 PM and from 9 PM to 2 AM. I worked 16 hours a day, clanking away at their old machines. I would make 800 rubles, which was also Kyril's salary.
YAAAAAAWN
CLANK
CLANK
CLANK
CLANK
CLANK
CLANK
CLANK

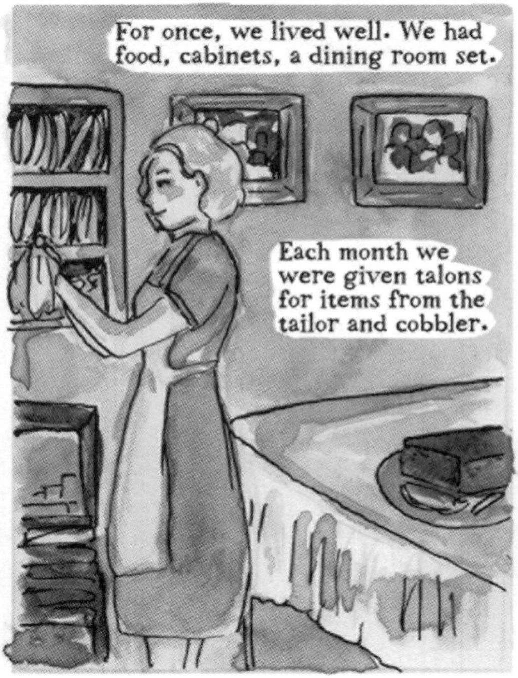
For once, we lived well. We had food, cabinets, a dining room set.
Each month we were given talons for items from the tailor and cobbler.

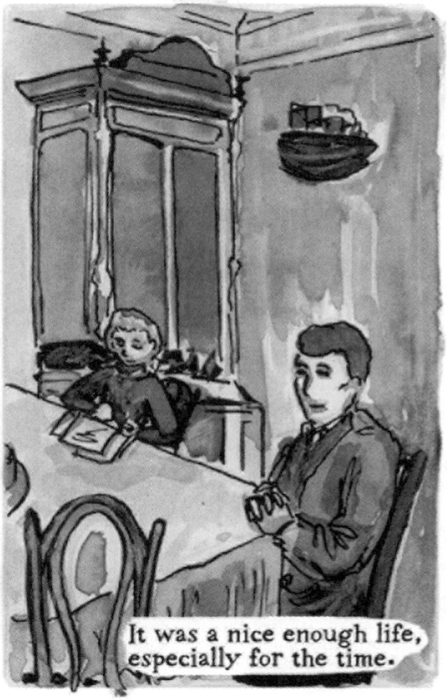
It was a nice enough life, especially for the time.

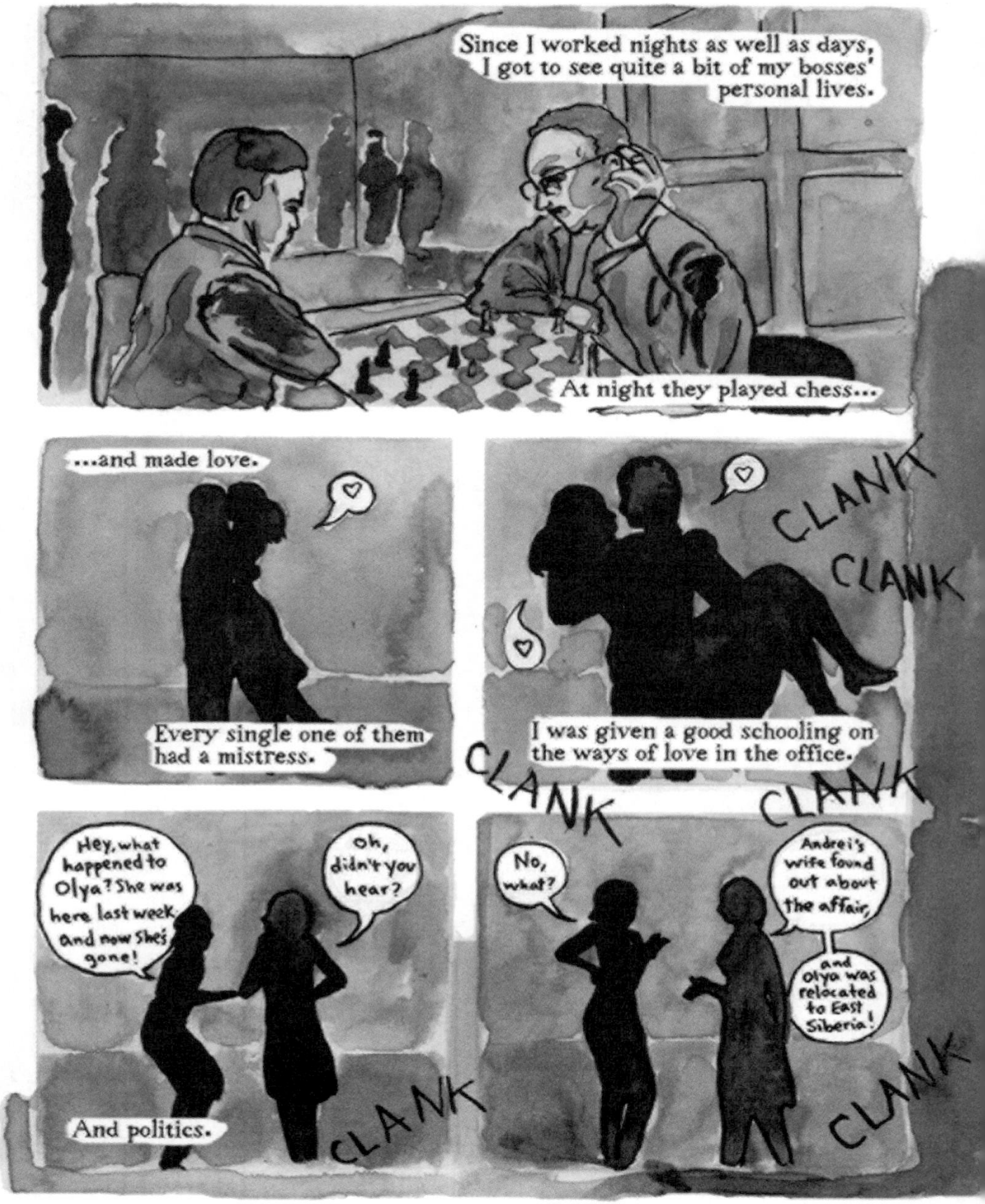

Since I worked nights as well as days, I got to see quite a bit of my bosses' personal lives.
At night they played chess...
...and made love.
Every single one of them had a mistress.
I was given a good schooling on the ways of love in the office.
CLANK
CLANK
CLANK
CLANK
And politics.
Hey, what happened to Olya? She was here last week and now she's gone!
Oh, didn't you hear?
CLANK
No, what?
Andrei's wife found out about the affair,
and Olya was relocated to East Siberia!
CLANK

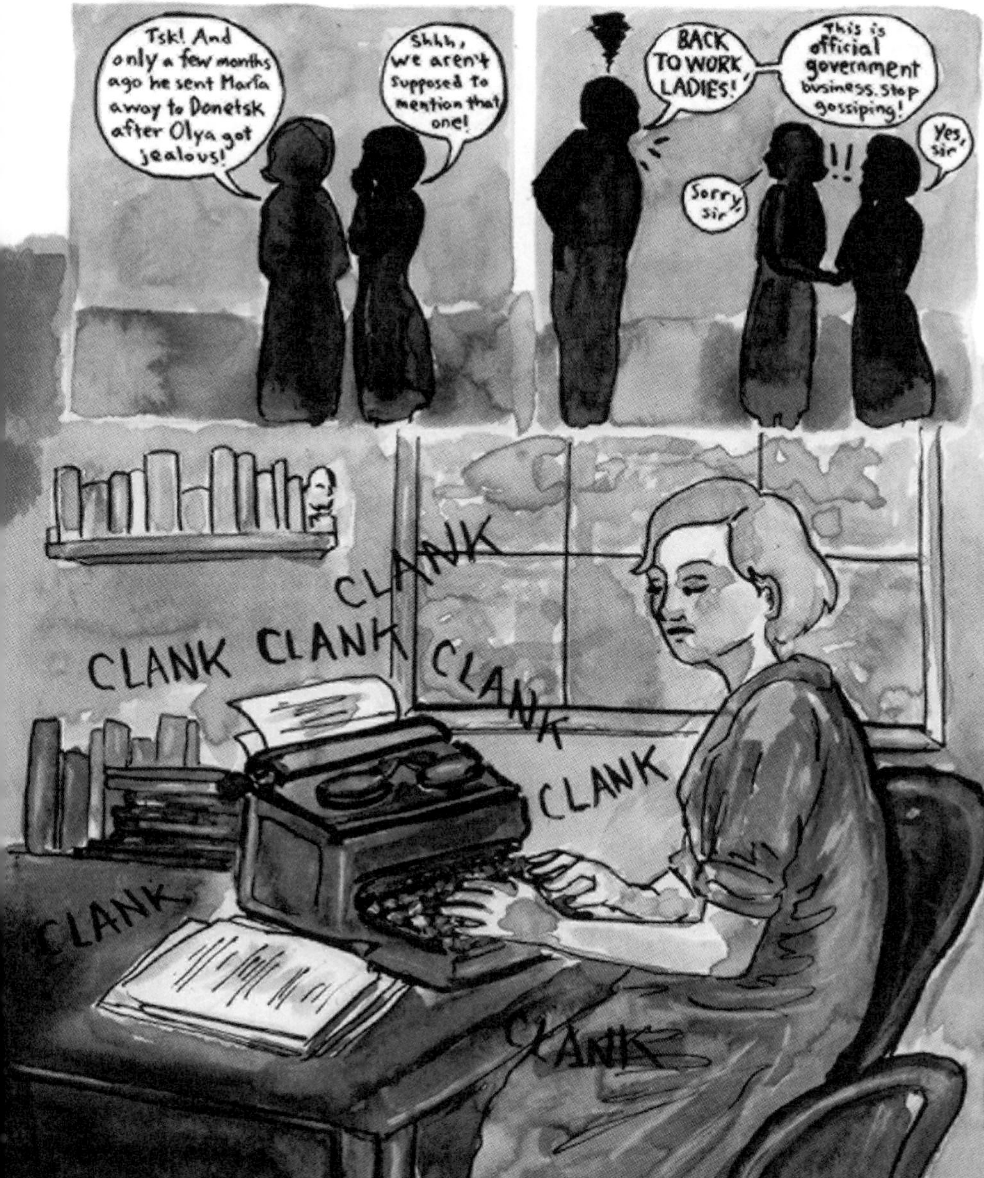

Tsk! And only a few months ago he sent Maria away to Donetsk after Olya got jealous!
Shhh, we aren't supposed to mention that one!
BACK TO WORK LADIES!
This is official government business. Stop gossiping!
!!
Sorry sir
Yes, sir
CLANK
CLANK
CLANK
CLANK
CLANK
CLANK
CLANK
CLANK

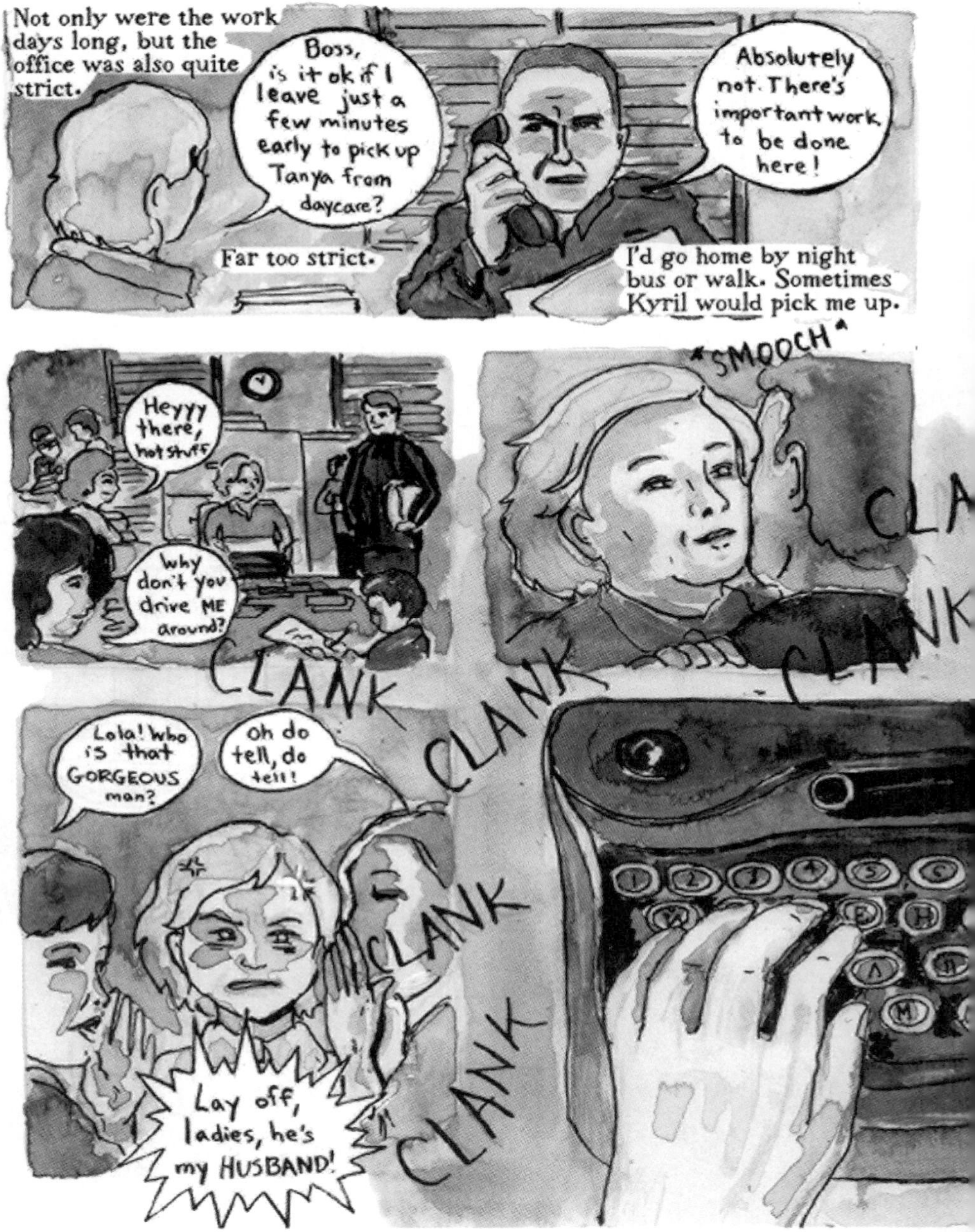
Not only were the work days long, but the office was also quite strict.
Boss, is it ok if I leave just a few minutes early to pick up Tanya from daycare?
Absolutely not. There's important work to be done here!
Far too strict.
I'd go home by night bus or walk. Sometimes Kyril would pick me up.
Heyyy there, hot stuff
why don't you drive ME around?
CLANK
SMOOCH
CLA
CLANK
CLANK
Lola! Who is that GORGEOUS man?
oh do tell, do tell!
CLANK
CLANK
CLANK
Lay off, ladies, he's my HUSBAND!

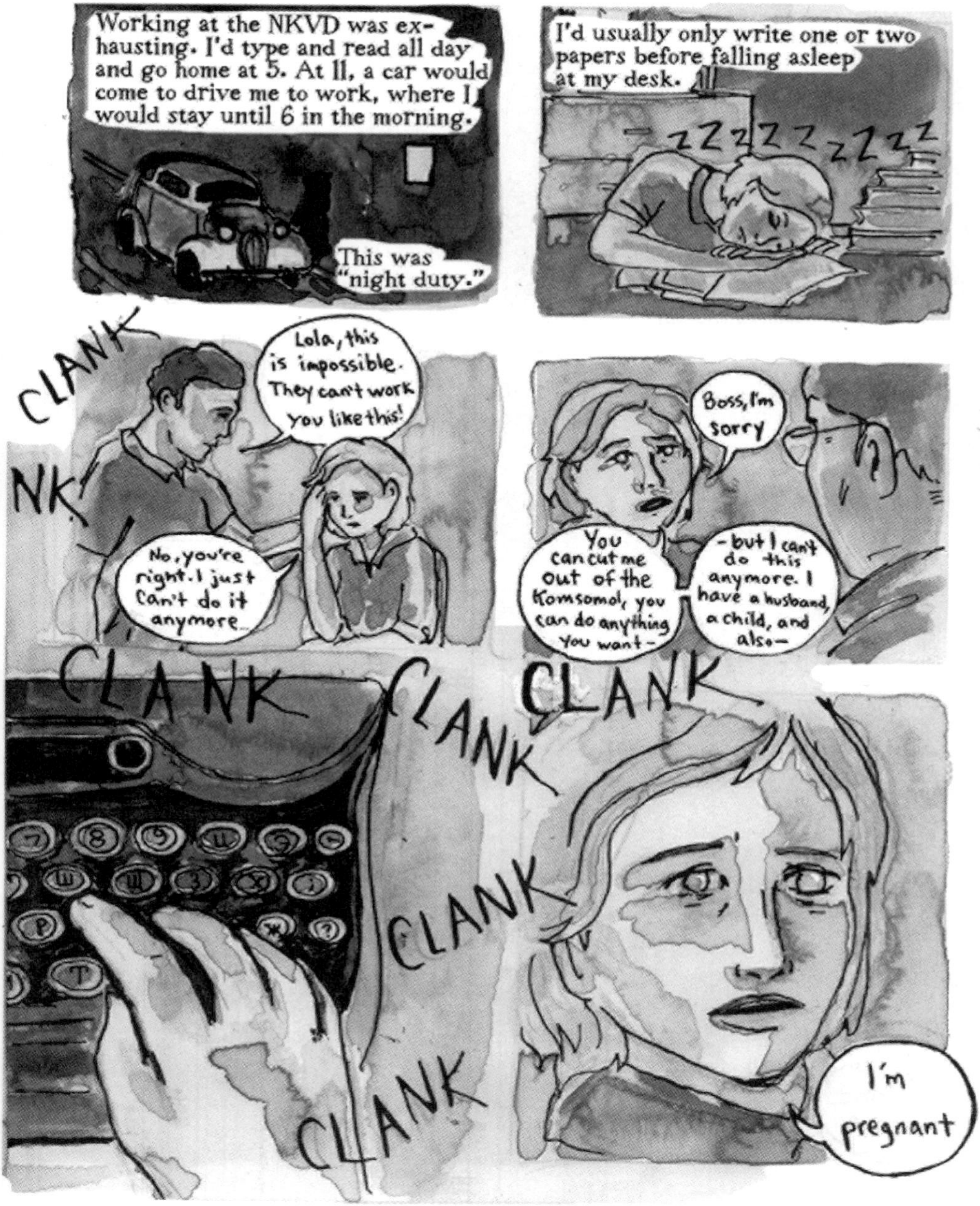
Working at the NKVD was exhausting. I'd type and read all day and go home at 5. At 11, a car would come to drive me to work, where I would stay until 6 in the morning.
This was "night duty."
I'd usually only write one or two papers before falling asleep at my desk.
zZzZZzZZzZ
CLANK
Lola, this is impossible. They can't work you like this!
NK
No, you're right. I just can't do it anymore...
Boss, I'm sorry
You can cut me out of the Komsomol, you can do anything you want-
-but I can't do this anymore. I have a husband, a child, and also-
CLANK
CLANK
CLANK
CLANK
CLANK
I'm pregnant

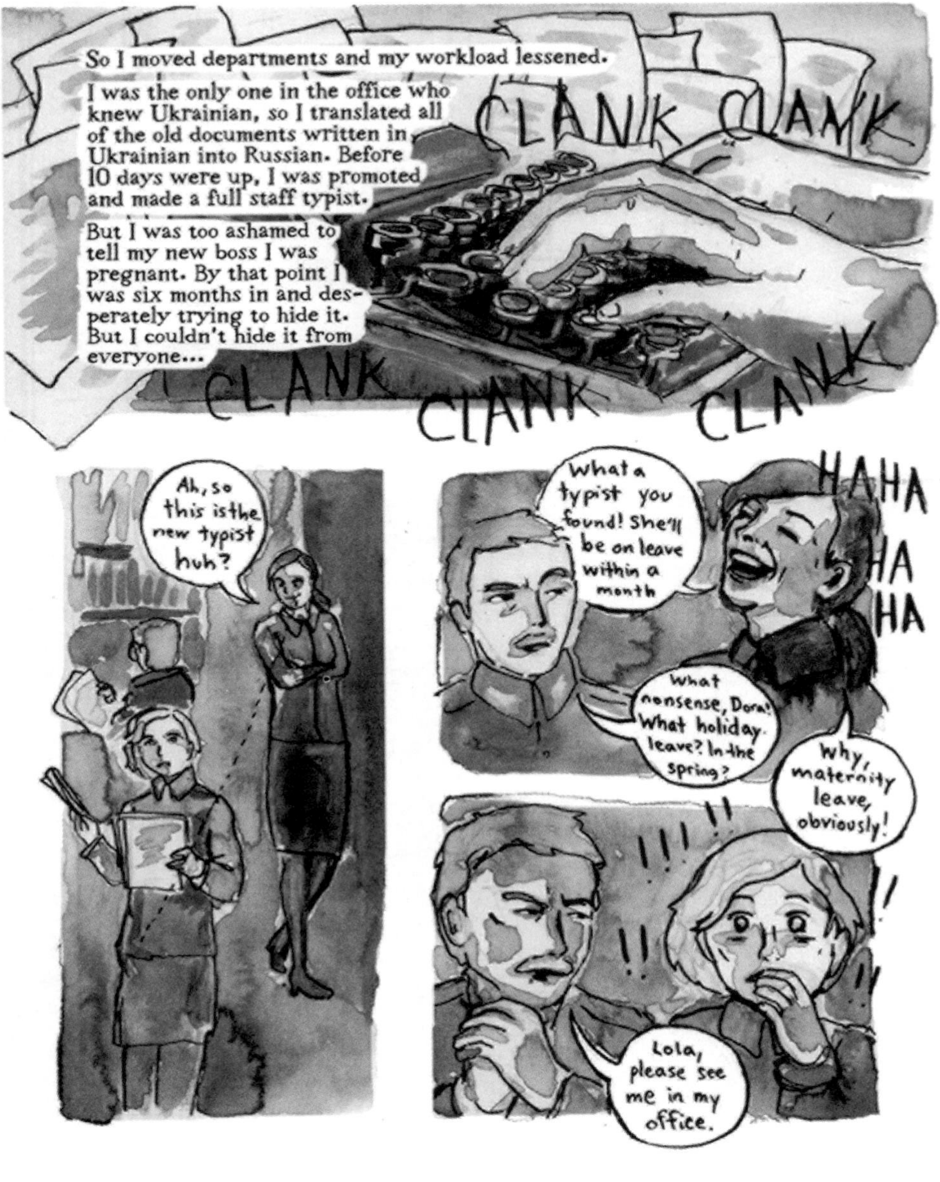
So I moved departments and my workload lessened.
I was the only one in the office who knew Ukrainian, so I translated all of the old documents written in Ukrainian into Russian. Before 10 days were up, I was promoted and made a full staff typist.
But I was too ashamed to tell my new boss I was pregnant. By that point I was six months in and desperately trying to hide it. But I couldn't hide it from everyone...
CLANK CLANK
CLANK CLANK CLANK
Ah, so this is the new typist huh?
What a typist you found! She'll be on leave within a month
HAHA HA HA
What nonsense, Dora! What holiday leave? In the spring?
Why, maternity leave, obviously!
!!! !! !! !! !!
Lola, please see me in my office.

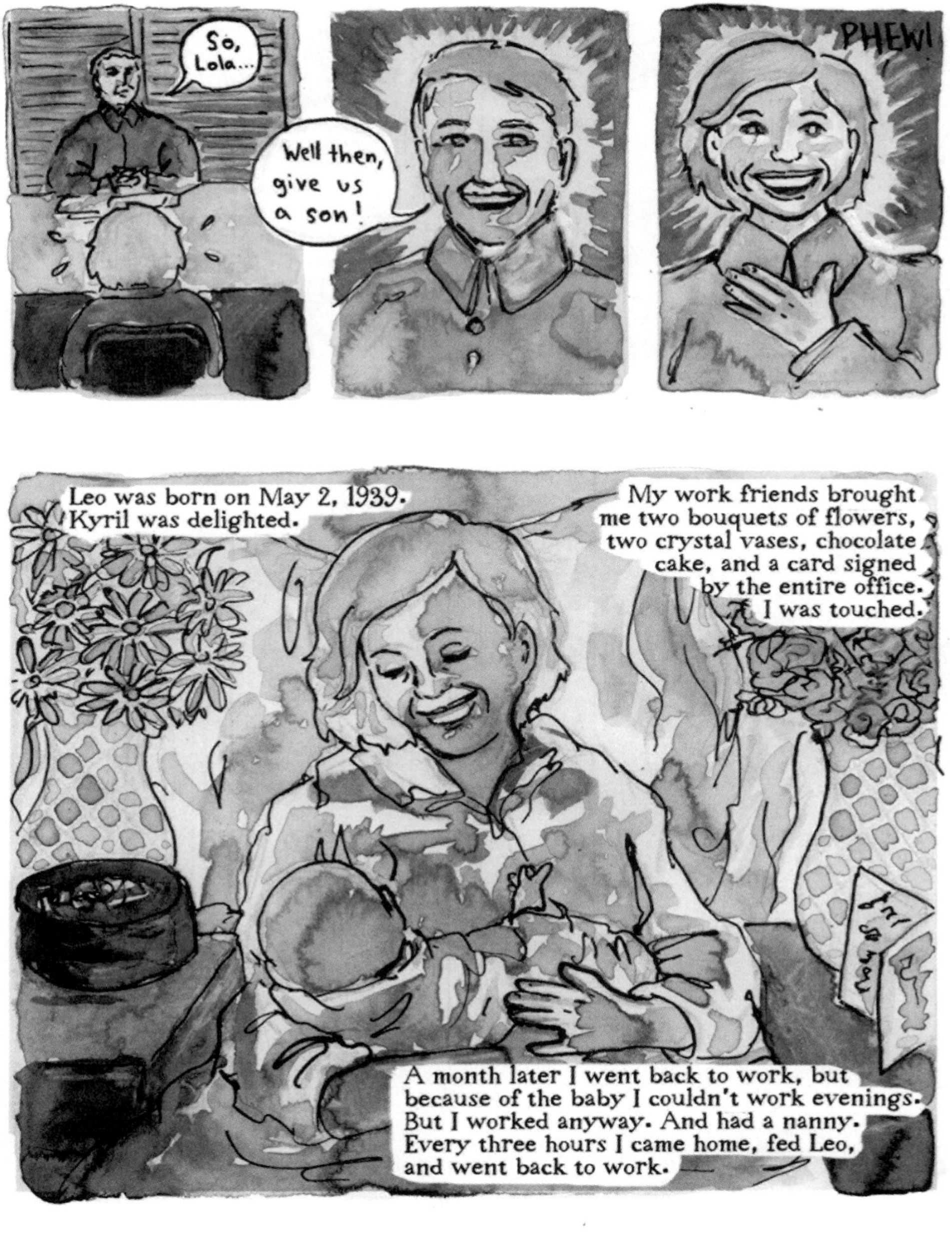
So, Lola...
Well then, give us a son!
PHEW!
Leo was born on May 2, 1939. Kyril was delighted.
My work friends brought me two bouquets of flowers, two crystal vases, chocolate cake, and a card signed by the entire office. I was touched.
A month later I went back to work, but because of the baby I couldn't work evenings. But I worked anyway. And had a nanny. Every three hours I came home, fed Leo, and went back to work.

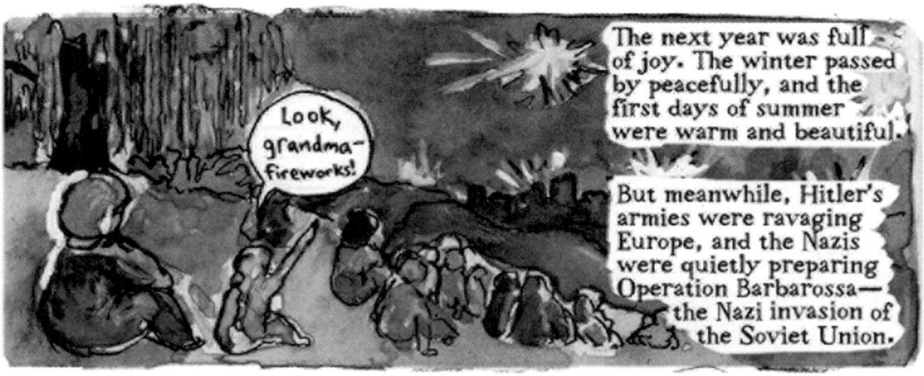
The next year was full of joy. The winter passed by peacefully, and the first days of summer were warm and beautiful.
Look, grandma— fireworks!
But meanwhile, Hitler's armies were ravaging Europe, and the Nazis were quietly preparing Operation Barbarossa— the Nazi invasion of the Soviet Union.

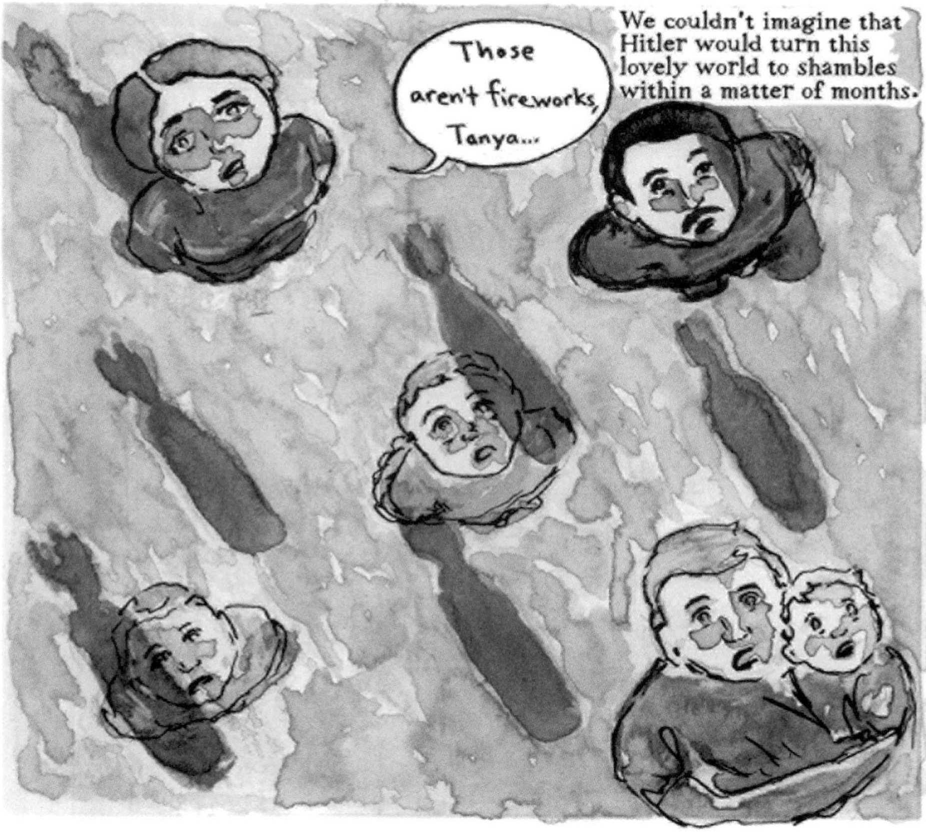
We couldn't imagine that Hitler would turn this lovely world to shambles within a matter of months.
Those aren't fireworks, Tanya...

Interlude

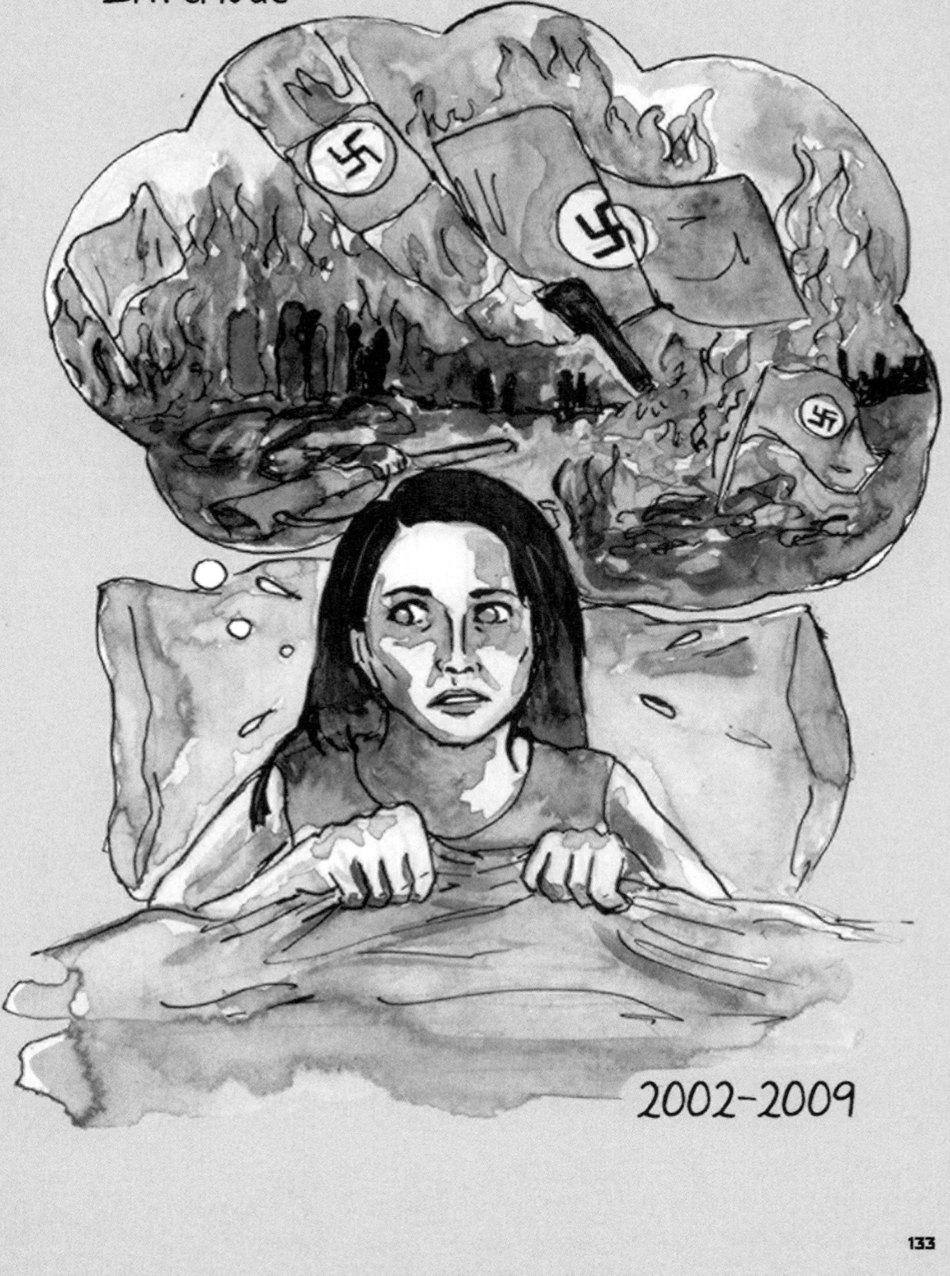
2002–2009

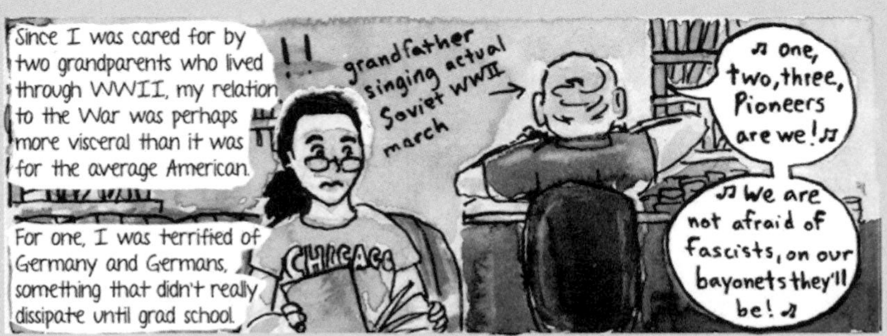
Since I was cared for by two grandparents who lived through WWII, my relation to the War was perhaps more visceral than it was for the average American.
!!
grandfather singing actual Soviet WWII march
♫ one, two, three, Pioneers are we! ♫
♫ We are not afraid of fascists, on our bayonets they'll be! ♫
CHICAGO
For one, I was terrified of Germany and Germans, something that didn't really dissipate until grad school.

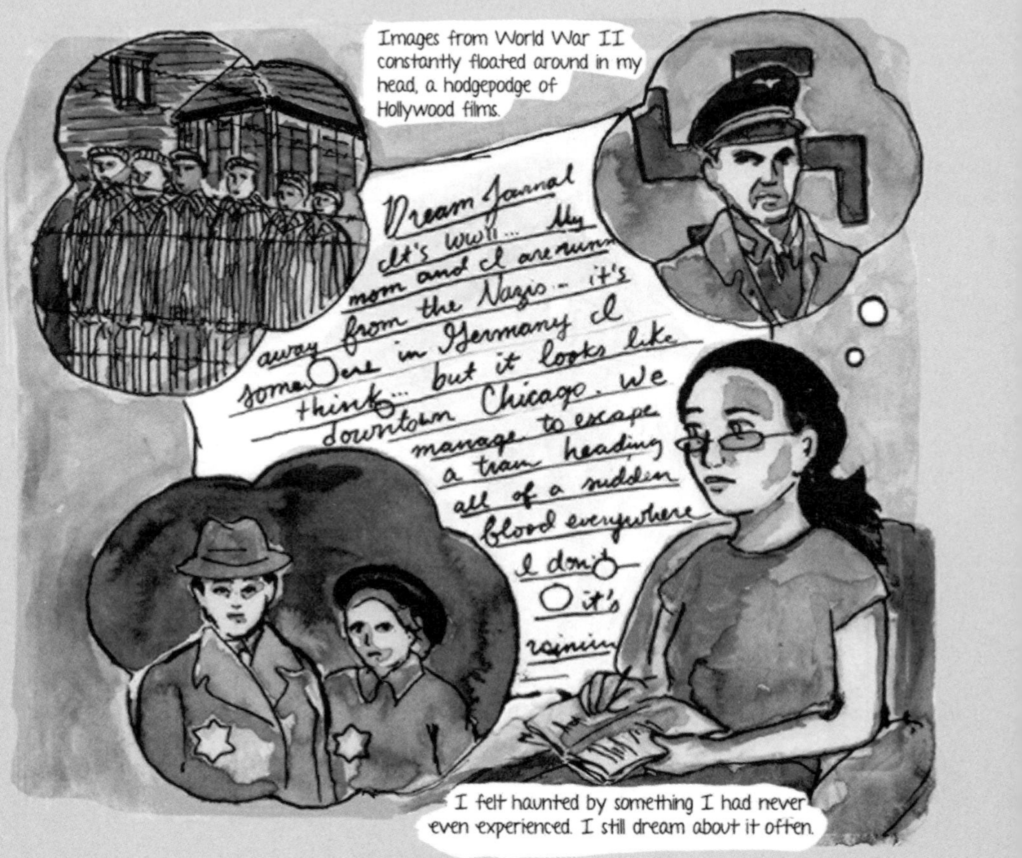
Images from World War II constantly floated around in my head, a hodgepodge of Hollywood films.
Dream Journal
It's WWII... My
mom and I are runn
away from the Nazis... it's
somewhere in Germany I
think... but it looks like
downtown Chicago. We
manage to escape
a train heading
all of a sudden
blood everywhere
I don't
it's
rainin
I felt haunted by something I had never even experienced. I still dream about it often.

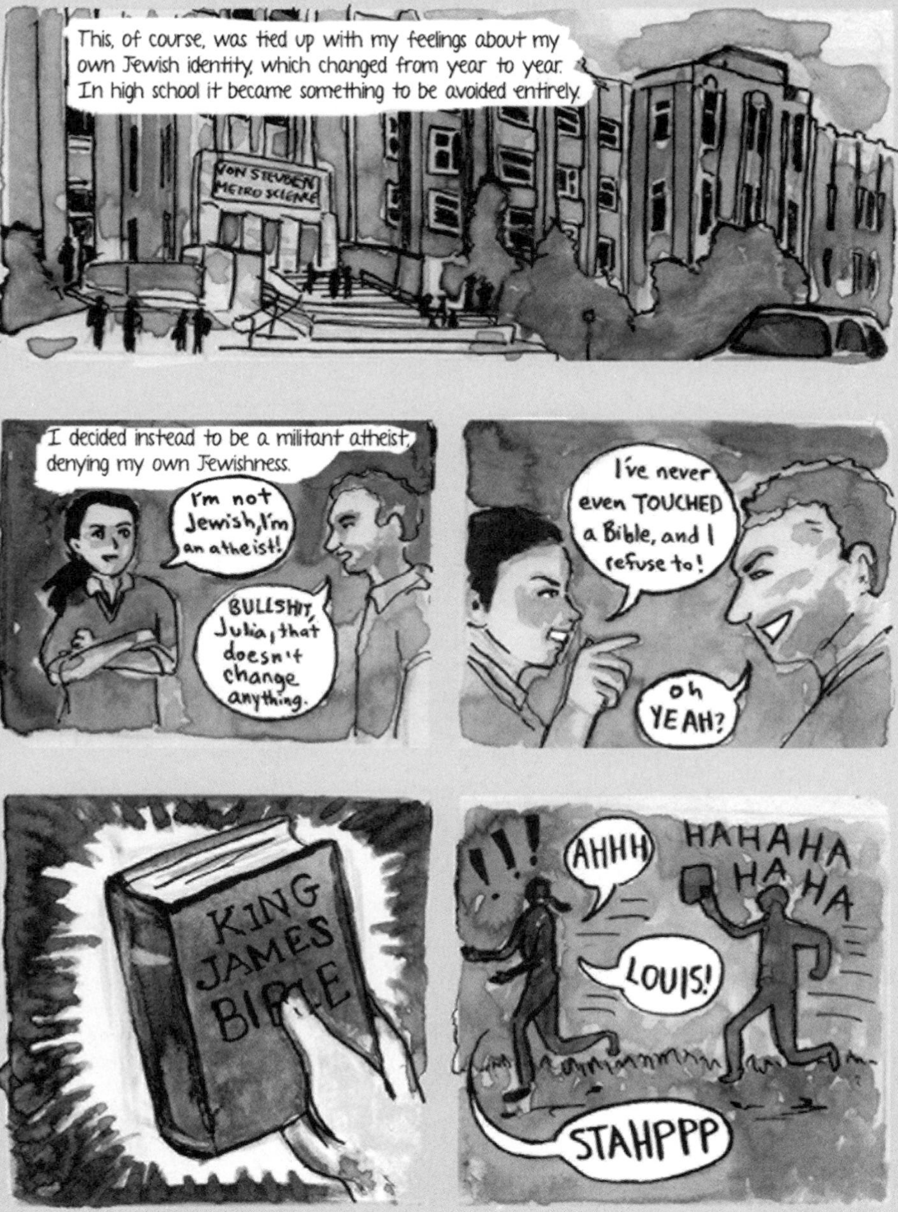
This, of course, was tied up with my feelings about my own Jewish identity, which changed from year to year. In high school it became something to be avoided entirely.
VON STEUBEN METRO SCIENCE
I decided instead to be a militant atheist, denying my own Jewishness.
I'm not Jewish, I'm an atheist!
BULLSHIT, Julia, that doesn't change anything.
I've never even TOUCHED a Bible, and I refuse to!
oh YEAH?
KING JAMES BIBLE
!!!
AHHH
HAHAHA HAHA HA
LOUIS!
STAHPPP

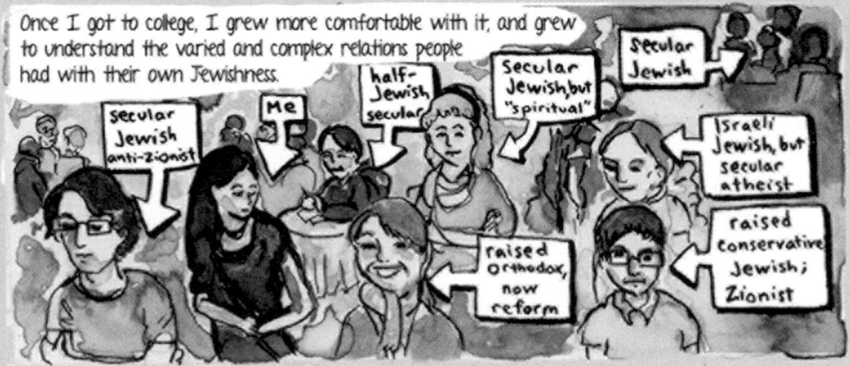
Once I got to college, I grew more comfortable with it, and grew to understand the varied and complex relations people had with their own Jewishness.
secular Jewish anti-zionist
Me
half-Jewish secular
Secular Jewish, but "spiritual"
Secular Jewish
Israeli Jewish, but secular atheist
raised orthodox, now reform
raised conservative Jewish; Zionist

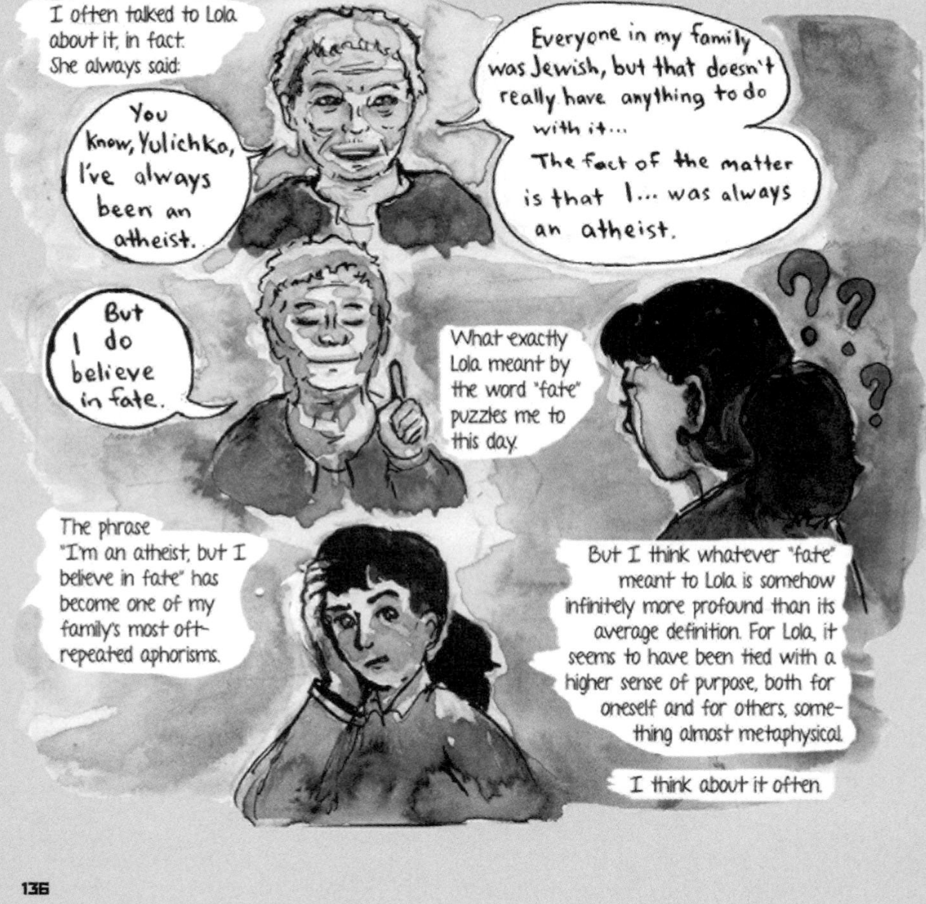
I often talked to Lola about it, in fact. She always said:
You know, Yulichka, I've always been an atheist.
Everyone in my family was Jewish, but that doesn't really have anything to do with it... The fact of the matter is that I... was always an atheist.
But I do believe in fate.
What exactly Lola meant by the word "fate" puzzles me to this day.
The phrase "I'm an atheist, but I believe in fate" has become one of my family's most oft-repeated aphorisms.
But I think whatever "fate" meant to Lola is somehow infinitely more profound than its average definition. For Lola, it seems to have been tied with a higher sense of purpose, both for oneself and for others, something almost metaphysical.
I think about it often.

Chapter 9: 1941-1942

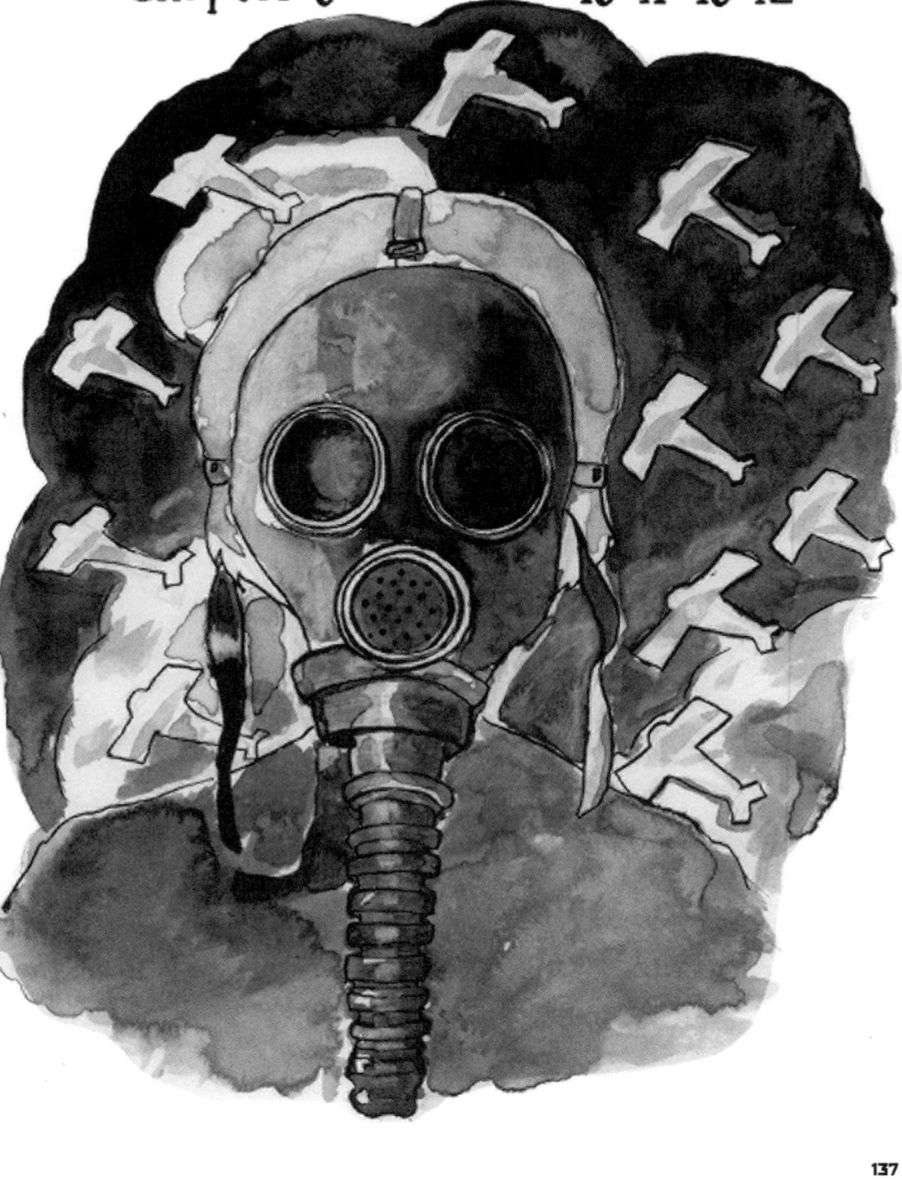

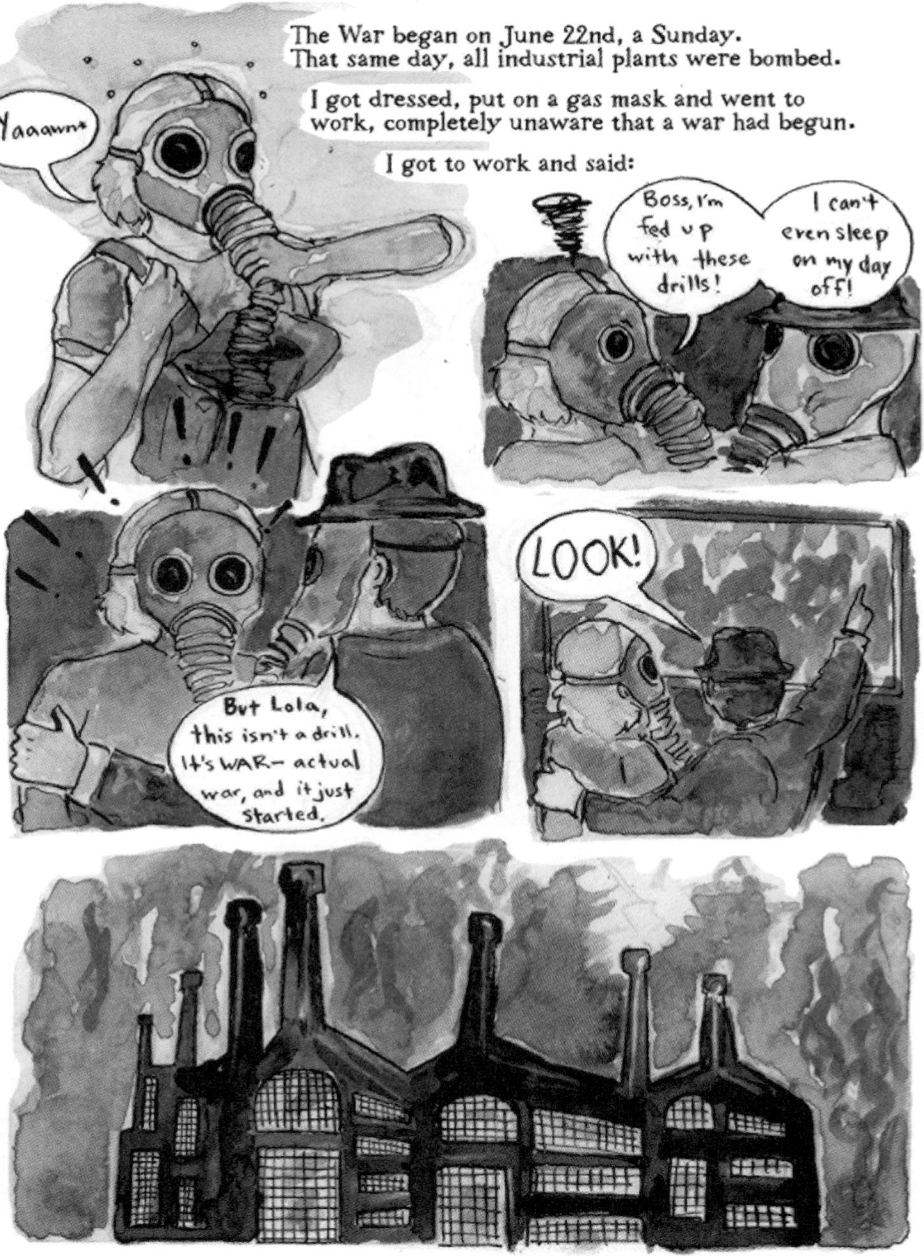
The War began on June 22nd, a Sunday.
That same day, all industrial plants were bombed.
Yaaawn
I got dressed, put on a gas mask and went to work, completely unaware that a war had begun.
I got to work and said:
Boss, I'm fed up with these drills!
I can't even sleep on my day off!
!!!
But Lola, this isn't a drill. It's WAR– actual war, and it just started.
LOOK!

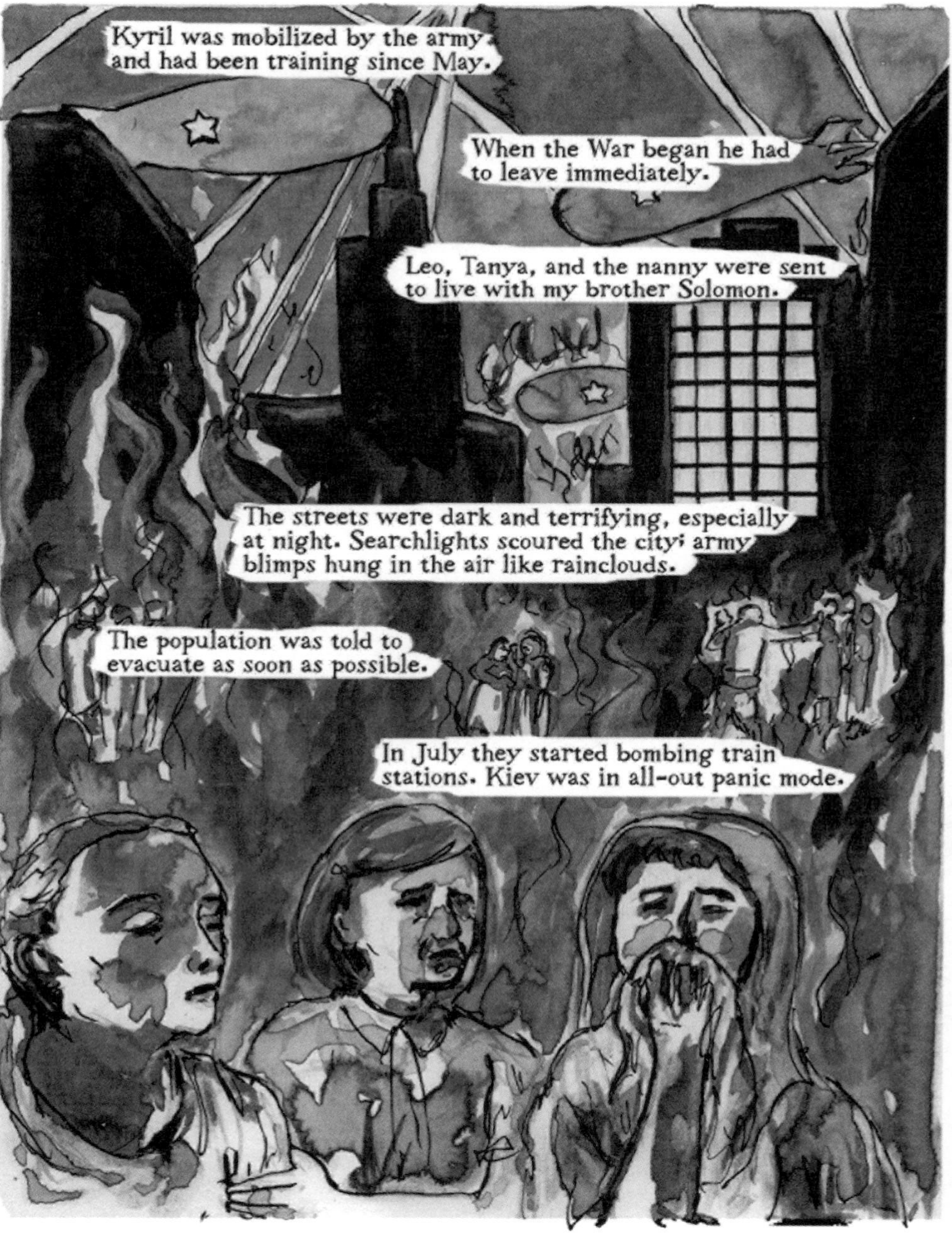
Kyril was mobilized by the army and had been training since May.
When the War began he had to leave immediately.
Leo, Tanya, and the nanny were sent to live with my brother Solomon.
The streets were dark and terrifying, especially at night. Searchlights scoured the city; army blimps hung in the air like rainclouds.
The population was told to evacuate as soon as possible.
In July they started bombing train stations. Kiev was in all-out panic mode.

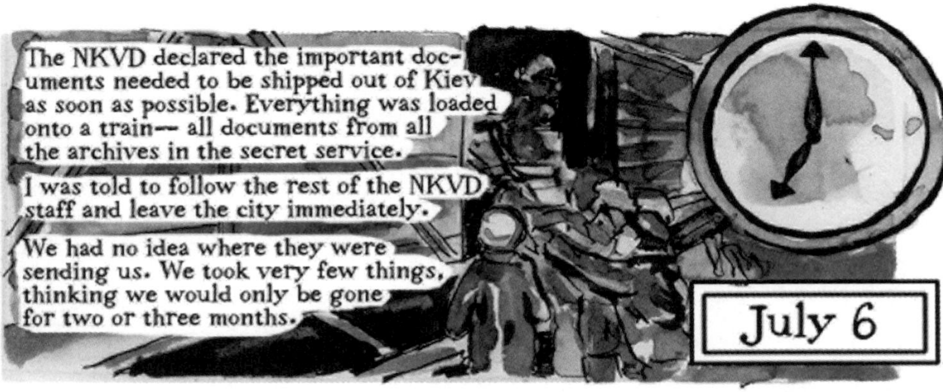
The NKVD declared the important documents needed to be shipped out of Kiev as soon as possible. Everything was loaded onto a train— all documents from all the archives in the secret service.
I was told to follow the rest of the NKVD staff and leave the city immediately.
We had no idea where they were sending us. We took very few things, thinking we would only be gone for two or three months.
July 6

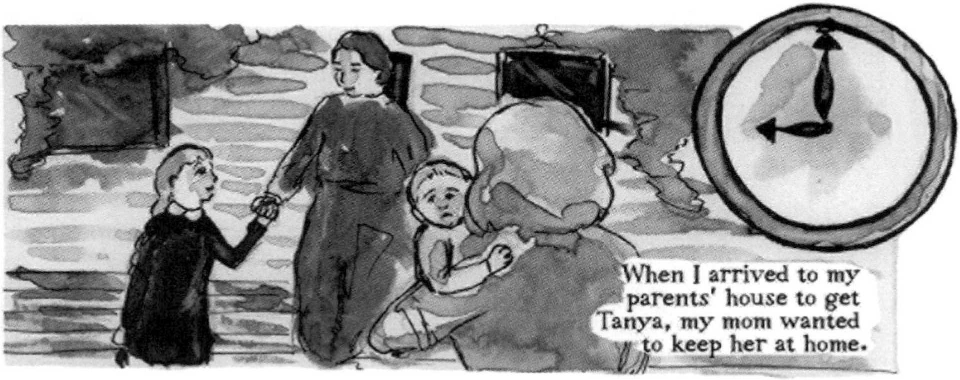
When I arrived to my parents' house to get Tanya, my mom wanted to keep her at home.

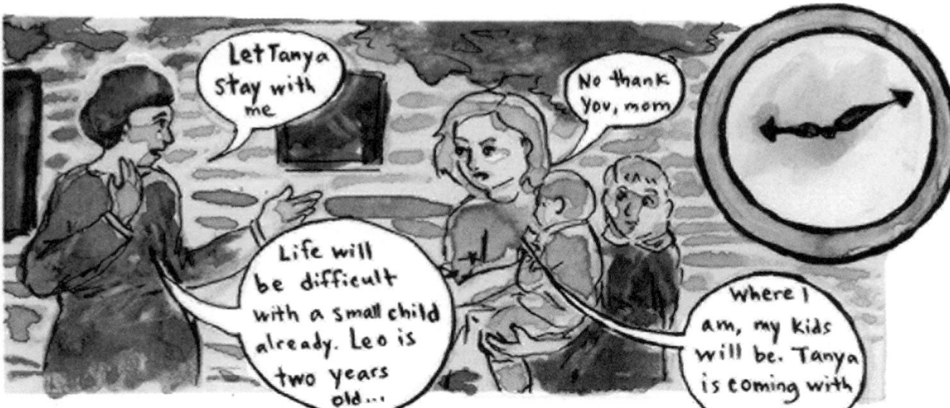
Let Tanya stay with me
No thank you, mom
Life will be difficult with a small child already. Leo is two years old...
Where I am, my kids will be. Tanya is coming with me.

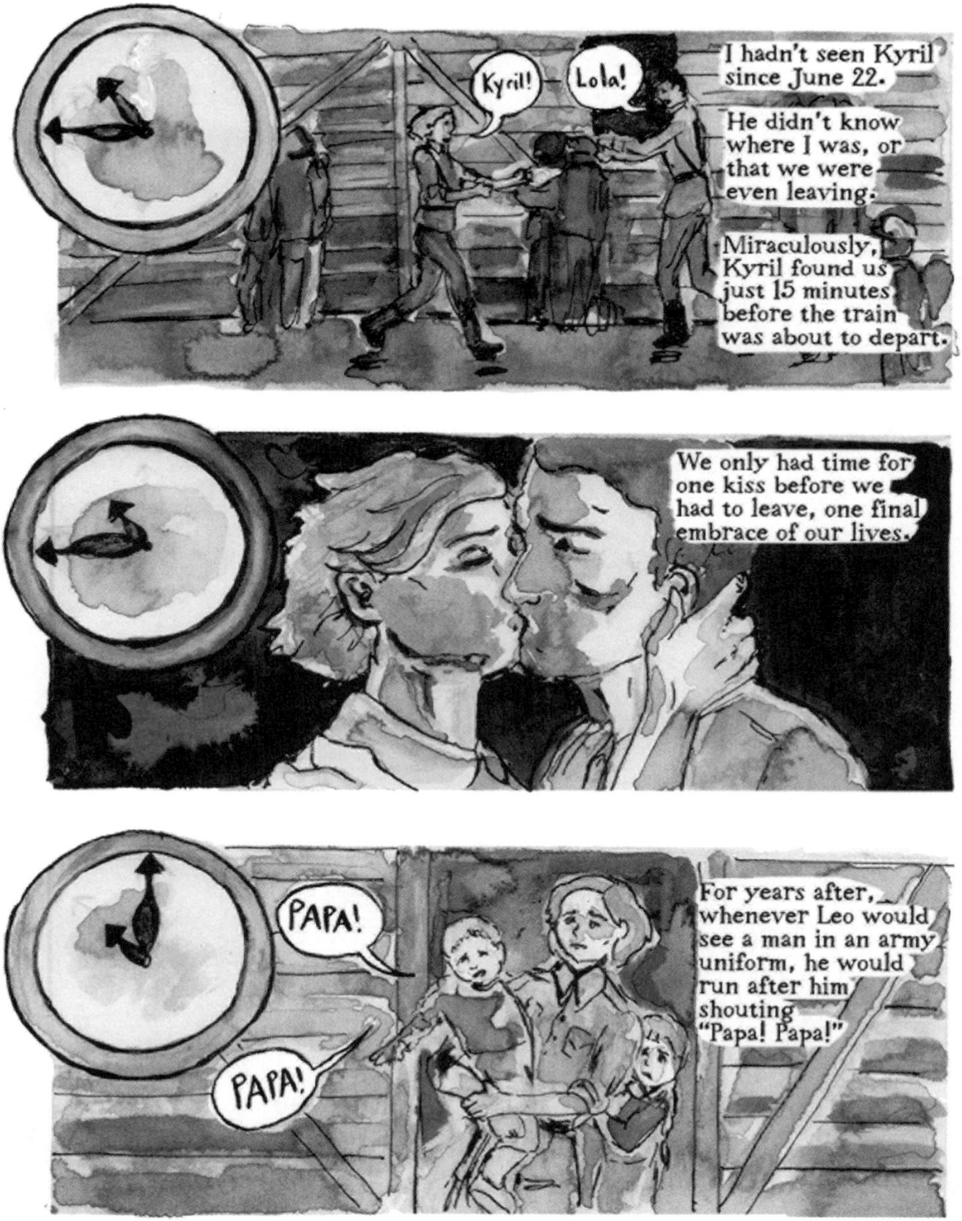
Kyril!
Lola!
I hadn't seen Kyril since June 22.
He didn't know where I was, or that we were even leaving.
Miraculously, Kyril found us just 15 minutes before the train was about to depart.
We only had time for one kiss before we had to leave, one final embrace of our lives.
PAPA!
PAPA!
For years after, whenever Leo would see a man in an army uniform, he would run after him shouting "Papa! Papa!"

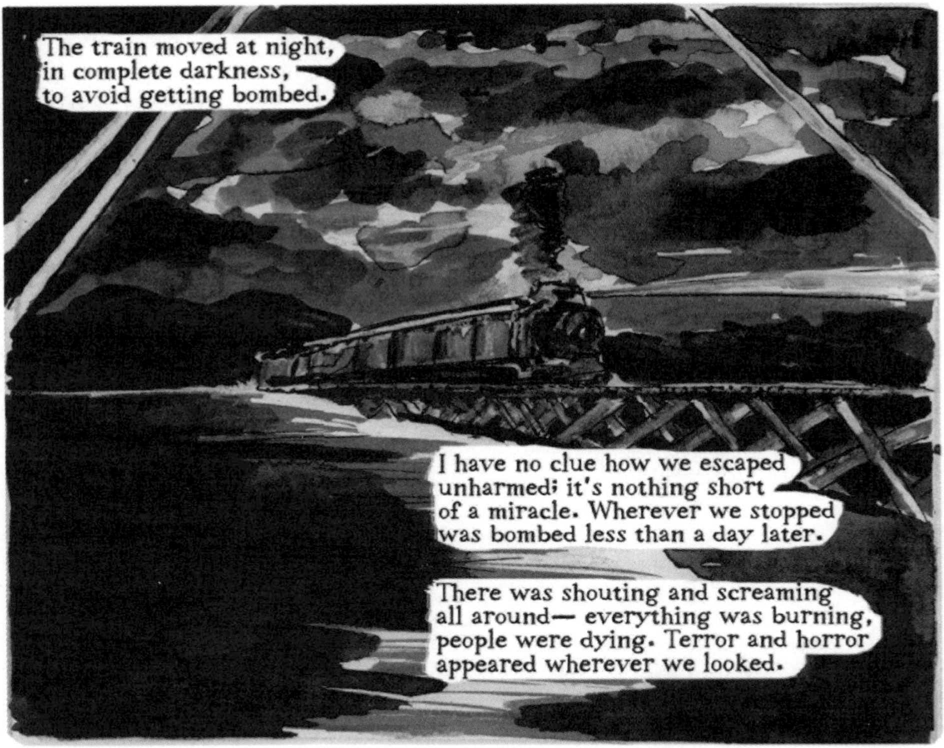
The train moved at night, in complete darkness, to avoid getting bombed.
I have no clue how we escaped unharmed; it's nothing short of a miracle. Wherever we stopped was bombed less than a day later.
There was shouting and screaming all around— everything was burning, people were dying. Terror and horror appeared wherever we looked.

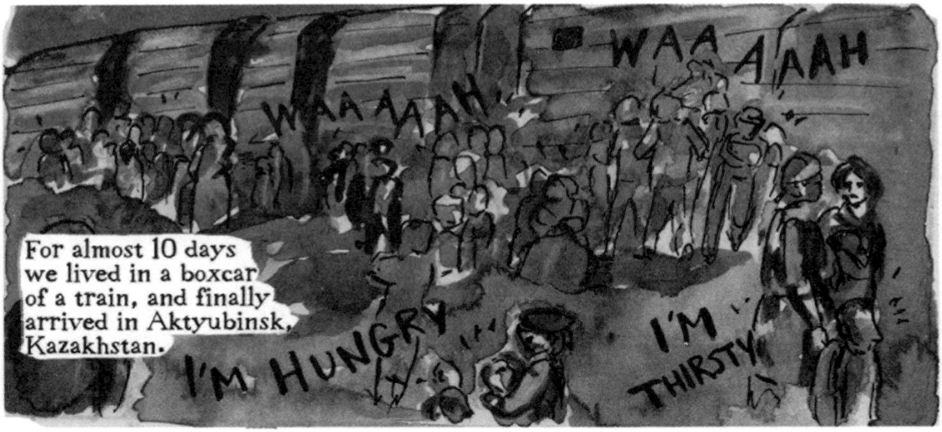
WAAAAAH
WAAAAAH
For almost 10 days we lived in a boxcar of a train, and finally arrived in Aktyubinsk, Kazakhstan.
I'M HUNGRY
I'M THIRSTY

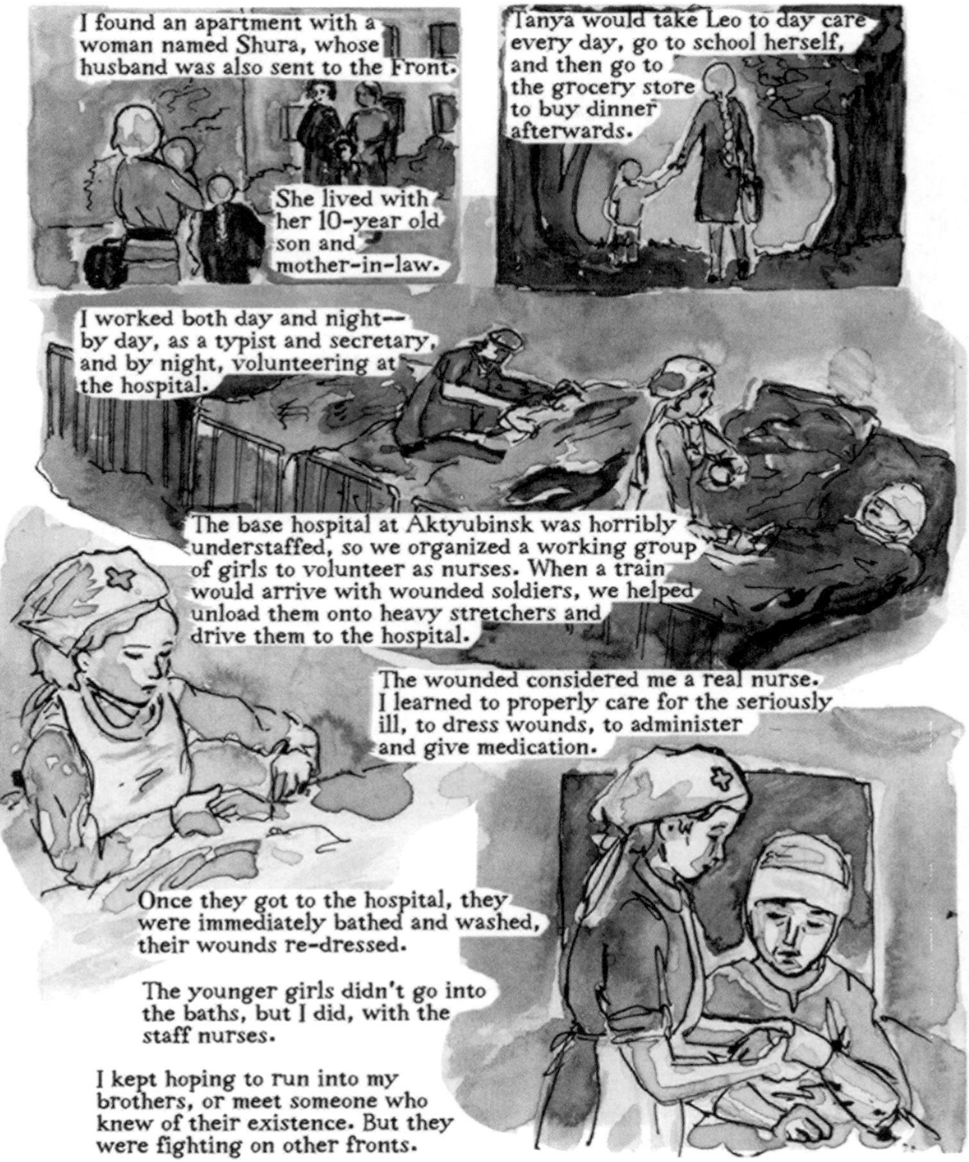
I found an apartment with a woman named Shura, whose husband was also sent to the Front.
She lived with her 10-year old son and mother-in-law.
Tanya would take Leo to day care every day, go to school herself, and then go to the grocery store to buy dinner afterwards.
I worked both day and night— by day, as a typist and secretary, and by night, volunteering at the hospital.
The base hospital at Aktyubinsk was horribly understaffed, so we organized a working group of girls to volunteer as nurses. When a train would arrive with wounded soldiers, we helped unload them onto heavy stretchers and drive them to the hospital.
The wounded considered me a real nurse. I learned to properly care for the seriously ill, to dress wounds, to administer and give medication.
Once they got to the hospital, they were immediately bathed and washed, their wounds re-dressed.
The younger girls didn't go into the baths, but I did, with the staff nurses.
I kept hoping to run into my brothers, or meet someone who knew of their existence. But they were fighting on other fronts.

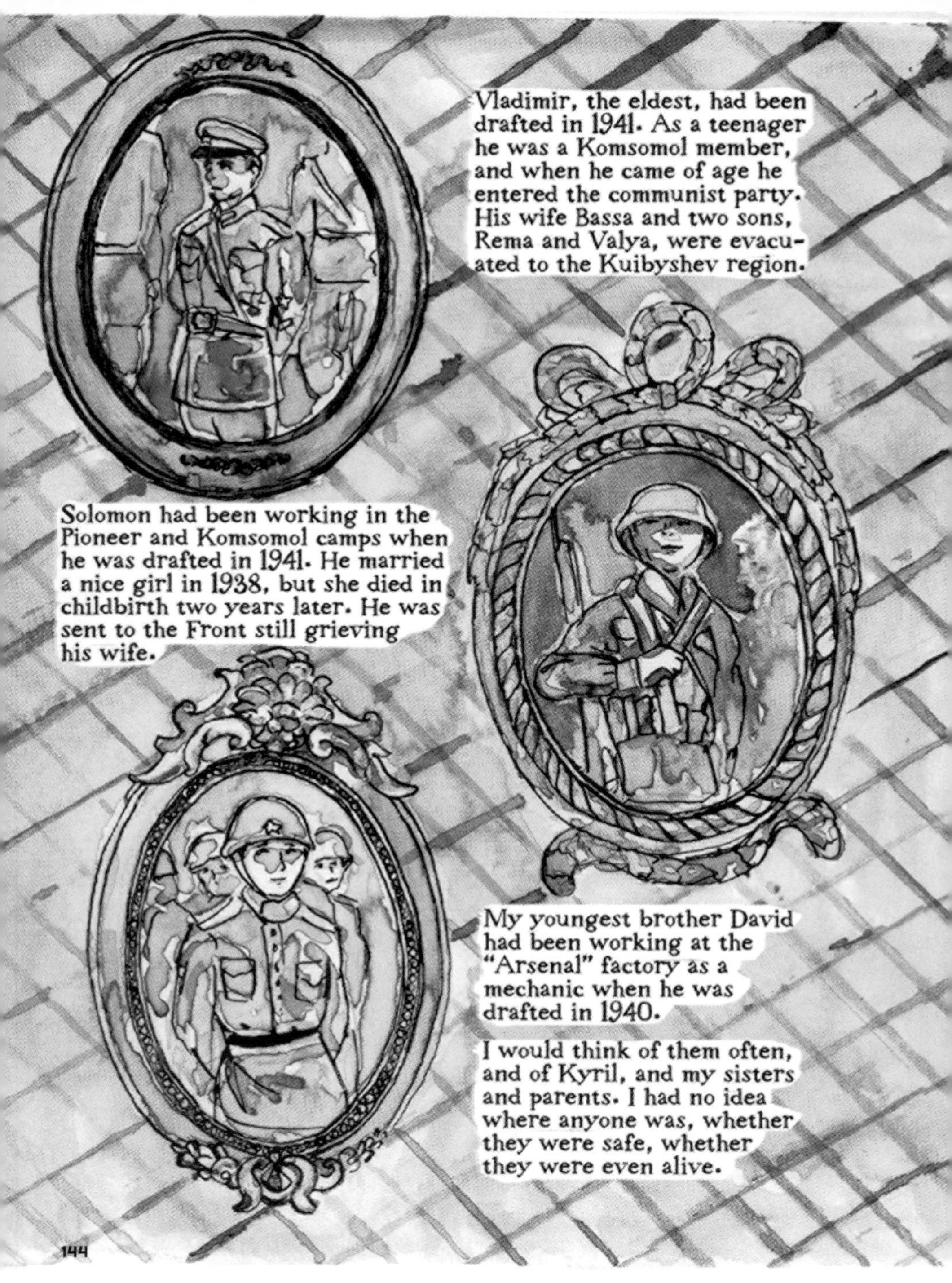
Vladimir, the eldest, had been drafted in 1941. As a teenager he was a Komsomol member, and when he came of age he entered the communist party. His wife Bassa and two sons, Rema and Valya, were evacuated to the Kuibyshev region.
Solomon had been working in the Pioneer and Komsomol camps when he was drafted in 1941. He married a nice girl in 1938, but she died in childbirth two years later. He was sent to the Front still grieving his wife.
My youngest brother David had been working at the "Arsenal" factory as a mechanic when he was drafted in 1940.
I would think of them often, and of Kyril, and my sisters and parents. I had no idea where anyone was, whether they were safe, whether they were even alive.

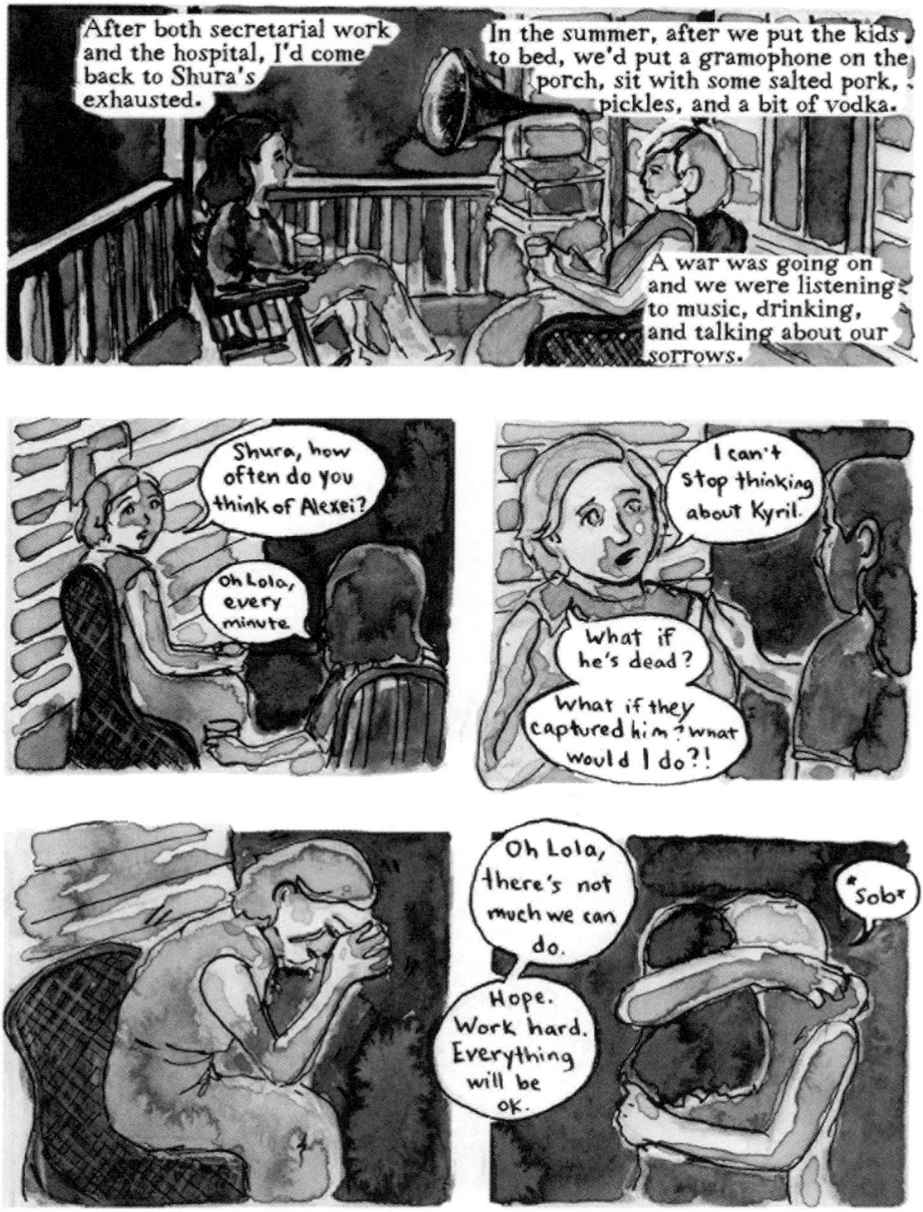
After both secretarial work and the hospital, I'd come back to Shura's exhausted.
In the summer, after we put the kids to bed, we'd put a gramophone on the porch, sit with some salted pork, pickles, and a bit of vodka.
A war was going on and we were listening to music, drinking, and talking about our sorrows.
Shura, how often do you think of Alexei?
Oh Lola, every minute
I can't stop thinking about Kyril.
What if he's dead?
What if they captured him? What would I do?!
Oh Lola, there's not much we can do.
Hope. Work hard. Everything will be ok.
Sob

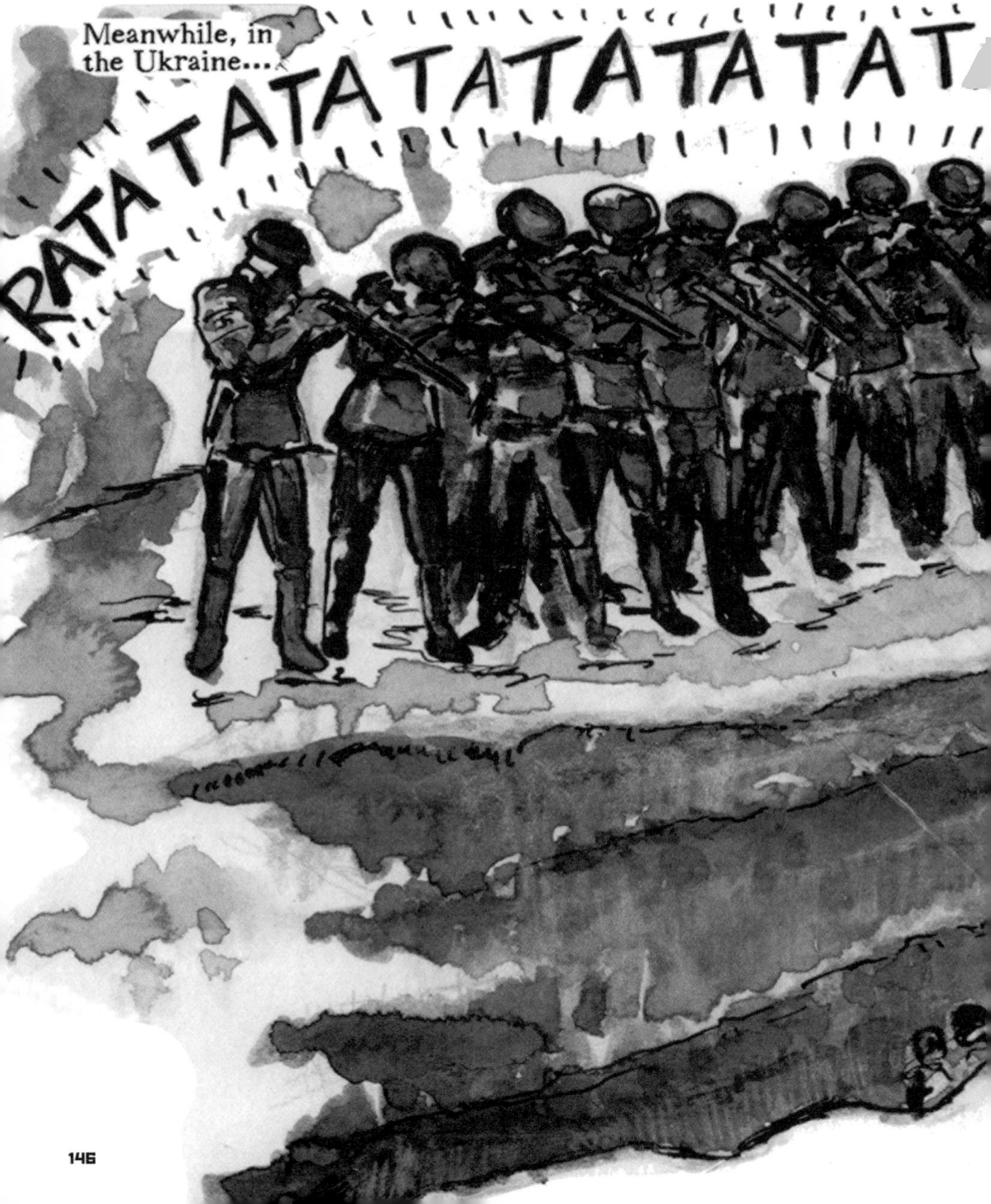
Meanwhile, in the Ukraine...
RATATATATATATATATAT

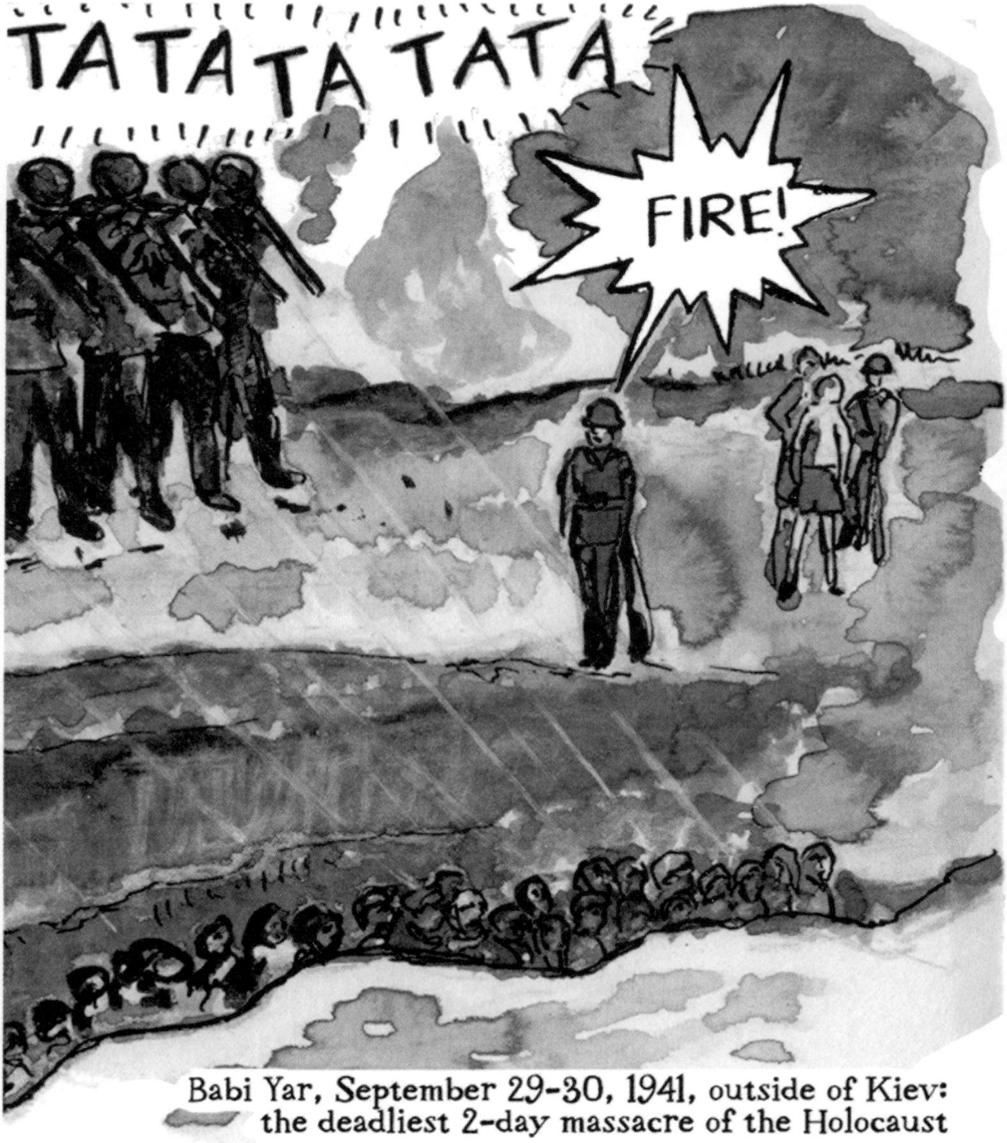
TATATATATATA
FIRE!

Babi Yar, September 29-30, 1941, outside of Kiev:
the deadliest 2-day massacre of the Holocaust

Interlude

January 2010

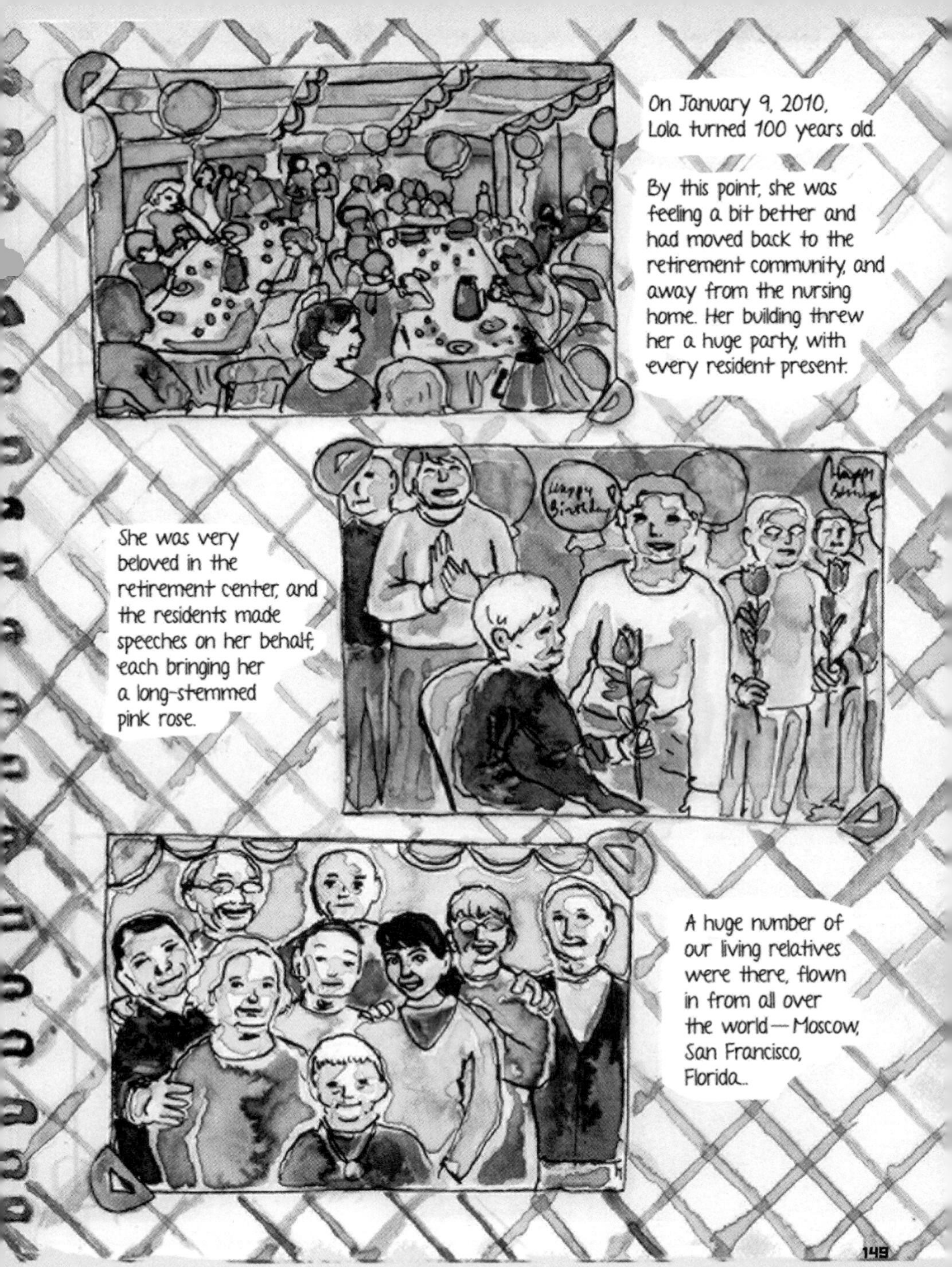
On January 9, 2010, Lola turned 100 years old.
By this point, she was feeling a bit better and had moved back to the retirement community, and away from the nursing home. Her building threw her a huge party, with every resident present.
She was very beloved in the retirement center, and the residents made speeches on her behalf, each bringing her a long-stemmed pink rose.
Happy Birthday
A huge number of our living relatives were there, flown in from all over the world—Moscow, San Francisco, Florida...

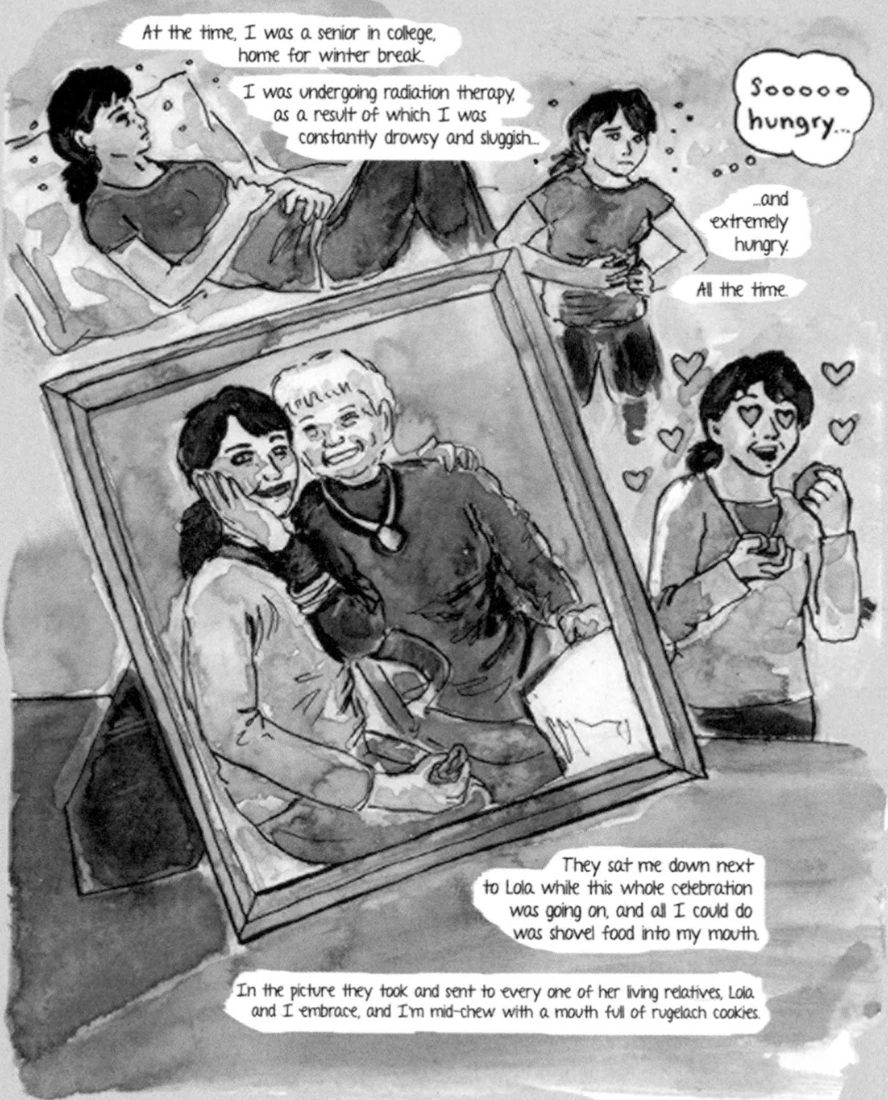
At the time, I was a senior in college, home for winter break.
I was undergoing radiation therapy, as a result of which I was constantly drowsy and sluggish...
Sooooo hungry...
...and extremely hungry.
All the time.
They sat me down next to Lola while this whole celebration was going on, and all I could do was shovel food into my mouth.
In the picture they took and sent to every one of her living relatives, Lola and I embrace, and I'm mid-chew with a mouth full of rugelach cookies.

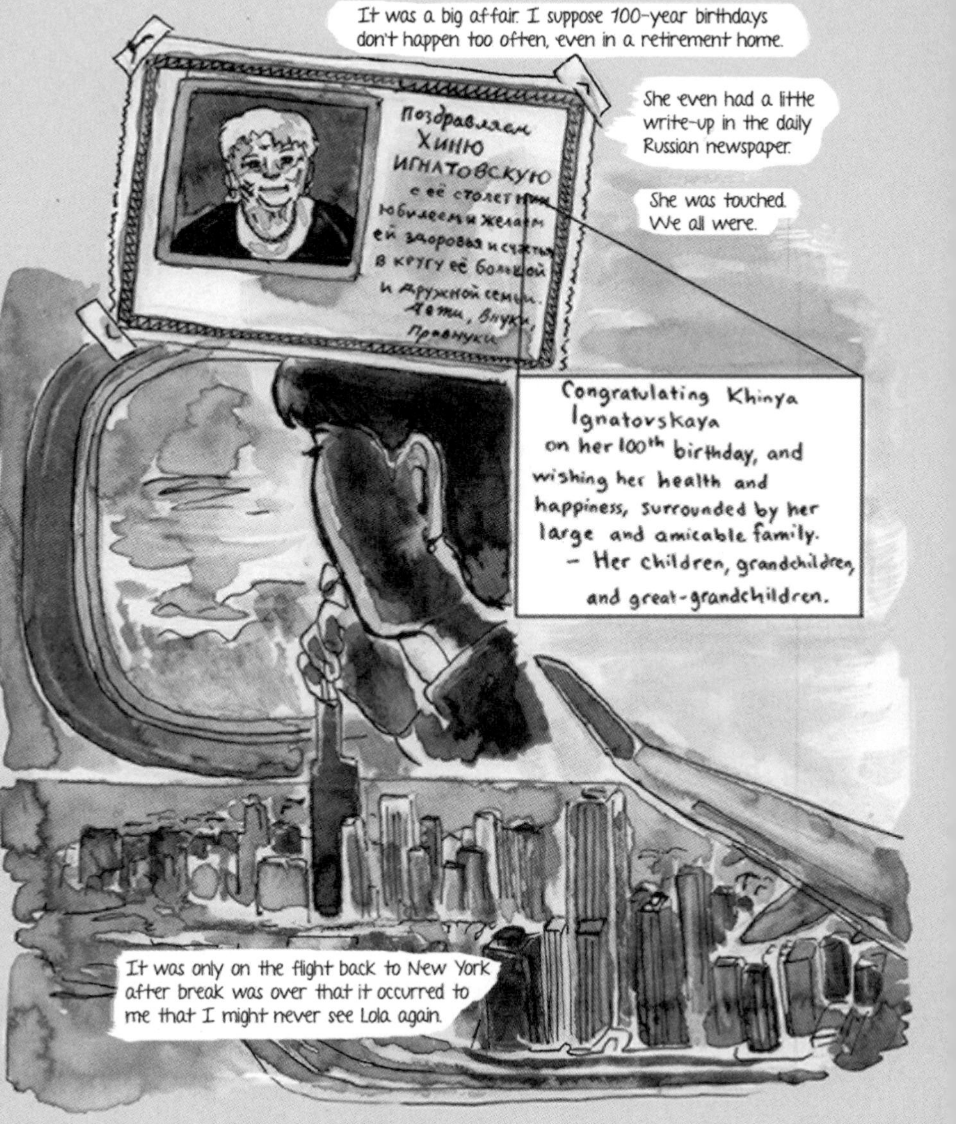
It was a big affair. I suppose 100-year birthdays don't happen too often, even in a retirement home.
Поздравляем
Хиню
Игнатовскую
с её столетним
юбилеем и желаем
ей здоровья и счастья
в кругу её большой
и дружной семьи.
Дети, Внуки,
Правнуки
She even had a little write-up in the daily Russian newspaper.
She was touched. We all were.
Congratulating Khinya Ignatovskaya on her 100th birthday, and wishing her health and happiness, surrounded by her large and amicable family.
– Her children, grandchildren, and great-grandchildren.
It was only on the flight back to New York after break was over that it occurred to me that I might never see Lola again.

Chapter 10: 1942-1943

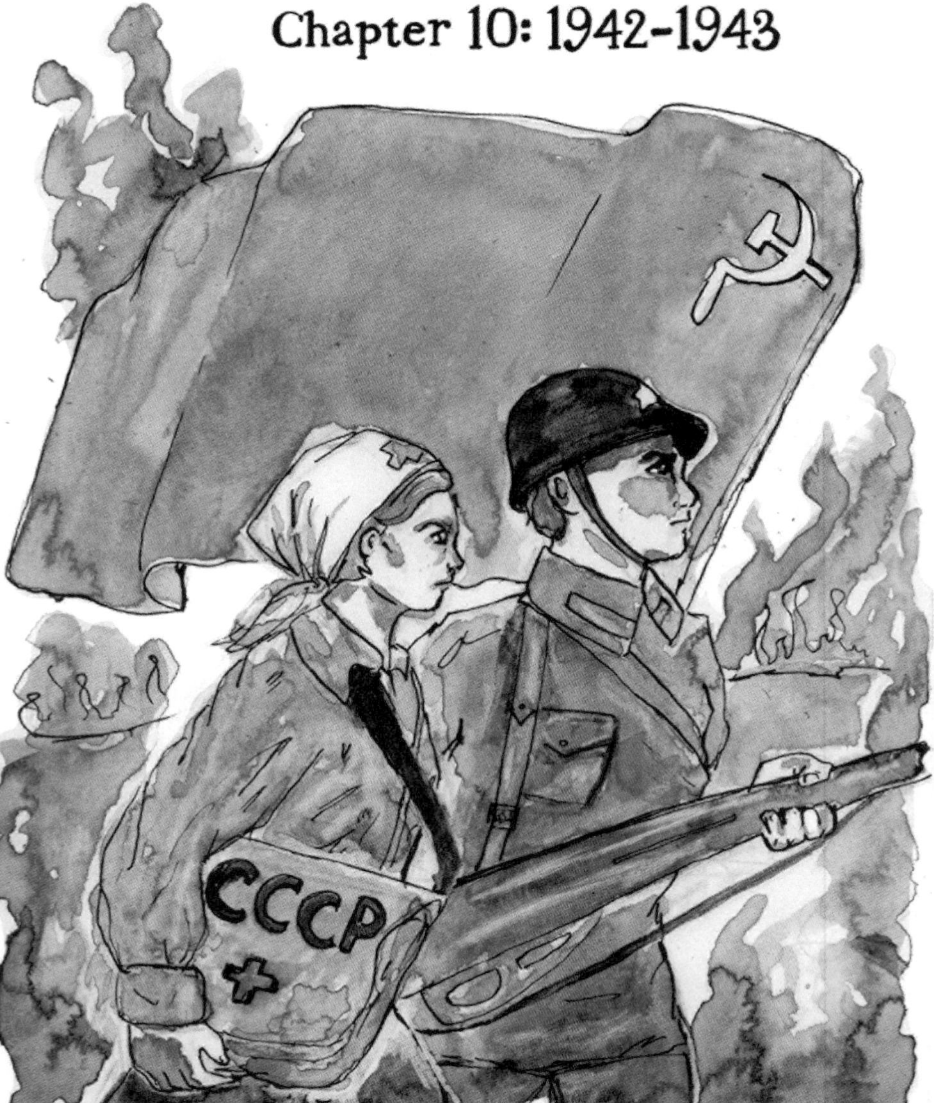
CCCP

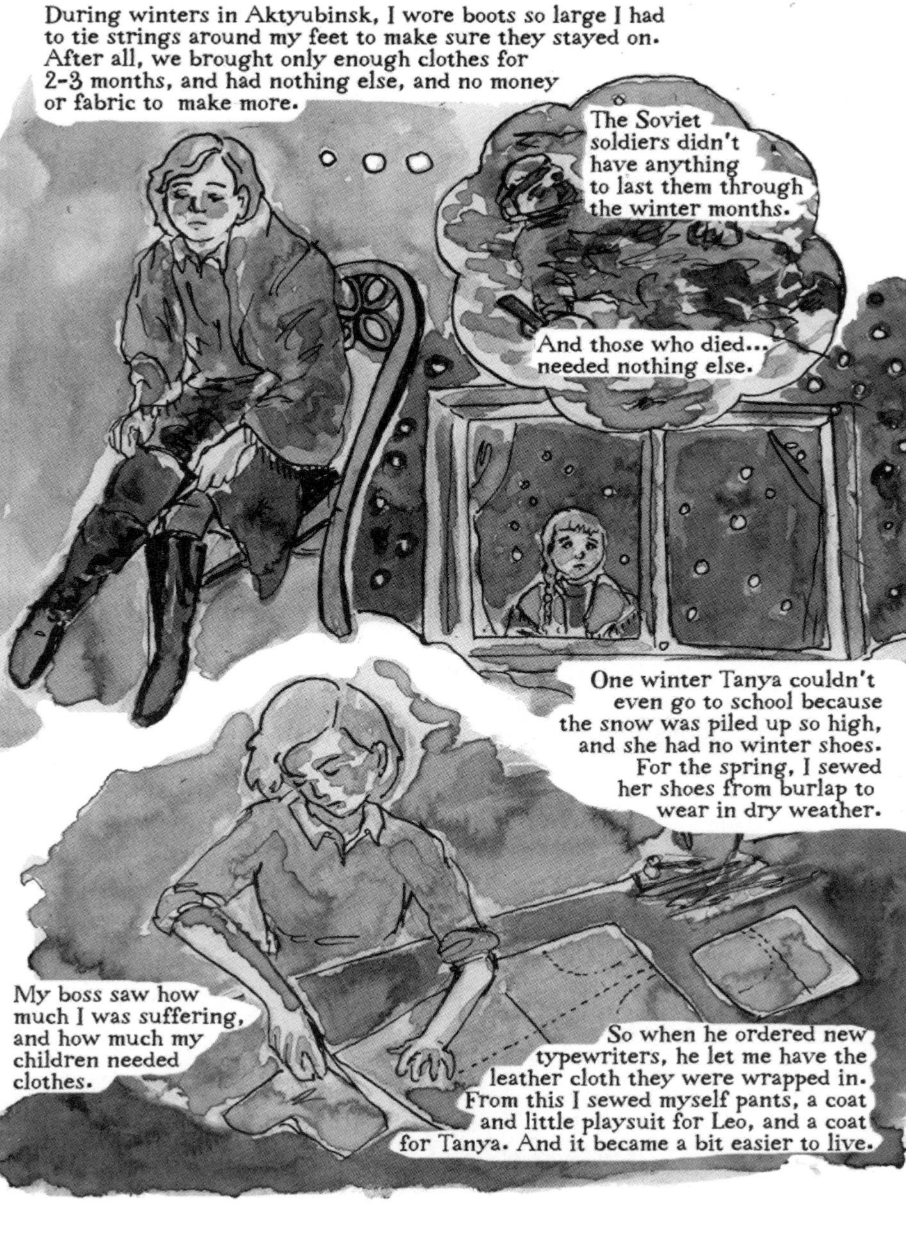
During winters in Aktyubinsk, I wore boots so large I had to tie strings around my feet to make sure they stayed on. After all, we brought only enough clothes for 2-3 months, and had nothing else, and no money or fabric to make more.
The Soviet soldiers didn't have anything to last them through the winter months.
And those who died... needed nothing else.
One winter Tanya couldn't even go to school because the snow was piled up so high, and she had no winter shoes. For the spring, I sewed her shoes from burlap to wear in dry weather.
My boss saw how much I was suffering, and how much my children needed clothes.
So when he ordered new typewriters, he let me have the leather cloth they were wrapped in. From this I sewed myself pants, a coat and little playsuit for Leo, and a coat for Tanya. And it became a bit easier to live.

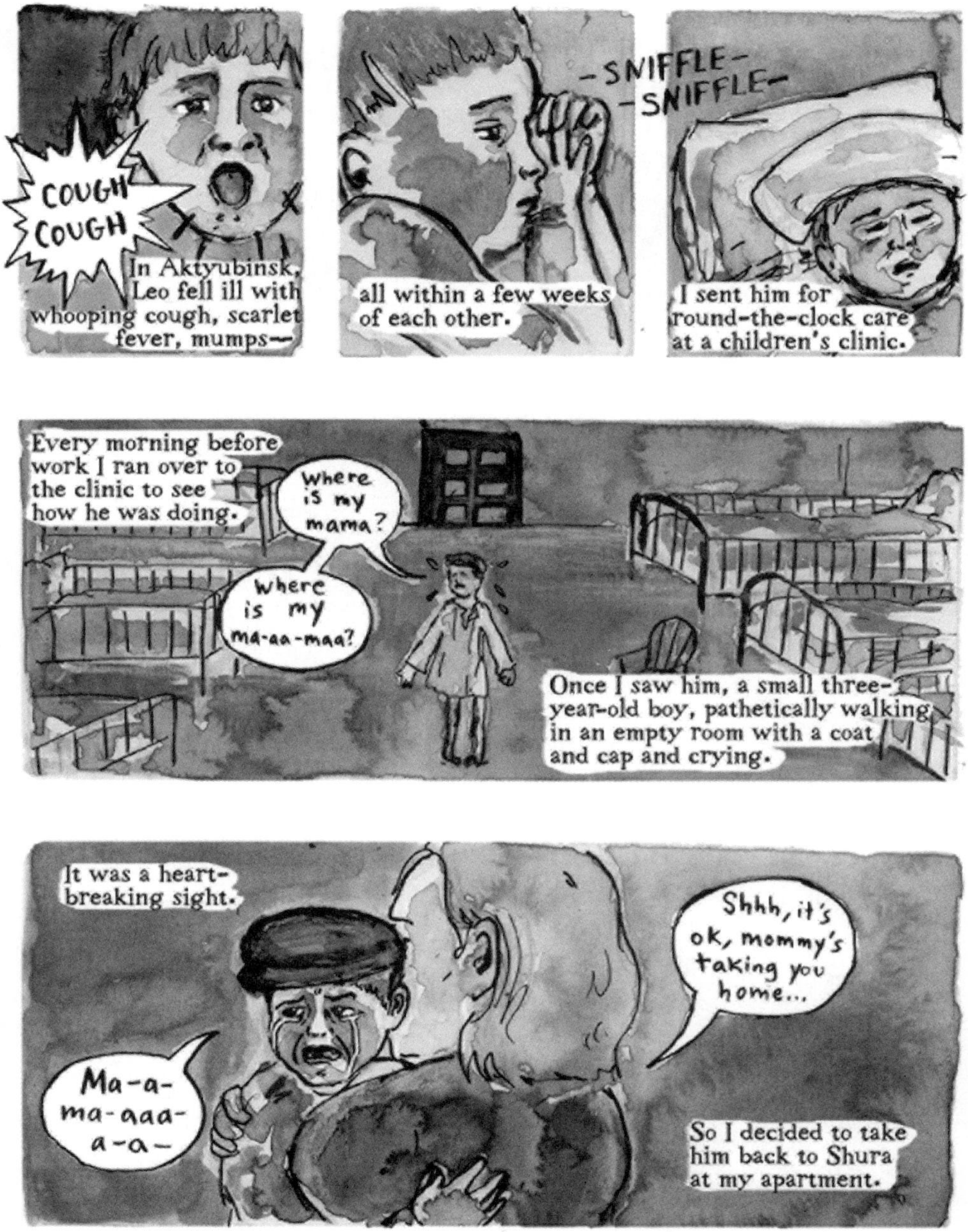
COUGH COUGH
In Aktyubinsk, Leo fell ill with whooping cough, scarlet fever, mumps—
-SNIFFLE-
-SNIFFLE-
all within a few weeks of each other.
I sent him for round-the-clock care at a children's clinic.
Every morning before work I ran over to the clinic to see how he was doing.
Where is my mama?
Where is my ma-aa-maa?
Once I saw him, a small three-year-old boy, pathetically walking in an empty room with a coat and cap and crying.
It was a heart-breaking sight.
Shhh, it's ok, mommy's taking you home...
Ma-a-ma-aaa-a-a-
So I decided to take him back to Shura at my apartment.

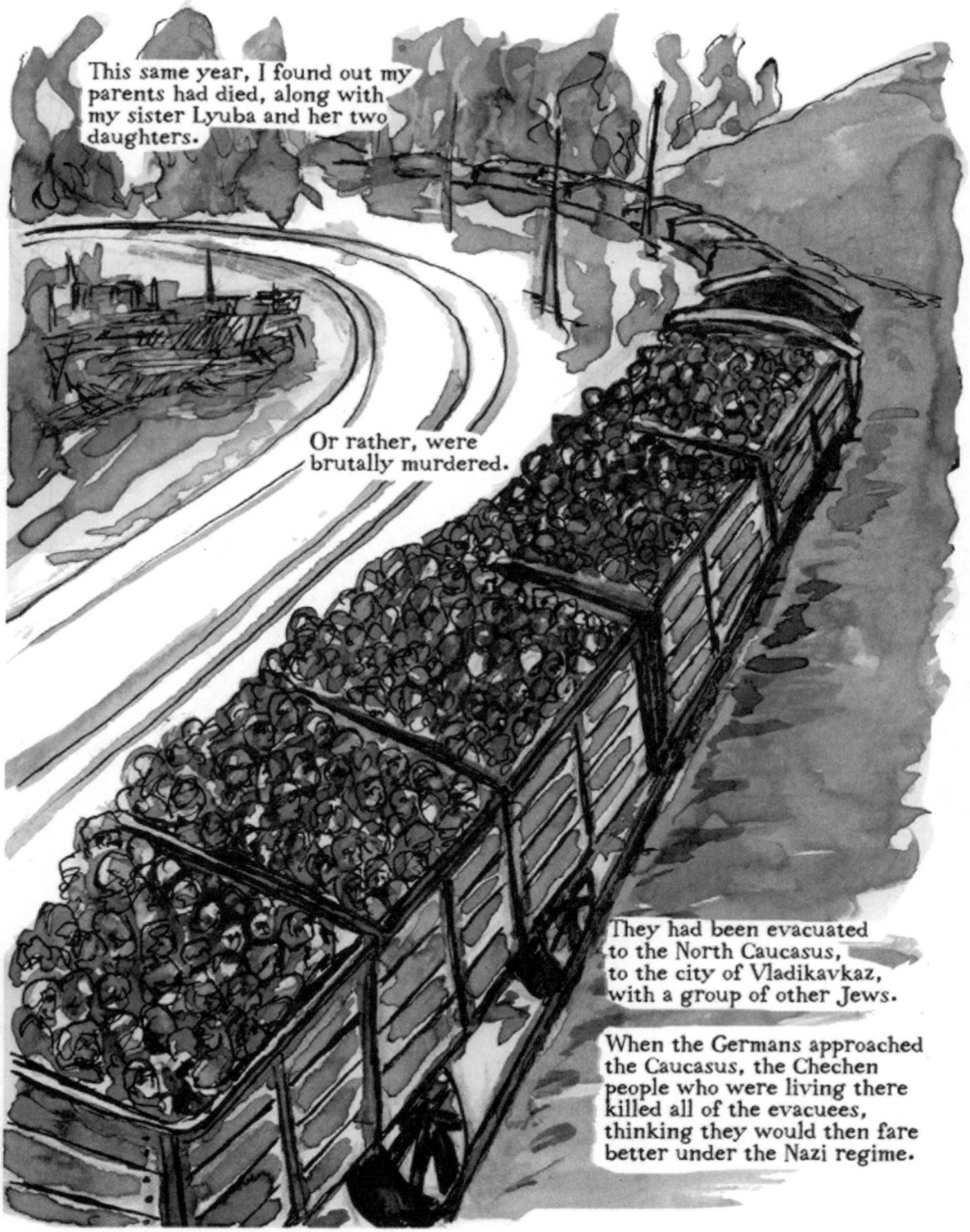
This same year, I found out my parents had died, along with my sister Lyuba and her two daughters.
Or rather, were brutally murdered.
They had been evacuated to the North Caucasus, to the city of Vladikavkaz, with a group of other Jews.
When the Germans approached the Caucasus, the Chechen people who were living there killed all of the evacuees, thinking they would then fare better under the Nazi regime.

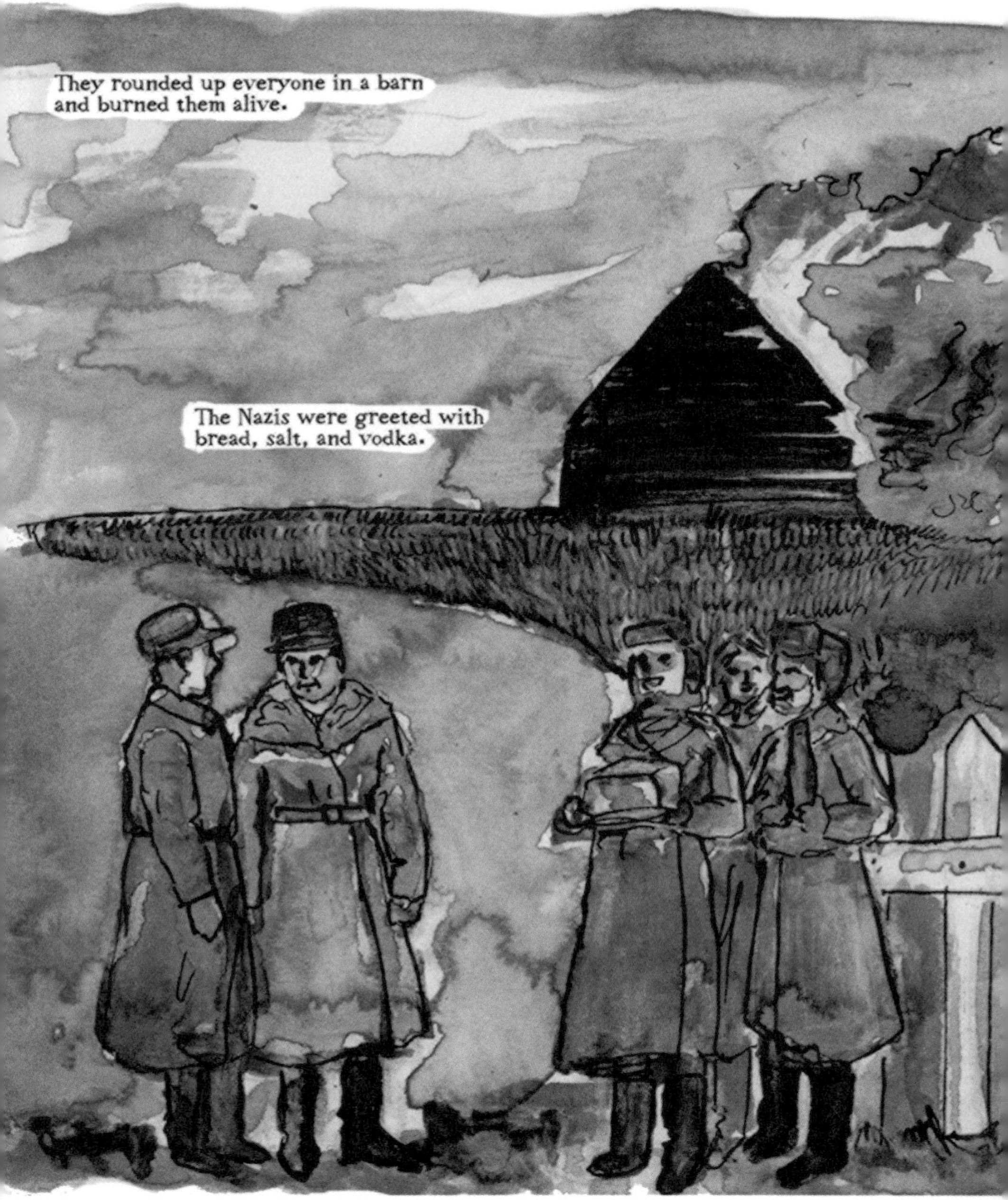
They rounded up everyone in a barn and burned them alive.
The Nazis were greeted with bread, salt, and vodka.

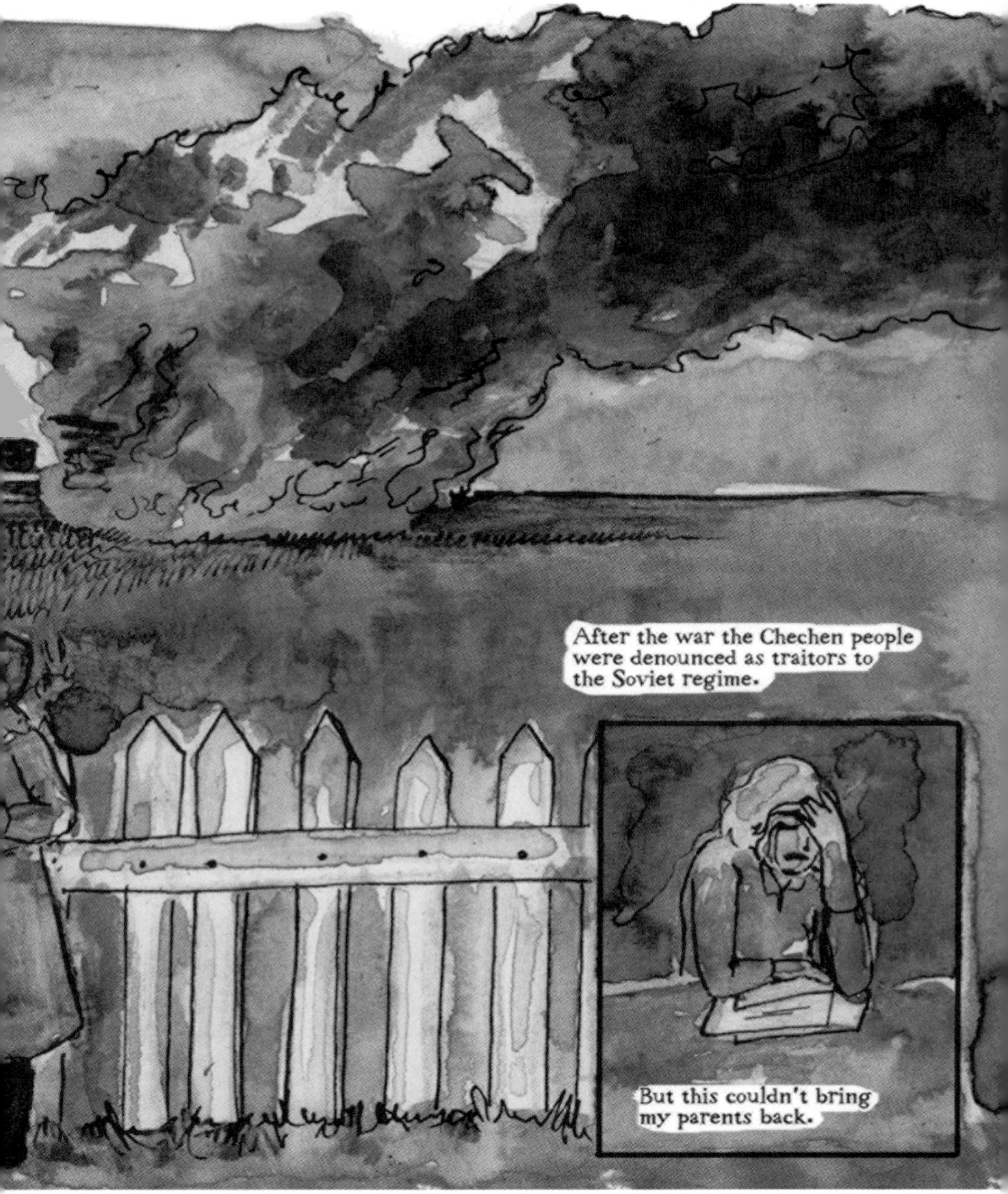
After the war the Chechen people were denounced as traitors to the Soviet regime.
But this couldn't bring my parents back.

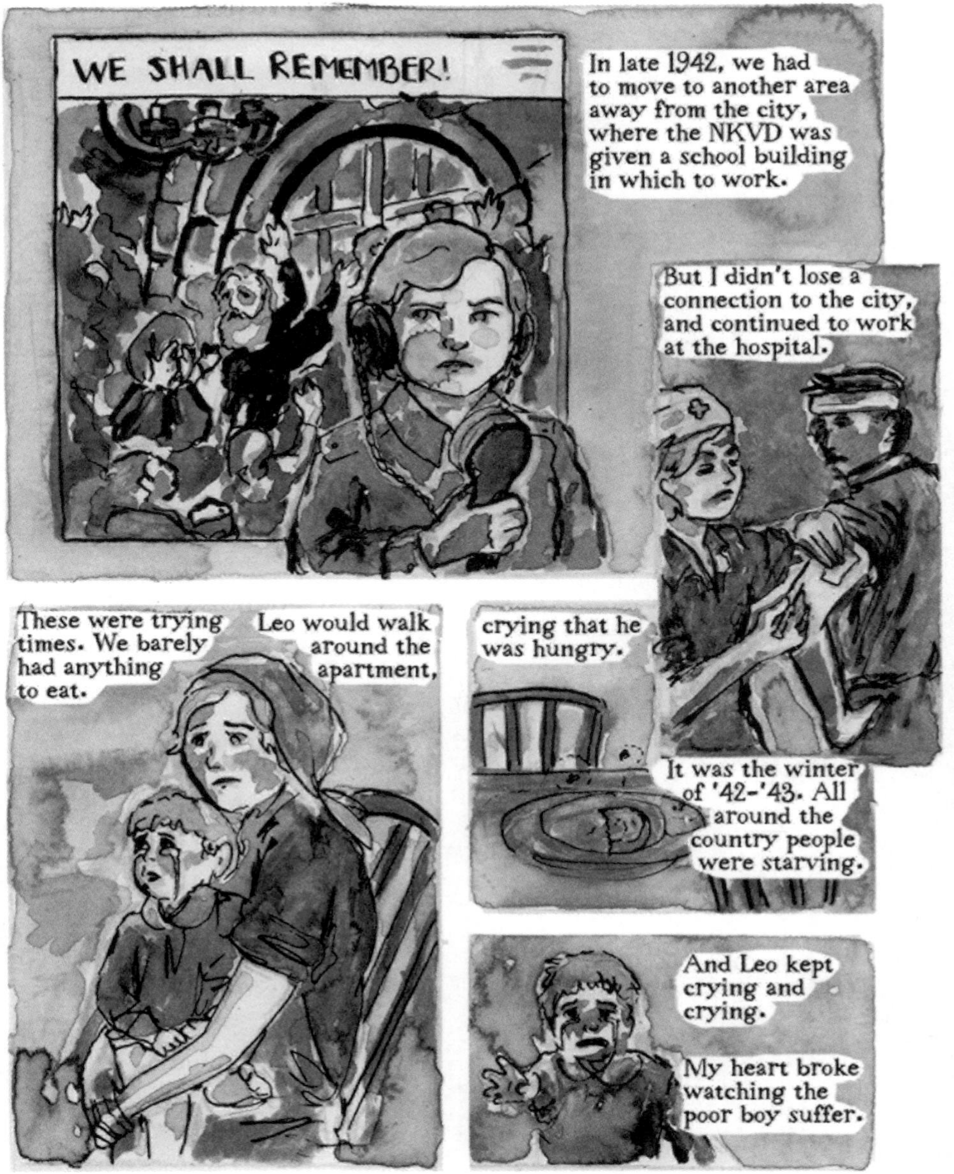

WE SHALL REMEMBER!
In late 1942, we had to move to another area away from the city, where the NKVD was given a school building in which to work.
But I didn't lose a connection to the city, and continued to work at the hospital.
These were trying times. We barely had anything to eat.
Leo would walk around the apartment,
crying that he was hungry.
It was the winter of '42-'43. All around the country people were starving.
And Leo kept crying and crying.
My heart broke watching the poor boy suffer.

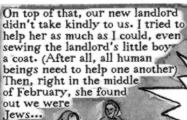

On top of that, our new landlord didn't take kindly to us. I tried to help her as much as I could, even sewing the landlord's little boy a coat. (After all, all human beings need to help one another) Then, right in the middle of February, she found out we were Jews...

GET OUT OF THIS ROOM!

GASP

I won't have any JEWS in here. It's because of YOU our husbands, sons, and brothers are being murdered in cold blood! Out! Get OUT!

So we were kicked out of the house, into the freezing cold, in the middle of nowhere...

Boss, please. Our landlady kicked us out for being Jews.. We have absolutely nowhere else to go...

Oh Lola!

Let's transfer you back to the city then.

159

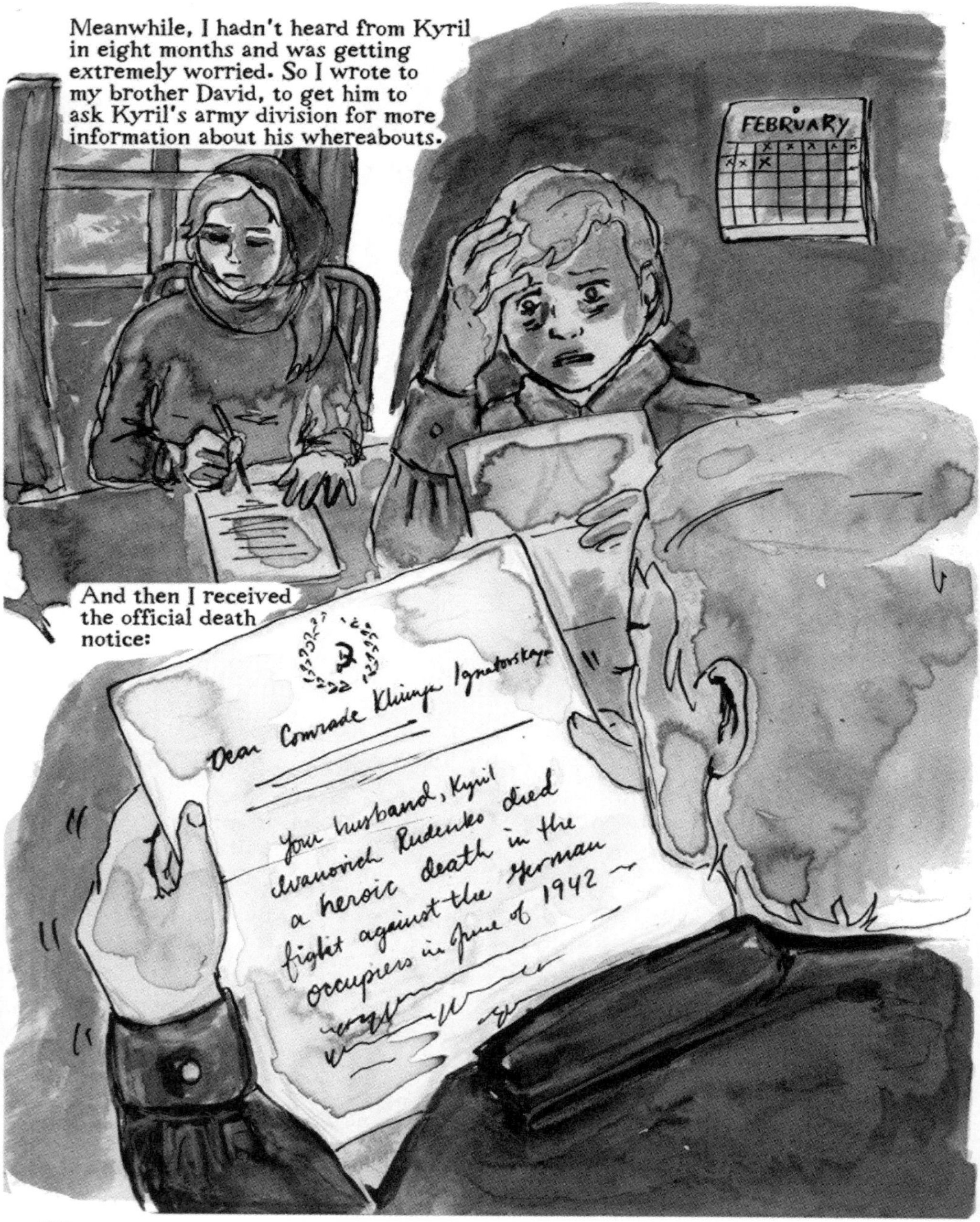
Meanwhile, I hadn't heard from Kyril in eight months and was getting extremely worried. So I wrote to my brother David, to get him to ask Kyril's army division for more information about his whereabouts.
FEBRUARY
And then I received the official death notice:
Dear Comrade Khinya Ignatovskaya
Your husband, Kyril Ivanovich Rudenko died a heroic death in the fight against the German occupiers in June of 1942

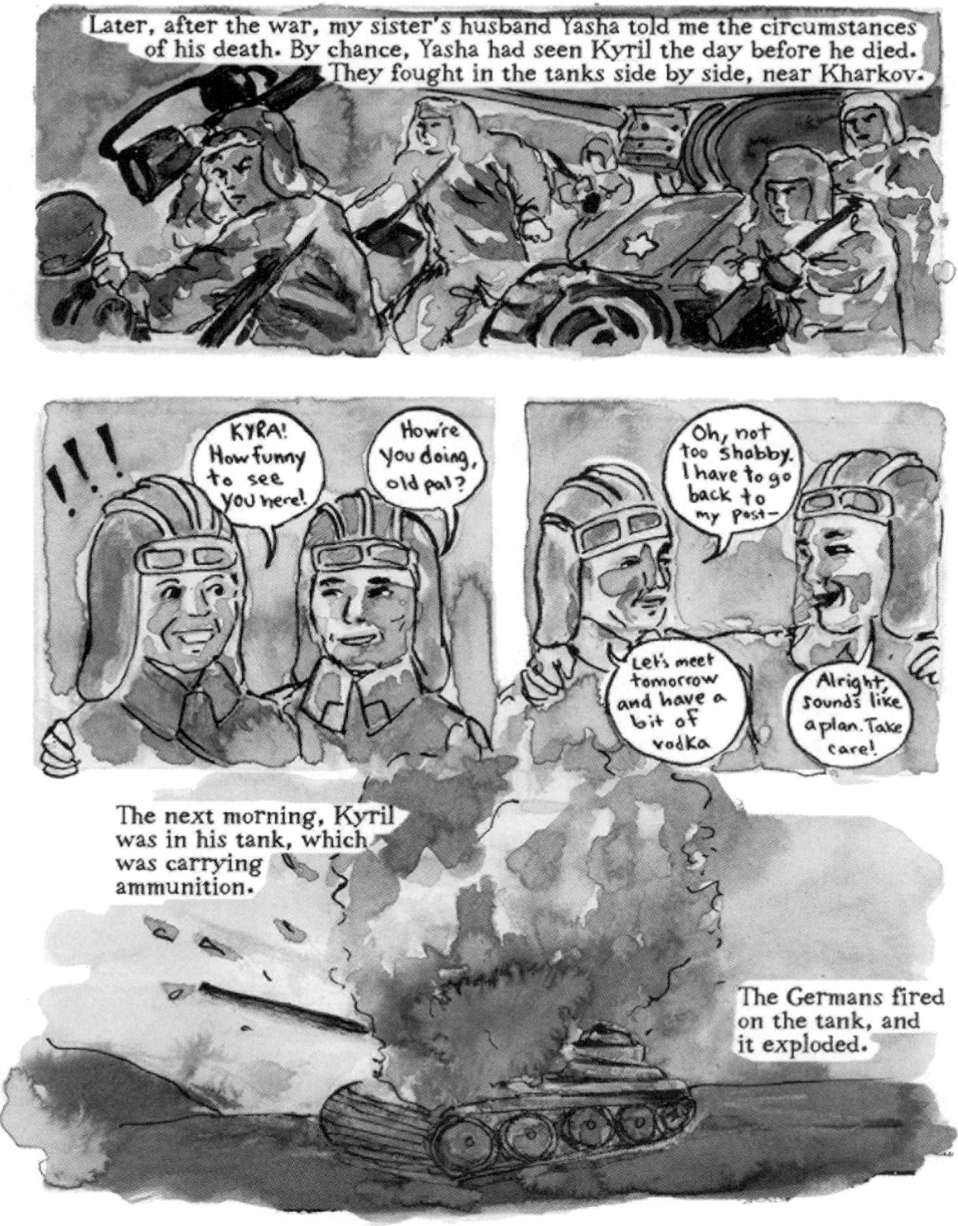
Later, after the war, my sister's husband Yasha told me the circumstances of his death. By chance, Yasha had seen Kyril the day before he died. They fought in the tanks side by side, near Kharkov.
!!!
KYRA! How funny to see you here!
How're you doing, old pal?
Oh, not too shabby. I have to go back to my post—
Let's meet tomorrow and have a bit of vodka
Alright, sounds like a plan. Take care!
The next morning, Kyril was in his tank, which was carrying ammunition.
The Germans fired on the tank, and it exploded.

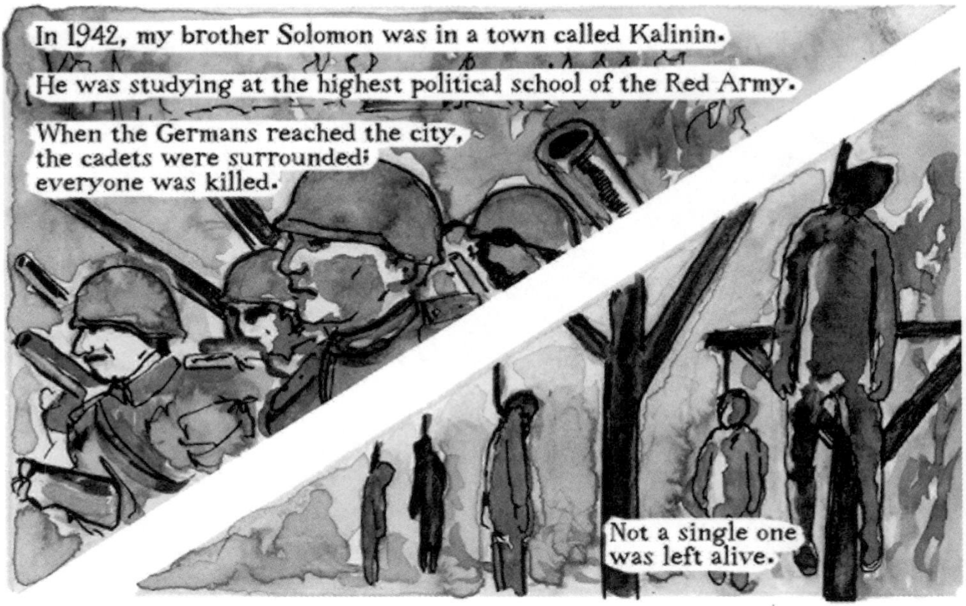
In 1942, my brother Solomon was in a town called Kalinin.
He was studying at the highest political school of the Red Army.
When the Germans reached the city, the cadets were surrounded; everyone was killed.
Not a single one was left alive.

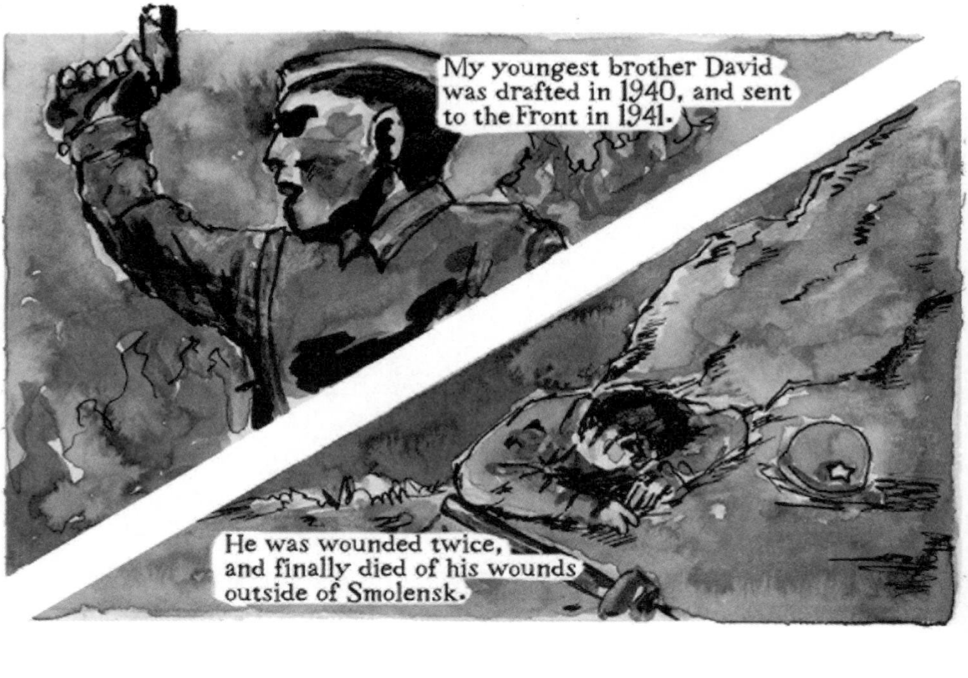
My youngest brother David was drafted in 1940, and sent to the Front in 1941.
He was wounded twice, and finally died of his wounds outside of Smolensk.

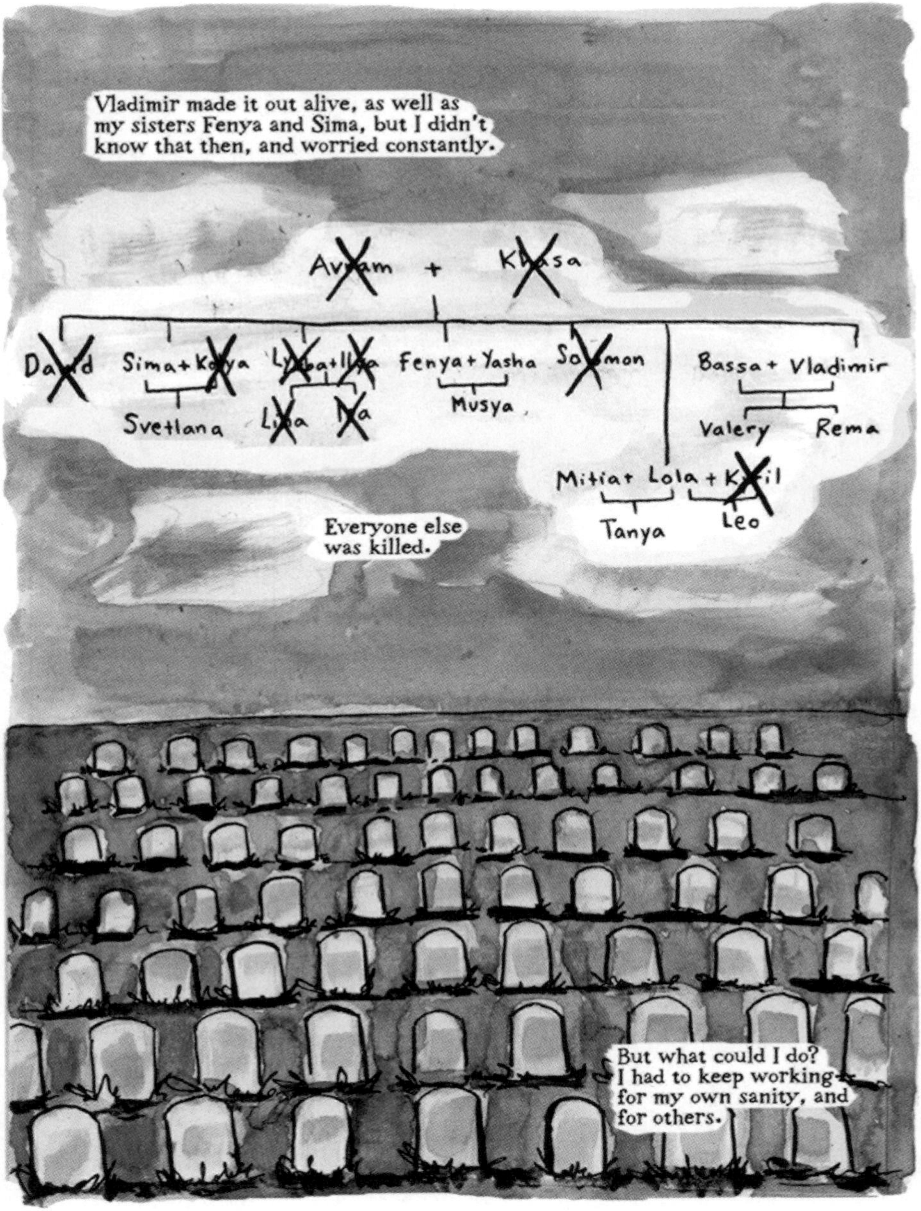
Vladimir made it out alive, as well as my sisters Fenya and Sima, but I didn't know that then, and worried constantly.
Sima +
Svetlana
Fenya + Yasha
Musya
Bassa + Vladimir
Valery
Rema
Mitia + Lola +
Tanya
Leo
Everyone else was killed.
But what could I do? I had to keep working for my own sanity, and for others.

Interlude

February 2010

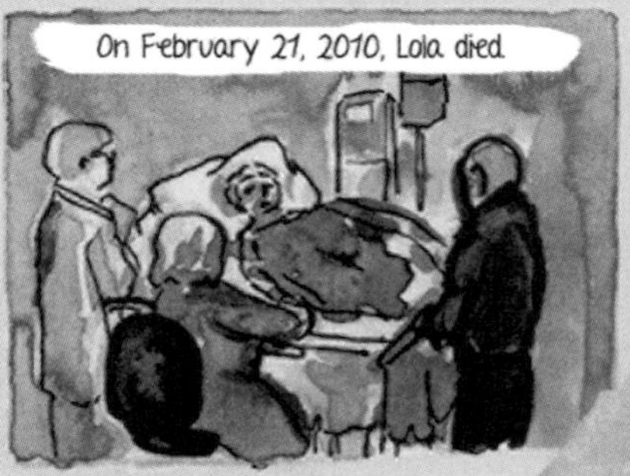
On February 21, 2010, Lola died.

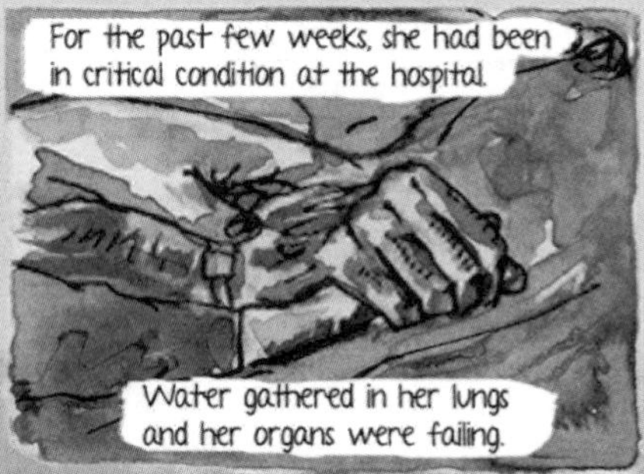
For the past few weeks, she had been in critical condition at the hospital.
Water gathered in her lungs and her organs were failing.

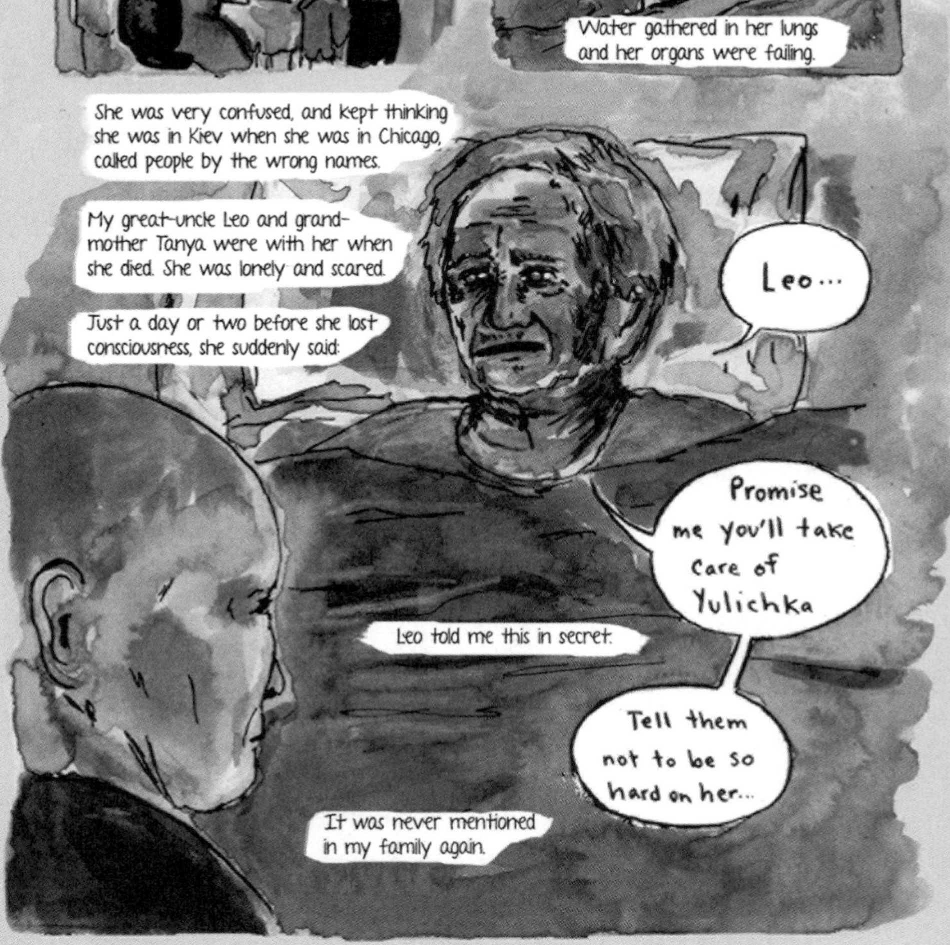
She was very confused, and kept thinking she was in Kiev when she was in Chicago, called people by the wrong names.
My great-uncle Leo and grandmother Tanya were with her when she died. She was lonely and scared.
Just a day or two before she lost consciousness, she suddenly said:
Leo...
Promise me you'll take care of Yulichka
Leo told me this in secret.
Tell them not to be so hard on her...
It was never mentioned in my family again.

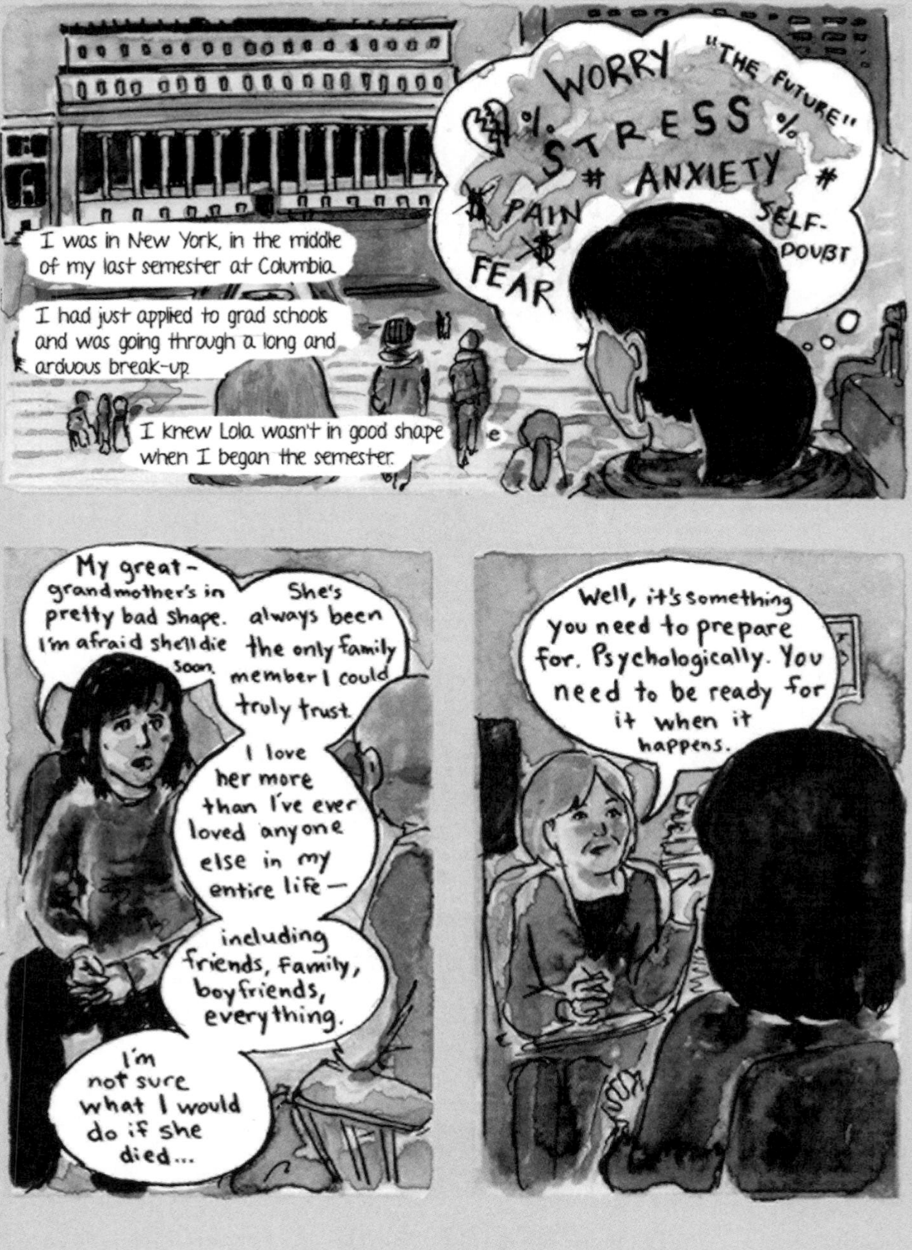
I was in New York, in the middle of my last semester at Columbia.
I had just applied to grad schools and was going through a long and arduous break-up.
I knew Lola wasn't in good shape when I began the semester.
WORRY
"THE FUTURE"
STRESS
ANXIETY
PAIN
SELF-DOUBT
FEAR
My great-grandmother's in pretty bad shape. I'm afraid she'll die soon.
She's always been the only family member I could truly trust.
I love her more than I've ever loved anyone else in my entire life—
including friends, family, boyfriends, everything.
I'm not sure what I would do if she died...
Well, it's something you need to prepare for. Psychologically. You need to be ready for it when it happens.

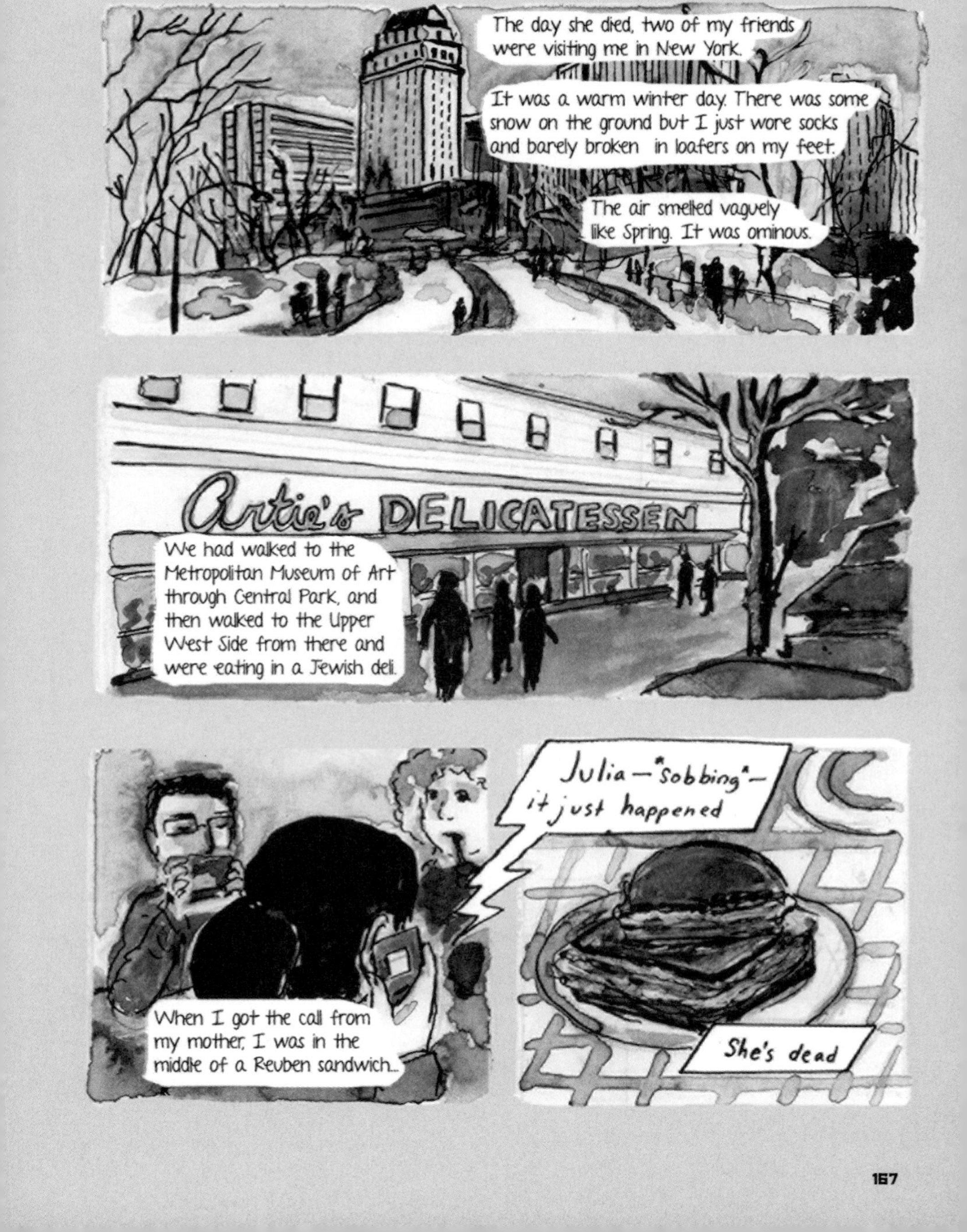
The day she died, two of my friends were visiting me in New York.
It was a warm winter day. There was some snow on the ground but I just wore socks and barely broken in loafers on my feet.
The air smelled vaguely like Spring. It was ominous.
Artie's DELICATESSEN
We had walked to the Metropolitan Museum of Art through Central Park, and then walked to the Upper West Side from there and were eating in a Jewish deli.
When I got the call from my mother, I was in the middle of a Reuben sandwich...
Julia—*sobbing*—it just happened
She's dead

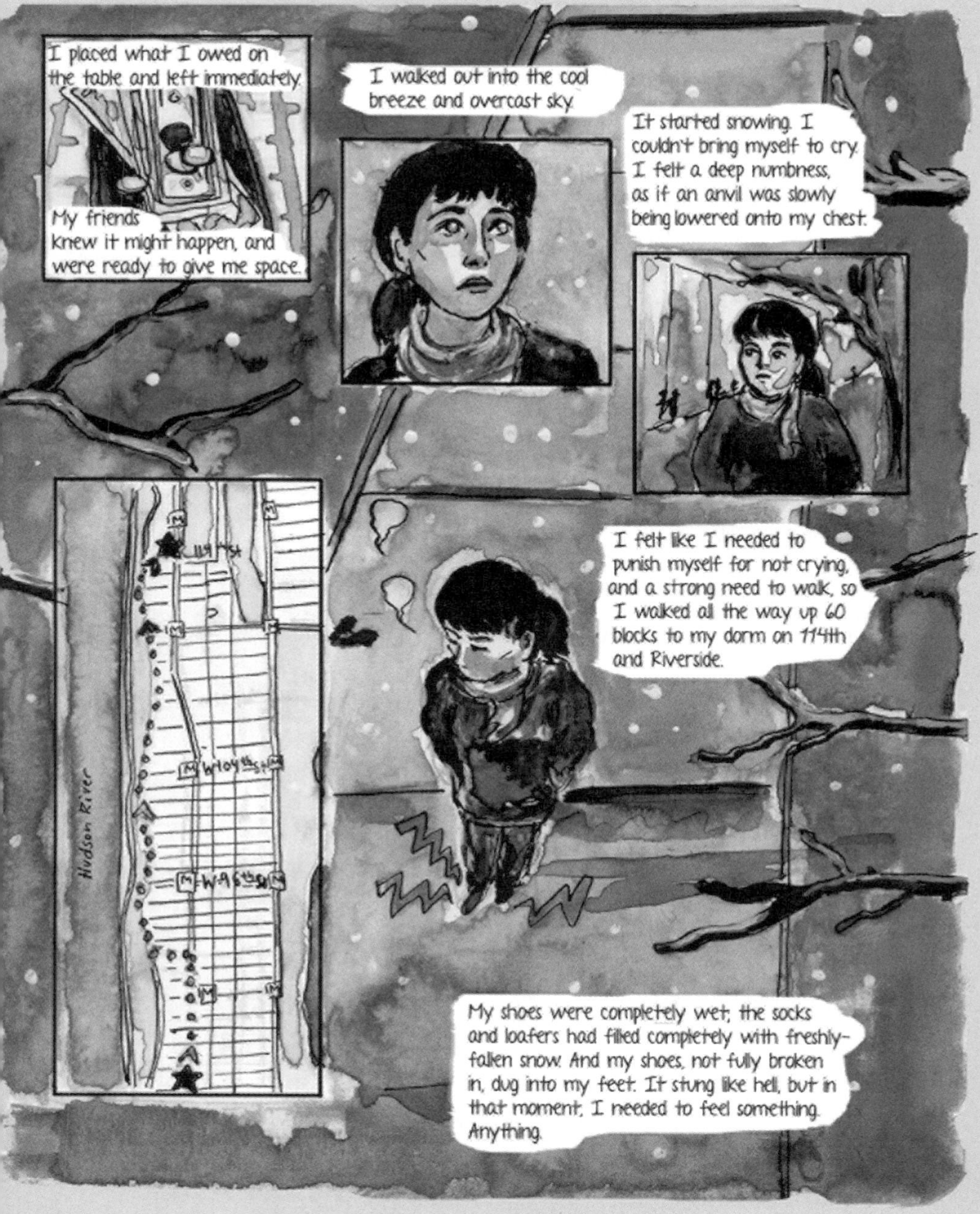
I placed what I owed on the table and left immediately.
My friends knew it might happen, and were ready to give me space.
I walked out into the cool breeze and overcast sky.
It started snowing. I couldn't bring myself to cry. I felt a deep numbness, as if an anvil was slowly being lowered onto my chest.
Hudson River
W 104th St
W 96th St
I felt like I needed to punish myself for not crying, and a strong need to walk, so I walked all the way up 60 blocks to my dorm on 114th and Riverside.
My shoes were completely wet; the socks and loafers had filled completely with freshly-fallen snow. And my shoes, not fully broken in, dug into my feet. It stung like hell, but in that moment, I needed to feel something. Anything.

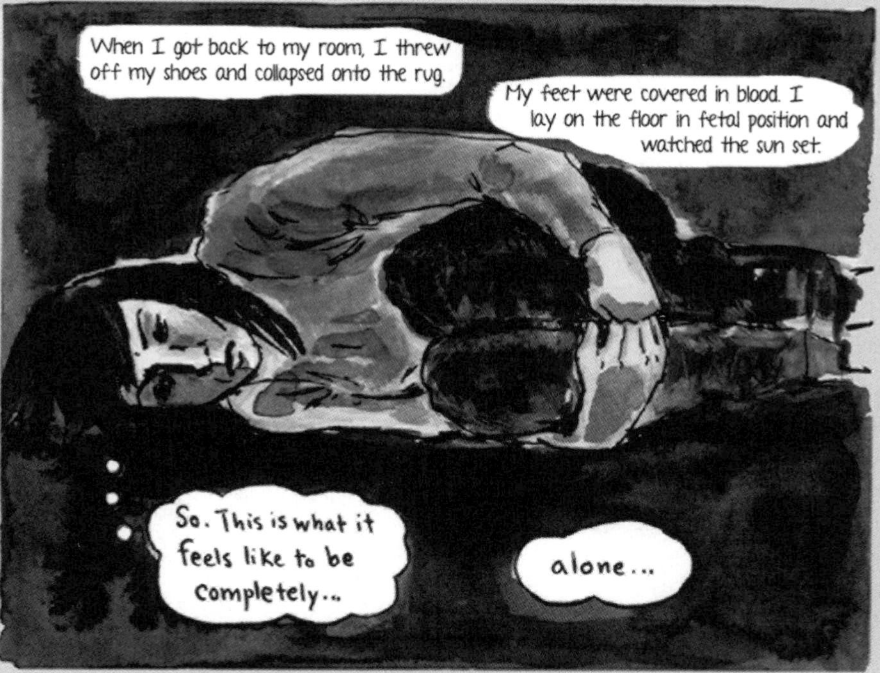
When I got back to my room, I threw off my shoes and collapsed onto the rug.
My feet were covered in blood. I lay on the floor in fetal position and watched the sun set.
So. This is what it feels like to be completely...
alone...

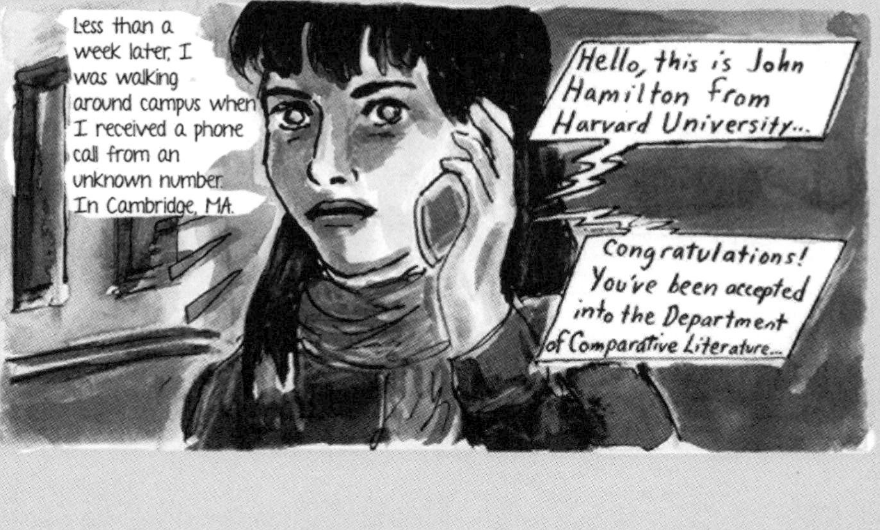
Less than a week later, I was walking around campus when I received a phone call from an unknown number. In Cambridge, MA.
Hello, this is John Hamilton from Harvard University...
Congratulations! You've been accepted into the Department of Comparative Literature...

Chapter 11: 1943-1945

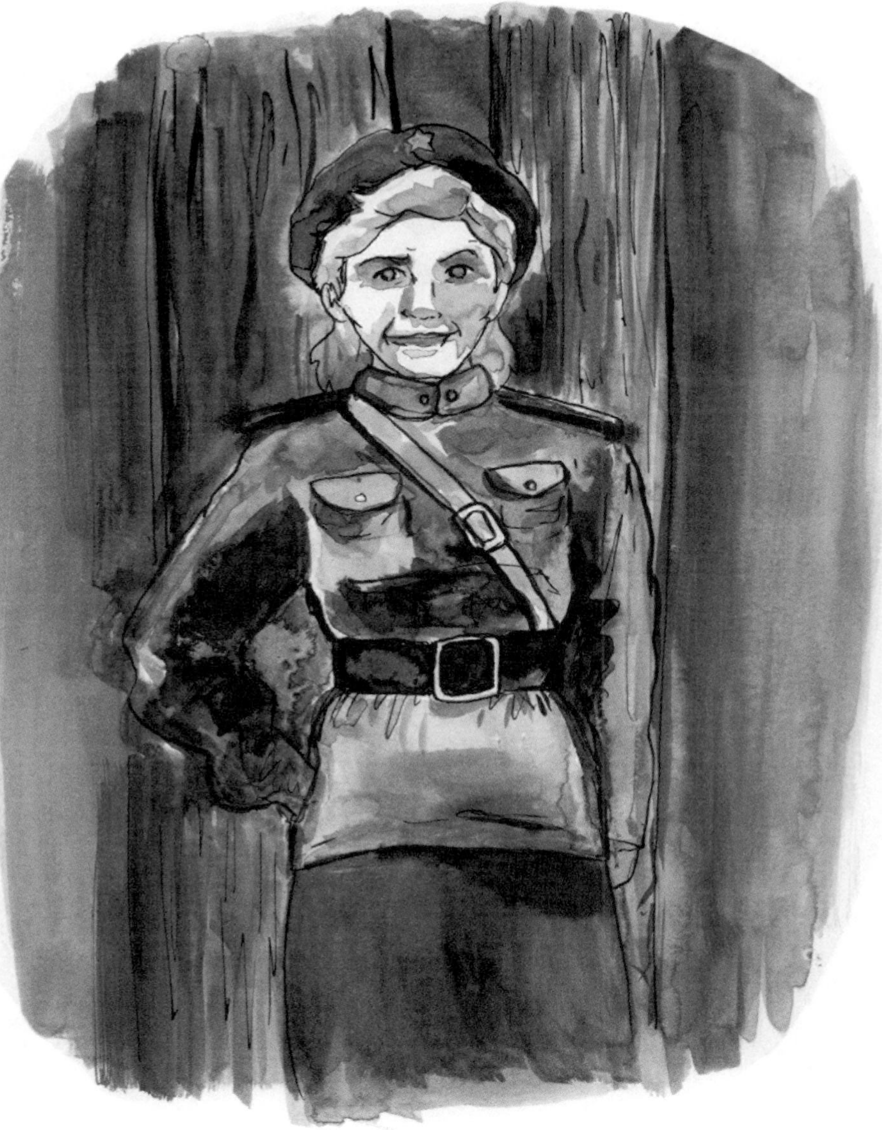

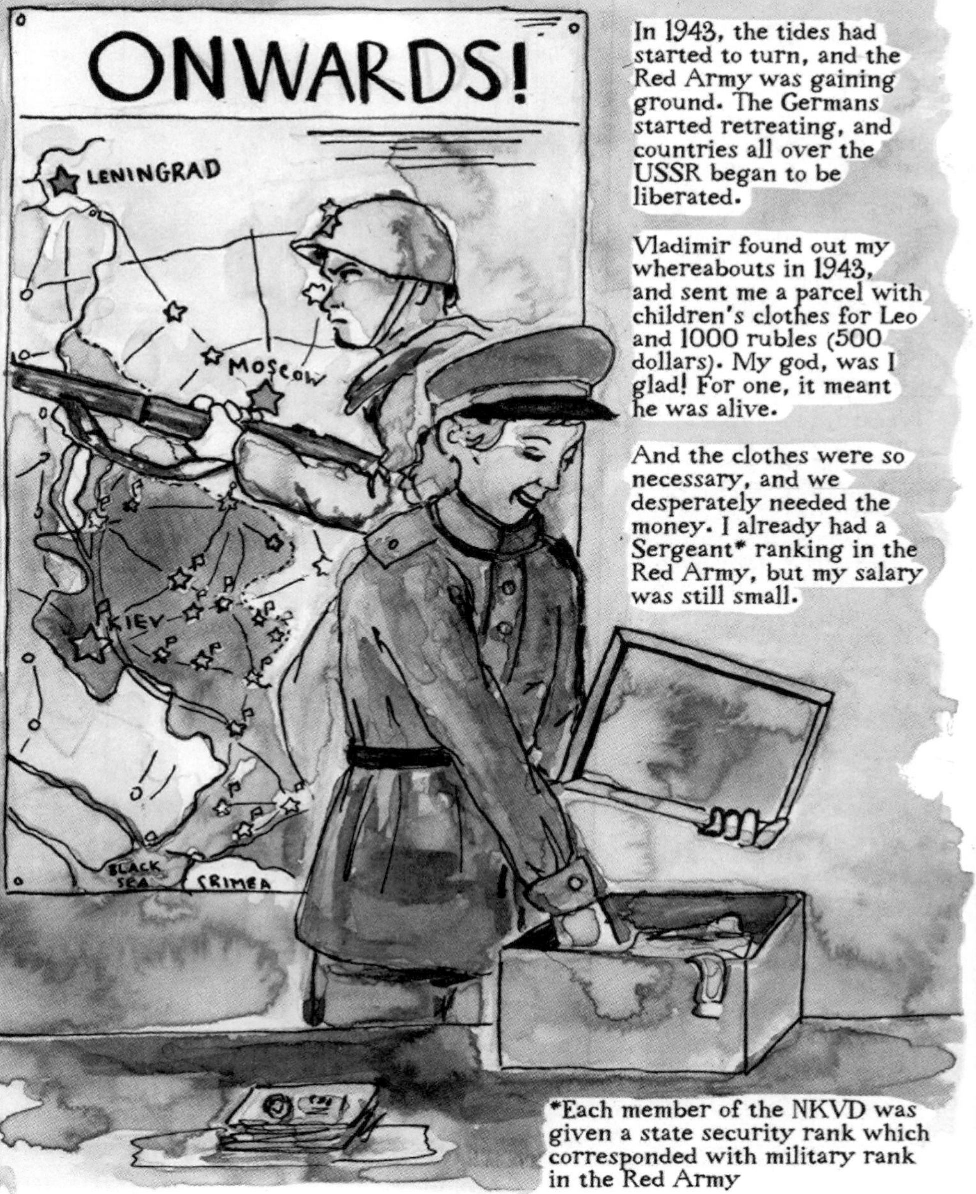
ONWARDS!
LENINGRAD
MOSCOW
KIEV
BLACK SEA
CRIMEA

In 1943, the tides had started to turn, and the Red Army was gaining ground. The Germans started retreating, and countries all over the USSR began to be liberated.

Vladimir found out my whereabouts in 1943, and sent me a parcel with children's clothes for Leo and 1000 rubles (500 dollars). My god, was I glad! For one, it meant he was alive.

And the clothes were so necessary, and we desperately needed the money. I already had a Sergeant* ranking in the Red Army, but my salary was still small.

*Each member of the NKVD was given a state security rank which corresponded with military rank in the Red Army

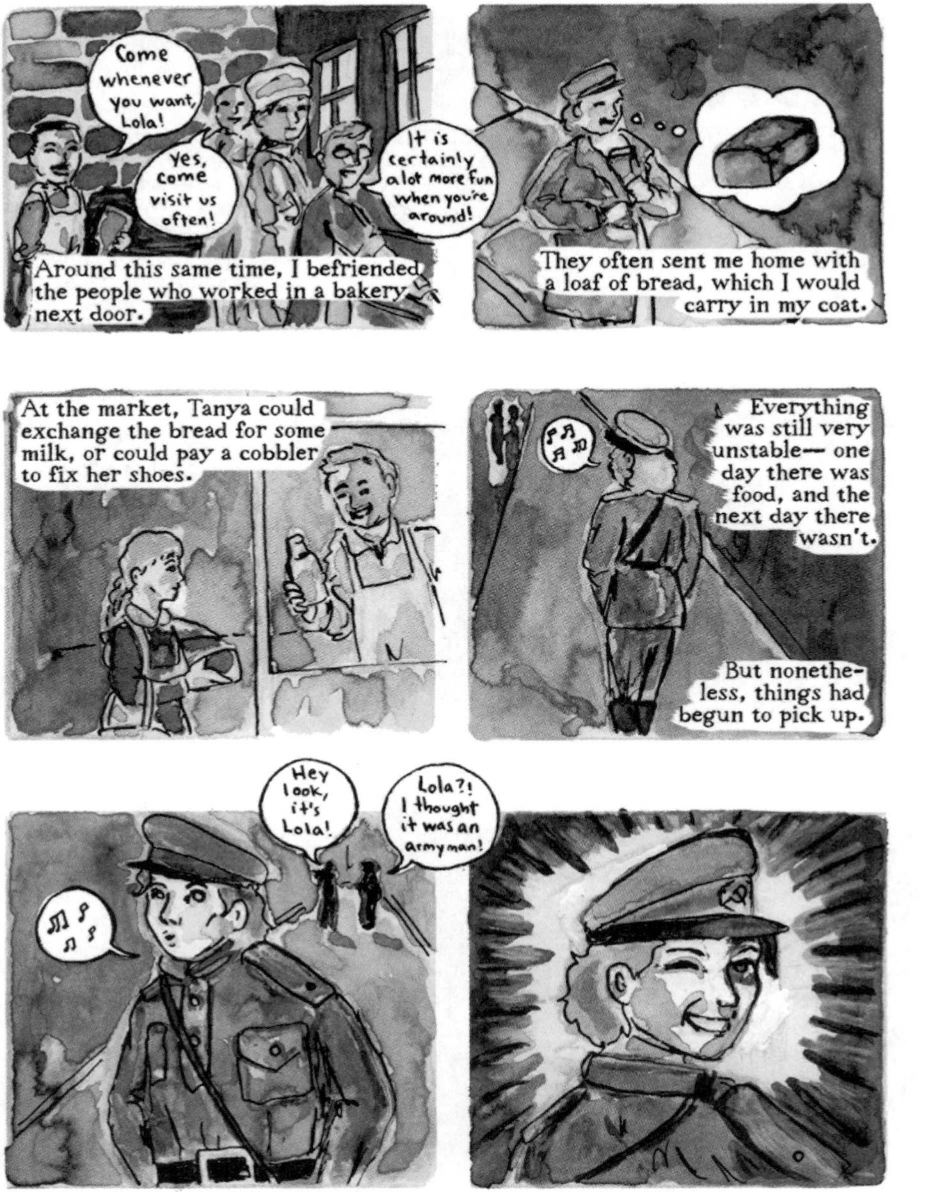
Come whenever you want, Lola!
Yes, come visit us often!
It is certainly alot more fun when you're around!
Around this same time, I befriended the people who worked in a bakery next door.
They often sent me home with a loaf of bread, which I would carry in my coat.
At the market, Tanya could exchange the bread for some milk, or could pay a cobbler to fix her shoes.
Everything was still very unstable— one day there was food, and the next day there wasn't.
But nonetheless, things had begun to pick up.
Hey look, it's Lola!
Lola?! I thought it was an armyman!

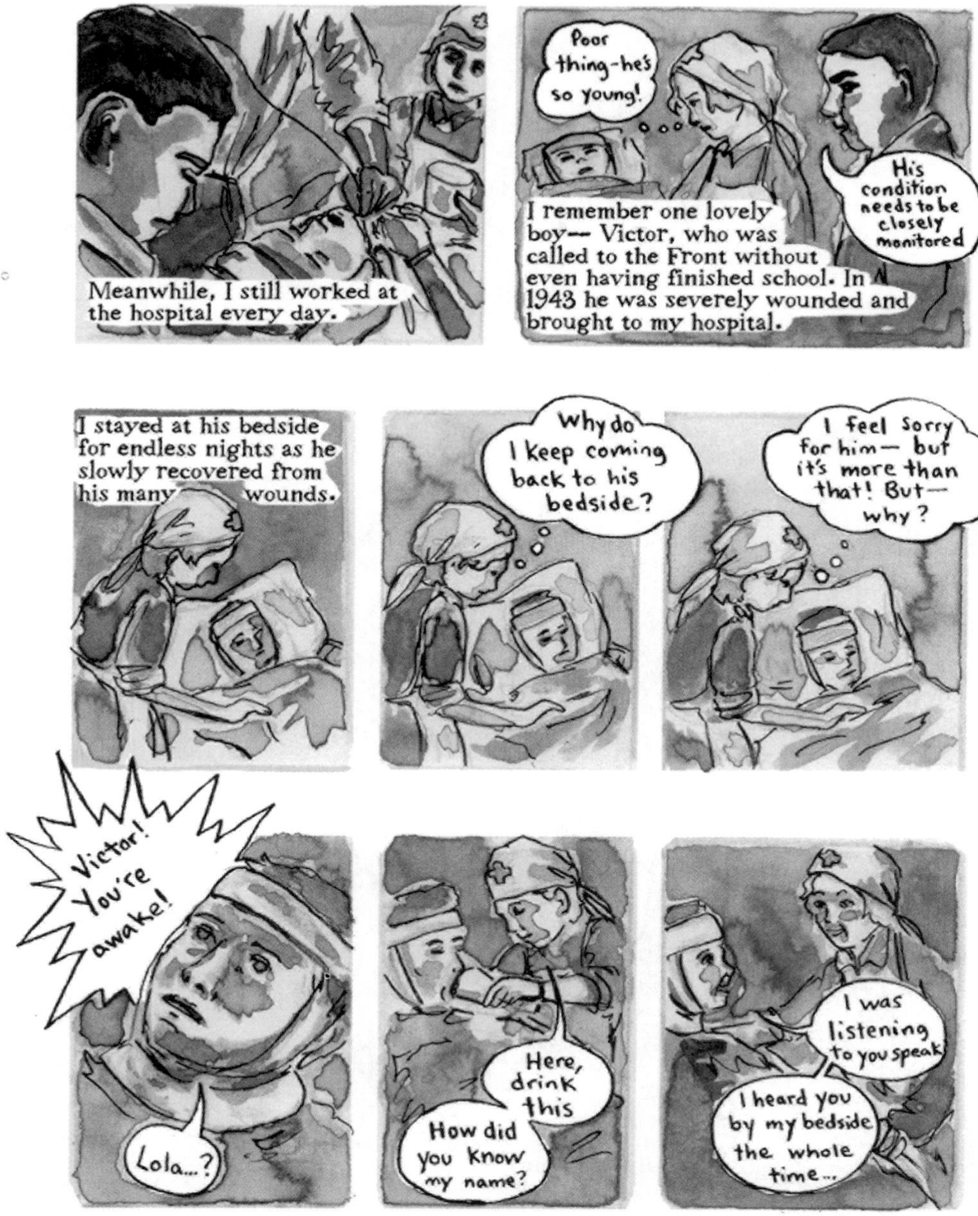
Meanwhile, I still worked at the hospital every day.
Poor thing-he's so young!
His condition needs to be closely monitored
I remember one lovely boy— Victor, who was called to the Front without even having finished school. In 1943 he was severely wounded and brought to my hospital.
I stayed at his bedside for endless nights as he slowly recovered from his many wounds.
Why do I keep coming back to his bedside?
I feel sorry for him— but it's more than that! But— why?
Victor! You're awake!
Lola...?
Here, drink this
How did you know my name?
I was listening to you speak
I heard you by my bedside the whole time...

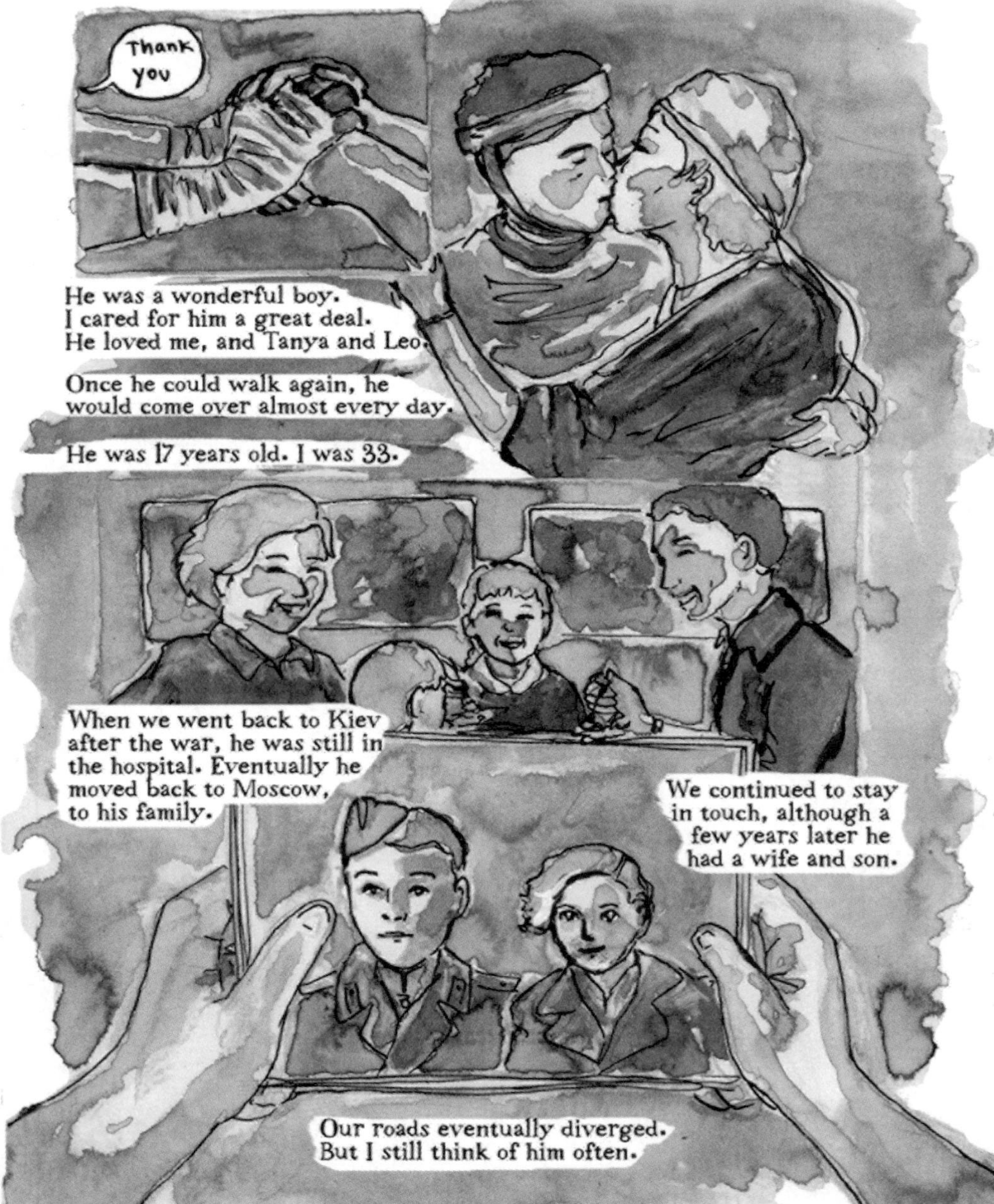

Thank you
He was a wonderful boy. I cared for him a great deal. He loved me, and Tanya and Leo.
Once he could walk again, he would come over almost every day.
He was 17 years old. I was 33.
When we went back to Kiev after the war, he was still in the hospital. Eventually he moved back to Moscow, to his family.
We continued to stay in touch, although a few years later he had a wife and son.
Our roads eventually diverged. But I still think of him often.

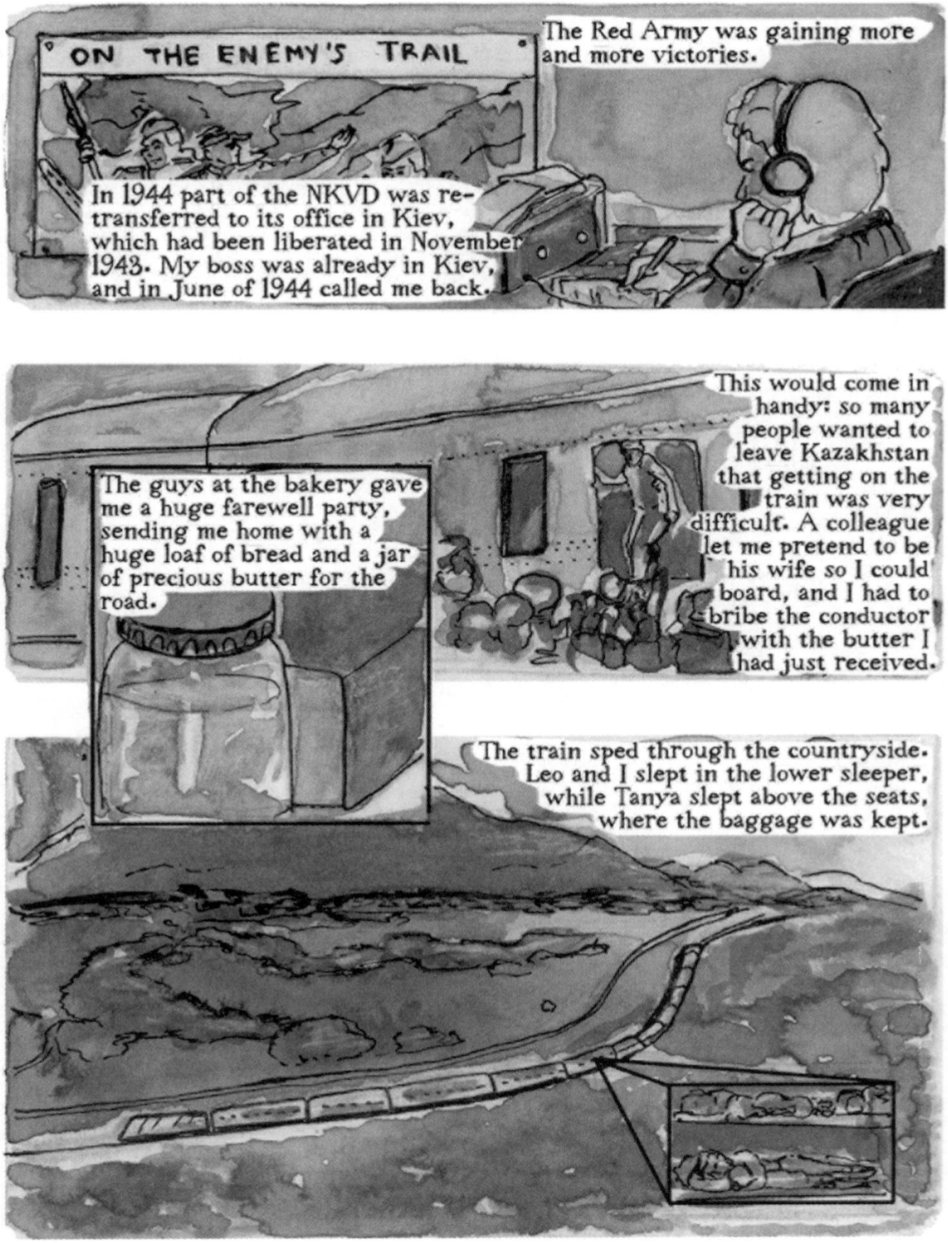
ON THE ENEMY'S TRAIL
The Red Army was gaining more and more victories.
In 1944 part of the NKVD was re-transferred to its office in Kiev, which had been liberated in November 1943. My boss was already in Kiev, and in June of 1944 called me back.
The guys at the bakery gave me a huge farewell party, sending me home with a huge loaf of bread and a jar of precious butter for the road.
This would come in handy: so many people wanted to leave Kazakhstan that getting on the train was very difficult. A colleague let me pretend to be his wife so I could board, and I had to bribe the conductor with the butter I had just received.
The train sped through the countryside. Leo and I slept in the lower sleeper, while Tanya slept above the seats, where the baggage was kept.

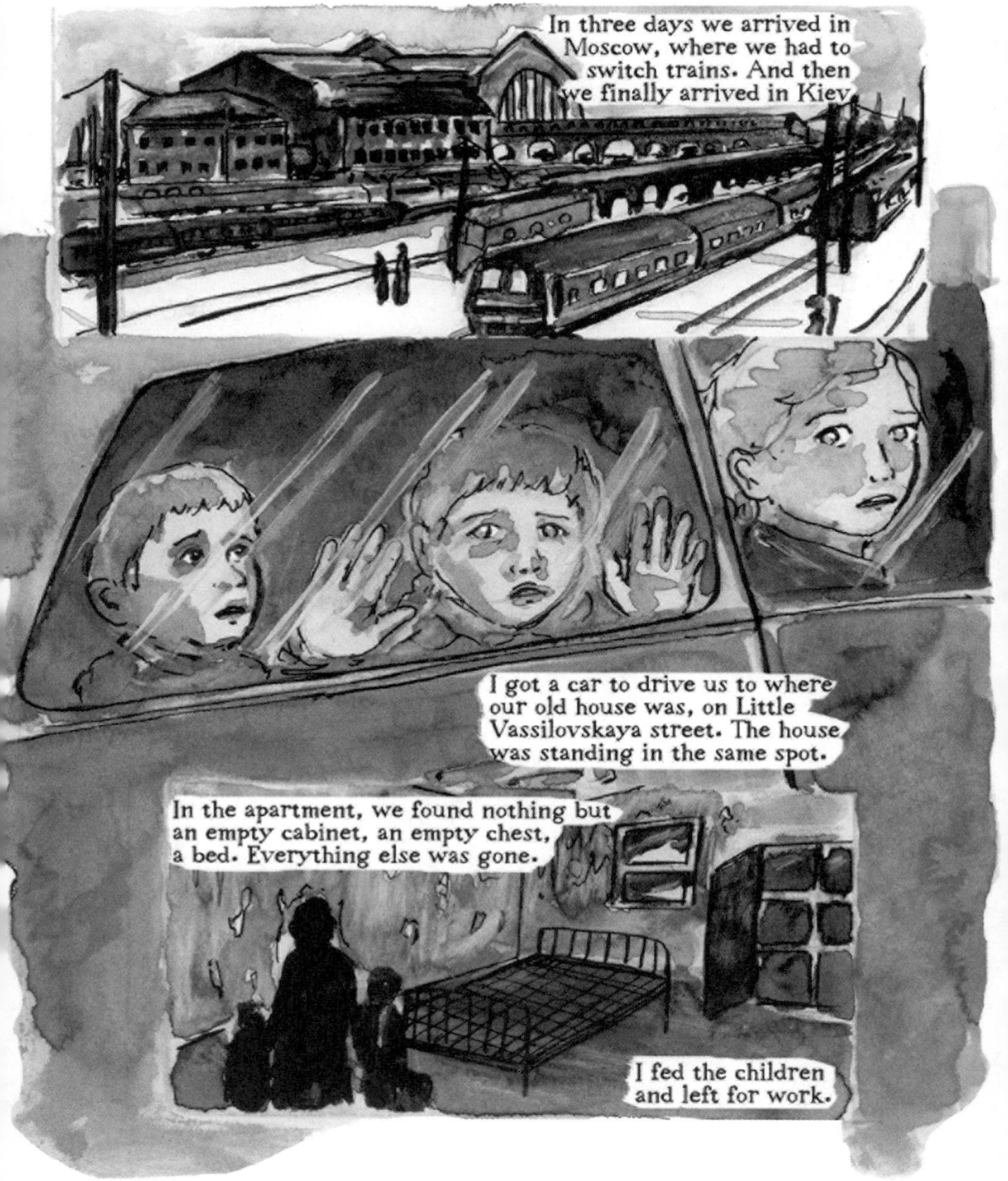
In three days we arrived in Moscow, where we had to switch trains. And then we finally arrived in Kiev.
I got a car to drive us to where our old house was, on Little Vassilovskaya street. The house was standing in the same spot.
In the apartment, we found nothing but an empty cabinet, an empty chest, a bed. Everything else was gone.
I fed the children and left for work.

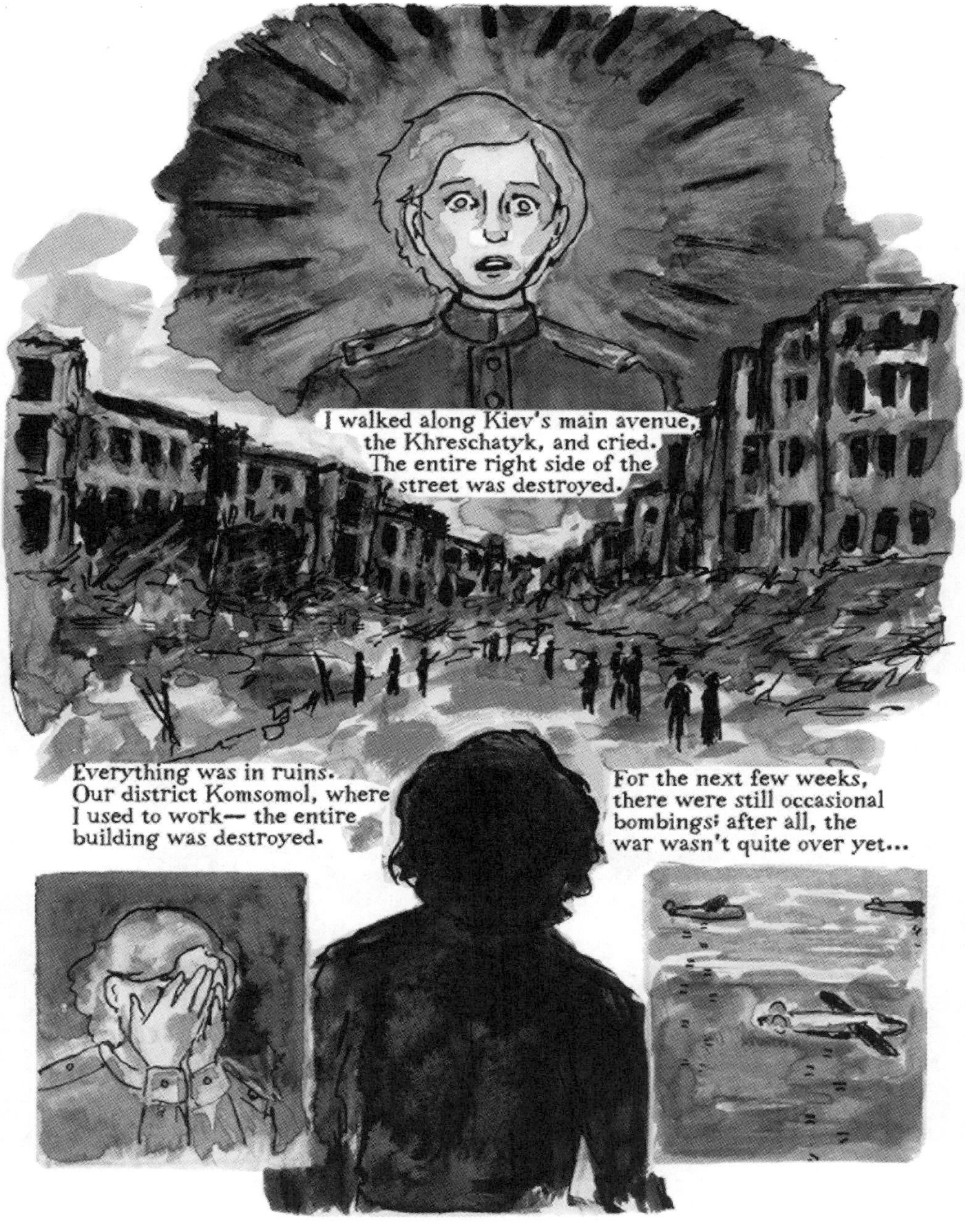
I walked along Kiev's main avenue, the Khreschatyk, and cried. The entire right side of the street was destroyed.
Everything was in ruins. Our district Komsomol, where I used to work— the entire building was destroyed.
For the next few weeks, there were still occasional bombings; after all, the war wasn't quite over yet...

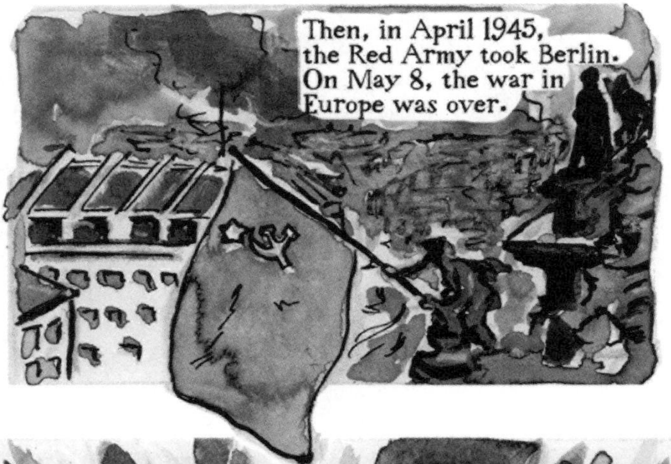
Then, in April 1945, the Red Army took Berlin. On May 8, the war in Europe was over.

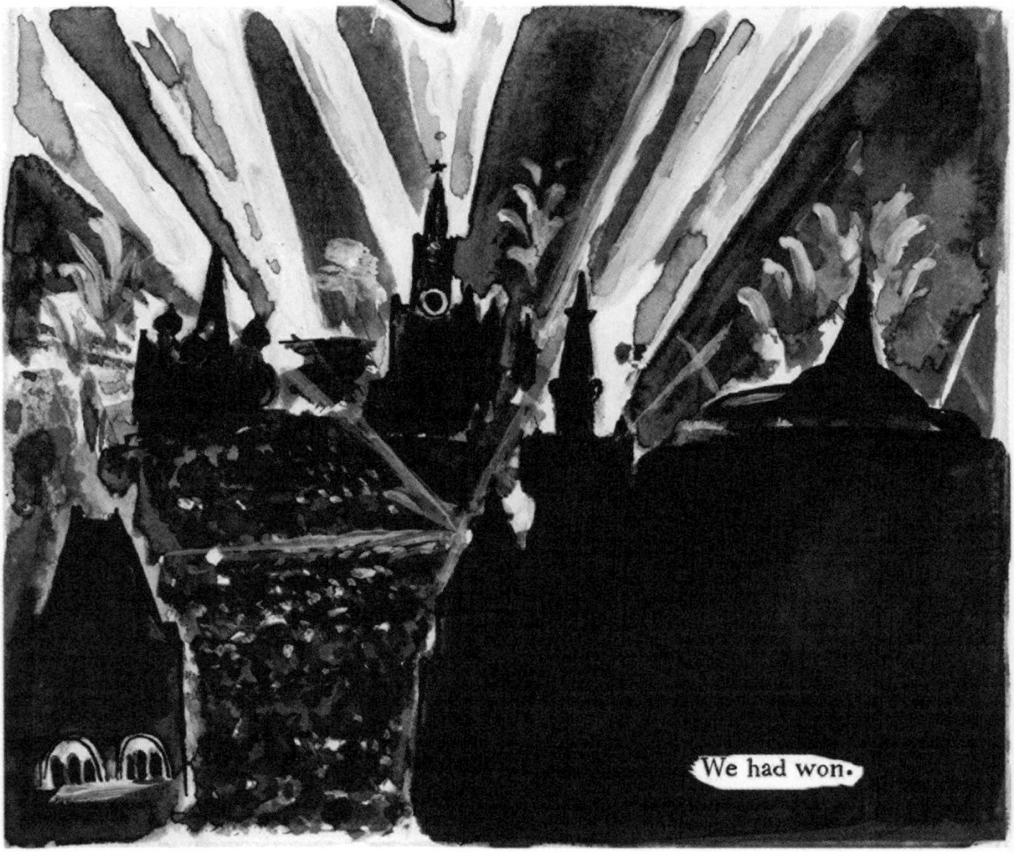
We had won.

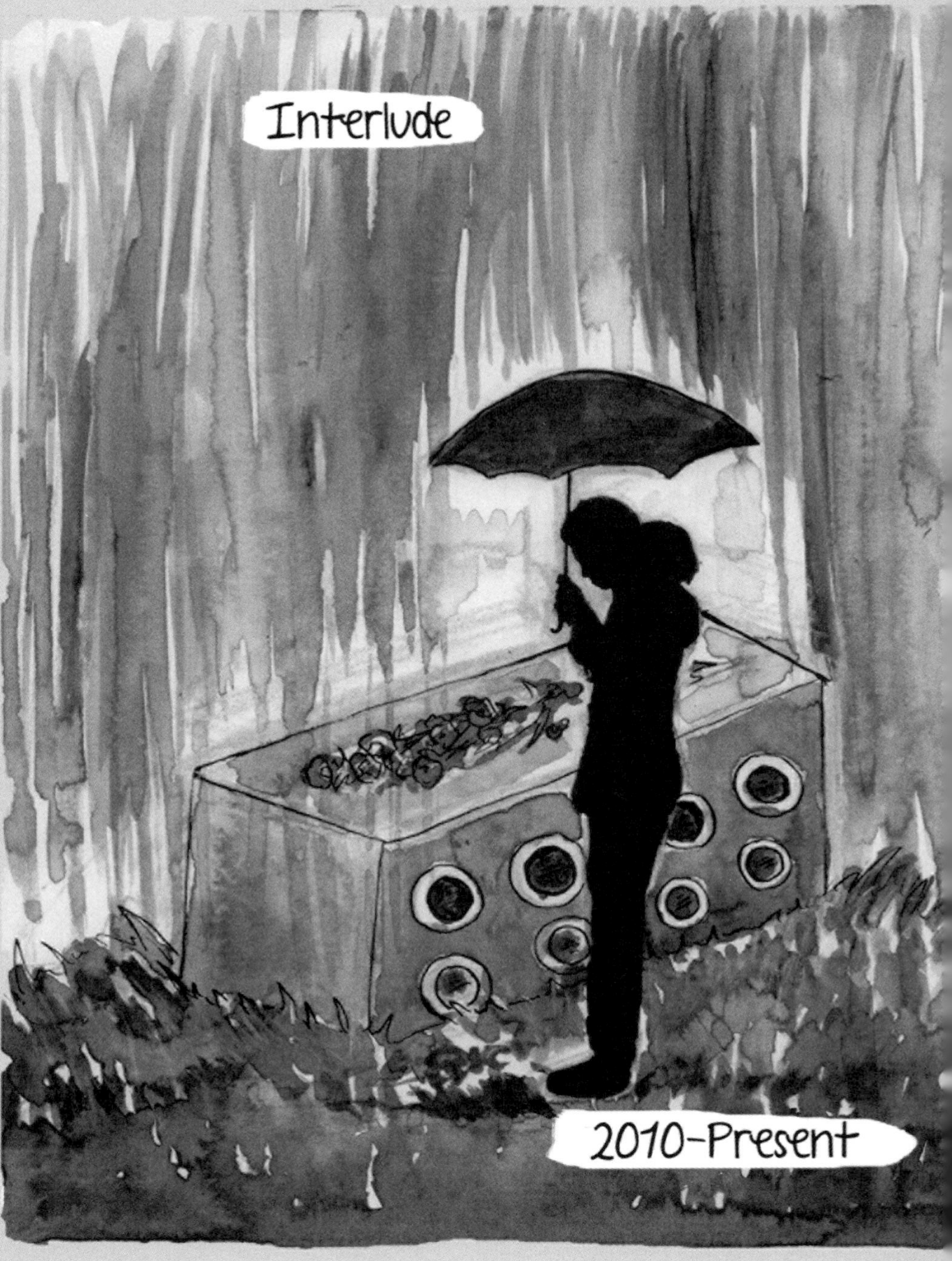
Interlude
2010–Present

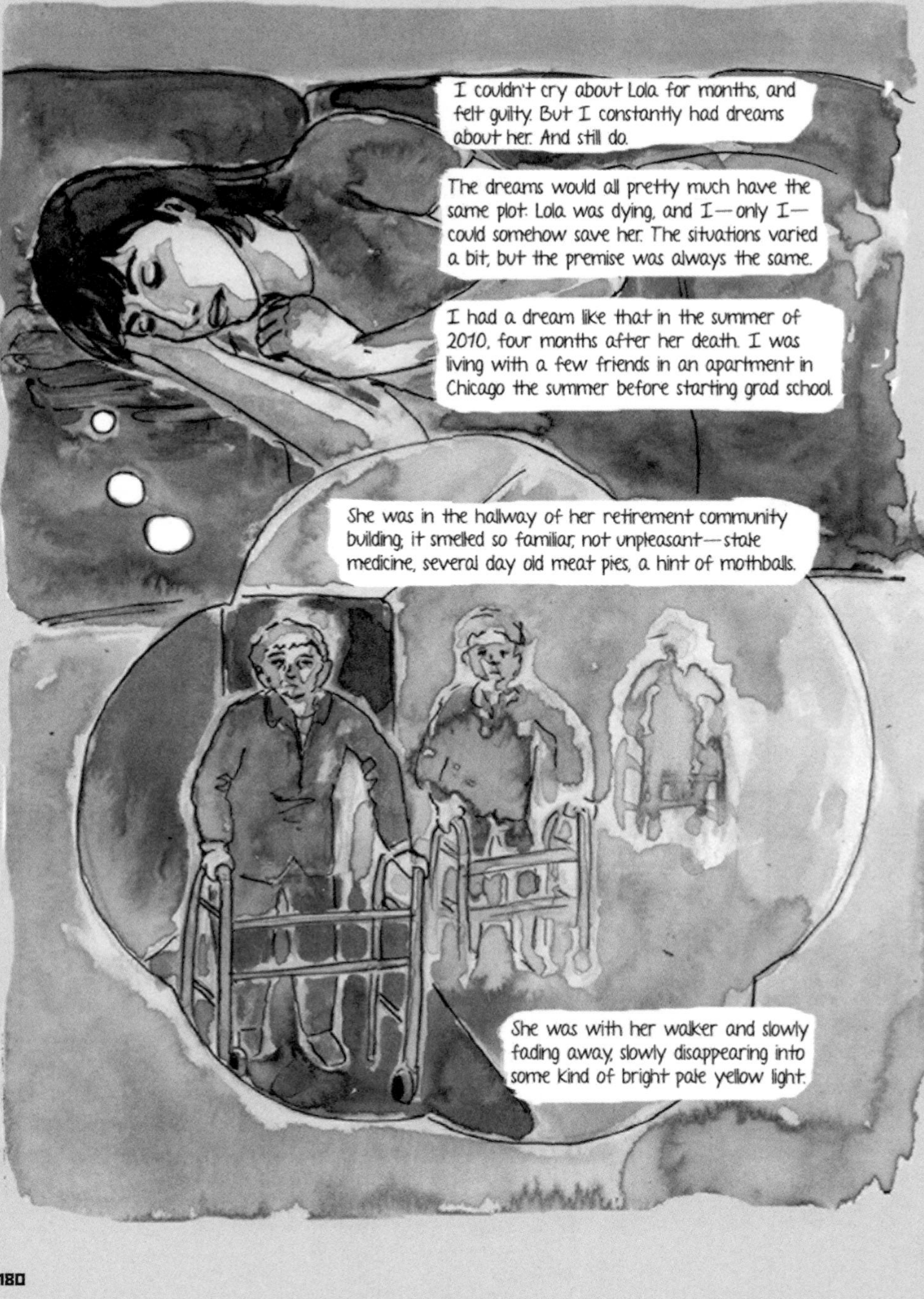
I couldn't cry about Lola for months, and felt guilty. But I constantly had dreams about her. And still do.
The dreams would all pretty much have the same plot: Lola was dying, and I—only I—could somehow save her. The situations varied a bit, but the premise was always the same.
I had a dream like that in the summer of 2010, four months after her death. I was living with a few friends in an apartment in Chicago the summer before starting grad school.
She was in the hallway of her retirement community building; it smelled so familiar, not unpleasant—stale medicine, several day old meat pies, a hint of mothballs.
She was with her walker and slowly fading away, slowly disappearing into some kind of bright pale yellow light.

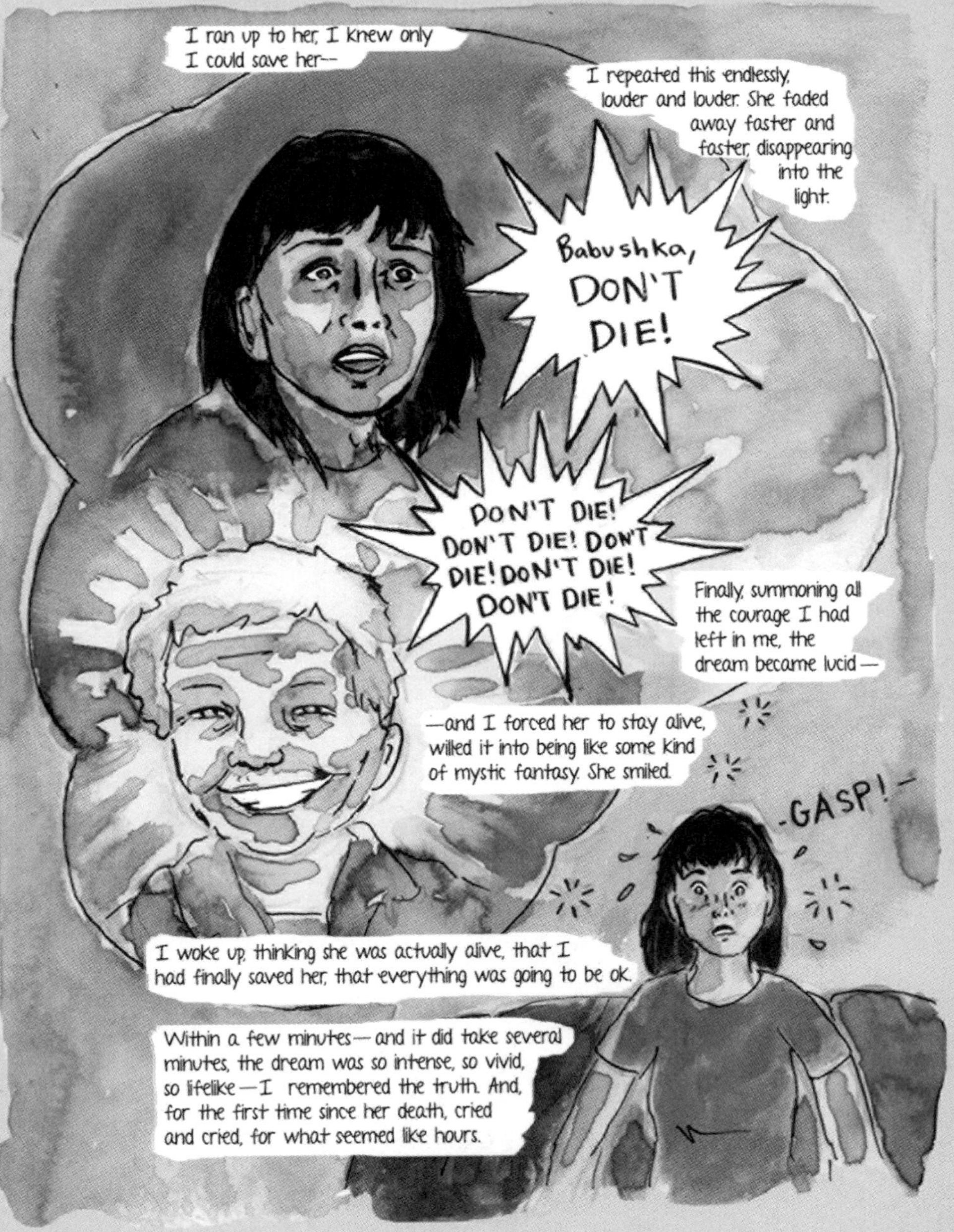

I ran up to her, I knew only I could save her--
I repeated this endlessly, louder and louder. She faded away faster and faster, disappearing into the light.
Babushka, DON'T DIE!
DON'T DIE! DON'T DIE! DON'T DIE! DON'T DIE! DON'T DIE!
Finally, summoning all the courage I had left in me, the dream became lucid—
—and I forced her to stay alive, willed it into being like some kind of mystic fantasy. She smiled.
-GASP!-
I woke up, thinking she was actually alive, that I had finally saved her, that everything was going to be ok.
Within a few minutes—and it did take several minutes, the dream was so intense, so vivid, so lifelike—I remembered the truth. And, for the first time since her death, cried and cried, for what seemed like hours.

Chapter 12:   1945-present

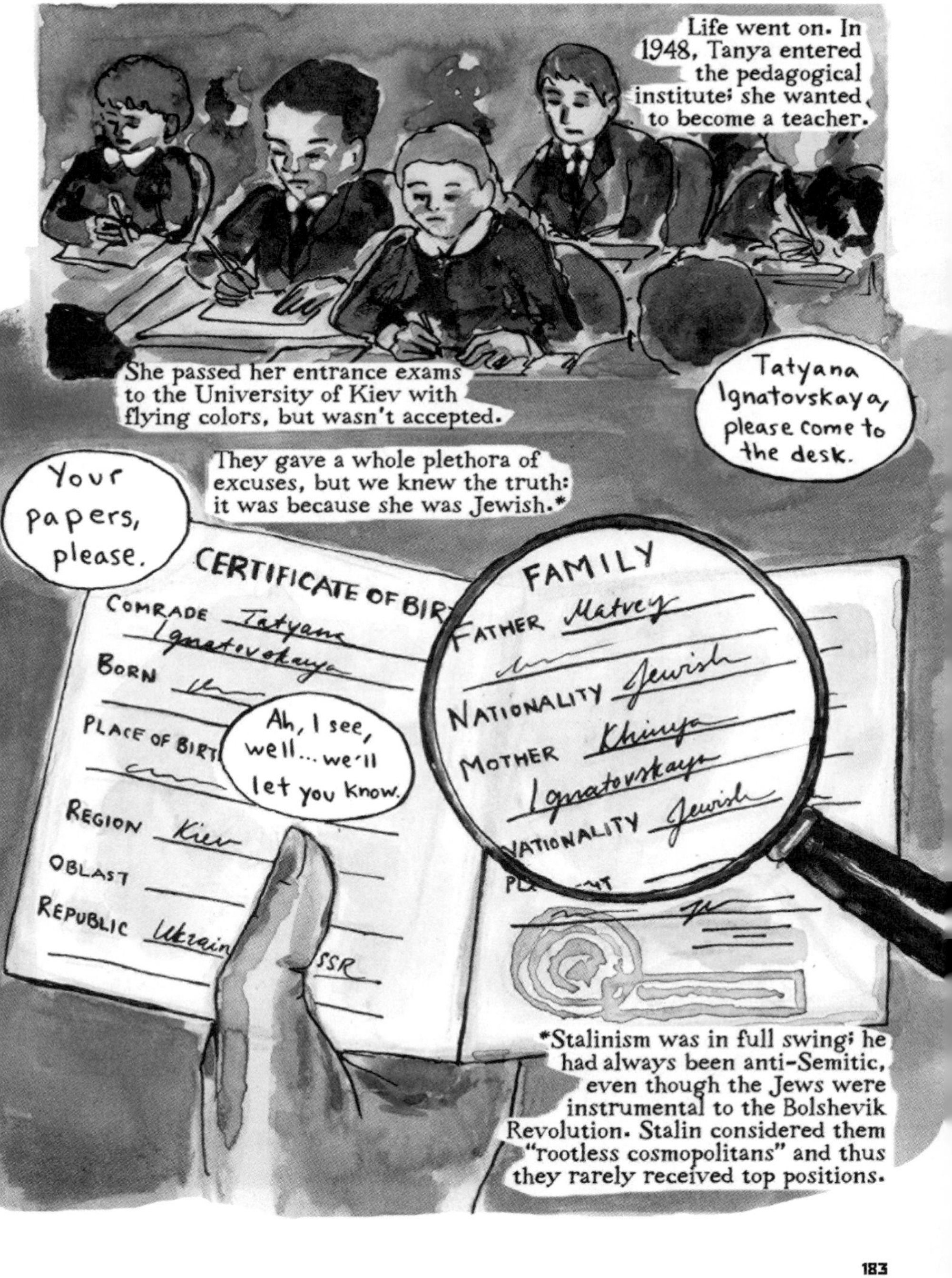
Life went on. In 1948, Tanya entered the pedagogical institute; she wanted to become a teacher.
She passed her entrance exams to the University of Kiev with flying colors, but wasn't accepted.
Tatyana Ignatovskaya, please come to the desk.
They gave a whole plethora of excuses, but we knew the truth: it was because she was Jewish.*
Your papers, please.
CERTIFICATE OF BIRT
COMRADE Tatyana Ignatovskaya
BORN
PLACE OF BIRT
REGION Kiev
OBLAST
REPUBLIC Ukrain SSR
Ah, I see, well... we'll let you know.
FAMILY
FATHER Matvey
NATIONALITY Jewish
MOTHER Khinya Ignatovskaya
NATIONALITY Jewish
*Stalinism was in full swing; he had always been anti-Semitic, even though the Jews were instrumental to the Bolshevik Revolution. Stalin considered them "rootless cosmopolitans" and thus they rarely received top positions.

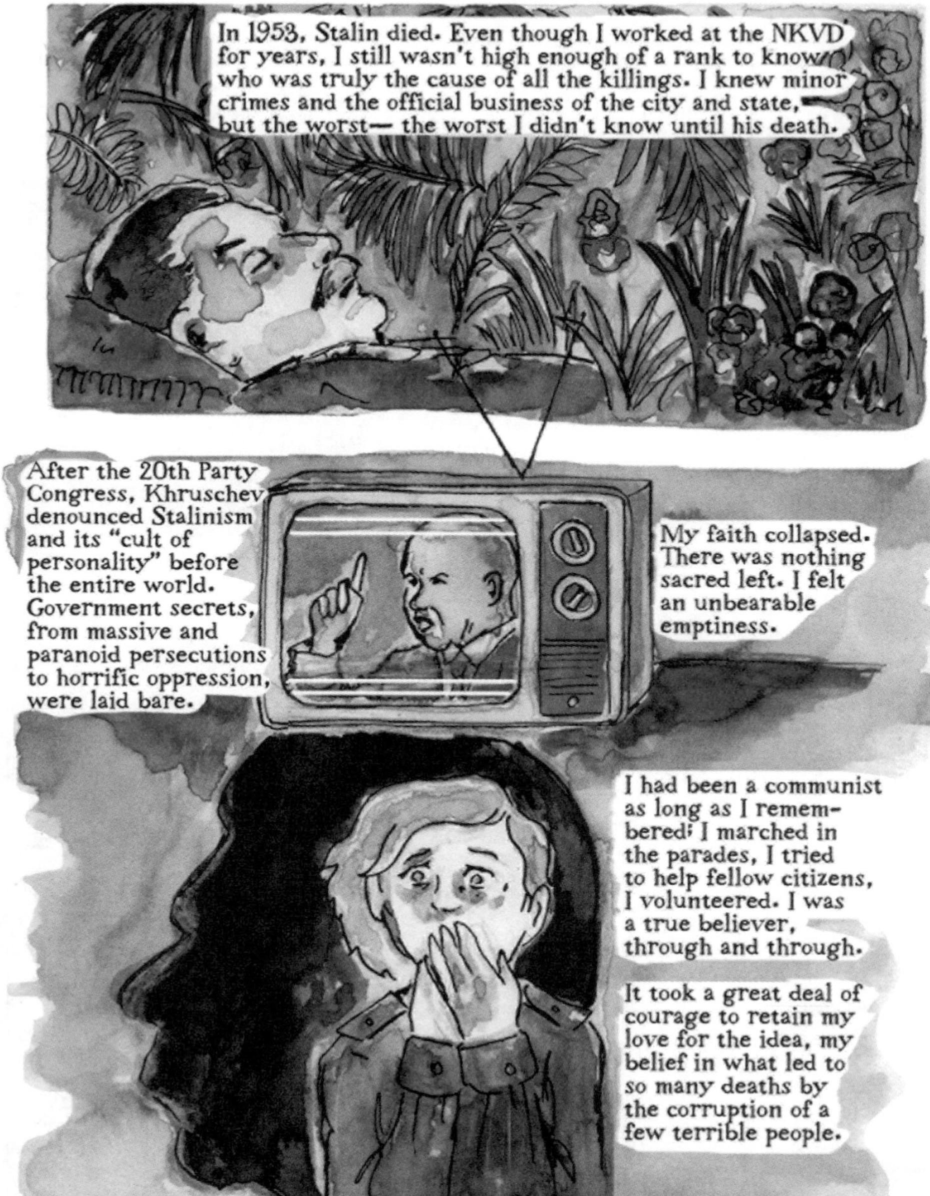
In 1953, Stalin died. Even though I worked at the NKVD for years, I still wasn't high enough of a rank to know who was truly the cause of all the killings. I knew minor crimes and the official business of the city and state, but the worst— the worst I didn't know until his death.
After the 20th Party Congress, Khruschev denounced Stalinism and its "cult of personality" before the entire world. Government secrets, from massive and paranoid persecutions to horrific oppression, were laid bare.
My faith collapsed. There was nothing sacred left. I felt an unbearable emptiness.
I had been a communist as long as I remembered; I marched in the parades, I tried to help fellow citizens, I volunteered. I was a true believer, through and through.
It took a great deal of courage to retain my love for the idea, my belief in what led to so many deaths by the corruption of a few terrible people.

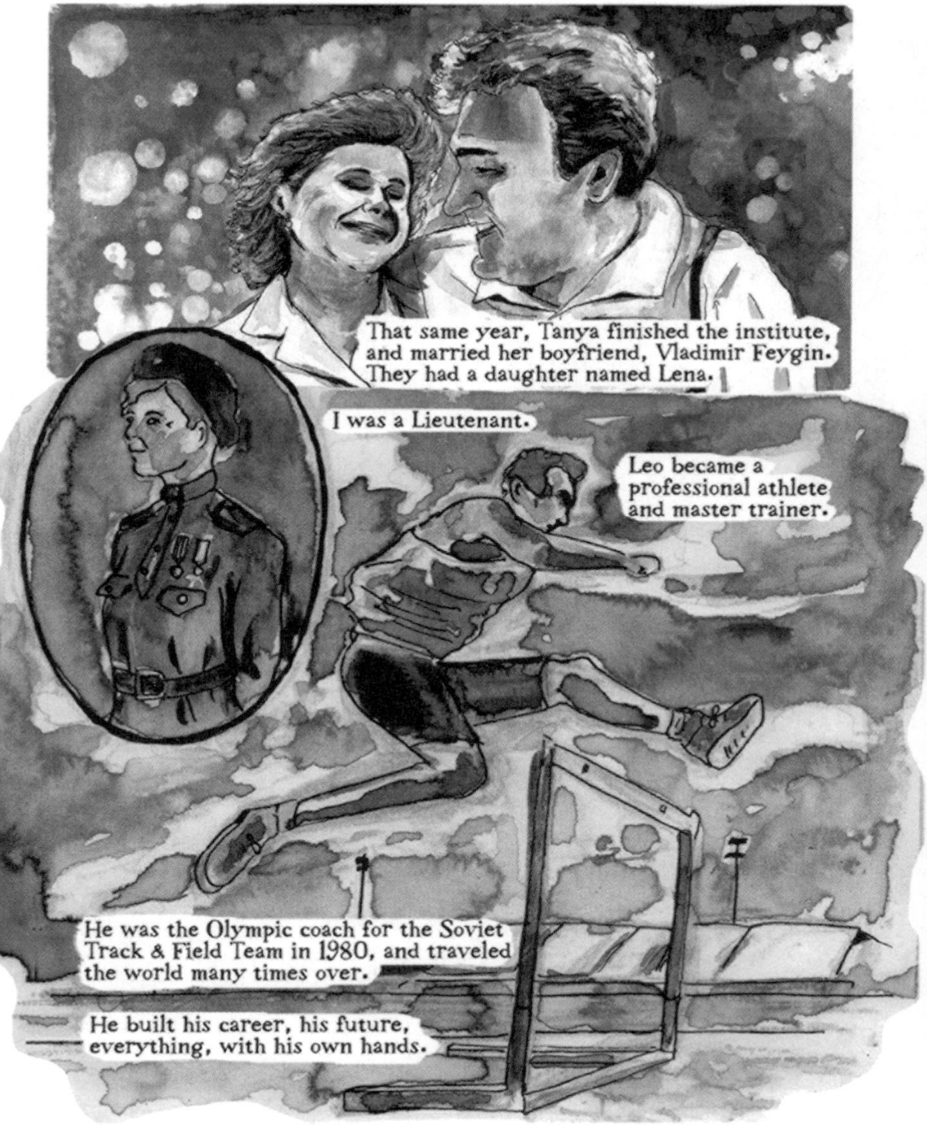
That same year, Tanya finished the institute, and married her boyfriend, Vladimir Feygin. They had a daughter named Lena.
I was a Lieutenant.
Leo became a professional athlete and master trainer.
He was the Olympic coach for the Soviet Track & Field Team in 1980, and traveled the world many times over.
He built his career, his future, everything, with his own hands.

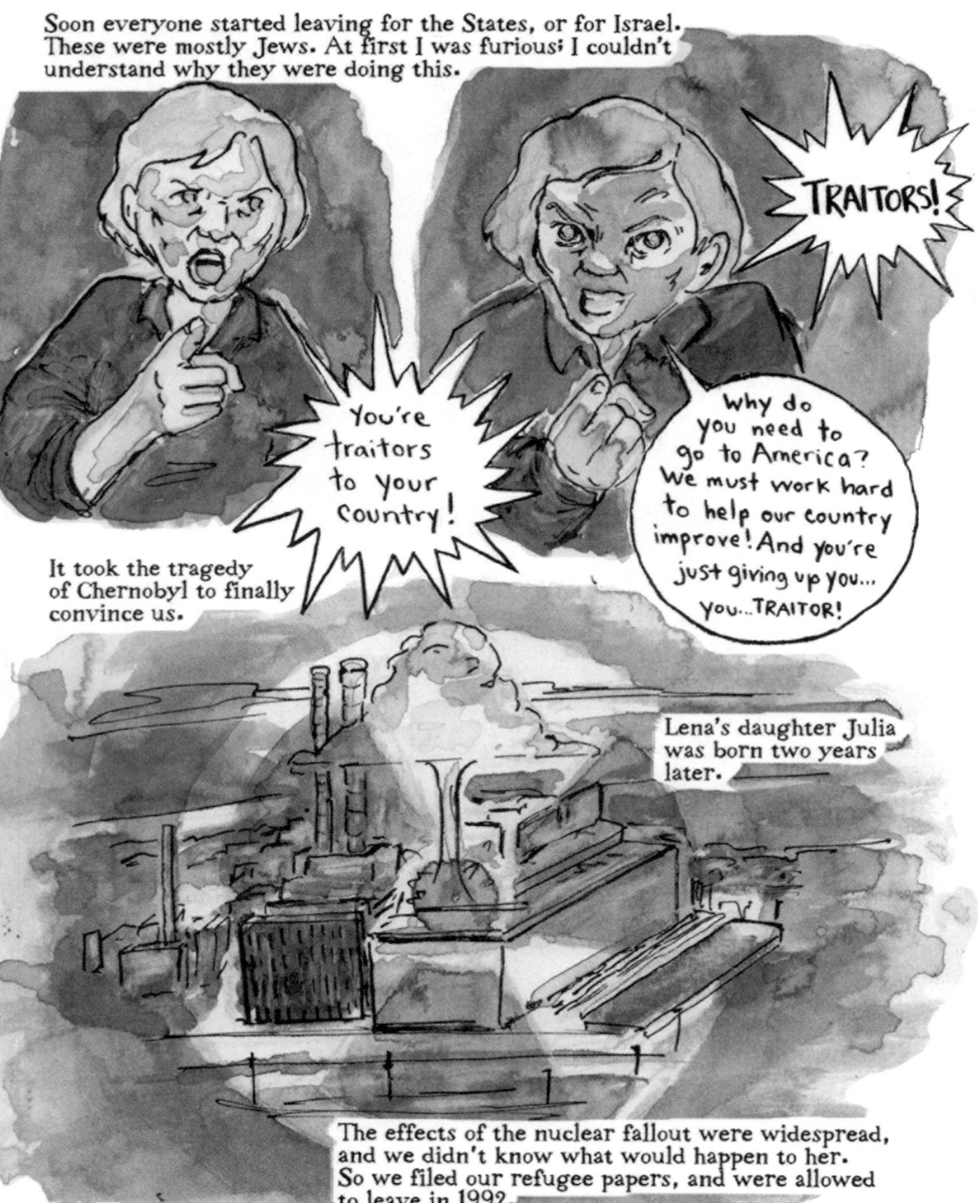
Soon everyone started leaving for the States, or for Israel. These were mostly Jews. At first I was furious; I couldn't understand why they were doing this.
You're traitors to your country!
TRAITORS!
Why do you need to go to America? We must work hard to help our country improve! And you're just giving up you... you...TRAITOR!
It took the tragedy of Chernobyl to finally convince us.
Lena's daughter Julia was born two years later.
The effects of the nuclear fallout were widespread, and we didn't know what would happen to her. So we filed our refugee papers, and were allowed to leave in 1992.

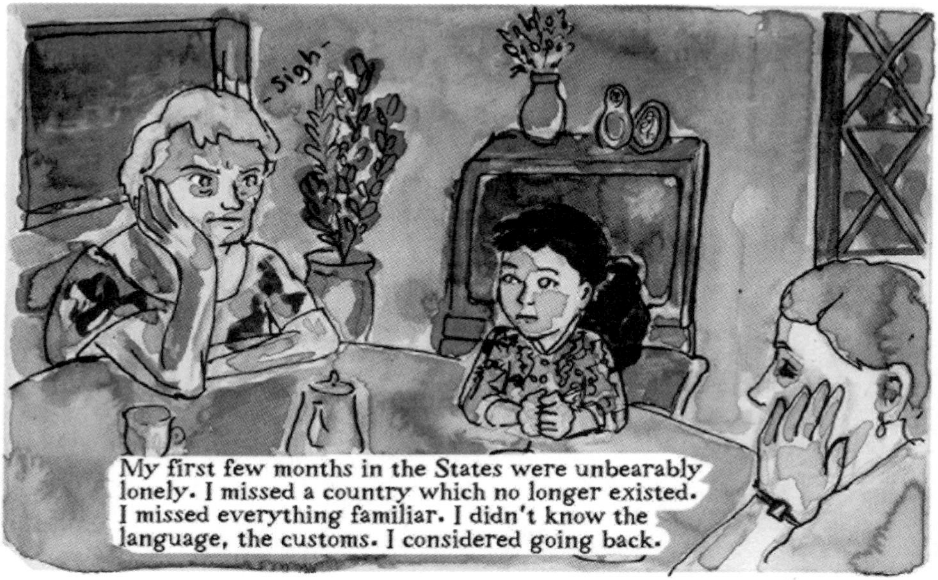
-Sigh-
My first few months in the States were unbearably lonely. I missed a country which no longer existed. I missed everything familiar. I didn't know the language, the customs. I considered going back.

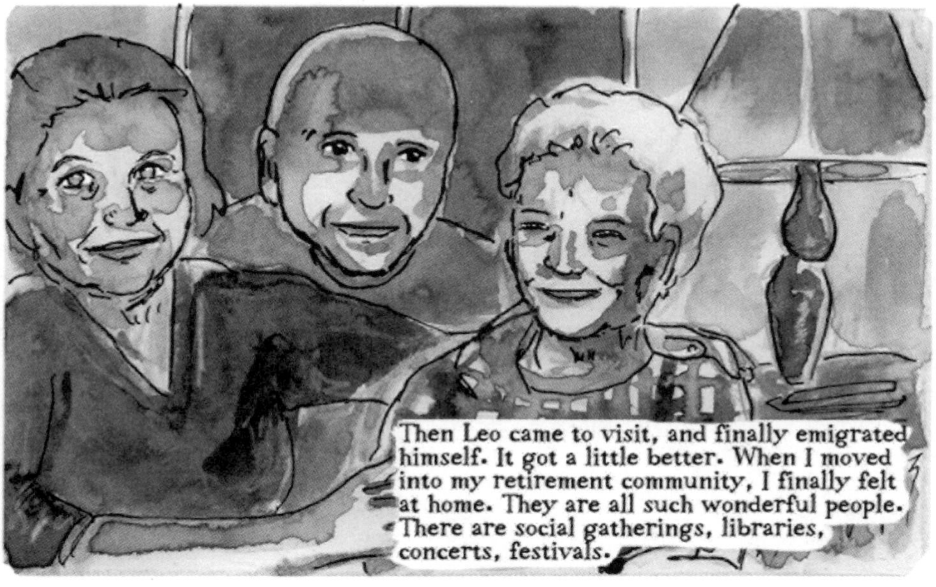
Then Leo came to visit, and finally emigrated himself. It got a little better. When I moved into my retirement community, I finally felt at home. They are all such wonderful people. There are social gatherings, libraries, concerts, festivals.

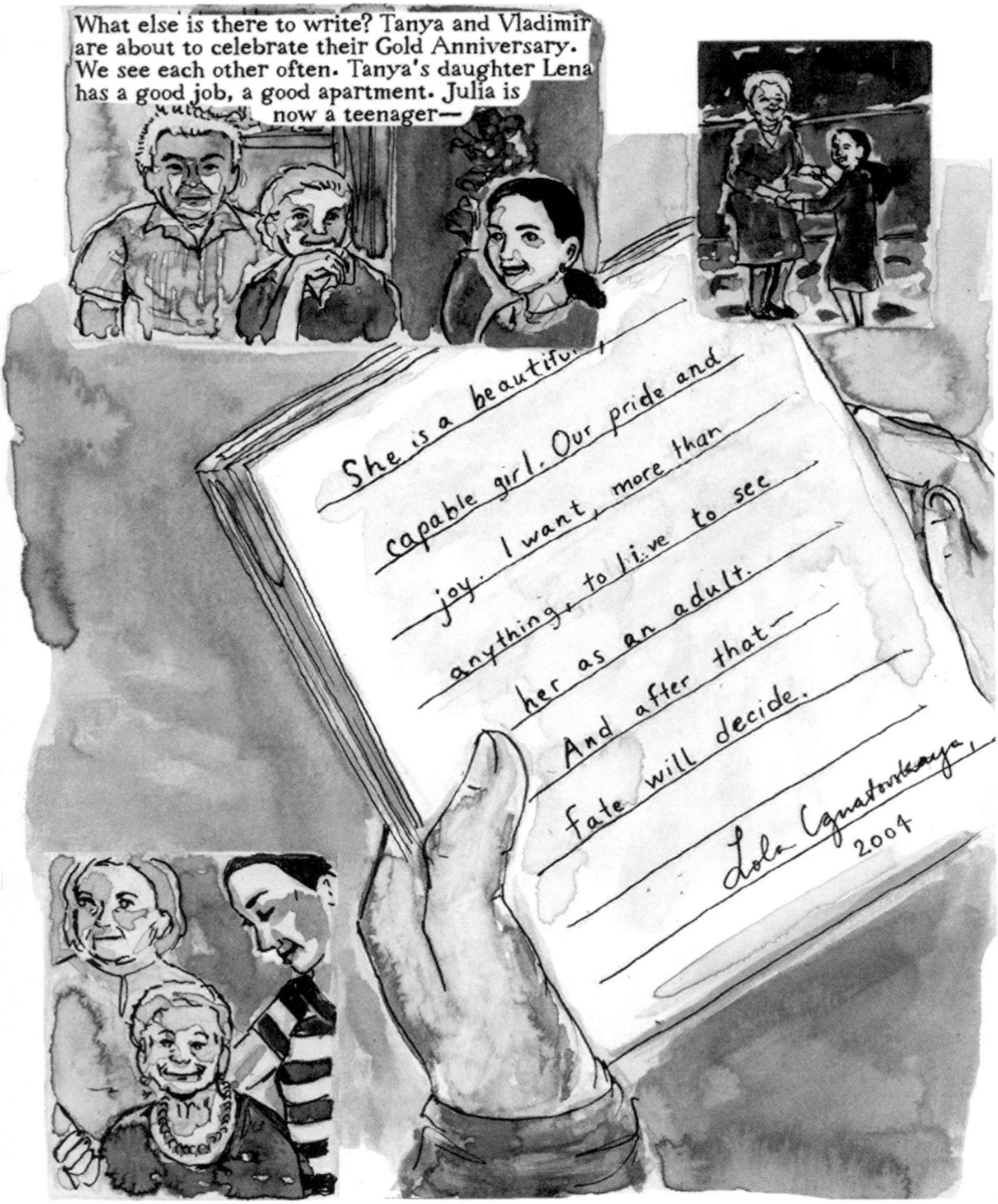
What else is there to write? Tanya and Vladimir are about to celebrate their Gold Anniversary. We see each other often. Tanya's daughter Lena has a good job, a good apartment. Julia is now a teenager—
She is a beautiful, capable girl. Our pride and joy. I want, more than anything, to live to see her as an adult. And after that— fate will decide.
Lola Ignatovskaya
2004

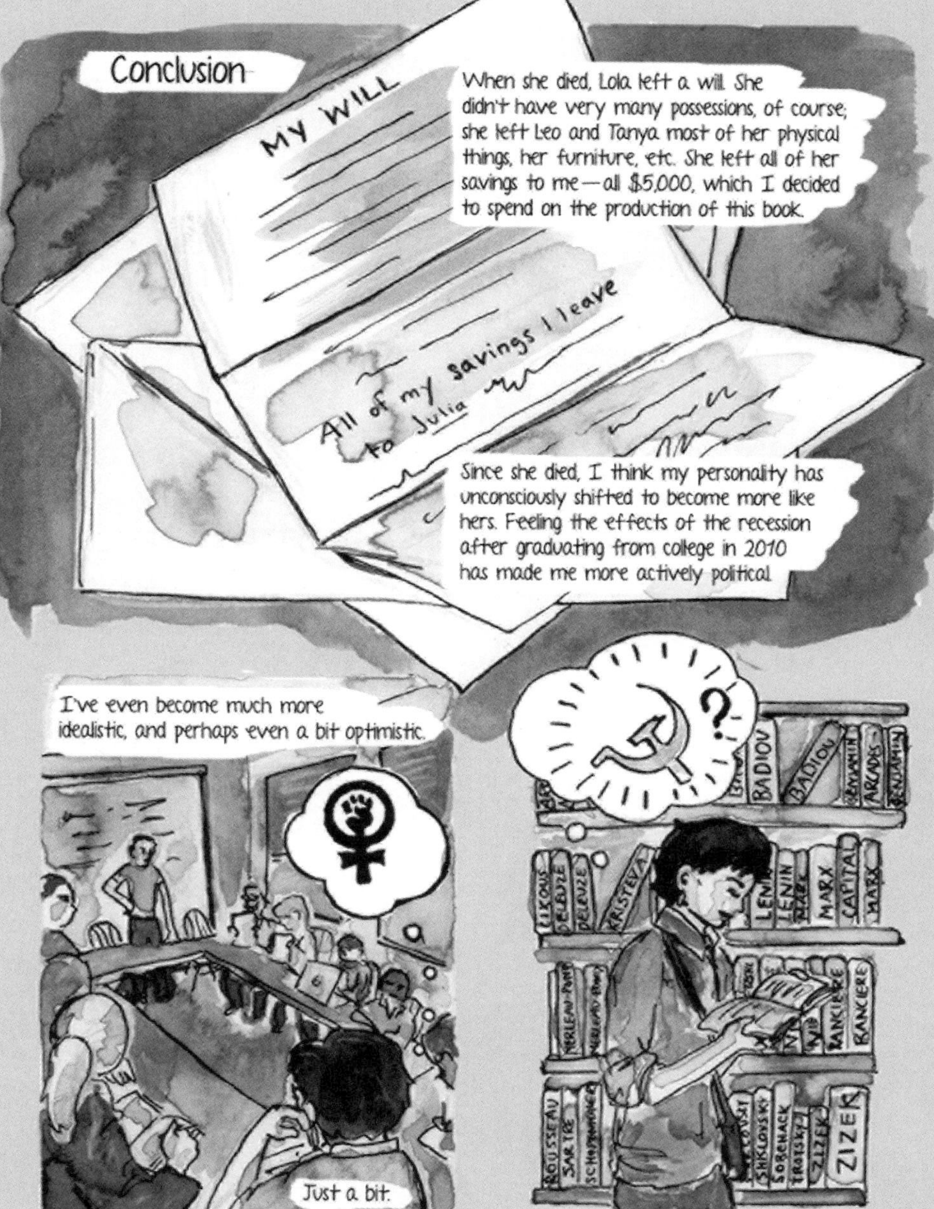
Conclusion
When she died, Lola left a will. She didn't have very many possessions, of course; she left Leo and Tanya most of her physical things, her furniture, etc. She left all of her savings to me—all $5,000, which I decided to spend on the production of this book.
MY WILL
All of my savings I leave to Julia
Since she died, I think my personality has unconsciously shifted to become more like hers. Feeling the effects of the recession after graduating from college in 2010 has made me more actively political.
I've even become much more idealistic, and perhaps even a bit optimistic.
Just a bit.
BADIOU
BADIOU
BENJAMIN
ARCADES
BENJAMIN
DELEUZE
DELEUZE
KRISTEVA
LENIN
LENIN
MARX
MARX
CAPITAL
MARX
RANCIERE
RANCIERE
ROUSSEAU
SARTRE
SHKLOVSKY
SOBCHACK
TROTSKY
ZIZEK
ZIZEK
ZIZEK

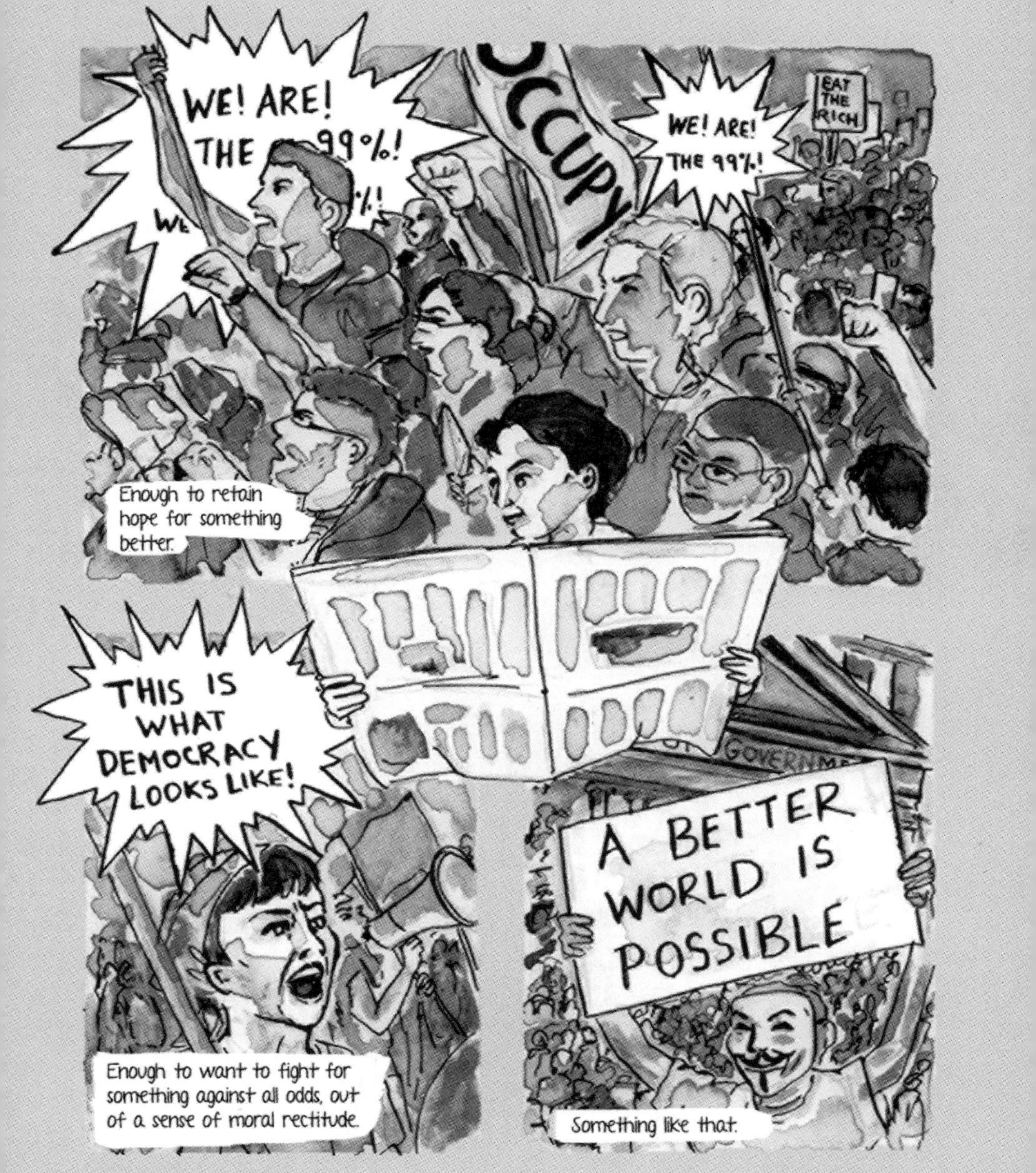
WE! ARE! THE 99%!
OCCUPY
WE! ARE! THE 99%!
EAT THE RICH
Enough to retain hope for something better.
THIS IS WHAT DEMOCRACY LOOKS LIKE!
GOVERNM
A BETTER WORLD IS POSSIBLE
Enough to want to fight for something against all odds, out of a sense of moral rectitude.
Something like that.

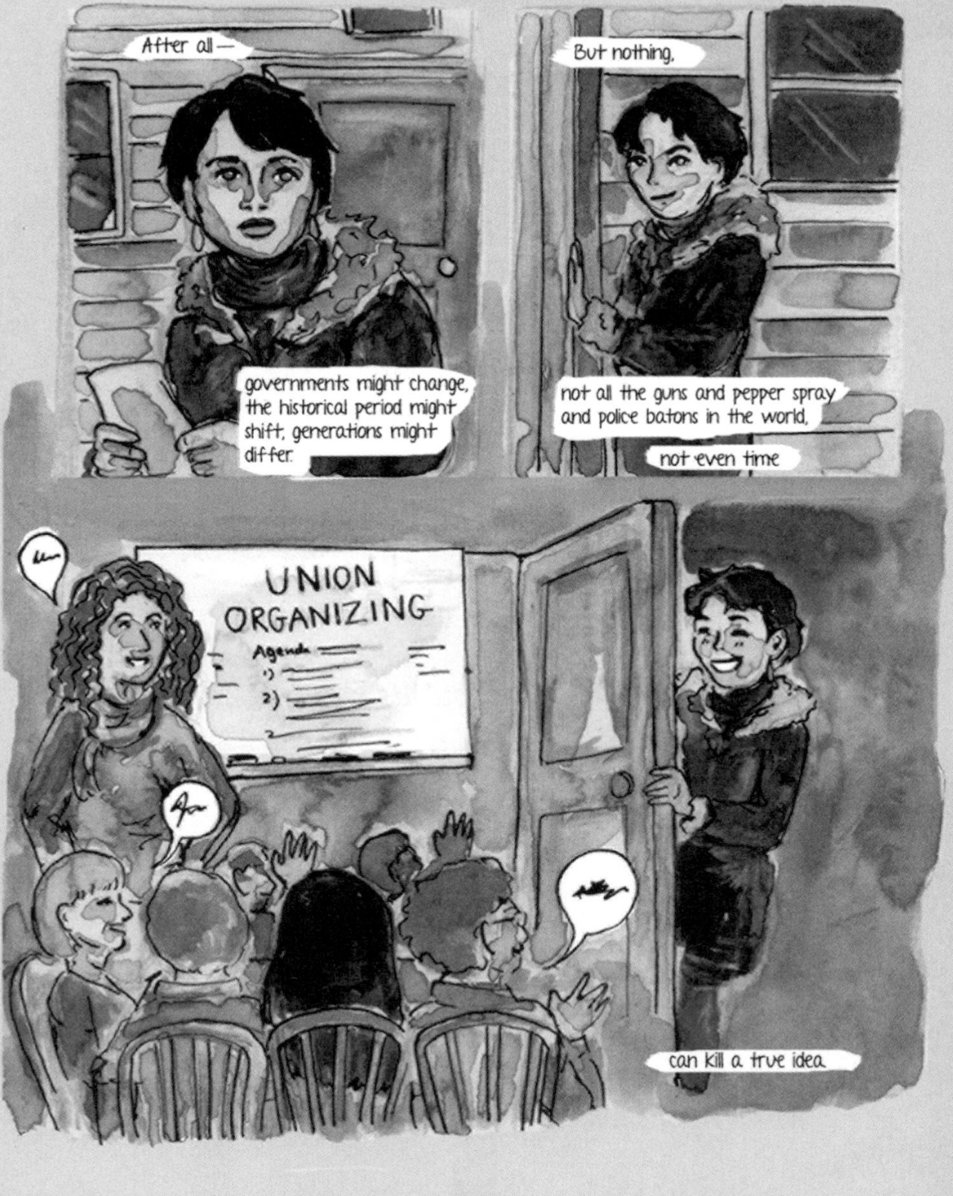
After all—
governments might change, the historical period might shift, generations might differ.
But nothing,
not all the guns and pepper spray and police batons in the world,
not even time
UNION ORGANIZING
Agenda
can kill a true idea

SUBSCRIBE TO EVERYTHING WE PUBLISH!

Do you love what Microcosm publishes?

Do you want us to publish more great stuff?

Would you like to receive each new title as it's published?

Subscribe as a BFF to our new titles and we'll mail them all to you as they are released!

$10-30/mo, pay what you can afford. Include your t-shirt size and month/date of birthday for a possible surprise! Subscription begins the month after it is purchased.

microcosmpublishing.com/bff

...AND HELP US GROW YOUR SMALL WORLD!

...and check out our other fine works of comics journalism: